Sustainable Development Seen Through the Lenses of Ethnoeconomics and the Circular Economy

Walter Leal Filho · Vladan Kuzmanović
Editors

Sustainable Development Seen Through the Lenses of Ethnoeconomics and the Circular Economy

Springer

Editors
Walter Leal Filho
Life Sciences
HAW Hamburg
Hamburg, Germany

Vladan Kuzmanović
Faculty of Economics
University of Belgrade
Belgrade, Serbia

ISBN 978-3-031-72675-0   ISBN 978-3-031-72676-7 (eBook)
https://doi.org/10.1007/978-3-031-72676-7

This Springer imprint is published by the registered company Springer Nature Switzerland AG
The registered company address is: Gewerbestrasse 11, 6330 Cham, Switzerland

Preface

In an era marked by unprecedented economic growth and technological advancement, the need for sustainable development has never been more critical. Our planet is experiencing profound environmental challenges, including climate change, resource depletion, and biodiversity loss, all of which threaten the well-being of current and future generations. In addressing these issues, two complementary approaches have gained prominence: ethnoeconomics and the circular economy. This book, "Sustainable Development Seen Through the Lenses of Ethnoeconomics and the Circular Economy", explores the intersections of these disciplines and their potential to foster a more sustainable and equitable world.

Ethnoeconomics, an emerging field, emphasises the economic practices and knowledge systems of indigenous and local communities. These communities have long thrived in harmony with their natural environments, employing sustainable resource management techniques passed down through generations. By integrating traditional ecological knowledge with modern economic theories, ethnoeconomics provides a unique perspective on sustainable development. It challenges conventional economic models that often prioritise short-term gains over long-term sustainability and offers valuable insights into creating resilient and adaptive communities.

The circular economy, on the other hand, reimagines our current linear economic model of "take, make, dispose". It advocates for a regenerative system where products, materials, and resources are reused, repaired, refurbished, and recycled, minimising waste and the environmental impacts. The circular economy not only addresses environmental concerns but also creates economic opportunities by fostering innovation, reducing costs, and generating new business models. By promoting closed-loop systems, the circular economy aligns closely with the principles of sustainability, encouraging us to rethink how we design, produce, and consume goods.

This book aims to bridge the gap between ethnoeconomics and the circular economy, highlighting how these approaches can complement and enhance each other. Through a series of case studies, theoretical explorations, and practical examples, we delve into the synergies between traditional knowledge systems and contemporary circular practices. The book also shows how different stakeholders are implementing these concepts to address local and global challenges, from resource management and waste reduction to social equity and economic resilience.

Throughout the book, the importance of cross-disciplinary collaboration is emphasised, recognising that sustainable development requires the integration of diverse perspectives and expertise. As we navigate the complexities of sustainable development, we are reminded that solutions must be context-specific, culturally sensitive, and inclusive.

Ethnoeconomics and the circular economy offer valuable tools for achieving these goals, providing pathways towards a more sustainable and just future. By embracing innovative circular practices, we can create a world where economic prosperity and environmental stewardship go hand in hand.

It is our hope that this book will inspire policymakers, academics, practitioners, and communities to explore the potential of ethnoeconomics and the circular economy in their efforts to build a sustainable future. Let us embark on this journey together, guided by the principles of respect, resilience, and regeneration, as we strive to create a world that is not only economically vibrant but also environmentally sound and socially equitable.

Hamburg, Germany — Walter Leal Filho
Belgrade, Serbia — Vladan Kuzmanović

Contents

The Growing Application Potential of Machine Learning in Healthcare Systems of Modernity

Reinaldo Padilha França, Rodrigo Bonacin, and Ana Carolina Borges Monteiro

Abstract Technology-related innovations come around the clock with new functionality, a new way of looking at the world, and getting things done. All areas are changing conceptions, and with health, machine learning is the landscape, which preserves its origins in the knowledge of related areas in artificial intelligence, such as pattern recognition and computational learning. Artificial Intelligence is the science applied in the development of technological devices that can simulate human reasoning and be employed in health, it provides benefits to hospitals and clinics concerning greater precision of diagnoses. Through AI, a larger database for early diagnosis is possible, associated with the data of patients in the Cloud, health institutions can process through this storage of patient information, assisting in the discovery of diagnoses. The benefits of Machine Learning in Health are related to reducing the time of diagnosis; the reduction exam costs, indicating the most decisive ones for obtaining the diagnosis; and even a doctor will be able to define the diagnosis more accurately and in a shorter consultation time, being able to serve more patients. For the patient, it considers the advantages of a more accurate diagnosis, with better monitoring of the evolution of the disease; superior quality of service, which is carried out in a more personalized way; the possibility of diseases detected in the early stages, understand how to prevent possible diseases. Thus, this chapter intends to offer an overview of Machine learning applied in Healthcare Systems, treating and exposing its success relationship, with a concise bibliographic background, explaining and distinguishing its technological potential.

Keywords Deep Learning · Big Data · Machine Learning · Data · Artificial Intelligence · Healthcare

---

R. P. França (✉) · R. Bonacin · A. C. B. Monteiro
Renato Archer Information Technology Center (CTI), São Paulo, Brazil
e-mail: reinaldo.franca@cti.gov.br

R. Bonacin
e-mail: rodrigo.bonacin@cti.gov.br

A. C. B. Monteiro
e-mail: ana.monteiro@cti.gov.br

W. Leal Filho and V. Kuzmanović (eds.), *Sustainable Development Seen Through the Lenses of Ethnoeconomics and the Circular Economy*,
https://doi.org/10.1007/978-3-031-72676-7_1

1 Introduction

Technology-related innovations come around the clock with new functionality, a new way of looking at the world, and getting things done. All areas are changing conceptions, and with the health machine learning the landscape, which is basically derived from artificial intelligence, which in turn pulls computer-related issues based on available data to continually learn and then make decisions. diverse without the need for human interaction. As things become more automated, many processes undergo true transformations and are open to new opportunities (Alpaydin, 2020; Neapolitan & Jiang, 2018).

In its essence, machine learning preserves its origins in the knowledge of related areas in artificial intelligence, such as pattern recognition and computational learning, basically, two types of approaches characterize machine learning, which are supervised and unsupervised learning; and two types of algorithms being classification and regression (Faul, 2019).

Through these faster diagnostic technologies, more assertive treatments, and better-calculated risks. Technology has become a great ally of doctors and patients. Studies have been done in several related areas, including ophthalmology, cardiology, pathology, and radiology. Technology is now trained to analyze images, identify trouble spots, and inform responsible professionals which areas need the most attention. Since the arrival of the third era of computing, the era of artificial intelligence, through machine learning techniques, neural networks, and natural processing language, the potential of these technologies in health is enormous (Bouchard, 2017; Stefano, 2019).

It is now possible to evaluate in a few minutes the genetic sequencing of a person, rank the most frequent and relevant mutations, crosscheck with the most up-to-date scientific literature, and generate differentiated treatment plans with more chances of cure (Hayre et al., 2019).

On the other hand, if analyzed traditionally, it would take about many hours. Whether in the office or the hospital, it is evident that time and data to be analyzed have become inversely proportional quantities in the daily life of the current doctor since the current commitment to work and good intentions of professionals in the sector are no longer enough to ensure care efficient and high quality. In this sense, it is clear that we need to dive into this ocean of data for insights to improve care, accelerate innovation, and reduce costs. In this context lies the greatest potential of Artificial Intelligence, cognitive computing, and machine learning (Monteiro, 2019; Monteiro et al., 2020).

Computers do not forget what they learn, are able to recognize changes and patterns in data more quickly and comprehensively than most humans, and have no judgmental bias, which makes it possible to predict conditions such as sepsis before it manifests clinically. Some of the most auspicious use cases for this technology encompass predictive analytics, predictive modeling, precision medicine, personalized medicine and health, and clinical decision support. The potential for working with data, analysis, and machine learning techniques in medicine is enormous, ranging from reduced operating costs and individual healthcare spending to people enjoying longer, healthier, more productive lives (França et al., 2020; Monteiro et al., 2020).

Thus, this chapter intends to offer an overview of Machine learning applied in Healthcare Systems, treating and exposing its success relationship, with a concise bibliographic background, explaining and distinguishing its technological potential.

2 Methodology

This research was developed based on the analysis of scientific papers and scientific journal sources referring to Machine Learning towards Healthcare Systems, concerning evolution and fundamental concepts of technology aiming to gather pertinent information regarding thematic. Thus this also enables more academic research through the background provided through this study.

3 Artificial Intelligence Concepts for Healthcare Systems

The technology is working to optimize the health sector, transforming digital medical records, streamlining patient care, and optimizing the procedures performed, allowing the collection of advanced data from patients, allowing more effective care, and even making diagnoses early, as well as modernizing as a research (França et al., 2019).

Artificial Intelligence (AI) applied in health offers benefits through the generation of data, teaching how to treat diseases and put patients in the health management center, helping in the prevention, and detection of diseases in individuals with disabilities, and identification of the best tests. It is a branch of Computer Science capable of creating devices that represent and operate in a similar way to a human capacity to perceive, reason, analyze, make decisions, understand analytically, and solve problems, considering the ability to learn, deliberate, and decide logically on the facts. Health AI goes beyond patient care but also extends to operational processes, helps to reduce unnecessary costs, and improves reactive planning (Maddox et al., 2019).

AI allows machines to learn from experiments, adjust to new data inputs, and perform tasks like humans, using Machine Learning (1980–2010), Deep Learning, and natural language processing algorithms, being trained to accomplish specific tasks when processing a large volume of data and recognize specific and individual patterns in that data. Still reflected in the neural network, a type of Machine Learning composed of interconnected units (such as neurons), this process requires restrictions on data to find connections and extract meanings from unused data, processing information, and responding to external inputs, relaying them between the units (Bengio et al., 2017; Goodfellow et al., 2016; Zhou et al., 2017).

AI analyzes more data, and in greater depth using neural networks that have many hidden layers, through a lot of data to train Machine Learning models since they learn directly from the data, following that the more data, the more accurate they become. AI can analyze Internet of Things (IoT) data that is transmitted from connected devices and connected devices to forecast demands using recurring networks, which are a specific type of Machine Learning network applied to sequential data (Li et al., 2018; Mohammadi, 2018; Tang, 2017).

AI achieves incredible accuracy through deep neural networks which continue to become more accurate as they are used. In the medical field, AI techniques based on Machine Learning, related to image classification and object recognition can now be used to find cancers in MRI scans with the same precision as well-trained radiologists (Akkus, 2017; Wang et al., 2016; Liu, 2018).

Machine Learning algorithms automate the construction of analytical models using statistical methods, neural networks, operations research, and physics by finding insights hidden in data, without being specifically programmed to look at a particular place or reach a certain conclusion. Training neural networks requires Big Data (big data) and computational power concerning graphic processing units, which are essential for AI, which is necessary for continuous processing (Beam & Kohane, 2018; Qiu, 2016; Zhang, 2018).

Another important aspect of AI is that, due to its ability to learn, it needs to be constantly fed with data so that it can continue to evolve, just like a person. It is possible with simple computing processes concerning structures for processing, categorizing, and effectively analyzing data (data model); having access to a large volume of data to be processed (Big Data); and as previously mentioned, the operational and logistical capacity to process information quickly and efficiently (processing power) (Min et al., 2017; Qiu, 2016; Zhou et al., 2017).

3.1 AI Applied to the Health

Artificial Intelligence is the science applied in the development of technological devices that can simulate human reasoning, and employed in health, it provides benefits to hospitals and clinics concerning greater precision of diagnoses; agile software and electronic medical records; optimization of data storage; creation of a wide database for early diagnosis; providing better resources in the treatment of cancer, reducing costs, seeking new resources to improve the experience of its patient and procedures, among many other aspects (Wahl et al., 2018).

Through Artificial Intelligence it is possible to achieve greater precision in diagnoses by performing diagnostics through software that provides images of organs internal organs of patients. Since there are Machine Learning algorithms that allow health professionals to process large amounts of image data instantly, it has the ability to identify medical conditions that would go unnoticed by doctors who are looking for some other immediate health problem. This makes the identification of medical problems much faster and more assertive than those performed manually, making it possible to detect conditions that would not be diagnosed without the help of technology (Kalis et al., 2018).

With Artificial Intelligence in health, optimization of data storage is achieved, derived from the fact that hospital data has the option of storage in the Cloud, related that many processes can be performed automatically, through easy access to information, some more complex processes can be carried out simply and quickly, helping to reduce costs, which provides greater safety for patients (Luxton, 2016).

Through AI, a larger database for early diagnosis is possible, encompassing the personal data of patients in the Cloud, care, and health institutions have the ability to process through this storage of patient information, assisting in the discovery of diagnoses, performing a tracking for evaluating the family history of people, determining the probability that they will acquire a disease, among other aspects, resulting in greater knowledge about the health status of these patients. This decreases the chances of preventing the disease from developing, in the same sense that it increases the chances of a cure, as well as, making disease prevention more accessible with the use of AI used in health (Yu et al., 2018).

The medical records of patients who were previously manual and limited, with the application of AI in health, use intelligent electronic records capable of quickly collecting, storing, and retrieving information from these patients. This facilitates the discovery of diseases and the development of treatment plans, resulting in more efficient management concerning patient information, because health institutions automate the maintenance of these records, and improve and increase the data source for the collection of patient information through sensors and devices. What is the context of a joint application with the IoT (Internet of things) it is possible to feed the database providing new information directly in the medical records of each patient (He, 2019; Mincholé & Rodriguez, 2019; Mintz & Brodie, 2019).

The AI in conjunction with the IoT it is possible to notify the doctor, in real-time, through devices considering the AI system, which through them perform real-time notification about changes in the patient's health status. Listing mainly in emergency cases, the doctor can record the occurrence in the medical record and the service will be faster and more effective. Also reflecting that as the data is stored in the cloud, access is easier from any device with internet access, and in cases of emergency, this consultation of patient data is faster (Shishvan et al., 2020).

Through the application of AI tools and techniques, it is possible to develop new methods of treatment for cancer-based on genomic changes, instead of the tumors present in patients, developing drugs based on genomic technology for other types of diseases (Baxevanis et al., 2020; Lesk, 2019; Xia, 2018).

Still considering that some diseases are hardly diagnosed in the beginning, decreasing the chances of cure, as is the case of skin, breast, and lung cancer, among others. With AI, analyses are safer and more accurate, facilitating the process of correct diagnosis of the disease, and reinforcing the diagnosis of patients. In the same sense radiographic, magnetic resonance, and tomography examinations are also benefited by greater assertiveness through Artificial Intelligence applied in the health area. For a doctor to get the diagnosis of a patient right it is generally not an easy task, as there are diseases that present very similar symptoms and that can delay the identification of the problem, which impairs the entire treatment. With AI, through data analysis associating symptoms and relating to the patient's history, as well as analysis of image exams, it is possible to issue a more assertive alert about the possible diseases that this patient has developed (Bi et al., 2019; Ho, 2020; Rodríguez-Ruiz, 2019).

A machine provided with AI, employing pattern recognition, identifies breast cancer, and pneumonia with reasonable precision, since for technology the disease is a set of pixels that it has been trained to find. Relating that technology can help in the process of making a diagnosis and the doctor has more time to be a doctor, to offer humane treatment. Still considering that a Machine Learning algorithm helps in the challenge of recycling, updating, taking into account that among more than n million medical publications, this algorithm can read all published articles, summarize and inform areas of interest related to the disease employing a recommendation algorithm (Krittanawong, 2018; Shah, 2019; Verghese et al., 2018).

It is worth noting that AI is an auxiliary and not a substitute for the physician, considering that many professionals in the field see this technology only as an abstract concept not realizing its real application, and therefore it should not be seen as a threat. AI empowers the doctor, transforming the profession. Reflecting on a typical VUCA scenario (Volatility, Uncertainty, Complexity, Ambiguity), assessing that the AI reaches or exceeds human levels of treatment in these four domains, however, the doctor's acceptance is the final and fundamental step, since the role AI consists of assisting decision making (Krittanawong, 2018; Shah, 2019; Verghese et al., 2018).

Still considering a technological context in case the diagnosis of a certain doctor and the prediction of AI diverge, the healthcare platform can send the original exam to other doctors for a report. In this way, eliminating possible human errors, this new final report is also used to re-train the entire neural network, making AI more and more accurate (Krittanawong, 2018; Shah, 2019; Verghese et al., 2018).

Artificial Intelligence is a powerful and revolutionary tool capable of empowering doctors and helping patients, especially when it comes to diagnostic medicine. However, it is not her final word, assessing the tendency to further 'humanize' technology over the years, but it is purely a mathematical model, which responds to patterns of behavior for which it was trained. Finally, using AI in Health empowers doctors, helping to save millions of lives (Miao, 2018).

3.2 Machine Learning Concepts for Healthcare Systems

Artificial Intelligence is currently able to identify pathologies with better accuracy than the human average, through a process of "machine learning", training the algorithm from a bank with more than millions of images and names of pathologies, which allows the understanding of what, and in which pixels, certain changes are present (Alpaydin, 2020; Charniak, 2019; Faul, 2019; Kim, 2017; Neapolitan & Jiang, 2018).

The first pillar of AI is Machine Learning by which computers become able to learn and evolve, with the logical processing of data and the identification of patterns generating intelligence. The operation occurs by identifying the patterns and recognizing whether there is a relationship between the data. In technical these patterns are identified in infinite webs so that there are thousands of points of intersection that consist of the connections between the information, enabling intelligence on a large scale (Alpaydin, 2020; Charniak, 2019; Faul, 2019; Kim, 2017; Neapolitan & Jiang, 2018).

Basically, Machine Learning is conceptualized as a tool based on a compilation of computerized systems and data insertion by users to facilitate decision-making. In the context of Health, using the equipment that already uses this methodology, it is possible to cross-check the clinical data of patients with the epidemiological references obtained in government health sites and formulate several hypotheses about a clinical event. Meaning that technical use in health is able to provide more accurate conclusions than if they were analyzed in isolation, bringing more security to the health professional when making decisions for the patient (Alpaydin, 2020; Charniak, 2019; Faul, 2019; Kim, 2017; Neapolitan & Jiang, 2018).

3.2.1 Supervised Machine Learning

Supervised Machine Learning is related to trying to perform prediction of a dependent variable from a set of independent variables. The basic characteristic is that the data used for training generally encompasses the expected response, i.e., it comprises the dependent variable ascertaining from the observed independent variables. In this context, there is a set of labeled data that is already known which is the correct output and that must be similar to the set, with the answers or classes to be predicted, having the premise that there is a relation between the input and the output of the algorithm (Fig. 1) (Lindholm et al., 2019).

Supervised learning problems are classified as "regression" problems, trying to predict the outcomes in a continuous output, implying the attempt to perform mapping of input variables to a given continuous function; and "classification", trying to predict the outcomes in a discrete output, implying the attempt perform mapping of input variables into different categories (Simeone, 2017).

3.2.2 Unsupervised Learning

Unsupervised learning is the attempt to obtain a more elucidative representation of the dataset, it allows addressing problems with little information or no information about what the outcomes should appear (Fig. 2), there is no feedback related to the forecast outcomes, that is, there is no "agent" for fix it. Generally, this best representation is also simpler, used to reduce the number of dimensions in a data set to concentrate only on the most useful attributes, or to detect trends, condensing the information into more relevant points (Jansen et al., 2018; Kulkarni, 2019; Li et al., 2019).

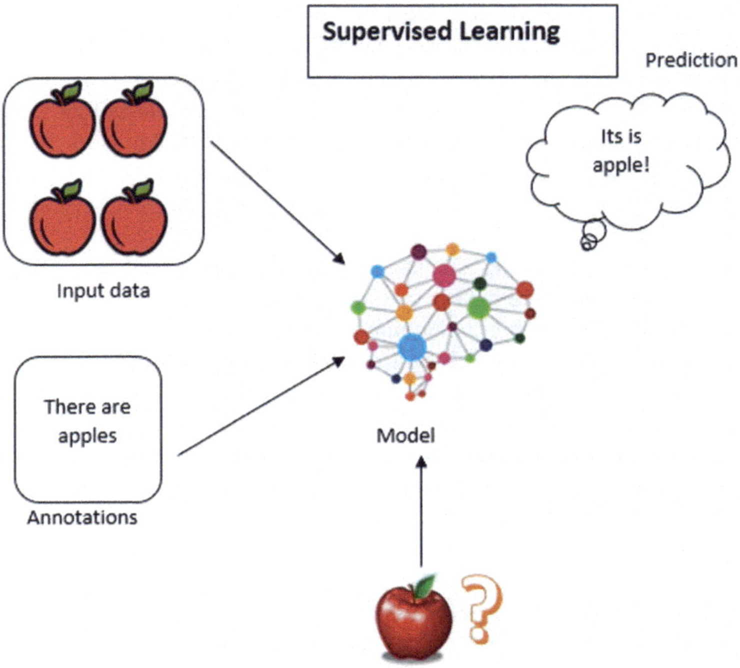

Fig. 1 Supervised Learning Illustration

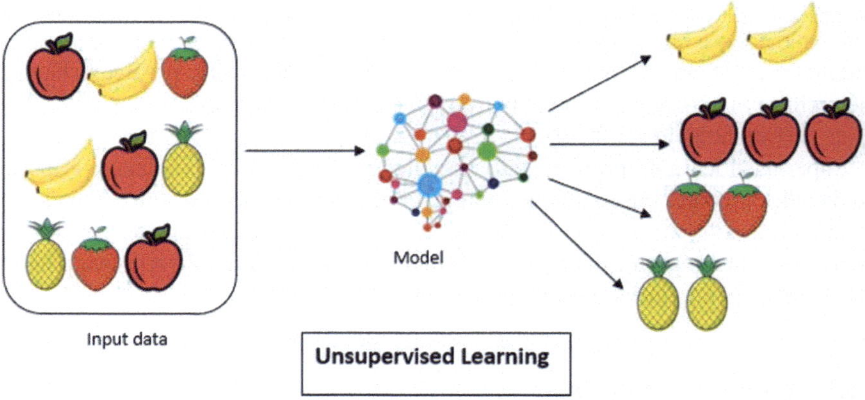

Fig. 2 Unsupervised learning illustration

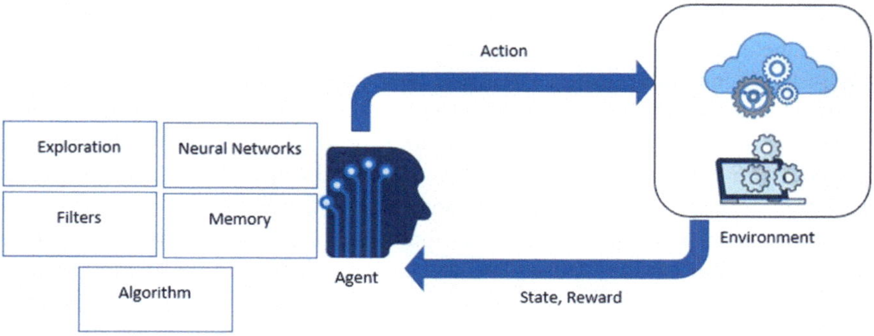

Fig. 3 Reinforcement learning

Amongst the best-known digital techniques for solving related problems, unsupervised learning is artificial neural networks (ANN), k-averaging clustering, expectation-maximization, K-means-expectation maximization clustering, support vector machine (SVM), word2vec, eclat, a priori, hierarchical clustering, principal component analysis, self-organized maps (SOM), insulating forests, restricted Boltzmann machines (RBM), T- distributed Stochastic Neighbor Embedding (t-SNE), among others (Jansen et al., 2018; Kulkarni, 2019; Li et al., 2019).

3.2.3 Reinforcement Learning

Reinforcement learning is the attempt to make the machine learn what is the best action to be taken, according to the decision made, with the time and repetition of the experiments analyzed, that is, in accordance with the circumstances (causality) in which this action will be executed. It is expected that the "agent" will be able to relate the actions that produce a greater reward for each circumstance that the current environment presents and start to prevent actions that produce punishment or lesser recompense (Fig. 3) (Li, 2017).

3.3 Machine Learning Application in Health

Health applications are supervised learning techniques for classification algorithms, meaning that, through a database of several patients containing the list of their symptoms and diagnoses, able to inform whether or not the patient has a certain disease, according to the symptoms he presents, seeking to find patterns of symptoms for each disease (Suzuki, 2017; Zhou et al., 2017).

This is an aspect of AI, that uses a method that unites data analysis and the construction of analytical models, enabling systems and software to learn from the information they receive, identify patterns, and even make decisions, based on models created from an interactive process based on the results obtained, it is possible to improve the algorithms in order to improve their performance (Tiwari, 2020).

It is worth mentioning that Big Data technology, which is due to the large volume of data and information stored on account of the new processing and storage systems, considerably increased the possibilities of Machine Learning, allowing the apprenticeship with previous computations and producing reliable and repeatable dispositions and results (Menasalvas & Gonzalo-Martin, 2016).

In the scenario of health, Machine Learning technology comes from a technological repertoire of responses that doctors and scientists achieve a model of efficiency much greater than any human being would be able to do. Showing that the techniques can be more accurate than the human evaluation for diagnostics in the medical field, since in urgent cases, which require quick medical intervention, the use of the tool for slight data analysis is even more necessary, so that, in a few minutes, a measure can be taken to avoid potential sequelae and even the death of patients (Weng et al., 2017).

The benefits of Machine Learning in Health are related to reducing the time of diagnosis; the reduction exam costs, indicating the most decisive ones for obtaining the diagnosis; and even the reduction of the operational team needed to meet the demand for exam analysis, since a doctor will be able to define the diagnosis more accurately and in a shorter consultation time, being able to serve more patients (Beaulieu-Jones, 2019).

The benefits of Machine Learning for the patient include the advantages of more accurate diagnosis, with better monitoring of the evolution of the disease; superior quality of service, which is carried out in a more personalized way; the possibility of diseases detected in the early stages, enabling greater chances of a cure or less drastic sequelae; as well as prevention concerning research based on previous diagnoses, making it possible to select the family of the disease and, with the supplementary exams, understand how to prevent possible diseases (Ravì, 2016).

A palpable example of the employment of Machine Learning is in the detection of skin cancer, concerning changes in pigmentation are the characteristics most considered in the detection, evaluating in diagnosis of melanomas and non-melanomas. Still considering that in general the way the image is registered, several factors must be taken into account so as not to confuse the detection algorithm, such as poor lighting, environment, and the instrument used in the registration causing bad image segmentation (Triantafyllidis & Tsanas, 2019).

Another example is the performance of imaging tests due to patient tremors, which impair the formation of the image. In this sense, through AI algorithms, it is possible to identify these movement patterns and reconstruct the image as if the patient were immobile. What results from discarding the alternative to sedation for this patient, that is, improves the access and application of this type of test for the population (Ker, 2017).

Still evaluating that with the evolution of technology over the years, computational processing became cheaper and more powerful, which opened the possibility of producing, more quickly and automatically, models capable of analyzing larger and more complex elements. As a result, results are generated that make it possible to discover opportunities and avoid unknown risks (Erickson, 2017).

4 Discussion

Other examples of applications of artificial intelligence in health can be related to virtual assistants in patient care; surgery using robots; accurate diagnoses through data analysis; prediction of risk factors; assertive guidance on treatments and development of new drugs; automated workflow assistance; system fraud detection, intelligent screening, as well as other aspects.

The patient's journey is the term related to the experiences that a person experiences when seeking medical care, this process is fundamental for obtaining better results both in the individual's quality of life and in reducing the costs of the health institution. AI can be applied to humanized processes in the patient's journey, including features of Machine Learning for chatbot (software capable of talking to a patient by text or audio, in a humanized way), or a virtual assistant, making it easier to obtain answers to questions health care and even treatment guidance, contributing to prevention, early diagnosis, treatment and quality of life through the collection, centralization and assertive analysis of all patient information.

Machine Learning applied to Health arises from the ability of machines to learn and use this knowledge in a functional way, arising from the premise that such systems can present data, identify specific patterns, and make decisions autonomously, taught through the construction of specific algorithms for each case. Reflecting on factors of increased data availability, the improvement of computational capacity, and the emergence of new algorithms for more complex problems that contribute to advances in this technology, stimulating the abilities of machines to contribute to health.

Machine Learning in health helps to improve health care and determine early diagnoses, bringing precision to care and diagnosis, predicting the patient's prognosis, and measuring the main therapeutic approaches in order to considerably minimize the chances of errors in doctors. In addition to proposing solutions to specific problems such as chatbot and virtual assistant who understand the text informed by the patient, anticipating common doubts and often excluding the need to open a call.

Faster diagnoses, more assertive treatments, and better-calculated risks show that the employment of Machine Learning in health reduces the margin of human error. Also through technology, it is possible to integrate services that cross data and allow mapping risk factors and analyzing genetic information, making it possible to anticipate diagnoses and adopt preventive measures.

Other ways of applying Machine Learning in Health are through algorithms capable of detecting signs of breast cancer in men and women, identifying cell patterns in human tissues, and being able to find abnormal cells. Another application is seen in a trained algorithm that can identify skin cancer or melanoma in patients, still evaluating that this type of initiative can remove this doubt from the professional who has an inconclusive evaluation.

It is important to consider that a large part of the world population lives in underdeveloped and developing countries, in certain situations, people live on less than one dollar a day, so this amount is incompatible with the minimum income for food and consequently, it is practically impossible to take care of health. Most countries in the world do not offer free and universal care to their population, the United States, even though it is a developed country, treats the health issue as something particular to each citizen, so the state is exempt from paying for the medical expenses of its citizens.

In other countries of the world, the government offers partial financial assistance to those who need medical care. The aid is beneficial for many savings but excludes 13.5 million people who live in extreme poverty. Brazil is a developing country and offers universal and totally free service to its population. In that country, medicines, medical consultations, births, and surgeries are totally free. However, this system called SUS (Unified Health System) is totally dependent on government transfers, which are generally insufficient to serve the entire country. This generates long queues for appointments and surgeries and even leads to the lack of destruction of free medicines for people with chronic diseases.

It is important to consider that some of the factors that increase the costs of accessing health care are the type of methodology used. Underdeveloped and developing countries are generally dependent on imports of medical equipment. Import costs are added to the cost of acquiring the device and consequently passed on to the patient or the health system. Thus, one of the alternatives is the replacement of traditional equipment with devices based on machine learning, as they have the ability to perform and even interpret the results.

Another solution is for underdeveloped and developing countries to redistribute GDP investments better, and allocate larger amounts to universities and research centers so that they develop medical devices dissociated from the need for traditional equipment and can perform medical examinations for cheaper equipment, accessible and easy to maintain such as smartphones and computers. It is important to consider that traditional equipment requires several reagents and even specialized technical assistance. Equipment based on Machine Learning, Deep Learning, and Artificial Intelligence techniques tends to have easy use and lower locking rates.

In addition, these techniques can be applied to monitor chronic diseases remotely, so that patients can be treated and monitored remotely without the need for long queues for care in Brazil. In the case of other countries, distance monitoring can be seen as a much cheaper and even free alternative for populations living in extreme poverty. Besides, remote monitoring can help people with low income and low school education to follow their treatments correctly. It is important to note that chronic diseases such as hypertension and diabetes when properly monitored by doctors tend to generate fewer complications and consequently generate fewer costs with hospitalizations.

Just as there are studies of Machine Learning in several related areas, including those of cardiology, ophthalmology, pathology, and radiology. Reflecting that nowadays, technology is already used and trained to analyze images, identify problem points, and inform the responsible professionals which are the areas that need more attention.

Yet another application context is related to the development of computational techniques capable of diagnosing eye diseases in their initial stages, capable of identifying normal and altered eyes through a simple retinal scan, using a bank of millions of anonymous eye scans, fighting blindness that can be prevented if treated early on. Or even a Machine Learning algorithm that helps to indicate cardiac risk or propensity to stroke (stroke) with an accuracy higher than humans, using computed tomography (CT) images through segmentation methods by similarity and mathematical morphology, including the data input of a neural network.

Artificial intelligence represents a true revolution in the personalization of health, through the impacts of Machine Learning on health can be seen in scientific knowledge in constant change, due to the discovery of new information, that refutes existing ones or complements knowledge in the optimization of work clinical professionals.

In addition, the Machine Learning tool brings differentiated learning to patient care professionals, the possibility of integrating systems and the statistical study of clinical problems, and the chances of diagnostic errors and conduct has greatly decreased, even facilitating faster communication among everyone involved.

From the patient's point of view, the implementation of Machine Learning in health is a revolution in the fields related to diagnosis, monitoring, and establishment of clinical conducts, which foresee clinical results in a shorter term, which was previously based on a long term, with scientific and statistical basis, which results in hope for patients with little expectation of cure or survival.

5 Conclusions

Through Machine Learning techniques, neural networks, and natural processing language applied to health, it is possible to evaluate a person's genetic sequencing, in a matter of minutes, ranking the most frequent and relevant mutations, crossing with the most up-to-date scientific literature, and generating different treatment plans with more chances of cure. In comparison the analysis of this information in a traditional way, i.e., without the use of technology, would take hundreds of hours, considering the tiredness and weariness of the team of human professionals.

As well as highlighting three points concerning technology such as processing capacity, cost, and access. Still evaluating another point related to better management of information and data related to health institutions, with technology and prevention, it is possible to bring this cost forward, to increase, improve, and upgrade the quality of life, reducing the cost of people's health.

Still considering that the application of Machine Learning in health, along with the adoption of new technologies and the development of analytical skills, brings numerous benefits ranging from clinical application to management. Thinking about machine learning in healthcare can seem distant.

From the point of view of medicine towards the patient, it is necessary to use and take advantage of all the technologies that allow 'seeing' the patient. Technology arrives to increase capacity and enhance human performance in what health professionals are good at, and which is not possible to program.

Assessing the modern point of view it is necessary to have this type of multidisciplinary, concerning Machine Learning (technology) in health, adding efforts and potential, which achieves the objectives more quickly, with less cost, and more quality delivery. In line with a comparative analogy linked to technology as the path to more sustainable, more personalized health, data can be considered the new oil, and artificial intelligence is the new electricity.

6 Trends

Machine Learning is a broad and very deep field when related to health, it will have greater performance concerning the personal assistant, monitoring patients in real-time and offering objective opinions about health, consequently, improving the quality of life of the patient who is in treatment (Buch et al., 2018; Desai, 2020; Wu, 2020).

In the same sense, the performance of technology will be even greater in relation to data integration with systems of health institutions, facilitating communication between specialist doctors and patients, and performing more precise and detailed patient screening, including even genetic information.

Assessing the broad potential of applicability of technology concerning predictive modeling by identifying molecules with the potential to be transformed into drugs to combat biological processes; or even monitoring laboratory tests to be done in real-time, with results obtained quickly, avoiding unnecessary delays or investments (Desai, 2020; França et al., 2021; Mittal & Hasija, 2020; Monteiro et al., 2021; Negrete et al., 2020; Wu, 2020).

The performance Deep Learning is a powerful method in many areas of medical imaging diagnosis, or even in the application to calculate, estimate, and determine a subject's age from hand x-ray digital images, eliminating the requirement for Atlas (medical encyclopedia) searches to improve and gain the time and cost (expense) of the digital process estimation. Even the Deep Learning-based neural network can be employed in reading medical records, memorizing disease trajectories and care processes, estimating current disease states, and even predicting future risks, which opens up a new principle-based approach to predictive medicine, among many applications (França et al., 2021; Mittal & Hasija, 2020; Monteiro et al., 2021, 2022; Negrete et al., 2020).

References

Akkus, Z., et al. (2017). Deep learning for brain MRI segmentation: state of the art and future directions. *Journal of Digital Imaging, 30*(4), 449–459.

Alpaydin, E. (2020). *Introduction to machine learning*. MIT Press.

Baxevanis, A. D., Bader, G. D., & Wishart, D. S. (Eds.). (2020). *Bioinformatics*. Wiley.

Beam, A. L., & Kohane, I. S. (2018). Big data and machine learning in health care. *JAMA, 319*(13), 1317–1318.

Beaulieu-Jones, B., et al. (2019). Trends and focus of machine learning applications for health research. *JAMA Network Open, 2*(10), e1914051-e1914051.

Bengio, Y., Goodfellow, I., & Courville, A. (2017). *Deep learning* (Vol. 1). MIT Press.

Bi, W. L., et al. (2019). Artificial intelligence in cancer imaging: clinical challenges and applications. *CA: A Cancer Journal for Clinicians, 69*(2), 127–157.

Blasimme, A., & Vayena, E. (2019, April 9). The Ethics of AI in Biomedical research, patient care and public health. *Oxford Handbook of Ethics of Artificial Intelligence*, Forthcoming.

Bouchard, B. (Ed.). (2017). *Smart technologies in healthcare*. CRC Press.

Buch, V. H., Ahmed, I., & Maruthappu, M. (2018). Artificial intelligence in medicine: Current trends and future possibilities. *British Journal of General Practice, 68*(668), 143–144.

Charniak, E. (2019). *Introduction to deep learning*. The MIT Press.

Desai, R. J., et al. (2020). Comparison of machine learning methods with traditional models for use of administrative claims with electronic medical records to predict heart failure outcomes. *JAMA Network Open, 3*(1), e1918962-e1918962.

De Stefano, L., et al. (2019). Newer Technologies, Better Healthcare. *Biomedical Journal of Scientific & Technical Research,* 14(4).

Erickson, B. J., et al. (2017). Machine learning for medical imaging. *Radiographics 37*(2), 505–515.

Faul, A. C. (2019). *A concise introduction to machine learning*. CRC Press.

França, R. P., et al. (2019). *Potential proposal to improvement of the data transmission in healthcare systems*.

França, R. P., et al. (2020). Potential proposal to improve data transmission in healthcare systems. In *Deep learning techniques for biomedical and health informatics* (pp. 267–283). Academic Press.

França, R. P., et al. (2021). An overview of deep learning in big data, image, and signal processing in the modern digital age. In *Trends in deep learning methodologies* (pp. 63–87). Elsevier.

Goodfellow, I., Bengio, Y., & Courville A. (2016). *Deep learning*. MIT Press

Hayre, C. M., Muller, D., & Scherer, M. (Eds.). (2019). *Everyday Technologies in Healthcare*. CRC Press.

He, J., et al. (2019). The practical implementation of artificial intelligence technologies in medicine. *Nature Medicine, 25*(1), 30–36.

He, L., Ota, K., & Dong, M. (2018). Learning IoT in edge: Deep learning for the Internet of Things with edge computing. *IEEE Network, 32*(1), 96–101.

Ho, D. (2020). Artificial intelligence in cancer therapy. *Science, 367*(6481), 982–983.

Jansen, A., et al. (2018). Unsupervised learning of semantic audio representations. In *2018 IEEE International Conference on Acoustics, Speech, and Signal Processing (ICASSP)*. IEEE.

Kalis, B., Collier, M., & Fu, R. (2018). *10 promising AI applications in health care*. Harvard Business Review.

Ker, J., et al. (2017). Deep learning applications in medical image analysis. *IEEE Access, 6*, 9375–9389.

Kim, P. (2017). Matlab deep learning. *With Machine Learning, Neural Networks, and Artificial Intelligence, 130.*

Krittanawong, C. (2018). The rise of artificial intelligence and the uncertain future for physicians. *European Journal of Internal Medicine, 48*, e13–e14.

Kulkarni, T. D., et al. (2019). Unsupervised learning of object key points for perception and control. *Advances in Neural Information Processing Systems.*

Lesk, A. (2019). *Introduction to bioinformatics*. Oxford University Press.
Li, X., & Wong, K.-C. (Eds.). (2019). *Natural computing for unsupervised learning*. Springer International Publishing.
Li, Y. (2017). *Deep reinforcement learning: An overview*. arXiv preprint arXiv:1701.07274.
Lindholm, A., et al. (2019). *Supervised machine learning*.
Liu, F., et al. (2018). Deep learning MR imaging-based attenuation correction for PET/MR imaging. *Radiology, 286*(2), 676–684.
Luxton, D. D. (2016). An introduction to artificial intelligence in behavioral and mental health care. In *Artificial intelligence in behavioral and mental health care* (pp. 1–26). Academic Press.
Maddox, T. M., Rumsfeld, J. S., & Payne, P. R. O. (2019). Questions for artificial intelligence in health care. *Jama, 321*(1) 31–32.
Menasalvas, E., & Gonzalo-Martin, C. (2016). Challenges of medical text and image processing: Machine learning approaches. In *Machine Learning for Health Informatics* (pp. 221–242). Springer.
Miao, C., et al. (2018). Humanized Artificial Intelligence: What, Why and How. *International Journal of Information Technology 24*(2).
Min, S., Lee, B., & Yoon, S. (2017). Deep learning in bioinformatics. *Briefings in Bioinformatics, 18*(5), 851–869.
Mincholé, A., & Rodriguez, B. (2019). Artificial intelligence for the electrocardiogram. *Nature Medicine, 25*(1), 22–23.
Mintz, Y., & Brodie, R. (2019). Introduction to artificial intelligence in medicine. *Minimally Invasive Therapy & Allied Technologies, 28*(2), 73–81.
Mittal, S., & Hasija, Y. (2020). Applications of deep learning in healthcare and biomedicine. In *Deep learning techniques for biomedical and health informatics* (pp. 57–77). Springer.
Mohammadi, M., et al. (2018). Deep learning for IoT big data and streaming analytics: A survey. *IEEE Communications Surveys & Tutorials, 20*(4), 2923–2960.
Monteiro, A. C. B. (2019). Proposta de uma metodologia de segmentação de imagens para detecção e contagem de hemácias e leucócitos através do algoritmo WT-MO.
Monteiro, A. C. B., et al. (2020). Development of a laboratory medical algorithm for simultaneous detection and counting of erythrocytes and leukocytes in digital images of a blood smear. In *Deep Learning Techniques for Biomedical and Health Informatics* (pp. 165–186). Academic Press.
Monteiro, A. C. B., et al. (2021). Deep learning methodology proposal for the classification of erythrocytes and leukocytes. In *Trends in deep learning methodologies* (pp. 129–156). Elsevier.
Monteiro, A. C. B., et al. (2022). An artificial intelligent cognitive approach for classification and recognition of white blood cells employing deep learning for medical applications. In *Deep learning for medical applications with unique data* (pp. 53–69). Academic Press.
Neapolitan, R. E., & X. Jiang. (2018). *Artificial intelligence: With an introduction to machine learning*. CRC Press.
Negrete, M., et al. (2020). Classification of dermoscopy skin images with the application of deep learning techniques. In *Proceedings of the 5th Brazilian Technology Symposium: Emerging Trends, Issues, and Challenges in the Brazilian Technology* (Vol. 2). Springer International Publishing.
Qiu, J., et al. (2016). A survey of machine learning for big data processing. *EURASIP Journal on Advances in Signal Processing, 1*, 67.
Ravì, D., et al. (2016). Deep learning for health informatics. *IEEE Journal of biomedical and health informatics, 21*(1), 4–21.
Rodríguez-Ruiz, A., et al. (2019). Detection of breast cancer with mammography: Effect of an artificial intelligence support system. *Radiology, 290*(2), 305–314.
Shah, N. R. (2019). Health care in 2030: Will artificial intelligence replace physicians? *Annals of Internal Medicine, 170*(6), 407–408.
Shishvan, O. R., Zois, D.-S., & Soyata, T. (2020). Incorporating artificial intelligence into medical cyber-physical systems: A survey. In *Connected Health in Smart Cities* (pp. 153–178). Springer.

Simeone, O. (2017). A brief introduction to machine learning for engineers. arXiv preprint arXiv: 1709.02840

Suzuki, K. (2017). Overview of deep learning in medical imaging. *Radiological Physics and Technology, 10*(3), 257–273.

Tang, J., et al. (2017). Enabling deep learning on IoT devices. *Computer, 50*(10), 92–96.

Tiwari, A. (2020, March 30). *Multidimensional medical imaging analysis alzheimer's disease via image processing and machine learning: A review, diagnosis and challenges.*

Triantafyllidis, A. K., & Tsanas, A. (2019). Applications of machine learning in real-life digital health interventions: Review of the literature. *Journal of Medical Internet Research, 21*(4), e12286.

Verghese, A., Shah, N. H., & Harrington, R. A. (2018). What this computer needs is a physician: Humanism and artificial intelligence. *JAMA, 319*(1), 19–20.

Wahl, B., et al. (2018). Artificial intelligence (AI) and global health: how can AI contribute to health in resource-poor settings? *BMJ Global Health, 3*(4), e000798.

Wang, S., et al. (2016). Accelerating magnetic resonance imaging via deep learning. In *2016 IEEE 13th International Symposium on Biomedical Imaging (ISBI).* IEEE.

Weng, S. F., et al. (2017). Can machine-learning improve cardiovascular risk prediction using routine clinical data? *PLOS One, 12*(4).

Wu, P., et al. (2020). Classification of lung nodules based on deep residual networks and migration learning. *Computational Intelligence and Neuroscience*, 1–10.

Xia, X. (2018). *Bioinformatics and the cell: modern computational approaches in genomics, proteomics and transcriptomics*. Springer.

Yu, K.-H., Beam, A. L., & Kohane, I. S. (2018). Artificial intelligence in healthcare. *Nature Biomedical Engineering, 2*(10), 719–731.

Zhang, Q., et al. (2018). A survey on deep learning for big data. *Information Fusion, 42*, 146–157.

Zhou, L., et al. (207). Machine learning on big data: Opportunities and challenges. *Neurocomputing 237*, 350–361.

Zhou, S. K., Greenspan, H., & Shen, D. (Eds.). (2017). *Deep learning for medical image analysis.* Academic Press.

Maritime Sustainability: Navigating Complex Challenges and Ecological Footprints

Serkan Karakas, A. Zafer Acar, and Mehmet Kirmizi

Abstract The maritime industry holds significant importance in facilitating international trade and contributing to the overall well-being of societies. Maritime activities encompass significant ecological and social results, in addition to their economic value. For instance, carbon emissions from maritime transportation remain a significant challenge, necessitating the implementation of various strategies and technologies to mitigate the issue. Nevertheless, the concept of maritime sustainability encompasses various complex aspects that have significant social and environmental implications. There are ongoing conflicts concerning the sharing of ocean resources among various maritime stakeholders. One additional concern pertains to the environmental inequality that exists between high-income and low-income countries in terms of ship recycling and demolition. Herewith, this chapter considers the various facets of sustainability in the maritime industry, including a recent term of blue economy, where sustainable economics intertwines with ecological well-being. Extensive discussion is also provided on contemporary technological and systems approaches aimed at mitigating the detrimental environmental effects of maritime operations. By interweaving ethnoeconomics and the welfare of coastal communities, this chapter also provides an in-depth discussion on recent issues such as ethical consumerism of maritime resources and environmental injustice.

Keywords Blue Economy · Sustainability · Maritime Transportation · Resource Management

---

S. Karakas (✉) · A. Z. Acar
Faculty of Applied Sciences, Bilgi University, 34440 Istanbul, Turkey
e-mail: serkan.karakas@bilgi.edu.tr

A. Z. Acar
e-mail: zafer.acar@bilgi.edu.tr

M. Kirmizi
Faculty of Economics and Administrative Sciences, Piri Reis University, 34940 Tuzla, Istanbul, Turkey
e-mail: mekirmizi@pirireis.edu.tr

W. Leal Filho and V. Kuzmanović (eds.), *Sustainable Development Seen Through the Lenses of Ethnoeconomics and the Circular Economy*,
https://doi.org/10.1007/978-3-031-72676-7_2

1 Introduction

Sustainability is a concept frequently heard from academic and industrial communities today. Beyond being a popular concept, thanks to the customers' awareness and their persistent pursuit of this issue, it influences the strategic decisions of high-level executives of the firms, particularly in the firms that operate in international scope and have a wide range of customers. In its simplest form, sustainability is concerned with the earth we will leave for our children and grandchildren (Yarrow, 2009). According to the most often cited sources (e.g. UN World Commission on Environment and Development, UCLA Sustainability Committee), sustainability seeks a balance between environmental health, social equity, and economic vitality (Boschmann & Kwan, 2008).

Sustainable practices promote the health and vitality of the environment, people, and the economy. Sustainability integrates these triple bottom-line factors (Agrawal & Singh, 2019) to create thriving, healthy, diverse, and resilient communities for the current generation and generations to come. Sustainability practices recognize how these challenges are interrelated and necessitate a systems perspective as well as an understanding of complexity. The experts on sustainability claim that when resources are scarce, they must be used wisely while keeping in mind long-term objectives and the consequences of how they are put to use.

Even in these simple definitions, it becomes clear that while we use natural resources for today's needs, we must assume the responsibility that our future heirs will also need them. In the context of sustainability, the concept of ethno-economy emerges at this point and emphasizes the need to display an ethical attitude toward the future while using resources within the framework of today's economic justifications. From a sustainable economics perspective, O'Hara (1998) delves into the influence of ethical considerations on the understanding and implementation of sustainable practices in economics and resource utilization. For this reason, it can be concluded that one of the focal issues of sustainable economics and ethnoeconomics is considered sustainable resource management.

Although it has not been a long time since the concept started to be used intensively, historically, the concept of sustainability has been viewed as a necessary element to strengthen brand extensions, especially by companies in the manufacturing sector. However, it was later realized that the impacts of sustainability initiatives go far beyond brand image and that it is an untouchable tangible resource with many benefits, such as risk management, cost reduction, revenue generation, and customer satisfaction in every facet of business operations. Thus, sustainability issues have started to be integrated with firms' strategies and implemented in their operations. During this above-mentioned development and maturation period of the concept, the logistics industry, together with all its transportation modes, has been stigmatised as the scapegoat of sustainability.

Throughout history, people have traded with each other to survive and create value, which means there has been an irrefutable need for transportation. Those transportation needs of goods subject to international trade have led to the development of the logistics industry. On the contrary, it has been observed that international trade has developed in regions with strong transportation infrastructure. Although phenomenal land routes such as the historical Silk Road maintained their popularity for a long time, maritime transport began to dominate international trade in parallel with the discovery of the Cape of Good Hope and the developments in the shipbuilding industry.

Today, approximately 80% of all goods traded internationally in volumetric numbers are transported by sea, and this figure is significantly greater for the majority of developing nations UNCTAD (2023). The world maritime fleet needed to transport these commercial goods subject to international trade consists of 105,493 ships of 100 gross tons and above as of January 2023 (Clarkson Research data cited in UNCTAD, 2023). With all kinds of ships, ports and terminals, shipyards, and other supporting institutions and infrastructure, maritime is more than just a transportation mode; it is a huge industry in itself. For instance, when we consider solely container transportation, whose popularity has increased in recent years, it is seen that it has generated a freight income of $300 billion before interest and taxes (EBIT) in 2022.

For an enormous portion of humanity, the marine environment-including all oceans, seas, and lakes-offers food, economic activity, and cultural value (Parsons et al., 2014). First, maritime transportation is an indispensable industry due to the financial value generated for its industry stakeholders, the large number of direct and indirect employees it employs, giving service to the world population, and the value it generates for economies by supporting international trade (Hernández et al., 2014; Merk, 2013). In addition to these macro-level reasons, when we look at it from a micro perspective, the maritime industry is indispensable due to the cost advantage it offers thanks to the economy of scale it creates for businesses that need international transportation. However, beyond the economic impacts of the maritime industry, it's a massive industry that consumes natural resources from shipbuilding to the construction of ports and terminals and has the potential to contaminate the environment during sailing and shipbreaking activities.

Herewith, the notion of sustainable resource management underscores the significance of utilizing natural resources in a cautious, responsible, and efficient manner (Kessler et al., 1992). From this point forth, Sect. 2 provides an in-depth analysis of this idea, specifically examining its application in the maritime industry. The subject matter encompasses a broad spectrum of themes, including environmental stewardship, ecosystem restoration, and sustainable fisheries management.

Putting an emphasis on resource recycling efficiency, the circular economy (CE) entails reorganizing business operations to align with sustainable principles (Preston, 2012). The term blue economy, first presented at the United Nations Conference on Sustainable Development, promotes sustainable economic growth by advocating for the minimization of waste production and the effective utilization of marine resources. Hence, the focus of Sect. 3 is on the blue economy and circularity, specifically examining reuse and remanufacturing in the shipbuilding industry and waste reduction strategies in port management.

To align with the 13th United Nations Sustainable Development Goal (SDG), it is necessary to enhance the use of diverse methodologies, systems, and technologies to reduce carbon emissions from maritime vessels. These are categorized into batteries and electric fuels, Cold Ironing (CI) technology, and Exhaust Gas Cleaning (EGCS) Systems. Nevertheless, carbon emissions are not the sole issue associated with maritime activities. The transportation of invasive species and microorganisms through ballast might enable their spread across different ecosystems, leading to ecological issues (Lv et al., 2022). For this purpose, there are various ballast water treatment systems (BWTS) available that utilize different treatment and filtration methods. In line with this, Sect. 4 explores the subject of decarbonization in maritime logistics and the preservation of ocean ecosystems in relatively technical terms.

The impacts arising from maritime activities extend beyond direct environmental consequences, such as increased emissions and marine pollution. These activities also have diverse direct or indirect effects on the communities living near and benefiting from oceanic regions. Accordingly, it is crucial to adequately address maritime social sustainability, ethical consumerism of maritime resources, and environmental injustice among high- and low-income economies. For instance, most of the commercial fleet worldwide is owned by firms based in well-developed nations. However, the process of dismantling ships that have reached the end of their economic lifespan occurs in developing countries, resulting in unfair and imbalanced exploitation of natural resources and the environment in low-income economies (Wan et al., 2021). Hence, Sect. 5 of the research is dedicated to exploring the ethical considerations in the maritime industry. Finally, in the Conclusions section, the key findings of the chapter are summarized.

This chapter employs a qualitative approach of thorough examination and evaluation of various reliable sources as part of our methodology. We extensively analyze scholarly literature to provide relevant academic perspectives. In addition, information is collected from a wide range of sources, such as the European Commission, the United Nations Conference on Trade and Development (UNCTAD), the International Maritime Organization (IMO), the International Transport Workers' Federation (ITF), classification societies (DNV), and maritime manufacturers.

From this point forth, this chapter provides an in-depth analysis of maritime activities, sustainability, the environment, and societies, focusing on the perspectives of sustainable economics and ethno-economics. In accordance with this structure, the remainder of the study is organized into the following sections: sustainable resource management in the maritime industry, blue economy and circularity, sustainable maritime transportation and logistics, ethical considerations in the maritime industry, and conclusions.

2 Sustainable Resource Management in the Maritime Industry

Sustainable resource management has been defined as the prudent, responsible, and effective use of natural resources to satisfy present requirements and ensure their preservation and availability for future generations (Kessler et al., 1992). Sustainable resource management seeks to reconcile the economic activities of human resources with the need to safeguard the environment, preserve ecosystem health, and advance societal well-being (Amrutha & Geetha, 2020; Järlström et al., 2018). It entails adopting practices that consider economic, social, and environmental aspects as well as making informed decisions (Epstein & Buhovac, 2014). Although it is a massive subject related to all industries, the current section gives fundamental insights into these aspects of sustainability in the maritime industry. Accordingly, the following subsections investigate environmental challenges and opportunities as well as economic and social aspects of sustainable resource management in the maritime domain.

2.1 Environmental Challenges and Opportunities in Sustainable Resource Management in the Maritime Industry

Every activity carried out by human beings, whether in, on, or near the seas or in terrestrial regions, directly or indirectly affects the marine ecosystem which provides many valuable services. For example, the wastes we discharge into rivers in inland terrestrial regions and the bilge and ballast waters discharged directly into the seas pollute the waters, which are among the most important resources for the future existence of human beings. Undoubtedly, the seas have a universal cycle for self-cleaning. However, in places -such as ports, terminals and economic zones- where the rate of pollution exceeds the rate of cleaning, marine life begins to disappear, giving priority to biological organisms that are sensitive to pollution.

For instance, Bullock et al. (2022) argued that the marine industry is distinguished by very significant levels of committed greenhouse gas (GHG) emissions. When the data in the International Maritime Organization's (IMO) fourth GHG study is examined, it is seen that international shipping contributed 2.89% of the world's greenhouse gas emissions in 2018, approximately 1076 $MtCO_2$ (IMO, 2020). The worst is that these emissions are expected to increase by 90–130% by 2050, despite improvements in carbon intensity. In fact, the industry would be the sixth-largest emitter in the world if it were a nation (Malmborg, 2023).

Moreover, fossil fuel resources are not the only resources used by the maritime transportation industry that should be taken into consideration in terms of sustainable resource management. When we examine the issue in depth from a supply chain perspective, raw materials that are used massively in the production of marine vessels and the construction of ports and terminals and often have the potential to leave hazardous wastes also become the subject of sustainable resource management. Therefore, the protection of the marine ecosystem, which is a crucial reservoir of biodiversity and of which the maritime transportation industry is a part, sustainable fisheries management, the use of greener technologies in transport infrastructure, and environmental stewardship from a sustainability perspective are the topics that should be taken into consideration.

In this respect, based on the facts provided by the scientific sources and the arguments of the experts in the area, which highlight the importance of sustainable resource management in the maritime industry and the environmental threats it faces, some possible actions that governments and maritime companies can take to protect the marine environment are summarized below. However, because it is one of the primary responsibilities of the maritime industry in terms of SDGs, the issues regarding clean technology and sustainable ship design will be given separately in a dedicated part.

Enhancing Marine Ecosystem Conversation Efforts: To effectively champion the cause of marine ecosystem protection, governments can adopt an ecosystem-based approach to marine resource management (Agardy et al., 2017). This approach recognizes the intricate web of connections between different species and habitats within marine environments, promoting a holistic perspective that acknowledges how the well-being of one species or habitat can impact the entire ecosystem. Moreover, governments and maritime companies can make significant investments in research initiatives aimed at better understanding the marine ecosystems within their regions. By doing so, they can identify vulnerable areas and species, enabling them to tailor their conservation efforts more effectively. Regular monitoring of water quality, species populations, and ecosystem health can complement these research endeavors by providing valuable data that inform conservation strategies (Palumbi et al., 2009). Additionally, governments should actively engage in international agreements and collaborations to address transboundary marine conservation issues (van Tatenhove, 2017). Simultaneously, maritime companies can contribute to these global efforts by adhering to international standards and best practices, thus minimizing their global impact on marine biodiversity.

Promoting Responsible Practices and Innovation in Maritime Industries: To foster a broader culture of responsibility towards marine ecosystems, governments and maritime companies can engage in public awareness campaigns and educational programs. These initiatives serve to promote responsible behavior and emphasize the crucial importance of marine biodiversity conservation. In recognition of environmentally conscious practices, governments can offer economic incentives and tax benefits to maritime companies that not only adopt eco-friendly practices but also invest in biodiversity conservation. In parallel, governments and maritime companies can join forces in research and development efforts, aiming to pioneer innovative technologies that reduce the environmental impact of maritime operations. As provided in Sect. 4, these technologies and applications encompass but are not limited to sustainable ship design and routing optimization, the utilization of shore-side electricity (i.e., cold ironing), and alternate fuels, contributing to sustainable practices in the industry.

Strategic Allocation of Resources for Marine Conservation: Given the constraints of limited resources, governments can strategically allocate funding and conservation efforts to regions that serve as hotspots of marine biodiversity and ecosystem services (Chan et al., 2006; Selig et al., 2014). This targeted approach, grounded in existing literature and scientific findings, ensures that available resources are optimally employed to safeguard our precious marine environments. These actions, when taken collectively and with a long-term perspective, can contribute to the protection and conservation of marine biodiversity while allowing for sustainable economic development in coastal regions. Also, they could be accepted as the opportunities before us to be more successful in this field.

Sustainable Fisheries Management: Despite the significant role of fisheries in the livelihoods of the world population, they are not an infinite resource. Thus, it is an undeniable subject of sustainability and sustainable development projects (Costello et al., 2010). However, the reduced numbers of fish have occurred not only in uncontrolled fisheries but also in contamination and the warming of the oceans and the seas. Therefore, it is a matter of the environmental and social aspects of sustainability. Thus, the failure of the related projects can affect the future of millions of people. Thanks to developing information technologies and information systems comprehensive data collection could be beneficial for significant projects based on reliable fish stocks.

Environmental Stewardship: Since roughly %71 of the world is covered by the sea and %80 of the internationally transported commercial goods are transported by the maritime industry, it plays a vital role not only in the global economy by facilitating international trade but also in the sustainable economic growth (Wang et al., 2020). Thus, the development of the maritime industry's human resources in an environmentally sensitive manner will be beneficial both for the industry and the sustainable growth efforts of the world itself based on robust environmental stewardship. Also, ensuring decent working conditions for seafarers is one of the responsibilities of the maritime industry which is not only related to SDG 11 but also embedded in many other SDGs (Wang et al., 2020).

Ecosystem Restoration: Even though the ecological crisis in the marine environment is prevented by regulations and environmentally sensitive actions in the maritime industry, in accordance with the spirit of the sustainability approach we should bring the marine ecosystem to our children and grandchildren as we take from our ancestors. So, it is not a matter of reducing carbon emissions and decontaminating the ports only. We need to change our approach to using natural resources environmentally starting from ship and port construction to ship routing to reduce fuel consumption. The problem is that we are still in the early stages of marine ecosystem restoration, and it's still costly. However, if we do not invest in restoration projects, it will be too late tomorrow. In this sense, coordinated efforts involving multiple stakeholders, long-term commitments to restoration, financial commitments, and/or legislative requirements will contribute to the success of restoration (Saunders et al., 2020b).

2.2 The Economic Necessity of Sustainable Resource Management in the Maritime Industry

It is common in the literature that priority is given to environmental impact while examining sustainability. Pursuing this habit, the abovementioned activities focus on environmental aspects of sustainable management of marine resources. However, the maritime transportation industry, including ports and terminals, creates economic value by contributing greatly to the delivery of commercial goods, moving along international supply chains to demand points at the lowest unit cost, benefiting from the economy of scale it creates. Although it is not possible to completely separate the sustainability dimensions from each other, it would be useful to examine the issue within the framework of sustainable resource management to create a consensus on what can be done without ignoring the negative environmental effects in return for the economic benefit created by the maritime transportation industry. So, after the environmental issues, now, it would be beneficial to examine the economic issues in the framework of sustainable resource management in the maritime industry.

In the contemporary world, sustainable resource management in the maritime industry is no longer just an environmental concern; it is now an economic imperative. This section explores the intrinsic link between economic well-being and responsible resource management in the maritime sector. It also delves into how policies such as the 8th Environment Action Programme of the European Union contribute to a vision of a climate-neutral, resource-efficient economy.

Economic Benefits of Sustainable Resource Management: In recent years, there has been a growing recognition of the economic imperatives associated with sustainable resource management within the maritime industry. The world's oceans and marine ecosystems play a vital role in supporting not only the well-being of marine life but also the global economy. As a result, safeguarding these valuable resources is not merely a moral or environmental duty but an economic necessity.

The global maritime industry, which encompasses shipping, fishing, and tourism, relies heavily on the health and abundance of marine ecosystems. Sustainable fisheries (Costello et al., 2010), clean and navigable waters, and vibrant coastal ecosystems are essential for the economic prosperity of many nations (UN, 2006). In this context, the sustainable management of maritime resources is not just about protecting the environment; it's also about securing the future economic stability of coastal regions and the industry as a whole (Neumann et al., 2017).

Effective sustainable resource management in the maritime industry can have direct economic benefits. For example, well-managed fisheries can maintain fish populations at healthy levels, ensuring a steady and predictable supply for commercial purposes (Costello et al., 2010). This reduces the risk of overfishing, stock collapse, and associated economic losses. Furthermore, the preservation of pristine marine environments can attract eco-tourism, providing a substantial source of income for coastal communities and businesses (Sangha et al., 2019).

Beyond these immediate economic gains, sustainable practices -including environmental entrepreneurship- can prevent the long-term costs associated with environmental degradation (Dean & McMullen, 2007). Polluted waters, declining fish stocks, and damaged ecosystems can lead to significant economic repercussions, including increased healthcare costs, reduced property values, and the loss of livelihoods in affected communities. By proactively engaging in sustainable resource management, the maritime industry can mitigate these potential economic pitfalls.

Cost-Benefit Analysis in the Maritime Industry: As the impact of long-term costs has been mentioned above, cost-benefit analysis is one of the key tools for understanding and revealing the economic necessity of sustainable resource management. This approach allows governments and industry stakeholders to evaluate the long-term economic impacts of their actions. It considers not just short-term gains but also the avoidance of future costs associated with environmental degradation and resource depletion. Incorporating these factors into decision-making processes is critical for the economic health of the maritime industry.

Market Forces and Sustainable Practices: Market forces are increasingly shaping the maritime industry's approach to sustainability. As consumers become more environmentally conscious, there is a growing demand for products and services that adhere to sustainable practices. This market-driven shift can provide economic incentives for maritime companies to invest in sustainable resource management. Embracing sustainable practices can enhance a company's reputation, attract more customers, and ensure long-term viability in a changing economic landscape.

In this respect, the 8th Environment Action Programme (EU, 2022), building on the European Green Deal, introduces a long-term vision for the European Union, aiming to accelerate the transition to a climate-neutral, resource-efficient economy. It recognizes that human well-being and prosperity depend on healthy ecosystems and defines objectives and priorities for environmental policy and well-living up to 2050. One of the six priority objectives of the Programme is "sustainable use of natural resources," articulated as "advancing toward a regenerative growth model, decoupling economic growth from resource use and environmental degradation, and accelerating the transition to a circular economy" (EU, 2022). This overarching approach aligns with the economic necessities of sustainable resource management in the maritime industry and reinforces its importance in shaping a prosperous future.

2.3 Social Dynamics of Sustainable Resource Management in the Maritime Industry

The social aspect of maritime sustainability is multifaceted and intricate. This perspective can be categorized into different themes, with a specific focus on key stakeholders such as fisheries, coastal communities, and seafarers. For instance, the coexistence of diverse stakeholders within the maritime environment often gives rise to conflicts pertaining to the allocation and utilization of ocean resources. Considering the multifaceted nature of the issue, this section offers an overview of the social dynamics related to sustainable resource management in the maritime industry.

Stakeholder Collaboration: Water (oceans, seas, etc.) covers 70½ of the planet (Maury et al., 2017), and these bodies of water have direct connections to many different socioeconomic stakeholders. Thus, to achieve a sustainable socio-ecological system is crucial (Maury et al., 2017). However, because no organization can survive alone and succeed alone (Kucukaltan et al., 2022), it's essential that stakeholders be engaged in any plan to succeed (Mackinson et al., 2011). Since, a sustainable marine environment is dependent largely on cooperation among the users of the marine space (Türkmen et al., 2021), effective sustainable resource management in the maritime industry requires collaboration amongst a variety of maritime stakeholders (Pomeroy & Douvere, 2008). The identification of key stakeholders based on their characteristics (urgency, power, and legitimacy) is the subject of an often-referenced theory of stakeholder salience (Järlström et al., 2018; Kucukaltan et al., 2022). Within the scope of sustainability in maritime resource management governmental agencies, shipping firms, fisheries, coastal communities, and environmental organizations can be considered as the salient stakeholders. Collaboration among maritime stakeholders is of course critical and beneficial as it guarantees the consideration of various viewpoints and interests, resulting in better-informed decisions, fewer conflicts, and the development of sustainable practices that are advantageous to the industry and the environment.

Coastal Community Engagement: One of the directly affected stakeholders of the maritime industry is the coastal community in any location of the world. Thus, involving coastal communities in decision-making processes and incorporating their traditional knowledge of local marine resources is vital to promoting sustainable practices and maintaining social harmony. Of course, this needs collaboration and cooperation among various stakeholders which also means conflicts. In this sense, collaboration and/or cooperation-based regulations foster collaboration among various stakeholders, ensuring that different perspectives and interests are considered in resource management decisions, contributing to harmonious social dynamics. Also, mechanisms for dispute resolution provided in the regulations help address conflicts that may arise in the maritime industry, preventing disruptions in social dynamics and promoting cooperative solutions.

Seafarer Welfare: Because humans are important stakeholders of coastal communities on the one hand and maritime companies on the other, seafarers are one of the vital or might be the pivotal stakeholders of the maritime industry. Ensuring the well-being of seafarers, including fair labor conditions, training, and safety, is a key component of the social dynamics within the maritime industry and influences resource management practices. In this sense, regulations related to "labor and welfare standards" set standards for labor conditions, ensuring that maritime workers have safe and fair working conditions, which is crucial for maintaining a skilled and motivated workforce in the maritime industry.

Concurrently, the adoption of advanced technologies for resource management requires training and skill development for the maritime workforce, impacting social dynamics within the industry. Generalizing the topic, safety, and security regulations are essential for protecting the lives and well-being of maritime workers and local communities, directly impacting social dynamics by minimizing accidents and risks.

Therefore, we can say that ensuring the well-being of seafarers and educating them about new and sustainable technologies has the potential to create a cycle that leads towards continuous well-being in terms of the social dimension of sustainability.

Social Responsibility of Maritime Companies: Companies in the maritime industry are increasingly expected to uphold social responsibility by considering the well-being of their employees, the communities they operate in, and the marine environment in their resource management strategies. Meanwhile, the principles of accountability and transparency, within the framework of social responsibility, required by various legal regulations ensure that social interests are considered in maritime decision-making processes, promoting trust and responsible resource management. Additionally, transparency in decision-making processes and ensuring accountability for all actions taken in resource management encourage responsible sourcing by helping to build trust and maintain positive social dynamics in the maritime industry.

Conflict Resolution Mechanisms: As it has been mentioned above, coordinating efforts among various stakeholders need to tackle the conflicts. Effective conflict resolution mechanisms are crucial for addressing disputes among maritime stakeholders, ensuring constructive social dynamics, and preventing conflicts that could disrupt resource management activities.

For example, promoting ethical fishing practices, including responsible fishing techniques and the prevention of overfishing, is essential for fostering positive social dynamics in the maritime sector. However, ethical fishing can cause conflict between coastal communities and fishing companies in various aspects and can create a dilemma in terms of choosing between meeting today's needs and protecting the future.

Undoubtedly, it will not be that easy to resolve conflicts and maintain the harmonious environment achieved in a structure with such a variety of stakeholders. In this case, legal regulations constitute another important topic, especially in terms of the concept of sustainability, which can mean investing in the future without giving up today.

Regulatory Compliance: These legal regulations in the maritime industry comprehensively tackle a spectrum of social issues such as labor rights, environmental protection, safety, community engagement, and sustainable development, all aimed at promoting responsible and socially conscious maritime practices. They are purposefully designed to align with the social dynamics of the maritime sector, encompassing various aspects and fostering inclusive, sustainable resource management practices that simultaneously benefit the industry and enhance the well-being of communities and the environment.

Adherence to maritime regulations and conventions related to resource management, such as the United Nations Convention on the Law of the Sea (UNCLOS), the International Labor Organization (ILO) Maritime Labor Convention, and legislations and the regulations of the International Maritime Organization (IMO) are fundamental regulatory aspects of the maritime industry's social dynamics.

Regulations emphasize sustainable practices, which are essential for ensuring that maritime activities do not harm the well-being and livelihoods of present and future generations in coastal communities. Meanwhile, regulations related to "environmental stewardship" address resource sustainability and environmental protection, aligning with the need for sustainable practices that consider the social impact on coastal communities, whose livelihoods often depend on these resources. In this sense, some regulations require engagement with local communities, recognizing the social importance of their involvement in decision-making processes and respecting their traditional knowledge of marine resources.

3 The Blue Economy and Circularity

The concept of circular economy (CE) emerged from industrial ecology and involves the reconfiguration of industrial systems to align with ecological principles and optimize resource recycling (Preston, 2012). Herewith, CE advocates for the recycling and reuse of limited and valuable resources in a closed loop. The circularity presents a proposed solution aimed at mitigating the environmental consequences of production, in contrast to the prevailing linear economic model characterized by a "take-use-dispose" approach (Bonsu, 2020; Fatimah et al., 2023). Within the framework of the circular economy, the preservation of the environment is achieved by the restoration of value that would otherwise be lost through the disposal practices inherent in the linear economic model. Hence, it is imperative to establish the circular economy as a supply chain ecosystem that remains engaged throughout the whole product life cycle. The notion of sustainability is rooted in the diminishing availability of natural resources and the interdependence of businesses on these resources. It posits that businesses should strive to maintain a harmonious equilibrium among economic, social, and environmental variables in order to ensure their long-term viability. The concept of circular economy places emphasis on the environmental dimensions of sustainability, namely by prioritizing the generation of value throughout the entire life cycle of products derived from available resources. Furthermore, it emphasizes the potential for these products to be reused in various capacities even after their economic usefulness has ceased.

The concept of the Blue Economy was initially introduced during the United Nations Conference on Sustainable Development, which took place in Rio de Janeiro in 2012. Smith-Godfrey (2016) further examined the definition of this novel concept as the sustainable industrialization of the marine environment, aiming to benefit all stakeholders. The blue economy facilitates the attainment of sustainable economic growth by harnessing and optimizing oceanic resources while minimizing waste production. Furthermore, the blue economy enhances income growth through the creation of new employment prospects (Rahman, 2017). The blue economy generates

31 million jobs worldwide and reaches an annual volume of US$1.5 trillion (Nham & Ha, 2023). When the principles of the circular economy are implemented within the context of the blue economy, a remarkable outcome emerges: the protection of the ocean ecosystem and the promotion of economic growth through the lens of sustainable resource management. Hence, the blue economy within circularity represents a significant stride towards addressing environmental challenges through a comprehensive lens. This approach not only fosters a harmonious equilibrium between economic and environmental factors but also safeguards against potential vulnerabilities in the long run. Herewith, efficient utilization of ocean resources via recycling can promote an inclusive and culturally sensitive sustainable economy, particularly in coastal regions. For instance, the proximity of recycling facilities to port areas in developing countries can enhance coastal communities' engagement in the blue economy by fostering employment opportunities and economic growth.

Hence, the subsequent sub-sections of the research are structured in accordance with the aforementioned links between blue economy, CE, and sustainable economics.

3.1 Circular Economy in Shipbuilding and Maritime Activities

The maritime industry and its operations have a crucial position in the global economy. The growing demands have resulted in a worldwide intricacy of supply chain activities, posing challenges for maritime activities to achieve a harmonious balance between economic and conservation principles. The blue economy encompasses other marine operations beyond the commonly recognized sectors of maritime trade, transportation, and shipbuilding. Notable activities include gathering food and nutrition, extracting energy resources, tourism, protecting coastal environments, and ensuring maritime security (Katila et al., 2019). The marine ecosystem has been significantly overutilized and subjected to unsustainable practices. It appears unavoidable that this utilization will persist due to causes such as population expansion, increasing energy consumption, and climate change. Hence, the efficient management and preservation of marine resources play a crucial role in establishing a sustainable blue economy (Du & Ni, 2023). The primary objective is not to hinder the growth of the maritime industry, but rather to direct its operations in a sustainable manner, guaranteeing that the development of the blue economy and the preservation of the marine environment are mutually supportive (Du & Ni, 2023).

Given the negative impact of shipbreaking on people and the environment (e.g., the release of toxic chemicals and heavy metals into nature), the utilization of recycling as a primary CE strategy may not be the only option for the shipping industry, while other various dimensions of CE offers prospective solutions. Currently, the extension of product life may be achieved through the practices of reuse and remanufacturing, while the recycling phase can be delayed to the greatest extent feasible

(Milios et al., 2019). The circular economy entails the implementation of the 6R principles (reduce, reuse, recycle, recover, redesign, and remanufacture) throughout the entire product life cycle. It aims to go beyond mere recycling and instead focuses on creating more value with less energy and waste by giving priority to other principles (Okumus et al., 2022). Specifically, the principles of "reuse and remanufacture" delay or substitute the recycling process or the "use-dispose" process, which is a prevalent kind of consumer behavior in present times. These positive benefits of sustainability include the reduction of raw material and labor usage in circular economies, as well as the protection of environmental issues such as low gas emissions. Moreover, the incorporation of circularity principles in the blue economy results in reduced equipment lead times, hence positively affecting the project schedule in shipbuilding projects. Additionally, it enables cost savings by offering lower expenses compared to purchasing new equipment (Okumus et al., 2022).

Yet, Milios et al. (2019) examine the obstacles hindering the use of "reuse and remanufacturing" in the shipbuilding industry. The authors propose that maritime corporations exhibit a lack of interest in reused equipment, and attribute this apathy, in part, to the stringent policies of maritime classification organizations. Currently, it is a good opportunity for the International Maritime Organization (IMO), government agencies, classification societies, remanufacturers, and ship owners to work together to ensure the safe use of reused equipment in the maritime industry.

3.2 Role of the Ports in Blue Circular Economy and Waste Reduction Strategies

Several investigations have been conducted thus far on the subject of sustainability and green ports. Nevertheless, the correlation between port business models and CE remains a relatively nascent area of study (Mańkowska et al., 2020). Herewith, seaports can be connected to the concept of circular economy (CE) by adopting strategies that focus on reducing inputs, eliminating waste and pollution, and promoting resource recycling in a closed-loop system. Moreover, ports possess the capacity to serve as global recycling hubs owing to their robust infrastructure and extensive maritime connectivity (Notteboom et al., 2020). For instance, the North Pacific Gyre serves as a significant location for the accumulation of plastic waste, which prompted the launch of the first Ocean Cleanup initiative at the port of San Francisco. Additionally, the port of Esbjerg in Denmark has the potential to function as a hub for garbage collection (van Giezen & Wiegmans, 2020).

According to van Giezen and Wiegmans (2020), the outsourcing of waste from developed countries to low-income economies is crucial for fostering a sustainable economy. This practice leads to the development of enhanced waste collection and recycling infrastructure, as well as the creation of new employment opportunities in port areas. It is important, however, to consider the well-being of individuals and the environment during this process. The ethical drawbacks of this are discussed in Chap. 5.

The function of ports extends beyond the mere collection, re-processing, and transportation of waste materials. They also play a crucial role in supporting the maintenance, repair, and potential enhancement of vessels engaged in ocean cleanup operations (e.g., Slat, 2018). Moreover, the port of Esbjerg plays a significant role in supporting the offshore wind industry in Denmark (Spalding et al., 2021). The port has significantly contributed to the inception of Denmark's initial large-scale offshore wind plant and currently holds responsibility for 80% of Europe's offshore wind potential (Edwards et al., 2023).

4 Sustainable Maritime Transportation and Logistics

The United Nations (UN) has designed 13 objectives to promote global sustainability, called Sustainable Development Goals (SDGs). The 13th of the SDGs refers to the actions against climate change, and IMO strategies on reducing GHG emissions from ships cooperate with this subject. In pursuit of this objective, IMO formulated an initial strategy in 2018 and subsequently implemented a comprehensive follow-up program in July 2023, aligning with its 2050 objectives of zero emissions from shipping activities (IMO, 2023b).

At present, a variety of technical alternatives are being investigated and implemented in order to meet the IMO's 2050 objectives, such as batteries, alternative fuels, and cold ironing (CI) technology. Implementing clean technologies and alternative fuels not only reduces the carbon footprint of the maritime industry but also fosters an ever more resilient economic model that benefits vulnerable coastal communities. Herewith, approximately 214 million individuals, accounting for 42% of the European Union's total population, reside in the coastal regions of Europe (European Commission, 2020), as fostering a sustainable blue economy has great relevance for the well-being of coastal communities (Fudge et al., 2023).

Accordingly, this section investigates the strategies employed to address the challenges associated with decarbonization and efficiency in maritime transportation. Specifically, it will focus on implementing clean technologies, alternative fuels, and optimized logistics systems to mitigate the environmental impact of shipping.

4.1 Clean Technologies and Alternate Fuels for Decarbonization in Maritime Logistics

Batteries and Alternative Fuels: Batteries are a component of both fully electric and hybrid ships' propulsion systems. Battery-electric ships do not release sulfur dioxide (SOx), nitrogen oxide (NOx), and particulate matter (PM) into the atmosphere, making them environmentally beneficial. Additionally, they play a significant role in mitigating underwater noise pollution (European Maritime Safety Agency, 2023). For instance, the Yara Birkeland, the first autonomous vessel, is outfitted with lithium-ion batteries and is projected to supplant approximately 40,000 diesel lorries annually, aligning with a zero-emission objective (Abu Bakar et al., 2023). On the other hand, hybrid ships utilize diesel generators to supply power to the onboard batteries, providing energy to the electric motors for propulsion (Abu Bakar et al., 2023).

Biofuels, methanol, hydrogen, liquefied petroleum gas (LPG), and liquefied natural gas (LNG) are being explored as viable substitutes for conventional marine fuels. Herewith, LNG exhibits a significantly better environmental profile when compared to conventional fuels, making it an ecologically sound alternative. For instance, Iannaccone et al. (2020) stress that LNG exhibits a 31% reduction in adverse economic effects and a 41% reduction in environmental impact compared to diesel within the cruise industry. The authors further highlight that the sustainability profile of LNG-based systems is 35% superior to that of diesel.

According to a previous report by DNV (2019), LNG has been found to have the least amount of CO_2 emissions when compared to other fossil fuels. However, the report further highlights that LNG produces unburnt methane, resulting in a considerably higher GHG impact when compared to CO_2. Yet, hydrogen, generated through the utilization of sustainable energy sources, is considered the most ecologically sound fuel option.

The utilization of battery-electric power systems for short-sea shipping, such as ferries, along with the adoption of hydrogen fuel technology, are increasingly being recognized as feasible environmentally-friendly alternatives. However, in the context of ocean transportation, the utilization of batteries is deemed unsuitable owing to their inability to meet substantial energy demands. Moreover, the limited energy density and substantial storage demands of hydrogen render it unsuitable for application in ocean transportation (DNV, 2019). Nevertheless, nuclear propulsion appears to be a theoretically feasible alternative, although it is accompanied by numerous potential challenges. Finally, despite its before-mentioned limitation, LNG presents itself as a promising and most ecologically sound substitute for ocean transportation, owing to its widespread accessibility on a global scale when compared to LPG and biofuels (DNV, 2019).

Cold Ironing (CI): Maritime vessels require primary propulsion systems to enable navigation, in addition to auxiliary units that provide the necessary energy for various onboard systems. Therefore, even when ships deactivate their primary propulsion engines while in port, there is still a need for energy to sustain various functions. To meet this requirement, auxiliary engines are activated, resulting in NOx and CO_2 emissions during the duration of the vessel's stay at the port.

Herewith, cold ironing, also known as onshore power supply (OPS), offers an alternative to a ship's auxiliary engines to supply cleaner shore-side electricity. The transmission cables provide a connection between the onshore electrical infrastructure and the ship's connecting point. However, it is imperative that the power provided to the ship aligns with its specific voltage and frequency requirements. Moreover, technical challenges such as power fluctuations, parameter optimization, and structural modifications must be addressed to utilize the technology efficiently (Zhao et al., 2023b). Consequently, the utilization of cold ironing systems is now (yet) inadequate, necessitating investment from both the port and shipping sectors. Nevertheless, as a result of legislative measures, it is anticipated that this practice will further proliferate (Abu Bakar et al., 2023).

Exhaust Gas Cleaning (EGCS) Systems: The International Maritime Organization (IMO), through MARPOL Annex VI, has set strict rules for the allowable limits on NOX, SOX, particulate matter (PM) emissions, and permissible sulfur concentration (% m/m) of maritime fuels (IMO, 2021). Moreover, regulations 13 and 14 of MARPOL Annex VI govern the special constraints imposed on three emissions (i.e., NOX, SOX, and PM) within designated emission control areas (ECAs). Accordingly, ship operators employ a range of strategies to adhere to the regulations outlined in these guidelines. One of the methods employed involves the utilization of ultra-low sulfur fuels such as LNG, Marine Diesel Oil, Marine Gas Oil, and Ultra-low Sulphur Heavy Fuel Oil-ULSHFO (Zis et al., 2022).

Another application involves the installment of scrubber systems on maritime vessels. Scrubber systems enable the utilization of conventional HFOs containing high levels of sulfur, segregating SOX from the emitted substances (Zis et al., 2022). There are two types of scrubbing technologies: dry scrubbing and wet scrubbing. Dry scrubbers employ chemical agents like calcium hydroxide, whereas wet scrubbers utilize seawater as well as fresh water to cleanse exhaust gases by removing sulfur (Wilailak et al., 2021). Traditional wet scrubbing comprises three main types of systems: closed-loop, open-loop, and hybrid. Open-loop scrubbers are designed to utilize seawater for the purpose of washing away sulfur and directly releasing it into the marine environment. On the other hand, closed-loop scrubbers have been specifically developed to operate in areas where discharge of any kind is prohibited (no-discharge areas), ensuring that sulfur is contained within the system and not released into the surrounding environment. Hybrid systems have the capability to be utilized interchangeably, with open-loop mode being employed at sea and closed-loop mode being utilized in ports (Wilailak et al., 2021).

While conventional wet scrubbing is preferred by commercial shipping over dry scrubbing by means of simplicity of operation and cost (Wilailak et al., 2021), it still encounters challenges when it comes to the effective separation of NOX gases from exhaust gases (Zhao et al., 2023a). However, the latest wet scrubber technology employs chlorine-based oxidants and exhibits significant potential in the removal of NOX and SOX pollutants (Zhao et al., 2023a).

4.2 Ballast Water Treatment for Protecting Ocean Ecosystems

Seawater has been utilized as ballast for ensuring the stability of ships during navigation ever since the advent of steel-hulled vessels. Ballast serves the purpose of enhancing the transverse stability of vessels and mitigating the strain exerted on the hull. Simultaneously, the ship's propulsion and maneuvering capabilities remain unaffected even when it is not loaded with cargo (IMO, 2023a).

In addition to the above-mentioned advantages, ballast water can result in detrimental ecological and economic consequences. Microorganisms and invasive species present in ballast water and sediments have the ability to endure extended voyages and can be introduced into the new ecosystem through water discharge (Lv et al., 2022). The transfer of invasive organisms via ballast water can result in harmful impacts on both the economy and the environment of the recipient ecosystem. Consequently, indigenous species may experience suppression from invasive species via predation or competition for food resources, disrupting biodiversity (Melnyk et al., 2023). Reduced species diversity or abundance can endanger ecosystem functions like nitrogen cycling or fisheries, as well as decrease the stability and resilience of the ecosystem as a whole (Fan et al., 2023; Selig et al., 2014; Worm et al., 2006). This decrease in diversity, beyond the disappearance of certain species, has direct negative effects on the food chain (Duffy, 2003; Selig et al., 2014).

Hence, the IMO introduced the Ballast Water Management (BWM) convention in 2004 as a means to address the issue of detrimental microorganisms and potentially invasive species in ballast water. The convention was globally enforced on September 8, 2017. Accordingly, all vessels are required to adhere to the Ballast Water and Sediments Management Plan, have an international BWM certificate, and keep a ballast water record book, as outlined in the convention (IMO, 2023a). The convention also requires ship operators to install an onboard ballast water treatment system to discharge ballast water in international waters.

A Ballast Water Treatment System (BWTS) is designed to eliminate microorganisms from ballast water effectively. As evolving systems, BWTSs are mostly designed using a dual-stage treatment, consisting of a chemical or physical filtration subsequent to a mechanical filtration. Ultraviolet (UV) and Electrochromatination (EC) are widely used technologies for the purpose of mechanical filtration (Wärtsilä, 2023).

4.3 Sustainable Ship Design and Ship Routing Optimization

In addition to the ballast regulations mandated by the IMO and the limits on sulfur emissions, the shipping industry has also implemented proactive and voluntary practices initiated by itself. One of these pertains to the field of sustainable ship design. Hull form optimization involves changing the maritime profile and hydrodynamic resistance of vessels, offering significant fuel savings. A well-optimized bulbous bow design can reduce the fuel consumption of a container vessel by over 5%. Herewith, the computational fluid dynamics (CFD) techniques have achieved a high level of maturity, enabling accurate prediction of hydrodynamic resistance and propulsion attributes for newly designed vessels (de Kat & Mouawad, 2019).

In a recent example of the CMA CGM Jacques Saade, to optimize hydrodynamic efficiency, the vessel's design has been modified to feature a straight bow instead of the conventional bulbous bow, and the ship's rudder and propeller have undergone a redesign. With a length of 400 m and a capacity of 23,112 TEU, CMA CGM Jacques Saade utilizes liquefied natural gas (LNG) as its fuel source, as opposed to conventional marine fuels with high sulfur content. The Energy Efficiency Design Index (EEDI) of the container ship exhibited a 20% improvement in comparison with traditional ships (CMA CGM, 2023). Another illustrative instance is the Environmental Passport for Design (EP-D) system, which has been effectively executed by Det Norske Veritas (DNV). EP-D is a voluntary classification notation that enables ship operators to validate their vessel's compliance beyond the current industry standards (DNV, 2023).

There is no question that designing and building greener ships is a costly long-term investment, but making better use of existing assets is also an environmentally viable and short-term strategy (Hellsten et al., 2019). Herewith, another potential application for mitigating greenhouse gas (GHG) emissions from maritime activities is the implementation of routing optimization and scheduling techniques. Accordingly, route and schedule optimization, a field of study within operations research (OR), is particularly applicable in the context of tramp shipping in the spot market, as OR techniques ranging from simple linear models to extensive nonlinear models are used for this purpose (Wang et al., 2019). The utilization of Machine Learning (ML) emerges as a promising solution for augmenting the efficiency of ships by means of optimizing their routes through the prediction of fuel consumption. Moreover, ML algorithms can further enable the optimization of ship routes by leveraging real-time meteorological data in an efficient manner (Huang et al., 2022). For instance, Planakis et al. (2022) proposed an ML-based predictive shipboard energy management system for a hybrid ship propulsion plant that led to a noteworthy reduction of NOX emissions by 8.5%. The authors involved realistic environmental conditions through a wave disturbance model.

Finally, even though the environmental value is becoming more recognized by policymakers as a tool to direct and assist biodiversity management and conservation (Beaumont et al., 2008), it is not economically possible to protect all oceans, seas, and inland waters against resource depletion at the same time. Nevertheless, resources must be focused on places where investment might best maintain areas of high marine biodiversity and its related ecosystem services due to a lack of funding and capability for conservation and management.

5 Ethical Considerations in the Maritime Industry

The present body of literature on sustainability predominantly focuses on the environmental facets of sustainability. Herewith, the social aspect of maritime sustainability has been insufficiently acknowledged and lacks comprehensive conceptualization, as noted by Karakasnaki et al. (2023). Similarly, criticism has been raised about the predominant focus of extant maritime spatial planning (MSP) research on the environmental context, with less attention given to the issue of social sustainability (Gilek et al., 2021). Hence, this section aims to investigate the concept of sustainability within the socio-economic framework, and in the maritime domain. Thus, the primary objective of this part is to investigate maritime social sustainability from the perspectives of labor inequality, equal share of marine resources, and environmental injustice.

5.1 Maritime Social Sustainability and Ethical Consumerism of Maritime Resources

The concept of social sustainability, as viewed through a maritime lens, encompasses a wide range of factors such as safety, security, equality, socio-cultural values, health, and employment (e.g., Benamara et al., 2019). At this moment, one may argue that there is no agreed-upon generic definition of maritime social sustainability, although it is worth noting that existing studies are largely concerned with the working conditions of seafarers. Herewith, Karakasnaki et al. (2023) investigated physical, functional, healthy, communication, and cultural aspects of maritime social sustainability. The authors focused on the well-being of seafarers in two groups that work on national and international flag vessels and didn't find any meaningful difference between those groups by means of their definition of maritime social sustainability. Nevertheless, there remains a prevailing notion that seafarers employed on vessels registered under flags of convenience (FoG) of lesser repute endure unfavorable working conditions, very low wages, and inadequate provisions such as food and safe drinking water (ITF, 2023). The practice of flying a flag of convenience (e.g., Mauritius, Bermuda) is commonly employed by shipowners as a means to capitalize on tax advantages and reduce regulatory scrutiny (Ford & Wilcox, 2019).

It is estimated that approximately 1.6 million individuals are employed in the global maritime industry. A considerable proportion of this workforce is employed on ships registered under foreign flags (Aspers & Sandberg, 2020). At this time, there are certain reservations, particularly about the working conditions and remuneration of foreign crew members. For instance, Jones et al. (2020)'s study whether non-native labor from non-European Economic Area (EEA) countries working on fishing vessels is paid less than the local labor force. The authors stress that the remuneration of non-EEA labor is determined by the economic conditions of the country of origin rather than the country of employment. However, the ethical implications of this practice remain a subject of debate. Finally, Zhang et al. (2020) identified several challenges faced by crew members onboard, including communication issues (e.g., telephone and online), restrictions on shore leave due to visa requirements, and an increasing workload, particularly in terms of paperwork. The authors' conclusion is derived from interviews conducted with seafarers.

The maritime spatial planning approach to maritime social sustainability is more comprehensive, taking into account the socio-cultural milieu and the interplay between the maritime domain and society (e.g., coastal communities), rather than solely focusing on the well-being of seafarers (e.g., McKinley et al., 2019; Saunders et al., 2020a). For instance, in their study, McKinley et al. (2019) examine the socio-cultural dimensions of maritime planning via the lens of ecosystem services, ocean literacy, marine citizenship, and human well-being. Ocean literacy is a contemporary concept that refers to the comprehension of the reciprocal influence between the ocean and human existence. Marine citizenship refers to the comprehension of one's rights and obligations pertaining to the ocean environment (McKinley et al., 2019).

Saunders et al. (2020a), theorized social sustainability through recognition, representation, and distribution from a "social justice" perspective. Herewith, social justice prioritizes strategies that promote equitable and sustainable economic blue growth without further marginalizing disadvantaged groups. The authors place considerable emphasis on the significance of social inclusivity, the enhancement of democracy, and the equitable and fair distribution of marine resources. For instance, the matter of resource sharing in Marine Protected Areas (MPAs) within the Mediterranean Sea gives rise to conflicts among diverse maritime stakeholders (Gómez et al., 2021). The presence of ongoing conflict and disputes between recreational, small-scale, and industrial fishing actors may be attributed, in part, to the absence of a comprehensive definition of recreational fishing (i.e., not being recognized as a maritime stakeholder and licensing-related issues) and a thorough evaluation of its effects on natural reserves. This dearth of definition of recreational fishing and lack of surveillance on its activities contribute to the ongoing disputes over the allocation of natural resources between different beneficiaries (Gómez et al., 2021).

5.2 *Maritime Social Sustainability and Environmental Injustice*

Ships deteriorate over time due to environmental factors such as salinity, rendering them economically impractical. According to Karvelis et al. (2021), the estimated lifespan of a vessel is 30 years. At the conclusion of this estimated period, ships are dismantled either through drydocking or beaching, resulting in a notable release of harmful pollutants (e.g., mercury, asbestos, oil residues, and heavy metals) into the environment, particularly in the case of the latter. Herewith, ship demolition and recycling pose significant environmental risks and consequences; furthermore, it is a pertinent concern in the realm of unequal consumption of natural resources.

For instance, over 90% of the vessels traversing the world's oceans are under the ownership of maritime enterprises hailing from high-income nations (Mathew, 2021). In contrast, Wan et al. (2021) report that South Asian countries (i.e., Bangladesh, India, and Pakistan) are frequently chosen for ship demolition activities due to their comparatively lenient regulations, which are being taken advantage of and exploited. This leads to an inequitable and disproportionate abuse of natural resources in developing countries. India alone accounts for approximately 20–30% of the global ship dismantling and recycling activities (Vivek et al., 2019). Another significant issue related to shipbreaking is the matter of human health. The absence of adequate occupational safety measures and protective equipment during the dismantling process can increase the risk of occupational diseases caused by exposure to harmful substances. For instance, in a clinical investigation conducted in Alang, India, in 2006 and 2007, it was observed that out of a total of 94 workers, 15 individuals were diagnosed with the initial stages of asbestos intoxication (Mathew, 2021).

As mentioned earlier, it is widely acknowledged that the commercial fleet of ships operated by companies in wealthy nations and subsequently recycled in low-income countries, often having inadequate standards, leads to significant environmental damage. However, it is important to note that international trade and elements of global ecology are interconnected but not isolated. For instance, India holds a significant position as one of the largest exporters of seafood in the world. The country primarily exports seafood products to the United States, China, and the European Union (India Ministry of Commerce & Industry, 2023). The irresponsible recycling of ships can lead to the release of harmful substances into the environment. These substances have the potential to contaminate the food supply chains of both affluent nations and the rest of the world.

One additional ethical concern regarding environmental inequality between developed and developing economies pertains to the practice of outsourcing recyclable waste to the latter. The practice of outsourcing recyclable waste to developing countries can be considered a favorable approach for fostering sustainable economies in these regions, as suggested by van Giezen and Wiegmans (2020). However, in practical implementation, the emergence of practices detrimental to the environment and local communities in developing nations has raised ethical concerns encompassing both ecological and societal aspects. For instance, it is not uncommon for an unsorted mix of rubbish, including domestic garbage, to come out from cargo containers meant to contain scrap materials such as plastic and paper imported for recycling. A form of "waste smuggling," this practice generates tension between countries of origin and countries of destination, those with low-income economies.

In conclusion of this chapter, the maritime industry is responsible for the transportation of a significant majority of the world's traded goods. Hence, it is undeniable that maritime activities currently play a significant role in the global economy and overall well-being. Nevertheless, these activities also give rise to diverse social implications, as elucidated in this section. These issues manifest themselves in the form of labor inequality, disputes over resource sharing among various stakeholders, and environmental injustice at the international level. It is imperative to acknowledge that a comprehensive sustainability analysis should consider these concerns in conjunction with the economic and environmental pillars of maritime sustainability.

6 Conclusions

Currently, maritime routes deliver the majority of traded goods. Nevertheless, the exploitation of marine resources extends beyond the realm of maritime transportation. Maritime-related activities involve a variety of endeavors, including recreational and commercial fishing, tourism, and shipbuilding, that depend on and negatively impact the maritime ecology. Therefore, it is crucial to engage in the effective and responsible utilization of ocean resources in order to achieve true sustainable economic development. Herewith, various methods, processes, and technologies are available to reduce GHG emissions and marine pollution resulting from maritime activities. However, the utilization of ocean resources extends beyond the realm of environmental sustainability. The lack of consideration for both human and ecological well-being during the dismantling of ships at the end of their commercial lives in low-income nations is an ethical dilemma within the current economic dynamics. Furthermore, there are other ethical concerns, including the unfair distribution of maritime resources and waste smuggling. Herewith, it is apparent that the economic and environmental aspects of sustainability outweigh the social dimension. In particular, the number of studies addressing concerns such as ethical issues in maritime sustainability is still fairly low, and it is critical that future studies focus on this area.

Thus far, this chapter has thoroughly examined the matters of sustainable economics and ethnoeconomics within the maritime setting, yielding significant findings. For instance, various strategies exist to mitigate carbon emissions in the marine industry. These options include the utilization of low-carbon fuels and batteries for primary propulsion, as well as ship route optimization and ship design. Selecting the suitable option necessitates a deliberative procedure that must consider several elements, including the availability of technology, financial resources, and existing and anticipated regulatory changes. Choosing the suitable technology and system to decrease emissions from ships is an investment choice that requires meticulous planning and foresight (Spalding et al., 2021). Although LNG is currently considered the most viable "clean" maritime fuel option due to its availability, it is important not to overlook the potential for other alternatives to become feasible in the near future. An illustrative instance is the deployment of Maersk's "Ane Maersk," the first vessel fueled by methanol, as of the composition of this chapter (TheLoadStar, 2024). Therefore, it would be beneficial for future studies to analyze different low-carbon fuels and batteries, with a specific focus on the financial aspects such as investment and return on investment (ROI) for ship owners and operating companies.

References

Abu Bakar, N. N., Bazmohammadi, N., Vasquez, J. C., & Guerrero, J. M. (2023). Electrification of onshore power systems in maritime transportation towards decarbonization of ports: A review of the cold ironing technology. *Renewable and Sustainable Energy Reviews, 178*, 113243. https://doi.org/10.1016/j.rser.2023.113243

Agardy, T., Davis, J., Sherwood, K., & Vestergaard, O. (2017). *Taking steps toward marine and coastal ecosystem-based management: An introductory guide.* UNEP Regional Seas Reports and Studies No. 189.

Agrawal, S., & Singh, R. K. (2019). Analyzing disposition decisions for sustainable reverse logistics: Triple Bottom Line approach. *Resources, Conservation and Recycling, 150*, 104448. https://doi.org/10.1016/j.resconrec.2019.104448

Amrutha, V. N., & Geetha, S. N. (2020). A systematic review on green human resource management: Implications for social sustainability. *Journal of Cleaner Production, 247*, 119131. https://doi.org/10.1016/j.jclepro.2019.119131

Aspers, P., & Sandberg, C. (2020). Sailing together from different shores: Labour markets and inequality on board merchant ships. *Global Networks, 20*(3), 454–471. https://doi.org/10.1111/glob.12252

Beaumont, N. J., Austen, M. C., Mangi, S. C., & Townsend, M. (2008). Economic valuation for the conservation of marine biodiversity. *Marine Pollution Bulletin, 56*(3), 386–396. https://doi.org/10.1016/j.marpolbul.2007.11.013

Benamara, H., Hoffmann, J., & Youssef, F. (2019). Maritime transport: The sustainability imperative. In H. N. Psaraftis (Ed.), *Sustainable shipping: A cross-disciplinary view* (pp. 1–31). Springer International Publishing.

Bonsu, N. O. (2020). Towards a circular and low-carbon economy: Insights from the transitioning to electric vehicles and net zero economy. *Journal of Cleaner Production, 256*, 120659. https://doi.org/10.1016/j.jclepro.2020.120659

Boschmann, E. E., & Kwan, M.-P. (2008). Toward socially sustainable urban transportation: Progress and potentials. *International Journal of Sustainable Transportation, 2*(3), 138–157. https://doi.org/10.1080/15568310701517265

Bullock, S., Mason, J., & Larkin, A. (2022). The urgent case for stronger climate targets for international shipping. *Climate Policy, 22*(3), 301–309. https://doi.org/10.1080/14693062.2021.1991876

Chan, K. M. A., Shaw, M. R., Cameron, D. R., Underwood, E. C., & Daily, G. C. (2006). Conservation planning for ecosystem services. *PLOS Biology, 4*(11), e379. https://doi.org/10.1371/journal.pbio.0040379

CMA CGM. (2023). *CMA CGM Jacques Saade.* https://www.cma-cgm.com/static/PL/attachments/CMA%20CGM%20Jacques%20Saade.pdf

Costello, C., Lynham, J., Lester, S. E., & Gaines, S. D. (2010). Economic incentives and glob-al fisheries sustainability. *Annual Review of Resource Economics, 2*(1), 299–318. https://doi.org/10.1146/annurev.resource.012809.103923

Dean, T. J., & McMullen, J. S. (2007). Toward a theory of sustainable entrepreneurship: Reducing environmental degradation through entrepreneurial action. *Journal of Business Venturing, 22*(1), 50–76. https://doi.org/10.1016/j.jbusvent.2005.09.003

de Kat, J. O., & Mouawad, J. (2019). Green ship technologies. In H. N. Psaraftis (Ed.), *Sustainable shipping: A cross-disciplinary view* (pp. 33–92). Springer International Publishing.

DNV. (2019). *Assessment of selected alternative fuels and technologies in shipping.* https://www.dnv.com/maritime/publications/alternative-fuel-assessment-download.html

DNV. (2023). *Environmental Passport for Design (EP-D).*

Duffy, J. E. (2003). Biodiversity loss, trophic skew and ecosystem functioning. *Ecology Letters, 6*(8), 680–687. https://doi.org/10.1046/j.1461-0248.2003.00494.x

Du, P., & Ni, Y. (2023). Higher hierarchical growth through the country's blue economy strategies. *Ocean & Coastal Management, 233*, 106467. https://doi.org/10.1016/j.ocecoaman.2022.106467

Edwards, A., Akinlade, I., & Hayashi, K. (2023). *Port Esbjerg: Deploying Offshore Wind*. https://www.hbs.edu/environment/blog/post/IFC-Port-Es-bjerg#:~:text=The%20port%20has%20been%20a,has%20passed%20through%20the%20port

Epstein, M., & Buhovac, A. (2014). *Making sustainability work: Best practices in managing and measuring corporate social, environmental, and economic impacts* (2nd ed.). Routledge.

EU. (2022). *The European Parliament and the Council of the European Union Decision (EU) 2022/591 of the European Parliament and of the Council of 6 April 2022 on a General Union Environment Action Programme to 2030*. https://eur-lex.europa.eu/legal-content/EN/TXT/?uri=CELEX:32022D0591

European Commission. (2020). *DG Maritime Affairs and Fisheries—Strategic Plan 2020–2024*. https://commission.europa.eu/publications/strategic-plan-2020-2024-maritime-affairs-and-fisheries_en

European Maritime Safety Agency. (2023). *Alternative technologies*. https://www.emsa.europa.eu/sustainable-shipping/new-technologies.html

Fan, H., Huang, M., Chen, Y., Zhou, W., Hu, Y., & Wei, F. (2023). Conservation priorities for global marine biodiversity across multiple dimensions. *National Science Review, 10*(6), nwac241. https://doi.org/10.1093/nsr/nwac241

Fatimah, Y. A., Kannan, D., Govindan, K., & Hasibuan, Z. A. (2023). Circular economy e-business model portfolio development for e-business applications: Impacts on ESG and sustainability performance. *Journal of Cleaner Production, 415*, 137528. https://doi.org/10.1016/j.jclepro.2023.137528

Ford, J. H., & Wilcox, C. (2019). Shedding light on the dark side of maritime trade—A new approach for identifying countries as flags of convenience. *Marine Policy, 99*, 298–303. https://doi.org/10.1016/j.marpol.2018.10.026

Fudge, M., Ogier, E., & Alexander, K. A. (2023). Marine and coastal places: Wellbeing in a blue economy. *Environmental Science & Policy, 144*, 64–73. https://doi.org/10.1016/j.envsci.2023.03.002

Gilek, M., Armoskaite, A., Gee, K., Saunders, F., Tafon, R., & Zaucha, J. (2021). In search of social sustainability in marine spatial planning: A review of scientific literature published 2005–2020. *Ocean & Coastal Management, 208*, 105618. https://doi.org/10.1016/j.ocecoaman.2021.105618

Gómez, S., Carreño, A., & Lloret, J. (2021). Cultural heritage and environmental, ethical values in governance models: Conflicts between recreational fisheries and other maritime activities in Mediterranean marine protected areas. *Marine Policy, 129*, 104529. https://doi.org/10.1016/j.marpol.2021.104529

Hellsten, E., Pisinger, D., Sacramento, D., & Vilhelmsen, C. (2019). Green liner shipping network design. In H. N. Psaraftis (Ed.), *Sustainable shipping: A cross-disciplinary view* (pp. 307–337). Springer International Publishing.

Hernández, R., Martínez-Piva, J., & Mulder, N. (2014). *Global value chains and world trade: Prospects and challenges for Latin America*. Economic Commission for Latin America and the Caribbean (ECLAC).

Huang, L., Pena, B., Liu, Y., & Anderlini, E. (2022). Machine learning in sustainable ship design and operation: A review. *Ocean Engineering, 266*, 112907. https://doi.org/10.1016/j.oceaneng.2022.112907

Iannaccone, T., Landucci, G., Tugnoli, A., Salzano, E., & Cozzani, V. (2020). Sustainability of cruise ship fuel systems: Comparison among LNG and diesel technologies. *Journal of Cleaner Production, 260*, 121069. https://doi.org/10.1016/j.jclepro.2020.121069

IMO. (2020). *Fourth IMO GHG study*. International Maritime Organisation, London, UK. https://www.imo.org/en/OurWork/Environment/Pages/Fourth-IMO-Greenhouse-Gas-Study-2020.aspx

IMO. (2021). *Revised MARPOL Annex VI (Resolution MEPC.328(76))*.

IMO. (2023a). *Ballast Water Management*. www.imo.org/en/OurWork/Environment/Pages/BallastWaterManagement.aspx

IMO. (2023b). *IMO Strategy on Reduction of GHG Emissions from Ships*. https://www.imo.org/en/OurWork/Environment/Pages/2023-IMO-Strategy-on-Reduction-of-GHG-Emissions-from-Ships.aspx

India Ministry of Commerce & Industry. (2023). *India's seafood exports*. pib.gov.in/PressReleaseIframePage.aspx?PRID=1932317

ITF. (2023). *Flags of Convenience*. www.itfglobal.org/en/sector/seafarers/flags-of-convenience

Järlström, M., Saru, E., & Vanhala, S. (2018). Sustainable human resource management with salience of stakeholders: A top management perspective. *Journal of Business Ethics, 152*(3), 703–724. https://doi.org/10.1007/s10551-016-3310-8

Jones, E., Botterill, K., Chikwama, C., Caveen, A., & Gray, T. (2020). Pay gaps between domestic and international fishers: An economic or ethical issue? *Maritime Studies, 19*(1), 15–27. https://doi.org/10.1007/s40152-019-00133-6

Karakasnaki, M., Pantouvakis, A., & Vlachos, I. (2023). Maritime social sustainability: Conceptualization and scale development. *Transportation Research Part D: Transport and Environment, 121*, 103804. https://doi.org/10.1016/j.trd.2023.103804

Karvelis, P., Georgoulas, G., Kappatos, V., & Stylios, C. (2021). Deep machine learning for structural health monitoring on ship hulls using acoustic emission method. *Ships and Offshore Structures, 16*(4), 440–448. https://doi.org/10.1080/17445302.2020.1735844

Katila, J., Ala-Rämi, K., Repka, S., Rendon, E., & Törrönen, J. (2019). Defining and quantifying the sea-based economy to support regional blue growth strategies—Case Gulf of Bothnia. *Marine Policy, 100*, 215–225. https://doi.org/10.1016/j.marpol.2018.11.035

Kessler, W. B., Salwasser, H., Cartwright, C. W., & Caplan, J. A. (1992). New perspectives for sustainable natural resources management. *Ecological Applications, 2*(3), 221–225. https://doi.org/10.2307/1941856

Kucukaltan, B., Irani, Z., & Acar, A. Z. (2022). Business model canvas for humanitarian operations of logistics service providers. *Production Planning & Control, 33*(6–7), 590–605. https://doi.org/10.1080/09537287.2020.1834128

Lv, B., Shi, J., Li, T., Ren, L., Tian, W., Lu, X., Han, Y., Cui, Y., & Jiang, T. (2022). Deciphering the characterization, ecological function and assembly processes of bacterial communities in ship ballast water and sediments. *Science of the Total Environment, 816*, 152721. https://doi.org/10.1016/j.scitotenv.2021.152721

Mackinson, S., Wilson, D. C., Galiay, P., & Deas, B. (2011). Engaging stakeholders in fisheries and marine research. *Marine Policy, 35*(1), 18–24. https://doi.org/10.1016/j.marpol.2010.07.003

Malmborg, Fv. (2023). Advocacy coalitions and policy change for decarbonisation of international maritime transport: The case of FuelEU maritime. *Maritime Transport Research, 4*, 100091. https://doi.org/10.1016/j.martra.2023.100091

Mańkowska, M., Kotowska, I., & Pluciński, M. (2020). Seaports as nodal points of circular supply chains: Opportunities and challenges for secondary ports. *Sustainability, 12*(9). https://doi.org/10.3390/su12093926

Mathew, E. (2021). Ship recycling, market imperfections and the relevance of a consortium of ship recycling nations in the Indian subcontinent. *Journal of International Maritime Safety, Environmental Affairs, and Shipping, 5*(2), 23–31. https://doi.org/10.1080/25725084.2021.1921994

Maury, O., Campling, L., Arrizabalaga, H., Aumont, O., Bopp, L., Merino, G., Squires, D., Cheung, W., Goujon, M., Guivarch, C., Lefort, S., Marsac, F., Monteagudo, P., Murtugudde, R., Österblom, H., Pulvenis, J. F., Ye, Y., & van Ruijven, B. J. (2017). From shared socio-economic pathways (SSPs) to oceanic system pathways (OSPs): Building policy-relevant scenarios for global oceanic ecosystems and fisheries. *Global Environmental Change, 45*, 203–216. https://doi.org/10.1016/j.gloenvcha.2017.06.007

McKinley, E., Acott, T., & Stojanovic, T. (2019). Socio-cultural dimensions of marine spatial planning. In J. Zaucha & K. Gee (Eds.), *Maritime spatial planning: Past, present, future* (pp. 151–174). Springer International Publishing.

Melnyk, O., Sagaydak, O., Shumylo, O., & Lohinov, O. (2023). Modern aspects of ship Bal-last water management and measures to enhance the ecological safety of shipping. In A. Zaporozhets (Ed.), *Systems, decision and control in energy V* (pp. 681–694). Springer Nature Switzerland.

Merk, O. (2013). *The competitiveness of global port-cities: Synthesis report.* https://doi.org/10.1787/5k40hdhp6t8s-en

Milios, L., Beqiri, B., Whalen, K. A., & Jelonek, S. H. (2019). Sailing towards a circular economy: Conditions for increased reuse and remanufacturing in the Scandinavian maritime sector. *Journal of Cleaner Production, 225*, 227–235. https://doi.org/10.1016/j.jclepro.2019.03.330

Neumann, B., Ott, K., & Kenchington, R. (2017). Strong sustainability in coastal areas: A conceptual interpretation of SDG 14. *Sustainability Science, 12*(6), 1019–1035. https://doi.org/10.1007/s11625-017-0472-y

Nham, N. T. H., & Ha, L. T. (2023). The role of financial development in improving marine living resources towards sustainable blue economy. *Journal of Sea Research, 195*, 102417. https://doi.org/10.1016/j.seares.2023.102417

Notteboom, T., van der Lugt, L., van Saase, N., Sel, S., & Neyens, K. (2020). The role of seaports in green supply chain management: Initiatives, attitudes, and perspectives in Rotterdam, Antwerp, North Sea Port, and Zeebrugge. *Sustainability, 12*(4). https://doi.org/10.3390/su12041688

O'Hara, S. U. (1998). Economics, ethics and sustainability: Redefining connections. *International Journal of Social Economics, 25*(1), 43–62. https://doi.org/10.1108/03068299810194893

Okumus, D., Gunbeyaz, S. A., Kurt, R. E., & Turan, O. (2022). *Circular economy approach in the maritime industry: Barriers and the path to sustainability.* Paper presented at the Transport Research Arena 2022, Lisbon, Portugal.

Palumbi, S. R., Sandifer, P. A., David Allan, J., Beck, M. W., Fautin, D. G., Fogarty, M. J., Halpern, B. S., Incze, L. S., Leong, J.-A., Norse, E., Stachowicz, J. J., & Wall, D. H. (2009). Managing for ocean biodiversity to sustain marine ecosystem services. *Frontiers in Ecology and the Environment, 7*(4), 204–211. https://doi.org/10.1890/070135

Parsons, E. C. M., Brett Favaro, A., Aguirre, A., Bauer, A. L., Blight, L. K., Cigliano, J. A., Coleman, M. A., Côté, I. M., Draheim, M., Fletcher, S., Foley, M. M., Jefferson, R., Jones, M. C., Kelaher, B. P., Lundquist, C. J., Mccarthy, J.-B., Nelson, A., Patterson, K., Walsh, L, … Sutherland, W. J. (2014). Seventy-one important questions for the conservation of marine biodiversity. *Conservation Biology, 28*(5), 1206–1214. https://doi.org/10.1111/cobi.12303

Planakis, N., Papalambrou, G., & Kyrtatos, N. (2022). Ship energy management system development and experimental evaluation utilizing marine loading cycles based on machine learning techniques. *Applied Energy, 307*, 118085. https://doi.org/10.1016/j.apenergy.2021.118085

Pomeroy, R., & Douvere, F. (2008). The engagement of stakeholders in the marine spatial planning process. *Marine Policy, 32*(5), 816–822. https://doi.org/10.1016/j.marpol.2008.03.017

Preston, F. (2012). *A Global Redesign? Shaping the Circular Economy.* https://www.chathamhouse.org/sites/default/files/public/Research/Energy%2C%20Environment%20and%20Development/bp0312_preston.pdf

Rahman, M. R. (2017). Blue economy and maritime cooperation in the Bay of Bengal: Role of Bangladesh. *Procedia Engineering, 194*, 356–361. https://doi.org/10.1016/j.proeng.2017.08.157

Sangha, K. K., Stoeckl, N., Crossman, N., & Costanza, R. (2019). A state-wide economic assessment of coastal and marine ecosystem services to inform sustainable development policies in the Northern Territory, Australia. *Marine Policy, 107*, 103595. https://doi.org/10.1016/j.marpol.2019.103595

Saunders, F., Gilek, M., Ikauniece, A., Tafon, R. V., Gee, K., & Zaucha, J. (2020a). Theorizing social sustainability and justice in marine spatial planning: Democracy, diversity, and equity. *Sustainability, 12*(6). https://doi.org/10.3390/su12062560

Saunders, M. I., Doropoulos, C., Bayraktarov, E., Babcock, R. C., Gorman, D., Eger, A. M., Vozzo, M. L., Gillies, C. L., Vanderklift, M. A., Steven, A. D. L., Bustamante, R. H., & Silliman, B. R. (2020b). Bright spots in coastal marine ecosystem restoration. *Current Biology, 30*(24), R1500–R1510. https://doi.org/10.1016/j.cub.2020.10.056

Selig, E. R., Turner, W. R., Troëng, S., Wallace, B. P., Halpern, B. S., Kaschner, K., Lascelles, B. G., Carpenter, K. E., & Mittermeier, R. A. (2014). Global priorities for marine biodiversity conservation. *PLOS One, 9*(1), e82898. https://doi.org/10.1371/journal.pone.0082898

Slat, B. (2018). *Wilson to return to port for repair and upgrade.* https://theoceancleanup.com/updates/wilson-to-return-to-port-for-repair-and-upgrade/

Smith-Godfrey, S. (2016). Defining the blue economy. *Maritime Affairs: Journal of the National Maritime Foundation of India, 12*(1), 58–64. https://doi.org/10.1080/09733159.2016.1175131

Spalding, M. J., Braestrup, A. E., & Refosco, A. (2021). Greening the blue economy: A transdisciplinary analysis. In A. Carpenter, T. M. Johansson, & J. A. Skinner (Eds.), *Sustainability in the maritime domain: Towards ocean governance and beyond* (pp. 27–59). Springer International Publishing.

TheLoadStar. (2024). *Maersk set to deploy its first large methanol-enabled box ship.* https://theloadstar.com/photo-blog-maersk-set-to-deploy-its-first-large-methanol-enabled-box-ship/

Türkmen, A., Salazar, E. R., Vlaswinkel, B., & Mahadeo, S. (2021). *Marine spatial planning and the sustainable blue economy: Policy brief*. UNESCO. https://unesdoc.unesco.org/ark:/48223/pf0000375720

UN. (2006). *Water: A shared responsibility* (Vol. 2). World Water Assessment Programme (United Nations): Berghahn Books.

UNCTAD. (2023). *Review of Maritime Transport 2023: Towards a Green and Just Transition.* https://unctad.org/system/files/official-document/rmt2023_en.pdf

van Giezen, A., & Wiegmans, B. (2020). Spoilt—Ocean Cleanup: Alternative logistics chains to accommodate plastic waste recycling: An economic evaluation. *Transportation Research Interdisciplinary Perspectives, 5*, 100115. https://doi.org/10.1016/j.trip.2020.100115

van Tatenhove, J. P. M. (2017). Transboundary marine spatial planning: A reflexive marine governance experiment? *Journal of Environmental Policy & Planning, 19*(6), 783–794. https://doi.org/10.1080/1523908X.2017.1292120

Vivek, J. M., Singh, R., & Asolekar, S. R. (2019). *Hazardous waste generation and management in ship recycling yards in India: A case study.* Paper presented at the Waste Management and Resource Efficiency, Singapore.

Wang, X., Norstad, I., Fagerholt, K., & Christiansen, M. (2019). Green tramp shipping routing and scheduling: Effects of market-based measures on CO2 reduction. In H. N. Psaraftis (Ed.), *Sustainable shipping: A cross-disciplinary view* (pp. 285–305). Springer International Publishing.

Wang, X., Yuen, K. F., Wong, Y. D., & Li, K. X. (2020). How can the maritime industry meet Sustainable Development Goals? An analysis of sustainability reports from the social entrepreneurship perspective. *Transportation Research Part D: Transport and Environment, 78*, 102173. https://doi.org/10.1016/j.trd.2019.11.002

Wan, Z., Wang, L., Chen, J., & Sperling, D. (2021). Ship scrappage records reveal disturbing environmental injustice. *Marine Policy, 130*, 104542. https://doi.org/10.1016/j.marpol.2021.104542

Wärtsilä. (2023). *Ballast Water Treatment Systems (BWTS).* https://www.wartsila.com/encyclopedia/term/ballast-water-treatment-systems-(bwts)#:~:text=Ballast%20Water%20Treatment%20System%20(BWTS,ever%2Dgrowing%20number%20of%20manufacturers

Wilailak, S., Yoo, B.-H., Kim, Y., & Lee, C.-J. (2021). Parametric analysis and design optimization of wet SOx scrubber system in marine industry. *Fuel, 304*, 121369. https://doi.org/10.1016/j.fuel.2021.121369

Worm, B., Barbier, E. B., Nicola Beaumont, J., Duffy, E., Folke, C., Halpern, B. S., Jackson, J. B. C., Lotze, H. K., Micheli, F., Palumbi, S. R., Sala, E., Selkoe, K. A., Stachowicz, J. J., & Watson, R. (2006). Impacts of biodiversity loss on ocean ecosystem services. *Science, 314*(5800), 787–790. https://doi.org/10.1126/science.1132294

Yarrow, A. (2009). Sustainability and Intergenerational Solidarity. *Generations, 33*(3), 103–104.

Zhang, P., Zhao, L., Vata, O., & Rajagopal, S. (2020). Restructuring seafarers' welfare under the Maritime Labour Convention: An empirical case study of Greece. *Maritime Business Review, 5*(4), 373–389. https://doi.org/10.1108/MABR-02-2020-0009

Zhao, J., Li, H., Zhao, R., Lei, C., Wei, Q., & Ren, X. (2023a). A new absorbent system for reducing chlorine gas escape and enhancing pollutants removal during ship exhaust wet scrubbing. *Chemical Engineering Journal, 468*, 143489. https://doi.org/10.1016/j.cej.2023.143489

Zhao, P., Ma, K., Yang, J., Yang, B., Guerrero, J. M., Dou, C., & Guan, X. (2023b). Distributed power sharing control based on adaptive virtual impedance in seaport microgrids with cold ironing. *IEEE Transactions on Transportation Electrification, 9*(2), 2472–2485. https://doi.org/10.1109/TTE.2022.3211204

Zis, T. P. V., Cullinane, K., & Ricci, S. (2022). Economic and environmental impacts of scrubbers investments in shipping: A multi-sectoral analysis. *Maritime Policy & Management, 49*(8), 1097–1115. https://doi.org/10.1080/03088839.2021.1937742

Exploring the Dimensions of Ethical Consumption, Civic Engagement, and the 4th Industrial Revolution

Felipe Fernandes, Ana Regina de Aguiar Dutra, and José Baltazar Salgueirinho Osório de Andrade Guerra

Abstract This research project aims to investigate the interactions between ethical consumption, civic engagement, and the impacts of the 4th Industrial and Social Revolutions. The research seeks to understand how these dimensions relate to and mutually influence each other in a socio-cultural and economic context that is constantly evolving. To achieve this objective, a systematic literature review will be conducted, encompassing multidisciplinary studies addressing the themes of ethical consumption, civic engagement, and the advancements of the 4th Industrial and Social Revolutions. The review will be grounded in theories and concepts that help elucidate the Finally, a framework will be presented outlining the potential impact of the key technologies of the 4th Industrial Revolution on the dimensions of ethical consumption and civic engagement. This framework may contribute to consumer awareness and the development of more conscious and sustainable consumption practices. Additionally, the study aims to identify effective ways to integrate ethical consumption and civic engagement within the context of the 4th Industrial Revolution, aiming to drive a positive transformation toward a more just, equitable society committed to ethical and civic values.

Keywords 4th Industrial Revolution · 4th Social Revolution · Ethical Consumption · Civic Engagement

---

F. Fernandes · A. R. de Aguiar Dutra · J. B. S. O. de Andrade Guerra (✉)
Center for Sustainable Development Research, University of Southern Santa Catarina, Graduate Program in Administration, Florianópolis 88010-010, Brazil
e-mail: jose.baltazarguerra@animaeducacao.com.br

F. Fernandes
e-mail: felipe.fernandes65@unisul.br

A. R. de Aguiar Dutra
e-mail: ana.aguiar@animaeducacao.com.br

W. Leal Filho and V. Kuzmanović (eds.), *Sustainable Development Seen Through the Lenses of Ethnoeconomics and the Circular Economy*,
https://doi.org/10.1007/978-3-031-72676-7_3

1 Introduction

According to Schwab (2017), the fourth industrial revolution brings forth vast possibilities for humanity. These possibilities encompass a wide range of new technologies that can alter the way we live, ushering in a 4th Social Revolution, as advocated by Cottam (2020).

Alves et al. (2020) state, "The increasing threat of global climate change induced by human activity requires climate change policies that address this issue at the levels of global, national, and local governance." Mercure et al. (2019) point out that "The water-food-energy nexus is one of the most complex sustainability challenges faced by the world," and according to Guerra (2020), "(...) global environmental change, resulting from unsustainable resource use and greenhouse gas emissions, will likely alter climate patterns significantly." Absolutely, considering the current economic and social studies, including the impacts of the 4th Industrial Revolution on societies, it's crucial not to detach them from their environmental dimension. To analyze this dimension, a starting point could be the United Nations' Sustainable Development Goals (SDG).

Adopted in 2015, the 17 goals and 169 targets for sustainable development form a significant part of the current United Nations (UN) agenda. According to the organization itself, "This agenda is a plan of action for people, planet, and prosperity. (...) We recognize that eradicating poverty in all its forms and dimensions, including extreme poverty, is the greatest global challenge and an indispensable requirement for sustainable development." Additionally, the UN proposal advocates that the sustainable development goals "...are integrated and indivisible, balancing the three dimensions of sustainable development: economic, social, and environmental."

As can be observed above, the UN itself understands that economic, social, and environmental challenges are inseparable. These challenges occur in an environment impacted by the effects and transformations of the 4th industrial revolution and the consequent 4th social revolution. Therefore, a holistic study capable of integrating studies related to the 4th Industrial Revolution and its social transformations with the paradigms advocated by the SDG and their impacts on ethical consumption and civic engagement is pertinent and necessary. Indeed, these new technologies emerge in fields such as artificial intelligence, robotics, the Internet of Things, autonomous vehicles, 3D printing, nanotechnology, material science, energy storage, quantum computing, among other technical capabilities. These innovations have the potential to transform the organization of our society significantly.

In the contemporary perspective, concerns about the environment and its relationship with consumption are growing. There's also a recognized need for coordination among states to implement this agenda. It's within this context that authors like Czeskleba-Dupont (2003), Mathai et al. (2021), and Biermann and Pattberg (2008) discuss the importance of aligning the theoretical mission of sustainable development to address the challenges of global system development, particularly its relevant economic aspects, including consumption. These authors highlight the necessity of integrating sustainability principles into the global development agenda to effectively tackle environmental concerns associated with consumption practices.

In this Regard, this analysis will primarily concentrate on delineating the impacts stemming from the Fourth Industrial and Social Revolutions on ethical consumption and civic engagement. It aims to scrutinize the contributing factors that foster alterations in consumption patterns and delineate the essence of these modifications. Moreover, it endeavors to probe into the individual influence of the key technologies within the ambit of the 4th Industrial Revolution on ethical consumption and civic engagement.

2 Theoretical Review

Conforming to Mathai et al. (2021), the sustainability of production and consumption practices is deeply influenced by politically and economically significant factors. On the production side, there's a multi-actor drive, including the financial system, the influential advertising industry, political priorities that sometimes prioritize economic expansion and opening new markets, and heavyweight buyers exerting their influence. Conversely, the act of consuming is densely embedded within the social sphere, rooted in the complex structures of social organization. Access to available resources and the socio-cultural construction of demand emerge as substantial forces shaping production-consumption systems.

The book "Great Reset" by Schwab and Malleret (2020) presents, influenced by the COVID-19 pandemic crisis, examples of how the transition to a green, circular, and inclusive economy can contribute to desired social changes and achieve sustainable development goals. According to the authors, "The green economy encompasses a variety of possibilities (…). For instance, shifting from a 'take-make-dispose' approach to a model that is 'restorative and regenerative by design'. Cruz (2021) states that the Great Reset proposes stimulating and subsidizing various economic activities that could, for a time, bring about greater social pacification. However, he criticizes that these proposals stem from the standpoint of the members of the World Economic Forum, who, according to him, are among the main beneficiaries of these propositions.

In the economic realm, the "Great Reset" offers significant insights into monetary and fiscal policies. The advancement of the pandemic led most central banks worldwide to adopt markedly expansionary monetary policies, at the expense of a substantial increase in fiscal deficits. Pezzuto (2020) and Mudassir (2020) both assert that crises, such as those underpinning the propositions of the "Great Reset," along with the impacts they cause, can contribute to building a sustainable future. This can manifest in noticeable shifts in consumption habits, societal lifestyles, and the values connected to them. Moreover, they emphasize that these transformations might stem from the accelerated pace of digitization, automation, restructuring of sustainable supply chains, and the emergence of novel business models.

Therefore, Czeskleba-Dupont (2003) argues that for sustainable development to be operationalized, four key aspects need to be taken into account in any development plan or policy: (a) "the need to maintain ecological integrity"; (b) "the need to maintain social integrity"; (c) "the need to maintain economic integrity"; and (d) "the need to maintain intergenerational equity". Biermann and Pattberg (2008) assert that the emergence of new entities and actors surpassing the boundaries of national governments, historically central in traditional international environmental politics, suggests the need for "global environmental governance." This concept, as outlined in the context, unfolds into three distinct conceptions: an analytical description capturing ongoing changes in global politics, an assertive political agenda, and a critical political program.

Mathai et al. (2021) support the propositions of Czeskleba-Dupont (2003) and Biermann and Pattberg (2008) by pointing out that conventional research in the field of sustainability tends to circumvent or negligently minimize critical issues related to power and political contention. This research paradigm often overly emphasizes technological, economic, and behavioral solutions, frequently stemming from an ideological commitment to managerialism, while neglecting a deeper analysis of the political and economic factors underpinning the dynamics of sustainable production and consumption practices.

In this context, it's essential to consider Bresser-Pereira's (2010) assertions, wherein Democracy, Social State, and Managerial Reform constitute interrelated entities in a dialectical manner. According to him, their interconnectedness evolved from events following World War II. Within this framework, democracy played a crucial role in enabling increased demands for social services by workers and the middle class, leading to a transformation from a Liberal Democratic State to a Social Democratic State. The 1980s Managerial Reform responded directly to the growing need for efficiency in delivering public services for collective consumption, playing a crucial role in legitimizing the Social State and interlinking these three entities. This is illustrated in Jenness's (2004) insights, focusing on social movement dynamics. He examines mobilization structures, framing processes, and the relationship between social movements and public policies. The aim is to outline how activists, groups, community networks, professionals, social movement organizations, and the state interact to shape public policies, including criminal legislation.

These assertions are supported by Wolfson's research (Brown, 2002), which argues that the increased social and legal control over tobacco consumption in the last two decades stems from the contemporary tobacco control movement. Wolfson provides a compelling analysis of how this movement utilized a pre-existing 'infrastructure' of health organizations and professionals, as well as the close collaborative relationship between movement organizations and state agencies. According to Mathai et al. (2021), substantial challenges arise on the horizon of sustainable production and consumption, marked by the tenacious persistence of inherently unsustainable systems—a reality that endures even after decades of dedicated research efforts and policy implementation in this field. Furthermore, there emerges the issue of avoiding or minimizing the consideration of intricate power dynamics and political contestation, often underestimated within conventional sustainability research.

In this context, according to authors such as Melnyk et al. (2019), Liao et al. (2018), and Bongomin et al. (2020a, 2020b), a relevant aspect of the 4th industrial revolution is the capacity for production to interact with manufactured products in a way that adapts to consumers' needs, with all production stages formed without human participation and further developed in this regard. This constitutes the production aspect of the Internet of Things, rapidly integrating into the fabric of consumer society. Mathai et al. (2021) who argue that the entrenched inclination towards prioritizing technological innovation, paradoxically often obscures and conceals the deeply embedded social relations of exploitation within production-consumption systems, which in turn drive continuous socioecological degradation. This complex scenario necessitates a critical reassessment and more holistic approaches to address the pressing challenges of Sustainability.

3 Methodology

This research evolved as an outcome of an extensive literature review, characterizing the Great Reset, the 4th Industrial Revolution, and the 4th Social Revolution through an unstructured qualitative and exploratory approach. The selection of this investigative model was motivated by the initial pursuit of describing the phenomena without imposing correlations with other factors.

Additionally, two structured literature reviews were conducted using the Pro-Know-C method, following the recommendations of Lacerda et al. (2012) and Tasca et al. (2010). These reviews employed keywords such as "social revolution," "social transformation," and "social change" in the first axis, along with "fourth industrial revolution" and "4th industrial Revolution" in the second axis, aiming to contextualize the relationship between the 4th Industrial Revolution and the 4th Social Revolution. This review took place between November and December 2021, resulting in an initial portfolio of 1,178 articles, later refined to a final portfolio of 60 articles. A second research inquiry, employing the same method, was conducted between September and October 2023, focusing on the keywords "Nation-State" and "Social Organization," yielding an initial portfolio of 929 results. From these, 44 articles were analyzed and included in the final portfolio.

At the end of the various literature reviews, the key conclusions were synthesized into a "theoretical framework" capable of proposing the main dimensions and subdimensions identified within the bibliographic portfolio concerning the relationship between 4th Industrial Revolution technologies and ethical consumption and civic engagement.

4 The Fourth Industrial and Social Revolution and Its Impacts on Ethical Consumption and Citizen Engagement

We will address here the main technologies of the 4th Industrial Revolution and their potential impacts on ethical consumption and citizen engagement. In this regard, we can start the analysis with the field of nanotechnology. According to Allhoff et al. (2007), there is an underlying environmental concern associated with these technologies. The authors highlight that the relatively large surface-to-volume ratio of nanomaterials tends to increase their chemical reactivity, and the consequences of this cannot yet be predicted. The authors highlight our limited knowledge regarding the lifecycle of structures and devices developed with nanomaterials. A precautionary approach may necessitate careful consideration before widespread use of materials about which we possess limited information. On the other hand, according to these authors, the impact of nanotechnology could result in transformations in energy consumption, with an expected reduction of 14.2% in the current energy consumption of the United States of America.

In the field of 3D printing technology, Ermilova et al. (2019) discuss how the 3D printer has been utilized for various purposes, ranging from manufacturing prosthetics and building houses to printing clothing. They are becoming accessible to the public, allowing them to create simple yet elegant designs. Gupta et al. (2020) and Kumar et al. (2021) highlight advantages such as low labor and material costs, material flexibility, the ability to assist underserved populations, time efficiency, reduced waste generation, and lowered material and energy consumption. All these aspects result in a reduced environmental impact compared to traditional manufacturing.

The Internet of Things (IoT) is described by Brous et al. (2020) as an expansive network of interconnected objects and devices, enabling remote communication and control via the internet. Grammatikis et al. (2019) envision an optimistic future, emphasizing intelligent collaboration between objects anywhere and at any time. In the healthcare sector, Pauget (2019) highlights the utility of IoT for elderly care, with connected objects serving as blood pressure sensors and fall prevention applications. Brous et al. (2020) exemplify its application in public transportation, emphasizing the risks associated with removing the human element. Moreover, IoT facilitates self-service in markets, reducing labor costs and enhancing customer satisfaction (Brous et al., 2020).

In the area of the IoT, Arvidsson (2010) points out that in the corporate world, there's an emergence of new forms of knowledge operations. Simultaneously, there's a development of purist forms of Open Source Software that arise outside or in opposition to the context of corporate capitalism. At the same time, processes linked to the production or manipulation of information and affections, such as experiences, events, and brand image, play a crucial role. These practices are significantly enhanced by the widespread dissemination of networked information and communication technologies, situating themselves at the apex of contemporary value chains. Closely associated with information technology, these practices emerge from expanded forms of cooperation facilitated by such technologies.

Rich (1988) defines Artificial Intelligence (AI) as: "The study of how to make computers perform tasks where, at the moment, people are better. (...) Since then, different schools of thought in AI have studied ways to establish 'intelligent' behaviors in machines." According to Kovacev (2020), this technological shift promises significant transformations in the economy, potentially leading to the massive displacement of human workers while undermining government revenues dependent on taxation from human employment and increasingly demanding social services.

From an ethical perspective, authors like Marcus (2012) and Bonnefon et al. (2016) challenge decisions made by algorithms and autonomous machines, presenting significant ethical dilemmas in consumer contexts. Imagining a scenario where a machine, in control with a human as a passenger, must make a critical decision sacrificing the passenger to prevent harm to multiple individuals poses a profound ethical question. Would you invest in an autonomous vehicle knowing its programming prioritizes utilitarian outcomes in such situations? De Wolf (2017) explores the social impacts of quantum technologies on cryptography, search algorithms, and material simulation, delving into the ethical concerns arising from these impacts. Quantum computing's ability to breach classical hardware encryption escalates data protection challenges, especially during the transition from classical to quantum systems. This has considerable implications for industries like banking and aviation, reliant on cryptographic technologies susceptible to compromise by quantum computers.

In materials science, Goncharov (2020) highlights its integration with other Fourth Industrial Revolution technologies. According to the author, digital production technologies can interact with the biological world as engineers, designers, and architects progressively merge computer-aided design systems, additive manufacturing, materials science, and synthetic biology. This fusion leads to the exploration of symbiotic relationships among microorganisms, our bodies, the substances we consume, and even the homes we inhabit.

In the context of these new technologies within the 4th Industrial Revolution, Mergelina González-Santander and Lemus-Aguilar (2021) emphasize energy storage, highlighting its idea of self-sufficiency at individual and community levels, thus creating mini-networks that allow for a virtual disconnection from the grid. This notably facilitates energy generation within the society where the technology is embedded. The authors also present that energy storage systems give the system the capacity to store electricity during periods of overproduction, providing stored energy during cycles when generation isn't sufficient to meet demand. Moreover, the Table 1 presents a Theoretical Framework, linking the key technologies of the 4th Industrial Revolution to the impacts caused by them on ethical consumption and citizen engagement. This framework underscores how ethical dimensions are inherently connected to responsible consumption, emphasizing the pivotal role of citizen engagement in defining ethical and sustainable practices within the context of the Fourth Industrial Revolution.

Table 1 Theoretical framework for the Fourth Industrial Revolution: impacts on ethical consumption and citizen engagement

Fourth Industrial Revolution (Technologies)	Impacts on ethical consumption and citizen engagement	
	Ethical consumption	Citizen engagement
Nanotechnology	Ethics in nanotechnology involves conscious consumer choices regarding products manufactured with nanomaterials, considering environmental and health impacts	Ethical consumption related to nanotechnology is driven by public awareness, encouraging informed choices and demands for transparency in corporate practices
3D Printing	Ethical consumption in 3D printing refers to the selection of personalized products and the consideration of social and environmental impacts in the decision-making process of printing objects	Communities engaged in 3D printing can foster ethical practices by sharing resources and knowledge, thereby contributing to a more collaborative consumption model
IoT	Ethical consumption in IoT involves selecting devices that prioritize data security and privacy, reflecting choices aligned with ethical values	Ethical citizens engage in discussions about IoT regulations and demand transparency in companies' practices, influencing the responsible development and usage of these technologies
Artificial Intelligence (AI)	Ethical consumption of AI involves selecting products and services based on ethical and transparent algorithms, avoiding discrimination and bias	Active consumer participation in public discussions about ethics in AI influences the shaping of policies and responsible practices within the industry
Quantum Technologies	Ethical consumption in quantum technologies involves concern for data security and privacy in an increasingly vulnerable environment to quantum cryptanalysis	Public awareness regarding the ethical implications of these technologies encourages the demand for ethical standards and stricter security practices

(continued)

Table 1 (continued)

Fourth Industrial Revolution (Technologies)	Impacts on ethical consumption and citizen engagement	
	Ethical consumption	Citizen engagement
Materials Science	Ethical consumption in this context involves informed choices regarding products developed through the intersection of materials science, sustainable design, and synthetic biology	The community actively engages in understanding the ethical applications of materials science, influencing the demand for products aligned with sustainable values
Energy Storage	Ethical consumption of decentralized energy storage solutions is related to choosing sustainable systems that contribute to energy autonomy	Communities involved in energy storage participate in community generation, promoting sustainable practices, and reducing dependence on traditional grids. Authors with research data (2023)

Source Authors with data from the research (2023)

5 Final Considerations

This research culminates from an extensive review of literature, contributing to an enhanced understanding of the intricate relationships between the emerging technologies of the Fourth Industrial Revolution and ethical consumption and citizen engagement. The various dimensions explored, encompassing seven identified pivotal technologies: Artificial Intelligence (AI), Internet of Things (IoT), Nanomaterials, Quantum Computing, Energy Storage, Materials Science, and 3D Printing, underscore the complex and interconnected nature of these technologies with the analyzed phenomena of ethical consumption and citizen engagement. A critical conclusion drawn from this review highlights the paramount importance of technological democratization and awareness regarding the usage of diverse technologies, coupling responsible consumption with community engagement. This approach enables the implementation of these technologies while considering their impacts on the environment and Society.

In the context of nanotechnology, ethics become crucial, demanding conscious consumer choices regarding products manufactured with nanomaterials, considering their environmental and health impacts. This ethical scenario intertwines with citizen engagement, driven by public awareness, fostering informed choices, and advocating for transparency in corporate practices. In the realm of 3D printing, the ethics of consumption are linked to the selection of personalized products, taking into account the social and environmental impacts involved. Within this context, citizen engagement is promoted by active communities utilizing 3D printing, sharing resources and knowledge, contributing to a more collaborative consumption approach.

The Internet of Things (IoT) presents ethical challenges, demanding the selection of devices that prioritize data security and privacy. Citizen engagement in this realm involves active participation in discussions regarding IoT regulations, advocating for transparency in corporate practices, and influencing the responsible development of these technologies. In the domain of Artificial Intelligence (AI), the ethics of consumption pertain to the choice of products and services based on ethical and transparent algorithms, avoiding discrimination and bias. Active consumer participation in public debates about AI ethics shapes responsible policies and practices within the industry.

In the ethical dimension of quantum technologies, there are concerns regarding data security and privacy. Citizen engagement, fueled by public awareness of the ethical implications of these technologies, drives the demand for ethical standards and stricter security practices. Within materials science, ethical consumption involves informed choices about products developed at the intersection of materials science, sustainable design, and synthetic biology. Citizen engagement is observed within the community, actively participating in understanding the ethical applications of materials science, influencing the demand for products aligned with sustainable values. Regarding energy storage, ethical consumption of decentralized solutions is linked to choosing sustainable systems that contribute to energy autonomy. Citizen engagement is evident through communities involved in this sector, actively participating in community generation, promoting sustainable practices, and reducing dependence on traditional grids.

These considerations underscore the need for a comprehensive, ethical, and citizen-oriented approach when considering the implications of the Fourth Industrial Revolution in each of these technologies. The study provides a foundation for future research and public and corporate policies aiming to build a fairer and more equitable society, considering not only general dimensions but also the ethical nuances and citizen engagement specific to each technological sector addressed.

Based on the conclusions presented, there are several opportunities for future research that could enhance the understanding of interactions between specific technologies and ethical dimensions along with citizen engagement. Some suggestions include delving deeper into the social impact of nanotechnology, considering not only the ethical aspects of consumption but also how these materials affect local communities, public health, and social dynamics.

Another promising area would be to investigate specific strategies of citizen engagement within the community regarding 3D printing, examining how communities can be mobilized to promote ethical and sustainable practices. Furthermore, analyzing existing or proposed ethical regulations for the Internet of Things (IoT) and assessing their effectiveness in protecting data privacy and promoting ethical choices by consumers is a relevant research direction. In the field of Artificial Intelligence (AI), delving deeper into the development and implementation of ethical algorithms, examining case studies and best practices to ensure algorithmic decisions are fair and transparent, would be intriguing. Additionally, evaluating the level of public awareness concerning the ethical implications of quantum technologies and identifying effective strategies to educate the public on these matters is an area deserving attention.

Exploring how civic participation integrates into the ethical development of materials, engaging the community in decision-making processes and defining sustainable priorities, represents another relevant research direction. Additionally, analyzing community-based energy storage initiatives and examining how these communities promote sustainable practices, local energy autonomy, and reduce reliance on traditional grids would be a significant field of study. A comparative approach to ethical strategies and citizen engagement across these technologies, identifying similarities, differences, and lessons learned applicable in various contexts, would also be valuable. Longitudinal studies to track the long-term impact of ethical consumption choices in each area, observing behavioral changes over time, are crucial for understanding the evolution of these practices.

Finally, a critical evaluation of the effectiveness of existing or proposed public policies to promote ethical consumption and citizen engagement in specific technologies, proposing adjustments as needed, can provide crucial insights for formulating more effective policies aligned with societal ethical demands. These research suggestions aim to deepen the understanding of ethical and citizen engagement issues in specific technologies, contributing to the development of more responsible and sustainable practices in a rapidly evolving technological landscape. In summary, this literature review underscores the complexity and interconnection of ethical consumption and citizen engagement dimensions in their relationship with emerging technologies of the Fourth Industrial Revolution. It provides a foundation for future research and public and corporate policies aiming to foster a fairer, more supportive, and environmentally sustainable society.

Acknowledgements We gratefully acknowledge the contributions of several institutions in the successful completion of this study. The research was carried out by the Centre for Sustainable Development (Greens) in collaboration with the Graduate Program in Administration at the University of Southern Santa Catarina (Unisul). We also extend our appreciation to the Fundação de Amparo à Pesquisa e Inovação do Estado de Santa Catarina (FAPESC), Ânima Institute (AI), Coordenação de Aperfeiçoamento de Pessoal de Nível Superior (CAPES), and the National Council for Scientific and Technological Development (CNPq) for their invaluable support and assistance throughout the research process.

References

Allhoff, F., et al. (2007). *Nanoethics: The ethical and social implications of nanotechnology*. Wiley.

Alves, F., Filho, W. L., Casaleiro, P., Nagy, G. J., Diaz, H., Al-Amin, A. Q., de Andrade Guerra, J. B. S. O., Hurlbert, M., Farooq, H., Klavins, M., Saroar, M., Lorencova, E. K., Jain, S., Soares, A., Morgado, F., O'Hare, P., Wolf, F., & Azeiteiro, U. M. (2020). Climate change policies and agendas: Facing implementation challenges and guiding responses. *Environmental Science & Policy, 104*, 190–198.

Arvidsson, A. (2010). Speaking out: The ethical economy: New forms of value in the information society? *Organization, 17*(5), 637–644.
Biermann, F., & Pattberg, P. (2008). Global environmental governance: Taking stock, moving forward. *Annual Review of Environment and Resources, 33*, 277–294.
Bongomin, O., Gilibrays Ocen, G., Oyondi Nganyi, E., Musinguzi, A., & Omara, T. (2020a). Exponential disruptive technologies and the required skills of industry 4.0. *Journal of Engineering, 2020*, 1–17.
Bongomin, O., Yemane, A., Kembabazi, B., Malanda, C., Chikonkolo Mwape, M., Sheron Mpofu, N., & Tigalana, D. (2020b). Industry 4.0 disruption and its neologisms in major industrial sectors: A state of the art. *Journal of Engineering, 2020*, 1–45.
Bonnefon, J. F., Shariff, A., & Rahwan, I. (2016). The social dilemma of autonomous vehicles. *Science, 352*(6293), 1573–1576.
Bresser-Pereira, L. C. (2010). Democracia, estado social e reforma gerencial. *Revista de Administração de Empresas, 50*, 112–116.
Brous, P., Janssen, M., & Herder, P. (2020). The dual effects of the Internet of Things (IoT): A systematic review of the benefits and risks of IoT adoption by organizations. *International Journal of Information Management, 51*, 101952.
Brown, P. (2002). Review of The Fight against Big Tobacco: The Movement, the State, and the Public's Health, by M. Wolfson. *American Journal of Sociology, 107*(5), 1359–1361. https://doi.org/10.1086/344846
Cottam, H. (2020). *Welfare 5.0: Why we need a social revolution and how to make it happen*. UCL Institute for Innovation and Public Purpose.
Cruz, J. M. (2021). *La Economía estresada*. UDL.
Czeskleba-Dupont, R. (2003). Sustainable world-system development: Restructuring societal metabolism. *Review* (Fernand Braudel Center), 221–239.
De Wolf, R. (2017). The potential impact of quantum computers on society. *Ethics and Information Technology, 19*(4), 271–276.
Ermilova, M., Maksimova, T., Zhdanova, O., & Zohrab, D. (2019). Improvement of innovation systems in sustainable economic development. In *E3S Web of Conferences* (Vol. 135, p. 04027). EDP Sciences.
Goncharov, V. V. (2020). The Fourth Industrial Revolution: Challenges, Risks and Opportunities. *ERUDITIO, 95*.
Grammatikis, P. I. R., Sarigiannidis, P. G., & Moscholios, I. D. (2019). Securing the Internet of Things: Challenges, threats and solutions. *Internet of Things, 5*, 41–70.
Guerra, J. B. S. O. A. (2020). Bridge–Construindo Resiliência Numa Economia Global Dinâmica: Complexidade Através De Escalas No Nexo Entre Alimentos, Água E Energia No Brasil. *Revista Gestão & Sustentabilidade Ambiental, 9*(1 esp), 1–2.
Gupta, S., Kumar, V., & Karam, E. (2020). New-age technologies-driven social innovation: What, how, where, and why? *Industrial Marketing Management, 89*, 499–516.
Jenness, V. (2004). Explaining criminalization: From demography and status politics to globalization and modernization. *Annual Review of Sociology, 30*, 147–171.
Kovacev, R. (2020). A taxing dilemma: Robot taxes and the challenges of effective taxation of AI, automation and robotics in the fourth industrial revolution. *Ohio State Technology Law Journal, 16*, 182.
Kumar, R., Rogall, C., Thiede, S., Herrmann, C., & Sangwan, K. S. (2021). Development of a decision support system for 3D printing processes based on cyber physical production systems. *Procedia CIRP, 98*, 348–353.
Lacerda, R. T. O., Ensslin, L., & Ensslin, S. R. (2012). Uma análise bibliométrica da literatura sobre estratégia e avaliação de desempenho. Gestão & Produção, [S.L.], *19*(1), 59–78. FapUNIFESP (SciELO). https://doi.org/10.1590/s0104-530x2012000100005
Liao, Y., Loures, E. R., Deschamps, F., Brezinski, G., & Venâncio, A. (2018). The impact of the fourth industrial revolution: A cross-country/region comparison. *Production, 28*.

Mathai, M. V., Isenhour, C., Stevis, D., Vergragt, P., Bengtsson, M., Lorek, S., Mortensen, L. F., Coscieme, L., Scott, D., Waheed, A., & Alfredsson, E. (2021). The political economy of (un) sustainable production and consumption: A multidisciplinary synthesis for research and action. *Resources, Conservation and Recycling, 167*, 105265.

Melnyk, L. H., Kubatko, O. V., Dehtyarova, I. B., Dehtiarova, I. B., Matsenko, O. M., & Rozhko, O. D. (2019). The effect of industrial revolutions on the transformation of social and economic systems. *Problems and Perspectives in Management, 17*(4), 381–391.

Mercure, J.-F., Paim, M. A., Bocquillon, P., Lindner, S., Salas, P., Martinelli, P., Berchin, I. I., de Andrade Guerra, J. B. S. O., Derani, C., de Albuquerque Junior, C. L., Ribeiro, J. M. P., Knobloch, F., Pollitt, H., Edwards, N. R., Holden, P. B., Foley, A., Schaphoff, S., Faraco, R. A., & Vinuales, J. E. (2019). System complexity and policy integration challenges: The Brazilian energy-water-food nexus. *Renewable and Sustainable Energy Reviews, 105*, 230–243.

Mergelina González-Santander de, P., & Lemus-Aguilar, I. (2021). Current innovation sources driving the Spanish electric power sector. *Ingeniería e Investigación, 41*(3), e85377–e85377.

Mudassir, H. (2020, March 16). *COVID-19 will fuel the next wave of innovation*. Entrepreneur.com. https://www.entrepreneur.com/article/347669

Pauget, B., & Dammak, A. (2019). The implementation of the Internet of Things: What impact on organizations? *Technological Forecasting and Social Change, 140*, 140–146.

Pezzuto, I. (2020). COVID-19: *The unexpected and disruptive event that will radically shake up and change the world as we know it*. Risk Governance and Control: Financial Markets & Institutions.

Rich, E. (1988). *Inteligência Artificial*. McGraw-Hill.

Schwab, K. (2017). *The fourth industrial revolution*. Currency.

Schwab, K., & Malleret, T. (2020). The great reset. In *World economic forum* (Vol. 22). Geneva.

Tasca, J. E., Ensslin, L., Rolim Ensslin, S., & Bernardete Martins Alves, M. (2010). An approach for selecting a theoretical framework for the evaluation of training programs. *Journal of European Industrial Training, 34*(7), 631–655.

Integrating the Circular Economy into the Surf Industry: A Vision Aligned with the Sustainable Development Goals

Carlos Eduardo de Morais, Rafael da Luz Lisboa, Victor Rafael Ribeiro, Ana Regina de Aguiar Dutra, Robert Birch, and José Baltazar Salgueirinho Osório de Andrade Guerra

Abstract One of the challenges of the surfing industry (SI), over time, has been the minimization of environmental impact. By embracing circular economy (CE) practices, SI not only promotes sustainability, but also aligns with the Sustainable Development Goals (SDGs). With the general objective of understanding the impact of CE on SI, this chapter investigates the incorporation of CE principles in SI and their relationship with the SDGs. To achieve the proposed objective, a narrative review was conducted with the purpose of examining current SI practices, including waste management, sustainable production and responsible consumption. The consonance between these practices and the SDGs themselves was assessed, and finally, a mapping of how SI can contribute to sustainable development goals based on the SDGs was carried out. Based on the results, recommendations are made for the effective integration of circular principles and SI in support of a more responsible future aligned with the SDGs.

Keywords Circular Economy · Surf Industry · SDGs · Sustainability · Oceans

---

C. E. de Morais · R. da Luz Lisboa · V. R. Ribeiro · A. R. de Aguiar Dutra ·
J. B. S. O. de Andrade Guerra (✉)
University of Southern Santa Catarina, Graduate Program in Administration, Florianópolis, Santa Catarina 88015-110, Brazil
e-mail: jose.baltazarguerra@animaeducacao.com.br

A. R. de Aguiar Dutra
e-mail: ana.aguiar@animaeducacao.com.br

V. R. Ribeiro · A. R. de Aguiar Dutra · R. Birch · J. B. S. O. de Andrade Guerra
Center for Sustainable Development Research, Florianópolis, Santa Catarina 88015-110, Brazil
e-mail: robsb@cybase.co.uk

R. Birch
School of Engineering, University of Liverpool, Liverpool L69 3BX, UK

W. Leal Filho and V. Kuzmanović (eds.), *Sustainable Development Seen Through the Lenses of Ethnoeconomics and the Circular Economy*,
https://doi.org/10.1007/978-3-031-72676-7_4

1 Introduction

Interest in nature-related research activities continues to expand steadily over the years (Coventry et al., 2021). However, the sustainability of these benefits still requires further investigation (Rodrigues Garcia et al., 2017). For example, carrying out marine industrial or even recreational activities in an unsustainable manner, such as increasing the disposal of waste that causes ocean pollution, can cause significant damage to ecosystems, making preserving the environment a challenging task (Rees et al., 2010; Wyles et al., 2017). The authors cited here deal with issues that are currently connected to what is now called the "blue economy". The blue economy, or ocean or maritime economy, which refers to the sustainable use of ocean resources for economic growth, improved livelihoods, and the health of the oceans. The blue economy encompasses a range of sectors, such as fisheries, aquaculture, maritime transport, energy, tourism and marine biotechnology. Its potential to contribute to sustainable development and poverty reduction has received the attention of policymakers, academics and stakeholders (Smith-Godfrey, 2016).

Surfing is one of the numerous recreational activities originating from the marine environment. The influence of this activity extends across several areas, including the socio-cultural, economic, and environmental, making it one of the most popular marine recreational activities globally (Orams & Towner, 2013). According to global industry analysts, in 2023, with a worldwide population of surfers estimated at 50 million (Manero, 2023), the related market accounts for over $4 billion in equipment and product sales. It is important to highlight that this number is possibly substantially higher when considering surfing fashion, which is marketed beyond specialized retail (Sportsvalue, 2023).

In Brazil, with the presence of numerous companies in the surfwear industry, the sport enjoys a significant number of practitioners and stands out in international competitions, where social and economic aspects exert a notable impact on the national surfing industry (SI). Currently, SI has a turnover of more than R$7 billion (US$1.4 billion) and has grown substantially, after the so-called "Brazilian Storm" was coined by the American press in 2011 to describe the new generation of Brazilian surfers that entered the world stage. But this singular moment has gone on to generate structuring projects for the country (Sportsvalue, 2023).

SI represents a multibillion-dollar population that strives for sustainable development in business, excelling at various stages of the supply chain, from the production and manufacture of durable and lightweight products to the distribution, consumption, disposal, and recycling of these items. However, considering the possibility of negative impacts, it is imperative to promote greater responsibility on the part of producers along the entire supply chain, holding accountable those who could be the main polluters (*The Guardian*, 2014). However, to achieve this goal, SI has adopted the process of transforming its waste into similar products for the industry or into other items with the result that energy and natural resources are saved. This makes it possible to reintegrate elements that would otherwise be discarded (Almeida et al., 2015; Fazenia et al., 2014; Ferreira et al., 2014; Jabbour et al., 2014). In this context, it is notable that several renowned brands, such as O'Neill, Finisterre, Quiksilver, Patagonia, Vissla, among others, show interest in the topic and seek alternatives to replace non-renewable materials with natural and recyclable materials. These well-known high-profile companies in the surfwear sector are already implementing plans that involve the substitution of materials and the implementation of reverse logistics. For example, the surfwear company Rip Curl started a process of recycling rubber products, such as wetsuits and flip-flops, in 2018. They are being recycled and turned into floor covering for the company's own offices. Mimi LaMontagne, who held the position of communications manager at Rip Curl, stated in an interview that the ultimate goal is to establish a global recycling program, allowing customers to return the materials to any retail store in the world (Stab Magazine, 2018). Another company in the sector, Soöruz, has also adopted the practice of reverse logistics in its system, launching the "2nd Life" program for its old wetsuits, which are recycled and turned into accessories.

It is undeniable that, over the years, the accessibility to obtaining new information has increased and has led to a growth in the number of consumers in SI who show concern about the origin of products before purchasing them. It is extremely important to consider the need to reduce the exploitation of the planet's natural resources and opt for products that cause the least possible impact on the environment, since irreversible damage is being caused with each passing year. This growing concern for environmental sustainability and the life cycle of products is reflected in the increase in studies that explore the relationship between surfing, as a nature-based activity, and sustainable development (Borne, 2023; Borne & Ponting, 2017). In this context, it is imperative to adopt the Circular Economy (CE) guidelines in SI. This approach involves a system that consists of transforming waste into recoverable resources through recycling and reuse (Gregson et al., 2015). In other words, it represents an alternative to improve efficiency in the use of materials and energy, promoting a more sustainable business model. The CE model is composed of four technical cycles: (i) product maintenance; (ii) reuse/redistribution of used products; (iii) updating/remanufacturing of the product; and (iv) product recycling (EMF, 2017).

In 2020, only 9% of the global economy can be considered circular, which implies that the planet reuses less than 10% of the 92.8 billion tons of minerals, fossil fuels, metals, and biomass consumed annually in production processes (BNDES, 2020). In the Brazilian scenario of 2017, 40.9% of the waste collected was inappropriately disposed of, which is equivalent to 29 million tons of waste deposited in dumps or controlled landfills, representing a risk to public health and the environment (Abrelpe, 2018). Among the challenges to be addressed are the high costs associated with operations, including waste collection, treatment, and disposal, along with the scarcity of resources allocated to the sector.

Annually, the world generates approximately two billion tons of municipal solid waste, with a conservative estimate pointing out that 33% of this amount is disposed of inappropriately from an environmental point of view, such as deposits in landfills (World Bank, 2020). In view of this worrisome scenario, it is imperative to implement public policies and adopt measures aimed at reducing waste generation, encouraging the promotion of CE through reuse and recycling. In cases where these practices are not viable, it is essential to consider the option of energy use (BNDES, 2020).

In this context, it is imperative to conduct urgent studies to evaluate the performance of activities involving the integration of CE in SI, with the purpose of verifying its sustainability. In addition, it is essential to ensure compliance with the United Nations (UN) 2030 Agenda for Sustainable Development (UN, 2015) and its 17 Sustainable Development Goals (SDGs) that aim to achieve sustainable development by 2030. It is relevant to highlight that this agenda is part of the United Nations Decade for the Protection of the Oceans Science for Sustainable Development (2021–2030) (Claudet et al., 2020), which is committed to meeting the SDGs (Ryabinin et al., 2019).

In addition to this introduction in Sect. 1, this chapter is organized into four distinct sections. Section 2 outlines the method selected to conduct the research, Sect. 3 examines prominent projects that incorporate CE into the SI. The affinities with the SDGs are discussed in Sect. 4, and finally, in Sect. 5, some discussion on this study and recommendations for future investigations are presented.

2 Methodology

This study is part of a qualitative narrative review, which is characterized as an appropriate method to examine the state of the art of a specific topic. This type of review involves a comprehensive analysis of the literature, without the imposition of a rigorous and easily replicable methodology to obtain quantitative data and specific responses (Vosgerau & Romanowski, 2014). Nevertheless, this approach plays a key role in acquiring and updating knowledge related to a specific theme, highlighting new ideas, methods, and sub-themes that vary in terms of emphasis in the selected literature (Elias et al., 2012). In this context, the research focuses on a literature review that explores the integration of CE in SI and its potential impact on the Sustainable Development Goals. The study was conducted throughout the month of October 2023, and its scope considers the last 20 years as the reference period.

In practice, strings such as "*Circular Economy*", "*Surf Industry*" *and* "*SDGs*" were used in the *Scopus, ScienceDirect, Web of Science* and *Willey* databases, combining or not these terms, without imposing a specific time interval. The inclusion of publications was determined based on the presence of the expressions used in the searches in the title, abstract, keywords or on the explicit relationship of the content with the integration of CE in the SI. Articles that did not meet these inclusion criteria and/or had duplicates, i.e., were retrieved from more than one of the databases, were excluded from the study. In addition, dissertations and theses were also excluded from the analysis. Even so, direct searches to the "google.com" search system from the above strings were also considered, sometimes in a combined way, sometimes isolated. After collecting the desired information, the first step consisted of reviewing the titles and abstracts, during which no publication was deleted. After this process, the selected documents were read in full.

For an analytical approach, the study initially sought to classify research based on two main categories: those that address samples related to CE, waste reuse, or recycling, and those that focus on SI innovation, production, or sustainable development. Based on this categorization, the analysis was extended to evaluate the theoretical basis of the studies, as well as to observe the general characteristics of the articles, including year of publication, language, and established objectives. Finally, the methodology used, the results achieved and the discussions were examined and presented. It should be emphasized that, for this analysis of the scientific literature identified in this research, an evaluation of each individual text was carried out without any specific qualitative or quantitative data processing techniques being applied.

3 Projects for Integrating the Circular Economy in the Surf Industry

This section describes two significant projects related to the integration of CE in SI that are underway currently in Brazil. The CE represents a model of sustainable production and consumption as opposed to the traditional linear model of "produce, use and discard". In this context, the integration of CE into SI involves the adoption of practices that aim to reduce the waste of resources, promote the reuse and recycling of materials, and encourage sustainable design in products and services. This move towards sustainability in SI not only helps preserve marine ecosystems but also offers a new business perspective that values environmental responsibility.

Two projects presented here are pioneering examples of this integration: The Ecological Surfboard—ECO Garopaba project (Sustainable Innovation in Surfing) and the Unbottling Minds project. Both projects demonstrate how innovation and creativity can be directed towards the production of surfing equipment and experiences that are not only environmentally friendly, but also economically viable and socially beneficial. These projects are explored in more detail here, highlighting their unique contributions to building a more sustainable future in the surf industry.

3.1 Ecological Surfboard—ECO Garopaba Project

This project represents a creative and sustainable response to the environmental challenges facing the oceans, particularly plastic pollution. This initiative fits into the broader context of circular economy and sustainability in the surf industry. ECO Garopaba's "Ecological Surfboard" project emerged in 2007 when Jairo Lumertz, a surfer from Rio Grande do Sul in Brazil, was living in Hawaii and created his first surfboard using used recycled PET bottles. In 2011, with his return to Brazil, he entered in partnership with Carolina Scorsin to create their first Ecological Surfboard in Garopaba, located in the Brazilian state of Santa Catarina, where they began to give lectures on sustainability. In 2023, they launched their 11th edition of their design at the Ecological Surfboard Surf Festival in Garopaba. This event promoted environmental sustainability in the sport with, for example, boards being manufactured using recycled materials as a remarkable example of how sustainable innovations can be integrated into SI. But, this project goes beyond creating boards from recycled PET bottles; it represents a multifaceted approach that addresses environmental sustainability, education, and social inclusion, thereby aligning with the United Nations SDGs.

The design of the eco-board is not only a creative response to plastic pollution, but also a means of engaging the local community and young people in sustainability practices. The choice of Garopaba as the epicentre of this project is no coincidence. This locality, known for its beaches and meeting point for surfing enthusiasts, offers the perfect setting for this initiative that combines water sports with environmental responsibility. At the heart of the project is the idea that active involvement in the manufacture of the boards can act as a catalyst for greater environmental awareness. Surfboards, made from recycled PET bottles, are not only tools for sport, but also tangible symbols of recycling and reuse of materials. This process of transforming waste into useful resources is a practical example of the circular economy in action, a concept that is increasingly relevant in discussions about sustainability. In addition to the production of eco-friendly surfboards, the project extends to several other areas, reflecting a broader commitment to sustainability. Environmental education is a central component, with the project providing lectures and workshops in local schools. Here, emphasis is placed on the importance of recycling and proper waste separation, teaching participants not only the importance of recycling but also how to do it effectively.

The multiplier training aspect is particularly noteworthy. Young people from public schools are trained in the construction of boards with PET bottles. This training is not only for the construction of boards, but also as an empowerment tool, allowing these young people to become entrepreneurs and community leaders in sustainability. They are encouraged to share their knowledge that, in turn, creates a growing network of individuals who are informed and engaged in sustainable practices. Social inclusion is also a crucial dimension of the project and the making of boards adapted for people with disabilities is a remarkable example of how the project seeks to include everyone in the surfing experience and environmental awareness. This aspect underlines the holistic nature of the project that seeks not only to address environmental issues but also to promote inclusion and equality. Additionally, the project has received significant recognition, reflecting its importance and impact. In 2018, it was a finalist for the Guga Kuerten Institute Award, an award that highlights innovative and effective social projects. This recognition is a testament to the positive impact the project has had on the local community and the surf industry.

Partnerships also play a vital role in broadening the reach and depth of the project. The collaboration, since 2017, with actor and activist Klebber Toledo is an example of this. Their participation not only raised the profile of the project, but also helped to establish broader connections and bring additional resources to the initiative. Toledo's presence at the annual PET Bottle Board Surf Festival adds an element of visibility and celebration, highlighting the community's unity around sustainability goals. In short, Garopaba's "Ecological Surfboard" is an exemplary project of how sustainable innovation can be incorporated effectively into specific sectors such as SI. It demonstrates that sustainability is not only a matter of environmental preservation, but also of education, social inclusion, and community empowerment. With its comprehensive and multifaceted approach, the project not only contributes to the reduction of plastic pollution but also inspires and empowers individuals and communities to adopt more sustainable lifestyles. This project represents a microcosm of how small, innovative actions can lead to meaningful change, positively influencing both local communities and the global environment. The importance of innovative approaches in the surf industry, aligned with the SDGs, is crucial to promote environmentally responsible and sustainable practices. Information about this project was found on the social network Facebook on the page of the Eco Garopaba Ecological Plank Project.

3.2 Unbottling Minds Project

The Unbottling Minds project, originated at Maresias Beach in São Sebastião, located in the Brazilian state of Santa Catarina, is a remarkable socio-environmental initiative that combines a passion for surfing with a deep commitment to sustainability and environmental education. This innovative project focuses on making surfboards from garbage, especially PET bottles and fabric scraps, serving as a powerful educational tool for young children and youths on the importance of sustainability and proper waste management. The origin of "Unbottling Minds" is a direct response to the negative impact humanity has on nature. Founded in 2016, the project was born out of the urgent need to act in favour of preserving the environment and to raise awareness among the local community and visitors about the environmental damage being caused in the Maresias region. The motivation for this initiative came from the contrast between the natural beauty of Maresias and the environmental problems faced, such as pollution and the accumulation of garbage, with the aim of changing this scenario for future generations.

The project was conceived by Thiago de Oliveira and has a multidisciplinary approach, incorporating art and culture into environmental education, and was designed to reach a wide range of ages and socioeconomic realities. Surfboards made from recycled materials are not only sports equipment but also tangible symbols of recycling and reuse, highlighting the importance of reducing rampant consumption and sustainable waste management. In addition to the manufacture of surfboards, the Unbottling Minds project has expanded to include other sustainability, socio-education and cultural projects, addressing solutions to various environmental and social problems. With a focus on children, adolescents, adults and the elderly, the project engages the entire community in pursuit of meaningful transformation.

The project's mission is to encourage the community to create a scenario, a new reality and a fairer world, with less impact on the environment and a vibrant street culture. Through its actions, the project seeks freedom, inclusion and dignity through sport, art, culture and citizenship. Among the project's notable initiatives are the community garden, which seeks to fight hunger and promote food sovereignty, and beach cleaning, a symbolic action that teaches the importance of environmental preservation. These actions, along with the community library, language teaching for children, and digital inclusion, are designed to promote inclusive education and social development as a means to reduce inequalities.

The Unbottling Minds project is an inspiring example of how local actions can generate meaningful change in the world. Through a simple and accessible language, it deals with current issues about the degradation of the planet, society's problematic relationship with waste, and the marginalization of street art. Through these actions, the desired change in the world is sought, emphasizing the need for individual and social transformations for a more sustainable future. In essence, the project is a powerful testimony that small groups of conscious, engaged people can, in fact, change the world. The preservation of the environment and the promotion of a fairer and more sustainable society is a common call.

4 Alignments with the Sustainable Development Goals

The contemporary global scenario, characterized by significant environmental and socio-economic challenges, requires innovative and sustainable solutions. Projects such as Ecological Board (ECO Garopaba) and Unbottling Minds demonstrate a deep alignment with the United Nations SDGs. In this context, four main alignments are evident.

1. **Quality Education (SDG 4)**

Education is key to promoting sustainability. The projects in question act as educational platforms, teaching about waste management and the importance of sustainability. By making surfboards from recycled materials, they offer a practical and engaging model for learning. This approach is in line with the understanding that education is a powerful tool for achieving sustainability (UNESCO, 2017).

2. **Responsible Consumption and Production (SDG 12)**

Both projects promote responsible consumption and production through the reuse of disposable materials, such as PET bottles, in the manufacture of surfboards. This practice exemplifies the circular economy, a crucial concept for achieving SDG 12. According to Geissdoerfer et al. (2017), the circular economy is not only an economic mechanism, but a response to the global environmental urgency. By turning waste into useful products, these projects demonstrate how responsible consumption and production can be incorporated into everyday life.

3. **Climate Action (SDG 13)**

Climate action is one of the most pressing challenges of our time. The projects "Ecological Board - ECO Garopaba" and "Unbottling Minds" contribute to this goal by promoting practices that reduce pollution and excessive consumption. According to the Intergovernmental Panel on Climate Change (IPCC, 2012), local initiatives that focus on sustainability are essential to mitigate climate change. By encouraging reuse and recycling, these projects help reduce the accumulation of waste, which is a significant factor in global warming.

4. **Life Below Water (SDG 14)**

The conservation of the oceans and marine life are critical to planetary sustainability. Both projects demonstrate a commitment to SDG 14, especially through beach clean-ups and marine pollution awareness. As stated by Worm et al. (2017), the health of marine ecosystems is intrinsically linked to human actions on land. By educating about and combating ocean pollution, these projects contribute directly to the health of aquatic ecosystems.

The Ecological Board—ECO Garopaba and Unbottling Minds projects are inspiring examples of how local initiatives can have a significant impact on achieving the SDGs. Not only do they provide practical solutions to environmental problems, but they also educate and inspire communities to adopt sustainable practices. As the UN emphasizes, the involvement of all sectors of society is crucial to achieving the SDGs (United Nations, 2015). These projects represent a microcosm of how innovative, community-based actions can lead to a more sustainable future for all.

Figure 1 shows the main alignments of CE in SI with the sustainable development goals.

5 Conclusions

This chapter sought to understand the impact of CE on SI, investigating the incorporation of CE principles in SI and their relationship with the SDGs. In view of the related projects, SI has a great potential to adapt to sustainable practices, and thus have a promising approach to achieve the SDGs, since it is intrinsically linked to best practices for the preservation of the environment.

As an academic contribution, this chapter not only brings together two topics that already have a significant representation for the scientific community and makes it possible to disseminate new ways to promote sustainability. The discussion promoted here allowed the creation of a promising avenue of knowledge not only for the disposal of waste and the principles of CE in SI, but also the bias of conditioning good practices aligned with the SDG agenda. In relation to the practical contribution, for companies and managers, the examples provided here enable a greater maturity in relation to the organizational context. In addition, encouraging the adoption of circular practices enables an interesting learning curve in the conscious use

Fig. 1 Chart of Key Alignments with the Sustainable Development Goals. *Source* Authors, 2023

of resources, investing in research and development of materials, a brand valuation, a better reputation in relation to stakeholders and a strategic positioning that ensures a greater competitive advantage.

With regard to social contribution, the incentive lies in supporting the adoption of circular practices in SI through projects, awareness campaigns and education. In this sense, there is an incentive to promote public policies that use the use of renewable and recycled materials in SI. Such recommendations can contribute to the development of a more sustainable and conscious SI, which has a positive impact on the entire ecosystem.

However, the effective integration of CE in SI requires the commitment of companies in the sector to sustainability, in addition to the support of government and civil society. This integration can drive the achievement of several SDGs, such as responsible consumption and production, combating climate change, preserving aquatic and terrestrial life. To achieve this, companies must adopt circular practices throughout the value chain, governments need to promote public policies that encourage such practices, and civil society must support awareness and education in this regard.

Finally, the limitations are conditioned to a study that addressed only two cases and was based only on narrative research activities. For future studies, it is suggested to expand this research to a greater number of projects at an international level with a deeper theoretical approach that seeks to mix qualitative and quantitative aspects.

Acknowledgements We gratefully acknowledge the contributions of several institutions in the successful completion of this study. The research was carried out by the Centre for Sustainable Development (Greens) in collaboration with the Graduate Program in Administration at the University of Southern Santa Catarina (Unisul). We also extend our appreciation to the Fundação de Amparo à Pesquisa e Inovação do Estado de Santa Catarina (FAPESC), Ânima Institute (AI), Coordenação de Aperfeiçoamento de Pessoal de Nível Superior (CAPES), and the National Council for Scientific and Technological Development (CNPq) for their invaluable support and assistance throughout the research process.

References

Abrelpe. (2018). *Solid Waste Standards in Brazil 2018/2019*. Retrieved on 11 February 2023 from: https://abrelpe.org.br/panorama/

Almeida, F. C. R., Sales, A., Moretti, J. P., & Mendes, P. C. D. (2015). Sugarcane bagasse ash sand (SBAS): Brazilian agroindustrial by-product for use in mortar. *Construction and Building Materials, 82*, 31–38.

BNDES. (2020). *Circular Economy: Waste that becomes an input*. Retrieved on 11 February 2023 from: https://agenciadenoticias.bndes.gov.br/blogdodesenvolvimento/detalhe/Economia-ircular-waste-turned-input/#:~:text=Second%20o%20report%C3%B3rio%20The%20circularity,consumed%20annually%20in%20processes%20productive

Borne, G. (2023). Sustainable transitions in the surfing sector. The role of risk and branding. *Business Strategy & Development, 6*(4), 610–623.

Borne, G., & Ponting, J. (2017). *Sustainable surfing*. Routledge.

Claudet, J., Bopp, L., Cheung, W. W. L., Devillers, R., Escobar-Briones, E., Haugan, P., et al. (2020). A roadmap for using the UN decade of ocean science for sustainable development in support of science, policy, and action. *One Earth, 2*, 34–42.

Coventry, P. A., Brown, J. V. E., Pervin, J., Brabyn, S., Pateman, R., Breedvelt, J., et al., 2021. Nature-based outdoor activities for mental and physical health: Systematic review and meta-analysis. *SSM—Population Health, 16*, 100934.

Elias, C. S. R., Silva, L. A., Martins, M. T. S. L., Ramos, N. A. P. R., Souza, M. G. G., & Hipólito, R. L. (2012). When does the end come? A narrative review of the end of school for mentally handicapped students. *SMAD: Electronic Journal on Mental Health, Alcohol and Drugs, 1*(8), 48–53.

Fazenia, K., Lindorfera, J., & Prammerb, H. (2014). Methodological advancements in Life Cycle Process Design: A preliminary outlook. *Resources, Conservation & Recycling, 92*, 66–77.

Ferreira, S., Cabral, M., Cruz, N. F., da Simões, P., Marques, R. C. (2014), Life cycle assessment of a packaging waste recycling system in Portugal. *Waste Management, 34*(9), 1725–1735.

Ellen Macarthur Foundation—EMF. (2017). *Circular Economy implementation in China*. Retrieved on 11 February 2023 from: https://www.ellenmacarthurfoundation.org/news/circular-economy-implementation-in-china

Geissdoerfer, M., Savaget, P., Bocken, N. M., & Hultink, E. J. (2017). The Circular Economy—A new sustainability paradigm? *Journal of Cleaner Production, 143*, 757–768.

Gregson, N., Crang, M., Fuller, S., & Holmes, H. (2015). Interrogating the circular economy: The moral economy of resource recovery in the EU. *Economy and Society, 2*(44), 218–243.

The Guardian. (2014). The surfing companies making waves with sustainable design. Retrieved on 11 February 2023 from: https://www.theguardian.com/sustainable-business/2014/nov/27/surfing-companies-making-waves-with-sustainable-design

Intergovernmental Panel on Climate Change (IPCC). (2012). *Global Warming of 1.5°C*. IPCC.

Jabbour, A. B., Jabbour, C., Govindan, K., Kannan, D., & Arantes, A. F. (2014). Mixed methodology to analyze the relationship between maturity of environmental management and the adoption of green supply chain management in Brazil. *Resources, Conservation & Recycling, 92*, 255–267.

Manero, A. (2023). A case for protecting the value of 'surfing ecosystems.' *NPJ Ocean Sustainability, 2*, 6.

Orams, M. B., & Towner, N. (2013). Riding the wave: History, definitions, and a proposed typology of surf-riding tourism. *Tourism in Marine Environments, 8*, 173–188.

Rees, S. E., Rodwell, L. D., Attrill, M. J., Austen, M. C., & Mangi, S. C. (2010). The value of marine biodiversity to the leisure and recreation industry and its application to marine spatial planning. *Marine Policy, 34*, 868–875.

Rodrigues Garcia, J., Conides, A. J., Rodriguez Rivero, S., Raicevich, S., Pita, P., Kleisner, K. M., et al. (2017). Marine and coastal cultural ecosystem services: Knowledge gaps and research priorities. *One Ecosystem, 2*, 4.

Ryabinin, V., Barbière, J., Haugan, P., Kullenberg, G., Smith, N., McLean, C., Troisi, A., Fischer, A., Aricò, S., Aarup, T., Pissierssens, P., Visbeck, M., Enevoldsen, H. O., & Rigaud, J. (2019). The UN decade of ocean science for sustainable development. *Frontiers in Marine Science, 6*, 470.

Smith-Godfrey, S. (2016). Defining the blue economy. *Maritime Affairs: Journal of the National Maritime Foundation of India, 12*(1), 58–64.

Sportsvalue. (2023). *Surf Business: Brazil, the New Epicenter of the Sport Worldwide*. Retrieved on 11 February 2023 from: https://www.sportsvalue.com.br/negocios-do-surfe-brasil-o-novo-epicentro-da-modalidade-no-mundo/#:~:text=Estimativas%20mais%20otimistas%20speak%20of,value%20aggregate%2C%20e%20impact%20market%C3%B3gico

Stab Magazine. (2018). *What do you do with your old wetsuits?* Retrieved on 11 February 2023 from: https://stabmag.com/news/what-do-you-do-with-your-old-wetsuits/

UNESCO. (2017). *Education for Sustainable Development Goals: Learning objectives*. UNESCO.

United Nations—UN. (2015). *Transforming our world: The 2030 agenda for sustainable development*. United Nations. Retrieved on 11 February 2023 from: https://sdgs.un.org/2030agenda

Vosgerau, D. S. A. R., & Romanowski, J. P. (2014). Review studies: Conceptual and methodological implications. *Journal of Educational Dialogue, 14*(41), 165–189.

World Bank. (2020). *What a Waste 2.0: A Global Snapshot of Solid Waste Management to 2050*. Retrieved on 11 February 2023 from: https://datatopics.worldbank.org/what-a-waste/trends_in_solid_waste_management.html

Worm, B., et al. (2017). Marine biodiversity and climate change. In *Climate change and marine and freshwater toxins* (pp. 33–56). Elsvier.

Wyles, K. J., Pahl, S., Holland, M., & Thompson, R. C. (2017). Can beach cleans do more than clean-up litter? Comparing Beach cleans to other coastal activities. *Environment and Behavior, 49*(5), 509–535.

Equality, Inequality and Industry 4.0: Proposing a Theoretical Framework

Felipe Fernandes, Robert Birch, and José Baltazar Salgueirinho Osório de Andrade Guerra

Abstract This research seeks to investigate the relationship between equality, inequality and the 4th Industrial Revolution (Industry 4.0) while exploring the dimensions that influence both the promotion of equality and the perpetuation of inequality in this context. The methodology adopted for this work was based on a structured literature review using, as the source, articles selected in Google Scholar in the period from 2017 to 2023. This article proposes a theoretical framework presenting six dimensions: Technological, Economic, Social, Environmental, Political and Global and Social Transformation. In addition, 11 sub-dimensions were presented, distributed in these categories of analysis. The theoretical contributions of this study include the systematization and integration of the various dimensions tangential to equality/inequality in the era of the Industry 4.0. The proposed framework offers a comprehensive conceptual framework for understanding these complex relationships and can equally serve as a basis for future research. Suggestions for future studies include empirical research that can apply the framework in specific contexts, evaluating both the effectiveness of policies and proposed strategies to promote equality and address inequality.

Keywords Equality · Inequality · Industry 4.0 · Social Transformation · Great Reset

---

F. Fernandes · J. B. S. O. de Andrade Guerra (✉)
Center for Sustainable Development Research, University of Southern Santa Catarina, Graduate Program in Administration, Florianópolis 88010-010, Brazil
e-mail: jose.baltazarguerra@animaeducacao.com.br

F. Fernandes
e-mail: felipe.fernandes65@unisul.br

R. Birch
School of Engineering, University of Liverpool, Liverpool L69 3BX, UK
e-mail: rsb123@liverpool.ac.uk

W. Leal Filho and V. Kuzmanović (eds.), *Sustainable Development Seen Through the Lenses of Ethnoeconomics and the Circular Economy*,
https://doi.org/10.1007/978-3-031-72676-7_5

1 Introduction

The analysis will focus on the dimensions of equality and inequality in the 4th Industrial Revolution (Industry 4.0). Factors that contribute to the promotion of equality, such as democratising access to advanced technologies, creating fair employment opportunities and digital inclusion, were examined in the work. In addition, elements that contribute to inequality in this context were investigated, such as the concentration of economic and technological power, the digital divide, and the polarization of the labour market.

This in-depth analysis sought to understand the main arguments related to equality and inequality in Industry 4.0. Theoretical and empirical approaches that discuss the socio-economic consequences of adopting disruptive technologies, such as artificial intelligence, automation, Internet of Things, and also social technologies such as the Platform Economy, were explored. The principal aim of this research is to build a theoretical framework that encompasses the main dimensions related to equality and inequality in Industry 4.0 while identifying key perspectives and debates. This theoretical framework is expected to offer a framework for understanding the socio-economic complexities and challenges related to equality and inequality in Industry 4.0 as well as providing valuable insights for the formulation of strategies and policies that seek to promote a more just and equitable society. Further to this, the results of this work will be useful for understanding the challenges and opportunities that arise in the context of Industry 4.0 as well as for developing policies and strategies that promote equal access, opportunities and benefits for all individuals, regardless of their socioeconomic background.

2 Literature Review

The Sustainable Development Goals (SDGs) present targets for diverse issues such as health, education, the environment, and sustainability and inequality. Several authors such as Andrade Guerra (2020), Mercure et al. (2019) and Alves et al. (2020), support the understanding that these problems can only be faced by taking into account their different aspects concomitantly and simultaneously. In this sense, the Welfare State emerges as one of the great achievements of societies throughout the twentieth century. This model of the State has made important contributions to the reduction of inequalities and to the provision of options for social mobility. Thus, in the face of two emerging phenomena, namely, Industry 4.0 and the social transformations that accompany it, the research is justified since it tries to synthesize these dimensions into a model capable of proposing the main changes provided by the adoption of disruptive technologies, i.e., artificial intelligence, automation, Internet of Things. Also included are the social technologies such as the Platform Economy both in the promotion of equality as well as in the perpetuation of inequality.

The framework conceived by Vestin et al. (2020), formulated from a comprehensive synthesis of 13 literature reviews related to Industry 4.0, reveals itself as a comprehensive structure that incorporates eleven distinct technologies and twelve design principles in a harmonious whole. The emphasis was placed on the most preponderant technologies, notably Cyber-Physical Systems, Internet of Things and Big Data, and the most salient design principles, such as the notion of the smart factory, service orientation and the imperative of sustainability and resource efficiency. In this way, a solid and holistic matrix representation of the landscape for Industry 4.0 was outlined.

According to Schwab (2017, p. 8), parallel to the technological development represented by Industry 4.0, it is still necessary to face inequality as a systemic challenge, since 1.3 billion people, approximately, (17% of the world's population) still does not have full access to electricity which is one of the defining technologies of the second industrial revolution. Moreover, according to the same author, the number of people who still do not have full access to the internet technology of the 3rd industrial revolution, is approximately three times higher than this. Cottam (2018) points out that, although the technologies employed in each of the industrial revolutions serve different purposes and have different impacts, a common thread can be observed between them in the way they stimulate and accelerate social transformations. These transformations, which might not otherwise happen or take much longer to occur, play a key role in the evolution of society.

For Bivar (2022), the 2008 financial crisis, which brought growing concerns about inequality and diminishing opportunities for all but the wealthiest, and the need to rethink the State's approach to economic growth are some of the main themes that drive research on the history of economic growth in contemporary times. According to Cottam (2018), we live in an interconnected world, with emerging technologies and welfare states designed to protect people. However, the same author argues that this project dates back to another century and is designed to deal with different types of technologies than those we have currently and are very different from those we will have in the future. This challenge becomes even more evident when we consider disruptive technologies already reaching a high degree of maturity in the laboratory that will require a significant adaptation of existing social structures.

Such concerns have been re-contextualized in the wake of the COVID-19 pandemic. For example, Patel and Phillips (2021) argue that historically, pandemics have led to profound social transformations after reaching societies. The authors, however, assert that such transformations are not an inevitable constant. Benach (2021), on the other hand, argues that the COVID-19 pandemic could potentially be associated with a pandemic of inequality and that profound social changes should be necessary to face this complex situation. According to Schwab and Malleret (2020), from a social point of view, the pandemic marks a return to "Big Government" and shows an exacerbation of previously existing inequalities and the fragility of institutions, especially in some of the developed countries where a more adequate response to this crisis was expected.

The inequality was evidenced by data from the "*Financial Times*" apud.in. Schwab and Malleret (2020), which pointed out that about 75% of workers in the finance and insurance industries could perform their jobs remotely, while in the food industry this figure was 3%. In addition, during the pandemic, some of the jobs most needed by our society, and that could not be interrupted during the "*lockdowns*" were those jobs carried out by workers whose earnings were relatively low, i.e., drivers, food workers, nursing professionals and carers of the elderly. From a racial point of view, during the pandemic, while black people accounted for 15% of the cases, they represented 40% of the fatalities.

Based on the circumstantial evidence arising from their review, Schwab and Malleret (2020) argue that the pandemic may widen inequalities rather than reduce them. The work of Finatto et al. (2021), who carried out a literature review on this specific topic, points towards this same trend. However, historical studies, such as that by Alfani (2020), present evidence that pandemics naturally reduce the labour contingent through a higher mortality among workers, especially the less qualified, and this has the same effect as causing a market scarcity of labour which consequently leads to a general increase remuneration. Ultimately, this effect goes on to cause an improvement in the distribution of wealth and income.

Schwab and Malleret (2020) concluded that these crises have also led to pressures for the redefinition of social contracts in different societies with one of the biggest "risks" being social disintegration. With widening inequalities and growing hopelessness, people can have a sense of having nothing to lose and easily turn against their government and governmental systems, which can lead to drastic social transformations such as violent revolutions. In addition, these same authors, noted the expansion of governmental social services that arose from a strong and urgent demand for social protection during the pandemic. This experience saw the expansion of the State and the discussions about its size and role in society return to the agenda with, subsequently, pressures for the redefinition of social contracts in different societies. Wilkinson (2016) also shares the concerns of these authors, arguing that the change in the future of work has implications for maintaining the social contract and raises uncomfortable questions about the sustainability of the social contract in all types of economies, from those still developing to the more advanced. This author suggests that this shift also raises fundamental questions about what it means to work, the metric of paid employment, the goal of full employment, as well as the focus on income inequality. In other words, the change in the future of work could affect how people carry out work and receive payment that, in turn, could have implications for how governments maintain a balance between the needs of citizens and the demands of the economy.

These assumptions also bring education to the centre of the equality/inequality debate. Smolentseva (2021) lays out a ranking of countries based on the proportion of their population that achieves tertiary education levels, identifying outstanding nations such as Russia, Canada, Japan, and the United States. These societies, where participation in higher education is significant, testify to the wide-ranging implications of higher education systems in various spheres, including the labour market, social mobility, and economic development. Aligning with Smolentseva's (2021) considerations, Green and Preston (2001) posit that education emerges as a powerful catalyst for social capital, leading more educated individuals to engage in a greater number of voluntary organizations, demonstrate greater interest in political issues, and engage more actively in political activities. However, the relationship between education and social cohesion is intricate and exhibits substantial variations between different societies. Within this context, the authors suggest that education influences social cohesion both directly, through effects related to socialization, and indirectly, by affecting skills disparities, which, in turn, are linked to income disparities. In addition, several alternative models are presented to understand how education affects social cohesion in diverse societies, based on analyses of aggregated data at the transnational level, incorporating information on skills, income distribution, and multiple indicators of social cohesion.

According to Mathai et al. (2021) The sustainability of production and consumption practices are profoundly influenced by political and economic factors of considerable relevance. On the production side, we find a drive driven by multiple actors, including the financial system, the influential advertising industry, political priorities that sometimes prioritize economic expansion and the opening of new markets, and the giant buyers who exert their weight. On the other hand, the act of consuming is prominent in the social sphere and rooted in the complex structures of social organization. Access to available resources and the socio-cultural construction of demand emerge as substantial forces that shape production-consumption systems.

According to Schwab and Malleret (2020), climate change and ecosystem collapse are the two main global risks today. Also for these authors, the impact represented by the pandemic demonstrated the implications of these risks, with the disruption of global production chains, demand and supply shocks and trade interruption that represented great risks (and in some cases opportunities) from an economic point of view, also amplifying global risks of other natures such as social, geopolitical and technological. Regarding global risks, Schwab and Malleret (2020) point out that they have the following characteristics:

- they are known and spread very quickly
- their effects are non-linear;
- their true impact and distribution are difficult to measure;
- they are global in nature and therefore require a joint global response;
- they affect disproportionately the most vulnerable countries and people.

In this regard, Bivar (2022) notes many academics argue that, instead of focusing on Gross Domestic Product (GDP) and aggregate growth, state policy should address inequality and wealth distribution. Therefore, it is essential that academics continue to work together to understand how the pursuit of economic growth has shaped our contemporary world and how we can address the challenges we currently face. Further, in this context, Morgen and Maskovsky (2003) argue that neoliberalism plays a fundamental role in shaping the restructuring of the welfare state, since it promotes the reduction of financial assistance programs and other programs aimed at satisfying the basic needs of economically disadvantaged groups. According to these authors, this results in a growing dependence on income and welfare benefits. As a result, economic insecurity intensifies among the most disadvantaged layers of society, while households with insufficient resources face difficulties, as privatized, market-based solutions fail to generate sufficient resources to meet their essential needs. This scenario perpetuates inequality, since poor populations are compelled to resort to market solutions that often fail to adequately meet their basic needs. Bouchard (2011) corroborates this view by arguing that anthropological research on the state underlines the importance of taking into account the perspectives of marginalized and subaltern communities, often affected by the policies and practices of the state. According to this author, the analysis of the State must contemplate the social inequalities and power dynamics that configure State policies and practices.

For growth to occur sustainably, Mathai et al. (2021) argue that it is necessary to pursue multifaceted alternatives, which encompass a wide range of approaches ranging from ideological and intellectual critiques to innovative initiatives and practical projects, permeating spheres involving programmatic entrepreneurship and political action. Therefore, research on sustainable production-consumption systems should proceed with an in-depth focus on issues of power and contestation, while simultaneously engaging with the various alternatives actively and fostering a constant and progressive dialogue between theory and practice. In line with this premise, Morgen and Maskovsky (2003) argue that analysis from the perspective of gender, race and, to a lesser extent, class, occupies a central place in ethnographic research concerning the restructuring of the welfare state as in the case of the United States. They conclude that research on inequality cannot be understood from a purely economic point of view and their research shows that social welfare policies often perpetuate gender and racial inequality. Given that women and racial minorities are in situations more susceptible to poverty and dependence on welfare programs, social welfare policies often entrench gender and race stereotypes, such as the conception that women are responsible for raising children and that racial minorities are idle and dependent on government support. These stereotypes can result in policies that penalize women and racial minorities, making the process of getting out of poverty and achieving economic independence more arduous.

From the perspective of technological transformation, Boyd and Holton (2018) argue that events of today are both distinct and similar to what has happened before in terms of profound technological and social transformations. According to these authors, technological change has transformative potential, while maintaining uncertainties and limits. Also, within the public debate, a rhetorical impulse in business and policymaking is behind what can be termed technological determinists, who, in contrast, take a lesser deterministic approach than would be when considering the sensitivity to power and uncertainty.

Liao et al. (2018) argue that Industry 4.0 goes beyond organizational and territorial boundaries, encompassing agility, intelligence, and networking, and that such a scenario triggers government efforts to define guidelines and standards. However, for these authors, the speed and complexity of the transition to this new era of digitalization in a globalized environment does not yet allow it. But, a common and coordinated understanding of the impacts of the actions undertaken within different countries and regions, points to the disruptive nature of this process. Therefore, it is necessary to understand the growing role of the platform economy and its impact on the equality/inequality theme.

Roblek et al. (2021) offer a further example of the platform economy by meticulously addressing the underlying potential of car-sharing in Europe, unfolding their analysis through in-depth consideration of diverse elements, including economic issues, business models, management systems, the feasibility of electric car sharing, the formulation of public policies related to this practice, and its implications for car-sharing experiences on travel. Despite the potential positive impacts of the sharing economy on sustainability, these authors argue that large global venture capital has gained such power and influence over the control of the platform economy that the risk of this economic model in promoting social inequalities can no longer be ignored. This same idea is supported by Hughes and Southern (2019), who resort to studies of the Marxist tradition, to analyse the scope of what they consider as a "crisis of capitalism", the tendency towards objectified work and the view that automation and the 'uberization' of the economy, form a tendency to accentuate the contradictions between capital and labour. Their analysis converges with that of Scully-Russ and Torraco (2020) and Dimitriev et al. (2016), who argue that there is empirical evidence in support of this assumption, which is presented in their respective works. Meanwhile, Cruddas and Pitts (2020) assert that in unfavourable political conditions, it would be strategically unwise to place too much hope in an overly optimistic approach to the future.

From a geopolitical perspective, Wilkinson (2016) presented an accurate reading in his research arguing that social change is complex and intertwined in a broader context of technological, economic, social, and environmental change, and that the interaction of a more diverse landscape of old and new actors—West vs. East—arises in the power of non-state actors and in a less benign multipolar geo-politics. This author suggests that national governments can use strategic forecasting methods to prepare for the job-scarcity economy. The article shares recent examples of global forecasting developed by the OECD to help national governments appreciate and prepare for this change, both individually and through international cooperation. Some of the strategic forecasting methods mentioned in the article include meta-analysis, scenario planning, megatrends, and insight.

Damijan et al. (2021) argue that the rapid pace of automation can lead to a dramatic increase in income inequality and result in revenue losses for the government. However, there is no consensus among economists on whether government intervention is necessary. According to these authors, a group of economists argue that taxing robots would be a self-defeating act that would discourage innovation and slow technological progress, while job losses from the use of robots by foreign competitors could still occur. Another group of economists advocates public intervention and the imposition of some kind of tax on robots or the work done by them. In addition, the authors maintain that while there is consensus among the first group of economists on the need for some kind of robot tax, there is still no agreement on the precise framework of fiscal policy to be introduced. In general, policy proposals fall into two categories: direct taxation of companies that benefit from automation, and indirect taxation to avoid possible stagnation of innovation. This group believes that such a tax could generate revenue to offset the drop in revenue from taxing labour when human labour is replaced by machines, and thus prevent or limit income and wealth inequality caused by automation. In addition to Dimitriev et al. (2016), Soh and Connolly (2020), point out that this phenomenon, although celebrated for creating new sources of value and innovation, also constitutes a serious threat because its main processes generate new forms of inequality and potentially undermine human dignity and agency. For those authors, human security is an important concept to analyse pre-emptively these emerging socioeconomic changes and consider measures and countermeasures capable of increasing social resilience.

In contrast to the findings of Dimitriev et al. (2016) and Soh and Connolly (2020), Vermeulen et al. (2017) argue that robotization and artificial intelligence (AI) can replace and complement jobs in the same application sector by polarizing the workforce, especially in sectors dominated by routine jobs in predictable environments. Also, a "multisectoral" perspective reveals many conceivable sources of new jobs which require education and training to adapt to new market needs. This substitution and improved productivity causes a decoupling between productivity and wages that is reflected on income distribution. Thus, for those authors, contrary to the assumptions of Dimitriev et al. (2016), the prospect of structural change is less pessimistic about the future of employment, with the creation of new sectors and more significant jobs.

From a human perspective, wearable Internet, big data analytics, sensor-based living, smart city implementations, or similar applications may become major focuses of community concern.

3 Methodology

This research was carried out through an extensive literature review process and sought to contextualize the relationship between the Industry 4.0 and the 4th Social Revolution. The studies carried out for the characterization of the *Great Reset*, Industry 4.0 and the 4th Social Revolution can be classified as an unstructured qualitative and exploratory literature review. In addition, two structured literature reviews were carried out that used the Pro-Know-C method, following the recommendations of Lacerda et al, 2012 and Tasca et al, 2010, with *keywords* "*social revolution*", "*social transformation*", "*social change*" as terms of one of the axes and the terms "*fourth industrial revolution*", and "*4th industrial Revolution*" in the second axis.

An initial search of the literature (conducted in November/December of 2023) resulted in an initial portfolio of 1,178 articles that reduced after analysis to a final portfolio of 60 articles. A second search (carried in September/October 2023) using the same method was conducted using the terms "*Nation-State + Social Organization*" *as keywords*, resulted in a portfolio of 929 articles which reduced to a portfolio of 44 articles after analysis. At the end of these literature reviews, the main conclusions were synthesized in a "theoretical framework" capable of proposing the main dimensions and sub-dimensions identified in the bibliographic portfolio of this research.

4 Theoretical Framework

The theoretical framework proposed here seeks to integrate the main dimensions of the relationship between Industry 4.0 and equality, providing a conceptual framework for analysis and action. Each dimension highlights specific challenges and opportunities and points to the need for interdisciplinary approaches and comprehensive policies. Research in this field should continue to explore these dimensions and develop practical strategies to promote equality in the context of the rapid technological evolution of Industry 4.0. Additionally, collaboration between governments, businesses, civil society, and international organizations is essential to address these complex challenges and create a more equitable and sustainable future.

Figure 1 shows the main dimensions consolidated from the literature review on studies on equality and inequality in the fourth industrial revolution. Therefore, we must consider the technological, economic, social, political, global and environmental dimensions in a holistic and non-escalated manner.

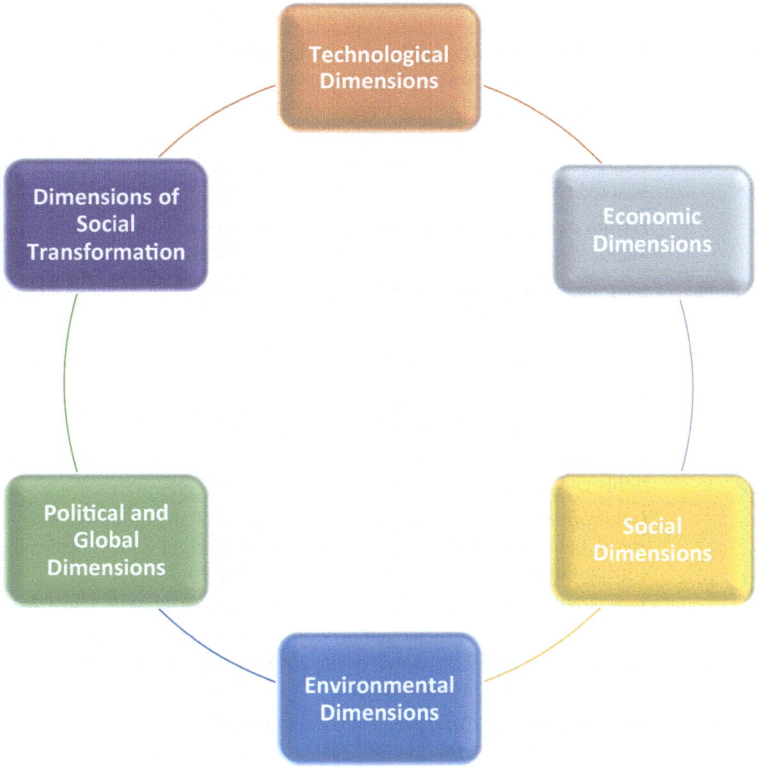

Fig. 1 Dimensions of analysis of the equality/inequality structure in Industry 4.0. *Source* The authors based on the literature review (2023)

Table 1 presents the descriptors referring to each of the dimensions proposed in the framework for the analysis of the complex relationship between equality, inequality and Industry 4.0, which is characterized by significant technological advances.

Table 1 Theoretical framework: Industry 4.0, equality/inequality

Dimensions	Descriptions
Technological	***Technological Democratization***: In this dimension, the importance of ensuring that emerging technologies are accessible to all, regardless of their socioeconomic background, is considered. Policies and initiatives that promote equal access to advanced technologies, such as AI and automation, are crucial
	Digital Inclusion: Addresses the need to ensure that all people have the ability to use and take advantage of the technologies of Industry 4.0. This includes internet access and digital enablement
Economic	***Employment and Labour Marke***: This dimension focuses on creating equitable employment opportunities in the context of automation and AI. The need to promote skills development and adaptation to changes in the labour market is critical
	Economic Inequality: Explores the issue of the concentration of economic and technological power, which can exacerbate inequality. Policies that aim to equitably distribute the economic benefits of Industry 4.0 are critical
Social	***Welfare State***: The need to rethink social welfare systems in the light of the transformations of Industry 4.0 is considered. How can these systems be adapted to address the emerging challenges of inequality and technology?
	Health and Education: Explores how technology can improve access to health and education while ensuring that disparities do not deepen
Environmental	***Sustainability and Climate Change***: The importance of the environmental dimension is recognised, which can both aggravate and mitigate inequality. Policies that pursue environmental sustainability can have significant impacts on social justice
Political and Global	***Governance and Regulation***: Emphasis is placed on the need for effective governance and regulation to guide the use of Industry 4.0 technologies. How can public policies balance technological innovation and the protection of the rights and interests of communities?
	International Cooperation: Recognizes that the challenges of Industry 4.0 are global. International cooperation is key to tackling issues such as the concentration of power and inequality on a global scale
Social Transformation	***Impact of Crises***: Addresses the role of pandemics and other types of major crises in accelerating social and economic transformation. How can lessons from the COVID-19 pandemic or the 2008 financial crisis be applied to address inequality in Industry 4.0?
	Redefining Social Contracts: Considers how current social transformations may require the redefinition of social contracts in different societies. How can society adapt to technological change and global risks?

Source The authors based on the literature review (2023)

In the technological dimension, the technological democratization is highlighted and supported by Schwab (2017), who, as mentioned previously, highlights the lack of global access to electricity, affecting some 17% of the world's population, and the limited access to the internet (one of the pillars of the 3rd Industrial Revolution) affecting an even greater number of people. These technological gaps highlight the importance of democratizing access to advanced technologies as part of the equality dimension. The digital inclusion emerges as a critical dimension of equality in the era of Industry 4.0. Chen and Liu (2021) emphasize the importance of developing capacity within the internet in a context of intense global competition in information and communication technologies.

In the economic dimension, the research addresses the need to create equitable employment opportunities, which is key to promoting equality in Industry 4.0. Authors such as Bivar (2022) highlight concerns about economic inequality and diminishing opportunities, emphasizing the importance of rethinking the State's approach to economic growth. Vermeulen et al. (2017) also explore the idea that robotization and AI can create new sectors and jobs, potentially impacting income distribution, while Dimitriev et al. (2016) and Soh and Connolly (2020) explore the complexities of automation, how it can polarize the workforce and affect income distribution. The concentration of economic and technological power is also a central concern. Authors such as Hughes and Southern (2019) argue that large global venture capital has gained influence over the control of the platform economy, raising questions about the potential impact on social inequality.

On social dimensions, Cottam (2018) discusses the implications of emerging technologies and their impact on social structures, contributing to the construction of the *theoretical framework* in the dimension of the Welfare State. His ideas contribute to the broader discussion on social and technological transformations in contemporary society. Authors such as Morgen and Maskovsky (2003) and Bouchard (2011) argue that it is essential to consider the perspectives of marginalized and subaltern communities when analysing the impact of state policies and practices, especially in relation to the restructuring of the welfare state. Related sub-items of health and education are the focus of authors such as Schwab (2017) who highlight the importance of addressing inequality as a systemic challenge including limited access to essential technologies, such as electricity and the internet, which affect access to education and health. Authors such as Patel and Phillips (2021) and Benach (2021) address the profound social transformations after pandemics, especially in the context of health inequalities, while Smolentseva (2021) and Green and Preston (2001) highlight the role of education in promoting social development and its contribution to equality.

In the dimension of the environment, sustainability is closely linked to equality. Schwab and Malleret (2020) argue that Industry 4.0 requires a major environmental reset. Vattikuti (2022) sees the pandemic as an opportunity for environmental change and social rehabilitation, emphasizing the importance of considering global environmental risks.

In the political and global dimension, Chen and Liu are mentioned in the text and point out challenges in the management of new technologies in China, including concerns about political stability and global competition in Information and Communication Technologies (ICT), which is related to the sub-dimension of governance and regulation. With regard to international cooperation, Schwab (2017) and Schwab and Malleret (2020) discuss the "Great Reset" and the need to redefine socioeconomic relations in different societies, which is related to international cooperation and governance to address issues of inequality on a global scale.

In the dimension of social transformation, it is understood that social exclusion and gender and racial inequality are also important dimensions of equality. Patel and Phillips (2021) highlight how pandemics can exacerbate inequalities, including those related to gender and race. Morgen and Maskovsky (2003) emphasize how social welfare policies can perpetuate gender and race stereotypes, affecting access to resources and economic independence. On the other hand, Wilkinson (2016) points out that the current transformations lead to a displacement of the comfort zone in relation to the social contracts currently in force.

These complex and interconnected dimensions provide the foundation for the development of a theoretical framework that seeks to understand the socio-economic complexities and challenges related to equality and inequality in the 4th Industrial Revolution, providing valuable insights for the formulation of policies and strategies that promote a more just and equitable society.

5 Discussion and Conclusions

The extensive literature review conducted in this study provided a deeper and more comprehensive understanding of the complex relationships between equality, inequality, and Industry 4.0. The multiple dimensions addressed, namely technological, economic, social, environmental, political, global, and social transformation, highlight the intricate and interconnected nature of these phenomena in the contemporary era.

One of the conclusions that emerge from this review is the critical importance of technological democratization, with an emphasis on the need to provide equitable access to technological advances, such as electricity and the internet, which have become fundamental infrastructures for education, health, employment, and participation in society. Digital inclusion, also considered in the review, appears as an essential dimension of equality, as lack of access to the internet can create significant barriers to full participation in Industry 4.0.

On the economic front, this review highlights the need to create equitable employment opportunities by addressing concerns about economic inequality and diminishing opportunities. The changes induced by robotization, artificial intelligence, and automation are pointed out as factors that can both create new jobs and polarize the workforce, affecting income distribution. In addition, the concentration of economic and technological power in the hands of a few actors also raises important questions.

In the social context, the transformation brought about by Industry 4.0 has profound implications for social structures, and it is crucial to consider the perspectives of marginalized and subaltern communities. The role of the welfare state, health and education are key areas that must be addressed to ensure that inequality does not increase. Gender equality and racial equality also emerge as critical dimensions to consider, given that pandemics and social changes can exacerbate already existing inequalities. The environmental and sustainability dimension is inextricably linked to equality, as global environmental risks can affect populations unequally, exacerbating inequality on a global scale.

At the political and global level, the management of new technologies, governance and international cooperation play a crucial role in promoting equality. Addressing the issues of inequality on a global scale requires a coordinated effort and a redefinition of socio-economic relations. With regard to social transformation, the ongoing changes lead to a displacement of existing social norms and contracts, requiring a reassessment of policies and practices to ensure a just and equitable society.

It is important to recognize that this literature review has its own limitations. It is based on the analysis of existing academic papers and research, and therefore reflects the state of knowledge up to the date of the review. Furthermore, the complexity of the interactions between equality and inequality in Industry 4.0 requires an interdisciplinary and holistic approach, which can be challenging to fully achieve in a single study. The theoretical contributions of this study include the systematization and integration of several dimensions that affect equality in the era of Industry 4.0. The proposed framework offers a comprehensive conceptual framework for understanding these complex relationships and can serve as a basis for future research.

Suggestions for future studies include empirical investigations that apply the framework in specific contexts, evaluating the effectiveness of proposed policies and strategies to promote equality. In addition, deepening the analysis of gender and race inequalities in the era of Industry 4.0 is a promising field of research. Investigating the impacts of pandemics and environmental events on inequality can also provide valuable insights for policymaking. Finally, studies on the influence of new technologies on governance and international cooperation are needed to address issues of inequality on a global scale.

In summary, this literature review highlights the complexity and interconnectedness of the dimensions that shape the relationship between equality and inequality in the 4th Industrial Revolution. It provides a solid foundation for future research and policy aimed at promoting a more just and equitable society in a context of rapid technological and social transformation.

Acknowledgements We gratefully acknowledge the contributions of several institutions in the successful completion of this study. The research was carried out by the Centre for Sustainable Development (Greens) in collaboration with the Graduate Program in Administration at the University of Southern Santa Catarina (Unisul). We also extend our appreciation to the Fundação de Amparo à Pesquisa e Inovação do Estado de Santa Catarina (FAPESC), Ânima Institute (AI), Coordenação de Aperfeiçoamento de Pessoal de Nível Superior (CAPES), and the National Council for Scientific and Technological Development (CNPq) for their invaluable support and assistance throughout the research process.

References

Alfani, G. (2020, October 15). *Pandemics and inequality: A historical overview*. VoxEU.

Alves, F., Filho, W. L., Casaleiro, P., Nagy, G. J., Diaz, H., Al-Amin, A. Q., de Andrade Guerra, J. B. S. O., Hurlbert, M., Farooq, H., Klavins, M., Saroar, M., Lorencova, E. K., Jain, S., Soares, A., Morgado, F., O'Hare, P., Wolf, F., & Azeiteiro, U. M. (2020). Climate change policies and agendas: Facing implementation challenges and guiding responses. *Environmental Science & Policy, 104*, 190–198.

Benach, J. (2021). We must take advantage of this pandemic to make a radical social change: The coronavirus as a global health, inequality, and eco-social problem. *International Journal of Health Services, 51*(1), 50–54.

Bivar, V. (2022). Historicizing economic growth: An overview of recent works. *The Historical Journal, 65*(5), 1–20.

Bouchard, M. (2011). The state of the study of the state in anthropology. *Reviews in Anthropology, 40*(3), 183–209.

Boyd, R., & Holton, R. J. (2018). Technology, innovation, employment and power: Does robotics and artificial intelligence really mean social transformation? *Journal of Sociology, 54*(3), 331–345.

Chen, Y., & Liu, Y. (2021). How biased technological progress sustainably improve the energy efficiency: An empirical research of manufacturing industry in China. *Energy, 230*, 120823. https://doi.org/10.1016/j.energy.2021.120823

Cottam, H. (2018). *Radical help: How we can remake the relationships between us and revolutionise the welfare state*. Hachette UK.

Cruddas, J., & Pitts, F. H. (2020). The politics of postcapitalism: Labour and our digital futures. *The Political Quarterly, 91*(2), 275–286.

Damijan, J., Damijan, S., & Vrh, N. (2021). *Tax on robots: Whether and how much*. GROWINPRO.

De Andrade Guerra, J. B. S. O. (2020). Bridge–building resilience in a dynamic global economy: Complexity across scales at the food, water, and energy Nexus in Brazil. *Environmental Management & Sustainability Journal, 9*(1 esp), 1–2.

Dmitriev, S., Kalinicheva, V., Shadoba, E., Nikonets, O., Pogonysheva, D., & Shvarova, E. (2016). On the impact of innovations on the social structure. *International Journal of Economics and Financial Issues, 6*(1), 107–113.

Finatto, C. P., da Silva, C. G., de Aguiar Dutra, A. R., Borchardt Deggau, A., Cubas, A. L. V., Moecke, E. H. S., Fernandez, F., & de Andrade Guerra, J. B. S. O. (2021). Sustainability in Covid-19 times: A human development perspective. In *COVID-19: Environmental Sustainability and Sustainable Development Goals* (pp. 1–34). Springer.

Green, A., & Preston, J. (2001). Education and social cohesion: Recentering the debate. *Peabody Journal of Education, 76*(3–4), 247–284.

Hughes, C., & Southern, A. (2019). The world of work and the crisis of capitalism: Marx and the Fourth Industrial Revolution. *Journal of Classical Sociology, 19*(1), 59–71.

Lacerda, R. T. O., Ensslin, L., & Ensslin, S. R. (2012). A bibliometric analysis of the literature on strategy and performance evaluation. *Management & Production [Online], 19*(1), 59–78.

Liao, Y., Loures, E. R., Deschamps, F., Brezinski, G., & Venâncio, A. (2018). The impact of the fourth industrial revolution: a cross-country/region comparison. *Production, 28*.

Mathai, M. V., Isenhour, C., Stevis, D., Vergragt, P., Bengtsson, M., Lorek, S., Mortensen, L. F., Coscieme, L., Scott, D., Waheed, A., & Alfredsson, E. (2021). The political economy of (un) sustainable production and consumption: A multidisciplinary synthesis for research and action. *Resources, Conservation and Recycling, 167*, 105265.

Mercure, J.-F., Paim, M. A., Bocquillon, P., Lindner, S., Salas, P., Martinelli, P., Berchin, I. I., de Andrade Guerra, J. S. B. O., Derani, C., de Albuquerque Junior, C. L., Ribeiro, J. M. P., Knobloch, F., Pollitt, H., Edwards, N. R., Holden, P. B., Foley, A., Schaphoff, S., Faraco, R. A., & Vinuales, J. E. (2019). System complexity and policy integration challenges: The Brazilian energy-water-food nexus. *Renewable and Sustainable Energy Reviews, 105*, 230–243.

Morgen, S., & Maskovsky, J. (2003). The anthropology of welfare "reform": New perspectives on US urban poverty in the post-welfare era. *Annual Review of Anthropology, 32*(1), 315–338.
Patel, M. S., & Phillips, C. B. (2021). COVID-19 and the moral imagination. *The Lancet, 397*.
Roblek, V., Meško, M., & Podbregar, I. (2021). Impact of car sharing on urban sustainability. *Sustainability, 13*(2), 905.
Schwab, K. (2017). *The fourth industrial revolution*. Currency.
Schwab, K., & Malleret, T. (2020). The great reset. In *World Economic Forum, Geneva* (Vol. 22).
Scully-Russ, E., & Torraco, R. (2020). The changing nature and organization of work: An integrative review of the literature. *Human Resource Development Review, 19*(1), 66–93.
Smolentseva, A. (2021). What is the emerging society with a high participation higher education system? In *Higher Education in the Next Decade* (pp. 186–204). Brill.
Soh, C., & Connolly, D. (2020). The human security implications of the fourth industrial revolution in East Asia. *Asian Perspective, 44*(3), 383–407.
Tasca, J. E., Ensslin, L., Ensslin, S. R., Alves, M. B. M. (2010). An approach for selecting a theoretical framework for the evaluation of training programs. *Journal of European Industrial Training, 34*(7), 631–655.
Vattikuti, S. (2022). The Great Green Reset of Global Economies: A Golden Opportunity for Environmental Change and Social Rehabilitation. *Authorea Preprints*.
Vermeulen, B., Pyka, A., & Omerovic, M. (2017). *The economic impact of robotics and artificial intelligence*. REELER Working Paper Series.
Vestin, A., Säfsten, K., & Löfving, M. (2020). Revealing the content of Industry 4.0: A review of literature. *SPS2020*, 563–574.
Wilkinson, A. (2016). Using strategic foresight methods to anticipate and prepare for the jobs-scarce economy. *European Journal of Futures Research, 4*(1), 1–11.

The Role of Ethnoeconomics in Promoting Sustainable Consumption and Production Patterns: A Pathway to Environmental Protection and Economic Prosperity

Harshit Mishra

Abstract Ethnoeconomics, a multidisciplinary field, is gaining prominence as a pivotal component in promoting sustainable consumption and production patterns (SCP). This chapter identifies the relationship between ethnoeconomics, environmental protection and economic prosperity, offering a comprehensive understanding of its theoretical framework, practical applications, and policy implications. Begins by elucidating the essence of ethnoeconomics, tracing its evolution, and emphasizing its interconnectedness with SCP. Theoretical models and approaches are explored, shedding light on the role ethnoeconomics plays in driving environmental sustainability and economic well-being. Indigenous knowledge, held by various communities, emerges as a cornerstone of SCP. This knowledge is invaluable in preserving biodiversity, advocating for food security, and underpinning cultural sustainability. Ethnoeconomics serves as a bridge to this traditional wisdom, contributing to sustainable agriculture, conservation, and resource management. Ethnoeconomics extends its influence into the realm of sustainable business and entrepreneurship, showcasing indigenous entrepreneurship models, ethical sourcing, and fair-trade practices. These initiatives empower indigenous communities while fostering environmental stewardship and green enterprises. Policy and governance implications are addressed, emphasizing the integration of ethnoeconomics into sustainable policy frameworks and the legal and regulatory aspects of its implementation. Challenges and opportunities on the path to ethnoeconomic sustainability are explored, along with the importance of international collaboration in this endeavour. Measuring the impact of ethnoeconomics on SCP becomes a focal point, involving the development of indicators and metrics, data collection, analysis, and assessing the environmental and economic outcomes. Long-term monitoring and evaluation are key to understanding the lasting effects of ethnoeconomic initiatives. Concludes by contemplating future directions

H. Mishra (✉)
Department of Agricultural Economics, College of Agriculture, Acharya Narendra Deva University of Agriculture and Technology, Kumarganj, Ayodhya, Uttar Pradesh 224 229, India
e-mail: wehars@gmail.com

W. Leal Filho and V. Kuzmanović (eds.), *Sustainable Development Seen Through the Lenses of Ethnoeconomics and the Circular Economy*,
https://doi.org/10.1007/978-3-031-72676-7_6

in ethnoeconomics, emerging trends, research gaps, and its implications for sustainable economics. Ethnoeconomics is positioned as a cornerstone of ecological footprint reduction, contributing to the global pursuit of a sustainable, environmentally friendly, and economically prosperous future.

Keywords Circular economy · Ethnoeconomics · Indigenous knowledge · Policy implications · SCP

1 Introduction

The quest for sustainable consumption and production patterns (SCP) is more critical than ever in our rapidly evolving world. As we grapple with environmental challenges and strive for economic prosperity, the role of ethnoeconomics in this pursuit emerges as a promising and multifaceted pathway. Current status of SCP in the world presents a mixed picture (Cavalcanti, 2002). On one hand, there is growing recognition of the importance of SCP for achieving sustainable development, and significant progress has been made in certain areas (Robert, 2019). Notably, the global rate of food waste has seen a reduction of 13% since 2015, a positive step toward conserving resources and reducing environmental impacts. However, on the flip side, overall consumption levels are still on the rise, and the world is far from achieving the Sustainable Development Goals (SDGs) related to SCP. An illustrative example is the global material footprint per capita, which has increased by 60% since 1980. This signifies a pressing need for more effective strategies to promote SCP patterns (Bliss & Egler, 2020; Lingham et al., 2022).

The global material footprint stood at a substantial 103.1 billion tonnes in 2019, emphasizing the immense scale of resource utilization. Additionally, global food loss and waste amounted to a staggering 1.3 billion tonnes per year in 2019, underlining the inefficiencies in the food supply chain (Guang, 2022). Global energy efficiency, at 0.1 kWh/dollar in 2015, indicates room for improvement in optimizing energy use. In contrast, the global renewable energy share, which reached 11.5% in 2020, demonstrates positive progress in transitioning to sustainable energy sources. Notably, these indicators vary significantly across countries, highlighting disparities in consumption and production. For instance, the material footprint per capita in high-income countries is ten times higher than that in low-income countries, emphasizing the need for equitable and inclusive approaches to SCP (Gould, 2016; Yahaya, 2012).

The economic benefits of SCP are substantial. A study by the International Resource Panel suggests that SCP could potentially boost global GDP by 2% and create 60 million new jobs by 2050. Furthermore, SCP can contribute to reducing pollution, improving public health, and conserving biodiversity, emphasizing its multifaceted advantages for society and the environment (Pushpangadan et al., 2016). Nonetheless, despite the evident advantages, many challenges hinder the widespread implementation of SCP. These challenges include a lack of awareness and understanding of SCP among businesses and consumers, market failures that often do not

Fig. 1 Challenges and solutions for promoting SCP patterns. *Source* GOAL 12: Sustainable Consumption and Production (n.d.)

reward sustainable behaviour, and policy barriers that can inadvertently discourage SCP (as shown in Fig. 1) (Adhikari, 2006).

SCP in India is still emerging, but it is growing rapidly. In 2022, the Indian government estimated that the SCP market was worth over $200 billion, and it is expected to reach $500 billion by 2030. This growth is indicative of the increasing importance of sustainability and environmental responsibility in India's economic landscape (Ignatov, 2011a; Singh & Mishra, 2023a). Many major sectors are driving the expansion of the SCP market in India. First and foremost, the renewable energy sector is making significant strides. India is one of the fastest-growing renewable energy markets globally, and this growth is creating new opportunities for SCP-compliant businesses. As the nation seeks to reduce its carbon footprint and dependence on fossil fuels, the demand for clean and sustainable energy sources is on the rise (Cheng, 2022).

Electric vehicles (EVs) represent another significant growth driver. The Indian government is actively promoting EV adoption, and this is expected to fuel demand for SCP-compliant batteries and other components. The shift towards electric mobility aligns with global efforts to reduce greenhouse gas emissions and combat air pollution, making it an essential component of SCP (Comaroff & Comaroff, 2022; Ignatov, 2011b). India is also a prominent market for green buildings, with a substantial focus on sustainable construction practices. This trend is generating demand for SCP-compliant construction materials and technologies. Green buildings not only conserve resources but also offer long-term economic benefits through reduced operational costs and enhanced property values (Cavalcanti, 2006a). Sustainable food production is a vital area of focus for India, given its status as a major agricultural producer. As consumers become more conscientious about their food choices, there is a growing demand for SCP-compliant food products. This shift towards sustainable agriculture not only promotes healthier eating but also supports environmentally friendly farming practices (Meagher, 2011; Singh & Mishra, 2023b).

Waste management presents another opportunity for SCP-compliant businesses. India is grappling with a substantial waste management challenge, and this creates a ripe environment for innovative solutions. SCP in this context involves reducing, reusing, and recycling waste, which not only has economic benefits but also contributes to a cleaner environment. The Indian government is also supportive of the SCP market (Slikkerveer, 2019). It has introduced a number of policies and incentives to promote SCP. For example, the government has offered tax breaks to businesses that invest in renewable energy and green buildings. It has also launched a number of programs to promote sustainable food production and waste management. The growth of the SCP market in India is having a positive impact on the economy (Nishad et al., 2023). It is creating new jobs and businesses, and it is helping to reduce India's environmental impact. Indian renewable energy, electric vehicle, green building, sustainable food, and waste management markets expected to create over 10 million jobs and reach $280 billion by 2030 (Mishra & Singh, 2023a; Roche, 2020).

Overall, the economic status of SCP in India is very positive. The market is growing rapidly, and the government is supportive of its development. SCP is also having a positive impact on the Indian economy, creating new jobs and businesses, and helping to reduce India's environmental impact. Ethnoeconomics is a field of study that examines the economic systems of indigenous and traditional societies (Turner, 2010). It can play a significant role in promoting SCP patterns by providing insights into how these societies have lived in harmony with nature for centuries. One of the main principles of ethnoeconomics is the concept of reciprocity. This means that members of a society give to and receive from each other in a mutually beneficial way. This principle is in stark contrast to the linear economic model of the modern world, which is based on the extraction, production, consumption, and disposal of resources (Aurenhammer & Aurenhammer, 2013). Another important principle of ethnoeconomics is the concept of sufficiency. This means that people are content with what they have and do not consume more than they need. This is in contrast to the consumerist culture of the modern world, which encourages people to constantly buy new things, even if they do not need them (Mishra & Singh, 2023a). Ethnoeconomic knowledge and practices can be applied to promote SCP in a number of ways. For example, ethnoeconomic insights can be used to design products and services that are more durable, repairable, and recyclable. They can also be used to develop more sustainable agricultural and production practices (Aponte Toro, 2000; McCarthy, 2011).

In this, we discuss a thorough examination of the interdependent connection between ethnoeconomics and SCP, uncovering the complex dynamics involving indigenous knowledge, environmental conservation, and economic development. To build a solid theoretical foundation, we begin by delving into the essence and evolution of ethnoeconomics, understanding its origins and how it has evolved over time (Masarek, 2010). Simultaneously, we dissect the intricacies of SCP, seeking to comprehend its frameworks and principles. This provides the context for our exploration of the interconnected nature of ethnoeconomics and SCP, highlighting the potential synergy between these two domains. Various theoretical models and approaches within this framework are also examined, demonstrating how they can be harnessed to drive sustainable practices. Moving forward, we embark on a journey into the world of indigenous knowledge. We investigate the pivotal role of indigenous communities in shaping SCP and how their ancient wisdom can be preserved, harnessed, and integrated into modern sustainability efforts (Chandler, 2006; Mishra & Singh, 2023a). Ethnoeconomics emerges as a bridge, connecting contemporary practices with traditional wisdom, ultimately contributing to cultural sustainability. The exploration extends into sustainable agriculture, uncovering indigenous agricultural practices that have, for generations, promoted biodiversity conservation and food security (Hisayasu, 2019). The rich tapestry of indigenous resource management practices, especially in forestry, wildlife, and land and water management, further demonstrates the invaluable lessons that can be gleaned from these age-old practices (Cavalcanti, 2006b).

In the era of the circular economy, we assess the relevance of this concept in SCP and unveil the ingenious indigenous approaches to waste reduction and recycling. The symbiosis between ethnoeconomics and the circular economy becomes evident, revealing their shared objectives of minimizing waste and maximizing resource efficiency (McCarthy, 2006). Exploring sustainable business and entrepreneurship, we examine indigenous entrepreneurial approaches, ethical sourcing, fair trade, and the rise of green enterprises. Ethnoeconomics not only empowers indigenous communities through business but also showcases the potential of sustainable economic growth. The policy and governance implications of ethnoeconomics are also addressed, emphasizing the need to integrate these principles into sustainable policy frameworks (Meagher et al., 2018). Legal and regulatory aspects, along with the challenges and opportunities in implementation, are illuminated, highlighting the necessity of international collaboration for the sustainability of ethnoeconomics. This culminates with a discussion on measuring the impact of ethnoeconomics on SCP, touching upon indicators, data collection, assessment of environmental and economic outcomes, and the importance of long-term monitoring and evaluation (Horta, 2019; Mishra & Mishra, 2023a). We conclude by pondering future directions, emerging trends, research gaps, and the profound implications of ethnoeconomics as a cornerstone in reducing our ecological footprint and promoting sustainable economics (Senehi et al., 2022).

2 Theoretical Framework

2.1 Concept and Evolution of Ethnoeconomics

Concept: Ethnoeconomics is an interdisciplinary field that examines the economic systems of different ethnic or cultural groups. It seeks to understand how culture, tradition, and social norms influence economic behaviour and decision-making. This field is rooted in anthropology, sociology, and economics, with a focus on the economic practices and strategies of specific communities.

Evolution: Ethnoeconomics has evolved over time, shifting from an anthropological interest in documenting the economic practices of indigenous societies to a broader exploration of how cultural factors impact economic development. Initially, it aimed to preserve the economic traditions of indigenous people. However, it has grown to encompass a more comprehensive analysis of how these practices can contribute to sustainability and economic prosperity in the modern world (Table 1).

Table 1 Evolution of ethnoeconomics (Source: Author's Compilation)

Period	Major contributors	Key developments
Early 20th Century	Franz Boas, George Peter Murdock, Karl Polanyi	Ethnoeconomics emerges as a subfield of anthropology, with a focus on the economic systems of indigenous peoples
Mid-20th Century	Harold Gould, Melville Herskovits, Raymond Firth	Ethnoeconomists begin to focus on the economic development of indigenous peoples, and the role of culture in economic decision-making
Late 20th Century	Stephen Gudeman, Michael Kearney, Eleanor Leacock	Ethnoeconomists become more critical of mainstream economic theory, and begin to develop their own theories and methodologies
21st Century	Aihwa Ong, Arturo Escobar, Grace Goodell	Ethnoeconomists continue to develop new theoretical perspectives, and to apply their research to a wider range of economic issues, including globalization, sustainable development, and gender inequality

2.2 *Sustainable Consumption and Production (SCP) Patterns*

Concept: SCP refers to the responsible and efficient use of resources in a manner that minimizes negative environmental impacts and supports long-term economic well-being. It involves reducing waste, conserving resources, and promoting environmentally friendly production and consumption practices. SCP is a critical component of sustainable development (as shown in Fig. 2).

Importance: SCP is vital for addressing global challenges like climate change, biodiversity loss, pollution, resource depletion, and environmental degradation. It promotes the creation of products and services that minimize harm to the environment, use resources more efficiently, and encourage responsible consumption patterns.

Fig. 2 Concept of SCP pattern

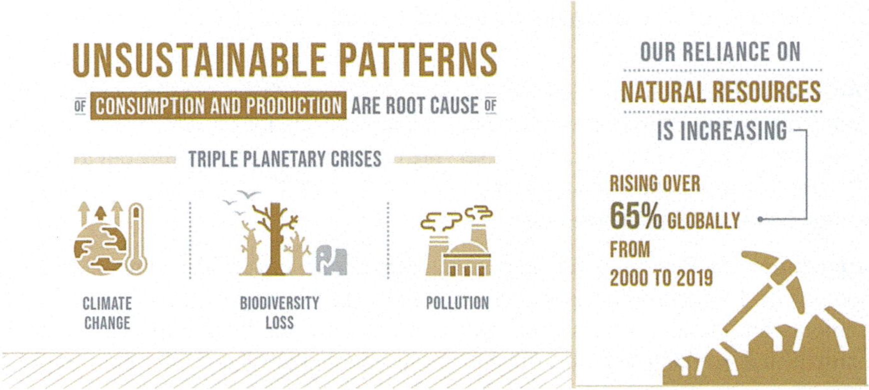

2.3 *Connection Between Ethnoeconomics and SCP*

- **Cultural practices and sustainability**: Ethnoeconomics studies how cultural practices and traditional knowledge can be harnessed to foster sustainable resource management. Indigenous communities, for example, often have time-tested methods of sustainable agriculture, fishing, and resource conservation that can be integrated into modern sustainability efforts.
- **Local knowledge and sustainable production**: Ethnoeconomics recognizes the value of local knowledge and practices. It suggests that incorporating these practices into modern production methods can improve sustainability. For instance, traditional agricultural techniques can reduce the need for harmful chemicals and enhance soil health.
- **Community-cantered approach**: Ethnoeconomics often emphasizes a community-cantered approach to economic activities. This aligns with the sustainability goal of promoting local economies, reducing the carbon footprint associated with global trade, and ensuring social well-being.

2.4 *Theoretical Models and Approaches*

- **Cultural economic models**: Researchers in ethnoeconomics often employ models that integrate cultural values and norms into economic decision-making processes. These models recognize the influence of culture on choices related to consumption and production.
- **Case studies**: Ethnoeconomics often relies on case studies to understand how specific cultural groups have managed their economic activities sustainably. These case studies may provide insights into best practices that can be applied more broadly.

- **Hybrid approaches**: Some scholars in this field adopt hybrid approaches, combining elements of ethnoeconomics with other economic theories. For example, they may merge cultural economics with neoclassical economics to better understand how cultural factors affect market behaviour.
- **Policy implications**: Theoretical models and approaches in ethnoeconomics can also inform policy development. They provide insights into how to leverage cultural knowledge and practices to promote SCP at both local and global levels.

The theoretical framework highlights the concept and evolution of ethnoeconomics, its relationship with SCP patterns, and the theoretical models and approaches used to study this intersection (Londoño Sulkin, 2017). This framework sets the stage for a comprehensive exploration of how cultural practices and traditional knowledge can contribute to environmental protection and economic prosperity through sustainable economic activities (Head et al., 2002).

3 Ethnoeconomics and Indigenous Knowledge

3.1 Role of Indigenous Communities in SCP

Indigenous communities play a crucial role in promoting SCP patterns. Their unique relationship with the environment and traditional resource management practices have enabled them to develop sustainable lifestyles over generations (as shown in Table 2). Indigenous knowledge systems are deeply rooted in their cultures, and they are often the custodians of ecosystems that are essential for the well-being of our planet. Indigenous communities offer valuable insights into SCP through their sustainable practices and their holistic understanding of the environment (Mishra & Mishra, 2023b).

Indigenous communities have long demonstrated SCP patterns by utilizing resources in ways that maintain ecological balance. They often rely on traditional farming methods, which involve crop rotation and agroforestry, ensuring soil fertility and preventing degradation. Traditional fishing practices, such as community-based management of marine resources, have sustained fish populations for centuries. Additionally, indigenous communities have unique perspectives on land management, focusing on preserving biodiversity and maintaining ecosystems for future generations (Soselisa, 2002).

Table 2 Role of indigenous communities in SCP with a focus on ethnoeconomics and indigenous knowledge (Source: Author's Compilation)

Aspect	Role of Indigenous Communities in SCP
Ethnoeconomics	**Traditional resource management**: Indigenous communities often possess deep knowledge of sustainable resource management practices, contributing to the conservation of natural resources and biodiversity
	Local economies: Indigenous economic activities, such as handicrafts, traditional agriculture, and eco-tourism, contribute to SCP by promoting local, sustainable economic development
	Knowledge transfer: Indigenous knowledge of plants, animals, and ecosystems can guide sustainable consumption practices, as it emphasizes the importance of balancing resource use with conservation
	Cultural sustainability: Ethnoeconomics supports cultural preservation and continuity, reinforcing the importance of local traditions and values in SCP
Indigenous Knowledge	**Natural resource management**: Indigenous knowledge systems help in sustainable harvesting, protecting against resource depletion and environmental degradation
	Climate adaptation: Indigenous knowledge often includes traditional weather forecasting and adaptive practices, which can aid in SCP efforts related to climate change
	Medicinal plants and traditional medicine: Indigenous knowledge of medicinal plants contributes to sustainable healthcare practices and reduces the reliance on pharmaceuticals
	Biodiversity conservation: Indigenous communities are custodians of biodiversity-rich areas and play a crucial role in conserving and protecting these areas
	Waste reduction: Indigenous communities often practice minimal waste generation and promote the use of natural and biodegradable materials, aligning with SCP principles

3.2 Preservation and Utilization of Indigenous Knowledge

The preservation and utilization of indigenous knowledge are vital for promoting SCP. Indigenous knowledge encompasses a wide range of practices related to sustainable resource management, traditional medicine, and ecological wisdom. To harness the benefits of this knowledge, it's essential to document and protect it from loss or exploitation (Cook, 2003). Many indigenous communities have oral traditions, which means that their knowledge is transmitted from generation to generation through storytelling and experiential learning. Efforts must be made to record and document this knowledge in a culturally sensitive and ethical manner (Tiwari et al., 2023).

Incorporating indigenous knowledge into SCP strategies can lead to innovative solutions for SCP. Indigenous practices, such as crop diversification, can help mitigate the negative impacts of monoculture farming. Traditional ecological knowledge about the timing of planting and harvesting can be adapted to modern agriculture to reduce waste and resource use. Additionally, indigenous medical practices can offer alternative, sustainable healthcare solutions that rely on local resources and traditional wisdom (Smith & Ouzman, 2004).

3.3 *Ethnoeconomics as a Bridge to Traditional Wisdom*

Ethnoeconomics serves as a bridge between indigenous knowledge and modern economic models. It enables the integration of traditional wisdom into contemporary sustainable development frameworks. Ethnoeconomics recognizes that indigenous communities have well-established economic systems that are deeply interwoven with their cultural and ecological values (Seppanen, 2014).

By acknowledging the economic aspects of indigenous knowledge and practices, ethnoeconomics helps to establish a dialogue between different worldviews. This bridge is essential for facilitating collaboration and mutual understanding (Kulbok-Lattik & Čopič, 2018). It allows for the incorporation of indigenous values, such as reciprocity, respect for nature, and community well-being, into SCP strategies. Ethnoeconomics thus plays a pivotal role in translating indigenous knowledge into practical policies and practices for achieving SCP patterns.

3.4 *Ethnoeconomics as a Tool for Cultural Sustainability*

Ethnoeconomics contributes to cultural sustainability by recognizing the economic value of indigenous traditions and practices. When these practices are integrated into SCP strategies, it not only benefits the environment but also supports the cultural heritage of indigenous communities. Cultural sustainability is essential for the well-being of indigenous peoples as it preserves their identity, strengthens social cohesion, and maintains a sense of belonging.

Furthermore, ethnoeconomics promotes economic prosperity within indigenous communities by valuing their traditional economies. It provides opportunities for sustainable economic development, such as eco-tourism, traditional handicrafts, and the marketing of indigenous products. This economic empowerment enhances the autonomy and self-determination of indigenous groups, enabling them to continue their sustainable practices while participating in the global economy (Keane, 2000; Mishra, 2021).

The integration of ethnoeconomics and indigenous knowledge into SCP strategies is a multifaceted approach that not only promotes environmental protection but also fosters economic prosperity and cultural sustainability. Recognizing the role of indigenous communities in SCP, preserving their knowledge, and incorporating their values through ethnoeconomics can lead us toward a more sustainable and equitable future (Cheng et al., 2003).

4 Ethnoeconomics in Sustainable Agriculture

4.1 Indigenous Agricultural Practices

Indigenous agricultural practices are deeply rooted in the traditions, knowledge, and cultural systems of various communities around the world. These practices have evolved over generations and have proven to be not only sustainable but also resilient in the face of environmental challenges. In the context of SCP, understanding and promoting indigenous agricultural practices is crucial.

- **Traditional farming techniques**: Indigenous communities often employ age-old techniques such as crop rotation, intercropping, and agroforestry, which contribute to soil fertility and reduce the need for synthetic inputs. These techniques not only enhance the sustainability of agriculture but also promote a balanced ecosystem.
- **Seed saving and biodiversity**: Indigenous farmers have a rich tradition of seed saving and maintaining a wide variety of crop species. This helps preserve biodiversity and ensures the availability of diverse food sources, which is vital for SCP.
- **Local knowledge**: Indigenous communities possess unique local knowledge about their ecosystems, which enables them to make informed decisions about planting, harvesting, and pest management. This knowledge is a valuable resource for sustainable agriculture.

4.2 Biodiversity Conservation in Agriculture

Biodiversity is fundamental to sustainable agriculture and SCP. Ethnoeconomics plays a critical role in conserving and promoting biodiversity within agricultural systems.

- **Traditional crop varieties**: Indigenous communities often cultivate a wide range of traditional crop varieties that are well adapted to local conditions. These varieties can withstand pests, diseases, and climate variations, reducing the need for chemical inputs.
- **Wild harvesting and foraging**: Many indigenous practices involve the sustainable harvesting of wild plants and animals. This promotes biodiversity conservation by ensuring that these resources are not overexploited.
- **Agrobiodiversity gardens**: Some indigenous communities create agrobiodiversity gardens that mimic natural ecosystems. These gardens support various plant and animal species, contributing to a healthier and more resilient environment.

4.3 Ethnoeconomics and Food Security

Ethnoeconomics plays a pivotal role in enhancing food security, a main component of SCP, especially in vulnerable communities.

- **Local food systems**: Indigenous communities often have localized food systems, relying on locally produced food. This reduces the carbon footprint associated with transportation and ensures access to fresh, nutritious food.
- **Diverse diets**: Traditional indigenous diets are often more diverse, incorporating a wide range of locally available foods. This diversity is essential for nutritional security and resilience in the face of changing environmental conditions.
- **Community resilience**: Ethnoeconomics fosters community-based approaches to food security, which rely on local knowledge, traditional seeds, and sustainable practices. This builds resilience against external shocks and economic fluctuations.

Integration of ethnoeconomics into sustainable agriculture is a powerful pathway toward SCP, environmental protection, and economic prosperity. Indigenous agricultural practices, biodiversity conservation, and food security strategies all contribute to more SCP patterns, which can help address the global challenges of environmental degradation and economic inequalities (Royters, 2022).

5 Ethnoeconomics and Sustainable Resource Management

Sustainable resource management is a critical component of promoting environmental protection and economic prosperity. Ethnoeconomics, a field that focuses on the economic activities and resource management practices of specific ethnic or cultural groups, plays a significant role in advancing sustainable resource management. In this section, we will explore the many ways that ethnoeconomics can be used to promote sustainable resource management. We will highlight indigenous resource management practices, the role of ethnoeconomics in forestry and wildlife management, and land and water resource management (Reid & Murphy, 2022). Furthermore, we will extract valuable lessons from indigenous resource management practices that can be applied to contemporary sustainability efforts.

5.1 Indigenous Resource Management Practices

Indigenous communities around the world have often demonstrated remarkable expertise in managing natural resources sustainably. Their resource management practices are deeply rooted in their cultural traditions and close connections to the land. These practices encompass a wide array of activities, such as agriculture, fishing, hunting, and gathering. Indigenous resource management systems are often characterized by their holistic and long-term approach, aiming to maintain the balance of ecosystems while meeting the needs of their communities (Vigilante & Bowman, 2004).

In many cases, indigenous resource management practices are intricately tied to the concept of reciprocity, where communities believe in giving back to the land as much as they take from it. This practice has been successful in preventing over-exploitation of resources and maintaining biodiversity. Moreover, indigenous resource management practices often rely on traditional knowledge passed down through generations, which has proven effective in adapting to changing environmental conditions (Craig, 1997).

5.2 Ethnoeconomics in Forestry and Wildlife Management

Ethnoeconomics has a significant role to play in the management of forests and wildlife. Indigenous communities often have a profound understanding of local ecosystems, which includes knowledge of specific plant and animal species, their habitats, and seasonal patterns. This knowledge allows them to effectively manage forests and wildlife for sustainable use.

Ethnoeconomic approaches to forestry and wildlife management can include practices like selective logging, controlled hunting, and the establishment of protected areas based on traditional ecological knowledge. These methods not only preserve biodiversity but also contribute to the economic well-being of indigenous communities, as they often generate income through the sustainable harvest and sale of forest products or wildlife resources (Kumar et al., 2023).

5.3 Land and Water Resource Management

Indigenous resource management also extends to land and water resources. Many indigenous communities have developed intricate systems for managing arable land, including crop rotation and agroforestry techniques that promote soil fertility and reduce erosion. Water resource management can involve the construction of sustainable irrigation systems, terracing, and the conservation of water sources, all of which help ensure the long-term availability of water for agriculture and domestic use.

By carefully tending to land and water resources, indigenous communities often avoid the environmental degradation associated with unsustainable land-use practices (Butcher & Hallward, 2019). Their approaches are not only ecologically sound but also economically viable, contributing to the resilience and prosperity of these communities.

5.4 Lessons from Indigenous Resource Management

One of the major takeaways from indigenous resource management practices is the importance of a holistic, long-term perspective. Indigenous communities prioritize the health of their ecosystems because they recognize that their well-being is intricately tied to the well-being of the environment. This underscores the need for a shift in modern resource management paradigms towards sustainability, rather than short-term exploitation.

Moreover, the knowledge and practices of indigenous resource management highlight the value of local and traditional knowledge in contemporary conservation and sustainability efforts. Collaboration and the integration of traditional practices into mainstream resource management strategies can significantly benefit both the environment and local economies (Frawley et al., 2002).

Combination of ethnoeconomics and sustainable resource management practices can safeguard the environment and boost the economy. Indigenous resource management practices provide valuable insights into how we can better manage our natural resources while promoting a harmonious relationship between people and the environment. By recognizing and learning from these practices, society can make strides toward a more sustainable and prosperous future (Callan & Coleman, 2018).

6 Ethnoeconomics and Circular Economy

6.1 Relevance of Circular Economy in SCP

The circular economy is a holistic and regenerative economic model that aims to minimize waste, maintain the value of products and materials, and promote resource efficiency. It is highly relevant to SCP as it emphasizes reducing the environmental impact of products and services while fostering economic growth. The circular economy framework encourages reusing, repairing, remanufacturing, and recycling products, which aligns with the principles of SCP. By extending the life cycle of products and materials, the circular economy reduces the need for resource extraction and waste generation (Nama, 2008).

Ethnoeconomics, rooted in traditional knowledge systems and practices, plays a crucial role in adapting and implementing circular economy principles in various cultural contexts (Cole, 2006). Indigenous communities have long practiced sustainable resource management and waste reduction, aligning with the circular economy's goals. They understand the importance of preserving the environment for future generations and have developed practices that contribute to SCP.

6.2 *Indigenous Approaches to Waste Reduction and Recycling*

Indigenous communities have developed innovative and sustainable approaches to waste reduction and recycling over centuries. These approaches are deeply rooted in their cultural and ecological knowledge. Examples of indigenous waste reduction and recycling practices include:

- **Upcycling and repurposing**: Indigenous communities often find creative ways to reuse items, turning discarded materials into valuable resources. This includes turning old clothing into quilts, using animal bones for tools, or converting waste materials into art and crafts.
- **Traditional knowledge of resource utilization**: Indigenous peoples have intricate knowledge of how to extract the most from available resources. This includes techniques for using all parts of plants and animals, reducing waste through careful resource management.
- **Waste avoidance**: Indigenous cultures often prioritize the avoidance of waste through mindful consumption. This includes practices like using reusable containers, avoiding excessive packaging, and making products that are designed to last.
- **Reciprocity and community sharing**: Many indigenous communities have traditions of sharing and communal ownership, which reduces the need for individual consumption and waste generation.

6.3 *Synergies Between Ethnoeconomics and Circular Economy*

The synergy between ethnoeconomics and the circular economy is evident in many ways:

- **Cultural alignment**: Ethnoeconomics is deeply rooted in cultural values and practices, and it often aligns with the principles of the circular economy, such as reducing waste and maintaining resource value.
- **Learning from indigenous wisdom**: The circular economy can benefit from the wisdom of indigenous communities by integrating their sustainable practices into broader economic systems. Collaborative efforts can adapt these practices to modern contexts.
- **Local resource utilization**: Ethnoeconomics emphasizes the sustainable use of local resources, reducing the reliance on global supply chains. This aligns with the circular economy's focus on localizing production and reducing transportation-related environmental impacts.

- **Holistic approach**: Both ethnoeconomics and the circular economy take a holistic approach to resource management, considering the social, economic, and environmental dimensions. This approach can lead to more resilient and sustainable economic systems.

By combining ethnoeconomics and the circular economy, we can create a promising pathway to SCP practices. By drawing from indigenous practices, cultural wisdom, and a shared commitment to waste reduction and resource efficiency, societies can move closer to the goal of environmental protection and economic prosperity through SCP. This synergy acknowledges the importance of respecting traditional knowledge while advancing towards a more sustainable and circular future (Robert, 2002).

7 Ethnoeconomics in Sustainable Business and Entrepreneurship

Ethnoeconomics is a multidisciplinary field that explores the economic practices, strategies, and traditions of various ethnic and indigenous groups. It offers valuable insights into sustainable business and entrepreneurship by emphasizing holistic and community-oriented approaches to economic activities (Slikkerveer et al., 2019). Here, we will discuss four major aspects of how ethnoeconomics contributes to sustainable business and entrepreneurship.

7.1 Indigenous Entrepreneurship Models

Indigenous entrepreneurship models are rooted in the traditions, values, and knowledge of indigenous communities. These models offer unique approaches to economic activities that are often more sustainable and socially responsible compared to conventional business models. They encompass practices such as:

- **Community-centered businesses**: Indigenous entrepreneurship frequently revolves around community well-being rather than individual profit. Businesses are often structured to benefit the entire community, with decision-making processes involving various community members.
- **Traditional knowledge-based enterprises**: Indigenous communities possess extensive knowledge about their natural surroundings and often incorporate this wisdom into their economic activities. This not only preserves traditional wisdom but also promotes sustainable resource management.
- **Cultural and artistic ventures**: Many indigenous communities engage in creative enterprises, such as traditional art and crafts, which not only provide economic opportunities but also contribute to the preservation of cultural heritage.

7.2 Ethical Sourcing and Fair Trade

Ethnoeconomics promotes ethical sourcing and fair-trade practices as a means of ensuring that indigenous and local communities benefit from economic activities while protecting their environment. These practices involve:

- **Fair compensation**: Ethical sourcing and fair trade prioritize paying producers and artisans a fair wage for their products, eliminating exploitative practices commonly seen in global supply chains.
- **Environmental responsibility**: Ethical sourcing often requires sustainable and environmentally friendly production methods, reducing the ecological footprint of products and services.
- **Cultural respect**: Ethical sourcing acknowledges and respects the cultural and traditional elements of products. This helps preserve and celebrate the heritage of indigenous and local communities.

7.3 Ethnoeconomics and Green Enterprises

Ethnoeconomics and green enterprises share a common focus on environmental sustainability. Ethnoeconomics can inform and enrich green business practices in many ways:

- **Traditional ecological knowledge**: Indigenous communities have often developed deep knowledge of their local ecosystems. Incorporating this knowledge can enhance sustainable and regenerative agricultural, forestry, and land management practices in green enterprises.
- **Community-based conservation**: Ethnoeconomics emphasizes community involvement in natural resource management, leading to more successful and sustainable conservation efforts. It showcases how local communities can play a vital role in preserving biodiversity and natural resources.
- **Low-impact production methods**: Many indigenous communities have traditionally employed low-impact production methods, which can serve as inspiration for developing sustainable and eco-friendly production processes in green enterprises.

7.4 Empowering Indigenous Communities Through Business

One of the most compelling aspects of ethnoeconomics is its potential to empower indigenous communities both economically and socially. This empowerment is achieved through:

- **Economic independence**: Indigenous entrepreneurship allows communities to rely less on external economic influences, giving them greater control over their financial well-being.
- **Preserving culture and identity**: By integrating cultural and traditional elements into business activities, ethnoeconomics helps preserve and celebrate indigenous cultures, preventing cultural erosion.
- **Reducing vulnerability**: Ethnoeconomics can make indigenous communities more resilient to economic and environmental shocks, providing them with the means to adapt and thrive.

Ethnoeconomics plays a crucial role in promoting SCP patterns by offering valuable insights into indigenous entrepreneurship models, ethical sourcing and fair trade, green enterprises, and empowering indigenous communities through business. These insights not only contribute to environmental protection but also enhance economic prosperity, offering a holistic and community-oriented approach to economic activities that benefits both people and the planet (Chapman, 2020).

8 Policy and Governance Implications

8.1 Integrating Ethnoeconomics into Sustainable Policy Frameworks

Integrating ethnoeconomics into sustainable policy frameworks is a critical step toward achieving environmental protection and economic prosperity. Ethnoeconomics, which refers to the study of how different ethnic or indigenous groups interact with their economic and natural environments, offers a unique perspective on SCP patterns (Meagher, 2006). To achieve this integration, many considerations and strategies must be taken into account:

- **Recognizing indigenous knowledge systems**: Indigenous communities often possess traditional knowledge systems that have been developed over centuries and are deeply attuned to their natural surroundings. Policy frameworks need to acknowledge the value of this indigenous knowledge and incorporate it into decision-making processes related to sustainability. This may include recognizing traditional land management practices, herbal medicine, and sustainable resource use as essential components of a holistic approach to sustainability.
- **Cultural respect and inclusivity**: Policies must respect and promote cultural diversity and inclusivity. Indigenous communities have distinct cultures, belief systems, and worldviews that are closely intertwined with their economic activities. The integration of ethnoeconomics into sustainable policies should embrace these diversities and ensure that no cultural group is marginalized in the process. Inclusivity can be achieved through meaningful consultation with indigenous leaders and communities.

- **Customized solutions**: Ethnoeconomic systems can vary significantly from one indigenous group to another. Therefore, policy frameworks should be flexible and adaptable, allowing for customized solutions that account for the unique circumstances and needs of each community. Standardized approaches may not be effective in all cases, and policies should be sensitive to these variations.
- **Land and resource rights**: Many indigenous communities have struggled with land and resource rights. Policymakers should focus on recognizing and securing these rights for indigenous peoples. Providing them with land tenure, resource management authority, and legal protection can empower these communities to sustainably manage their resources, promoting both environmental conservation and economic well-being.
- **Support for sustainable practices**: Governments can promote ethnoeconomic practices that align with sustainability by providing financial and technical support to indigenous communities. This can include funding for traditional agricultural practices, sustainable fishing, and non-timber forest products. Incentives and subsidies can encourage the preservation of indigenous knowledge and practices.

8.2 Legal and Regulatory Aspects

The legal and regulatory aspects of integrating ethnoeconomics into sustainable policy frameworks play a pivotal role in ensuring the protection of indigenous rights and the environment (Pandey, 2002). Here's a detailed discussion of the legal and regulatory considerations:

- **Recognition of indigenous rights**: At the heart of legal and regulatory aspects is the recognition of indigenous rights. This involves acknowledging the right of indigenous communities to control and manage their lands, territories, and resources. Many countries have adopted international conventions and treaties that protect these rights, and domestic laws should be brought into alignment with these international obligations.
- **Free, Prior, and Informed Consent (FPIC)**: FPIC is a fundamental principle when it comes to indigenous involvement in development projects that impact their lands and resources. It requires that governments, corporations, and other stakeholders seek the consent of indigenous communities before undertaking any project that could affect their environment or livelihoods. The legal framework must mandate FPIC and enforce its implementation rigorously.
- **Biodiversity protection**: Ethnoeconomics often intersects with biodiversity conservation. Laws and regulations should be in place to protect and preserve the biodiversity that indigenous communities rely on. This includes regulations to prevent overexploitation of resources, habitat protection, and measures to combat illegal trade in endangered species.
- **Intellectual property rights**: Many indigenous communities hold unique traditional knowledge related to plant-based medicines, sustainable agriculture, and resource management. Legal frameworks should address the issue of intellectual

property rights, ensuring that indigenous knowledge is protected from misappropriation and that communities benefit from any commercial use of their knowledge.
- **Access to justice**: Access to justice is a crucial aspect of legal and regulatory frameworks. Indigenous communities must have access to legal remedies when their rights are violated. This includes establishing specialized courts or dispute resolution mechanisms that are culturally sensitive and provide a level playing field for indigenous people.
- **Monitoring and compliance**: Legal frameworks should include mechanisms for monitoring compliance with ethnoeconomic integration policies. This could involve regular reporting, third-party audits, and penalties for non-compliance. Enforcement is critical to ensure that these policies translate into meaningful protection for indigenous communities and the environment.

8.3 *Challenges and Opportunities in Implementation*

Implementing ethnoeconomics as a tool for promoting SCP patterns presents a host of challenges and opportunities. This section explores these factors in detail.

a. Challenges in implementing ethnoeconomics

- **Cultural and ethical sensitivity**: One of the primary challenges in implementing ethnoeconomics is respecting and preserving the cultural and ethical aspects of indigenous communities. Often, the traditional practices and knowledge of these communities are at risk of being commodified and exploited. Striking a balance between economic development and cultural preservation is a significant challenge.
- **Legal and regulatory frameworks**: Ethnoeconomic initiatives may encounter legal and regulatory obstacles, such as intellectual property rights and land tenure issues. Indigenous knowledge is often not formally recognized, making it vulnerable to misappropriation. Developing appropriate legal frameworks to protect indigenous rights is crucial.
- **Knowledge transfer and capacity building**: Transferring indigenous knowledge to mainstream economic and environmental practices is challenging. Many indigenous communities have oral traditions, and the lack of written records makes it difficult to codify and share this knowledge. Effective capacity-building programs are essential to bridge this gap.
- **Resistance to change**: Convincing stakeholders and policy-makers to embrace ethnoeconomics can be met with resistance. This is often due to entrenched economic interests and the belief that traditional practices may hinder economic development. Overcoming this resistance requires robust advocacy and evidence-based demonstrations.

b. Opportunities in implementing ethnoeconomics

- **Biodiversity conservation**: Indigenous knowledge often includes sustainable land and resource management practices. Utilizing this knowledge can help preserve biodiversity, a critical component of SCP patterns.
- **Poverty alleviation**: Ethnoeconomic initiatives can contribute to poverty reduction among indigenous communities by providing economic opportunities based on traditional practices. This supports the United Nations' Sustainable Development Goals (SDGs) by improving livelihoods and well-being.
- **Local economic development**: Ethnoeconomics can stimulate local economies by promoting traditional crafts, agricultural methods, and products. This not only creates economic opportunities but also reinforces the importance of local ecosystems.
- **Cultural revitalization**: Ethnoeconomic initiatives provide a platform for the revitalization of indigenous cultures and traditions. This not only enhances cultural diversity but also enriches societies with valuable knowledge (Table 3).

8.4 International Collaboration for Ethnoeconomic Sustainability

a. Leveraging global partnerships

International collaboration is essential for the success of ethnoeconomic sustainability. Various stakeholders, including governments, NGOs, and indigenous communities, should come together to work towards common goals.

- **Knowledge sharing**: One of the primary aspects of international collaboration is the sharing of knowledge and best practices related to ethnoeconomics. This can be facilitated through international conferences, workshops, and online platforms.
- **Policy harmonization**: Collaborative efforts should focus on harmonizing policies at the international level. This includes the protection of intellectual property rights, land rights, and the recognition of indigenous knowledge in various international agreements.
- **Funding Mechanisms**: International collaboration can also involve the creation of funding mechanisms to support ethnoeconomic initiatives. These mechanisms can provide financial assistance for capacity building, infrastructure development, and sustainable projects in indigenous communities.

b. Indigenous representation

Indigenous communities should be active participants in international collaborations. Their voices and perspectives must be central to any decision-making processes (Markaryan et al., 2020). This ensures that ethnoeconomic sustainability initiatives are culturally sensitive and in alignment with the needs and desires of indigenous peoples.

Table 3 Overview of the challenges and opportunities in implementing ethnoeconomics for promoting SCP patterns (Source: Author's Compilation)

Challenges in Implementing Ethnoeconomics	Opportunities in Implementing Ethnoeconomics
1. Cultural and ethical sensitivity:	**1. Biodiversity conservation**:
Balancing economic development with cultural preservation	Preserving biodiversity through indigenous knowledge
Preventing commodification and exploitation of indigenous practices	
2. Legal and regulatory frameworks:	**2. Poverty alleviation**:
Intellectual property rights and land tenure issues	Contributing to poverty reduction among indigenous communities
Lack of formal recognition of indigenous knowledge	Aligning with Sustainable Development Goals (SDGs)
Need for appropriate legal protections	Improving livelihoods and well-being
3. Knowledge transfer and capacity building:	**3. Local economic development**:
Difficulty in transferring oral traditions to mainstream practices	Stimulating local economies through traditional practices
Lack of written records for indigenous knowledge	Promoting traditional crafts, agriculture, and products
Importance of effective capacity-building programs	Reinforcing local ecosystem significance
4. Resistance to change:	**4. Cultural revitalization**:
Stakeholder and policy-maker resistance	Revitalizing indigenous cultures and traditions
Entrenched economic interests	Enhancing cultural diversity and preserving valuable knowledge
Need for advocacy and evidence-based demonstrations	

Indigenous leadership: Indigenous leaders and representatives should be actively involved in negotiations and discussions on ethnoeconomic sustainability. Their inclusion is vital for building trust and ensuring the success of international collaborations.
Capacity building: International collaborations should also focus on capacity building within indigenous communities, empowering them to engage effectively in these initiatives and advocate for their rights and interests on a global scale.

c. Monitoring and evaluation

A robust monitoring and evaluation framework is crucial to track the progress and impact of international collaborations for ethnoeconomic sustainability. This involves the establishment of clear indicators and reporting mechanisms to ensure transparency and accountability.

- **Data collection and analysis**: Comprehensive data collection and analysis tools should be developed to measure the economic, environmental, and cultural impacts of ethnoeconomic initiatives. This data is essential for evidence-based decision-making and future planning.
- **Regular reporting**: Regular reporting on the progress of ethnoeconomic sustainability initiatives should be mandatory. This includes sharing both successes and challenges faced during the implementation of projects.

Crucial to promoting SCP, and achieving both environmental protection and economic prosperity, is the integration of ethnoeconomics into sustainable policy frameworks, the legal and regulatory aspects of this integration, the challenges and opportunities in its implementation, and international collaboration (Gewald et al., 2009). By recognizing the value of traditional knowledge and community practices, societies can move toward a more sustainable and equitable future.

9 Measuring the Impact of Ethnoeconomics on SCP

SCP is a critical component of achieving environmental sustainability and economic prosperity. Ethnoeconomics, as a multidisciplinary field, plays an essential role in understanding and promoting SCP patterns. To measure the impact of ethnoeconomics on SCP, one needs to consider a range of indicators, metrics, data collection methods, and analysis techniques (Veth et al., 2018).

9.1 Indicators and Metrics

Measuring the impact of ethnoeconomics on SCP requires a well-defined set of indicators and metrics that can capture the complex relationship between culture, economics, and sustainability (Belshaw, 2014). Some indicators and metrics include:

- **Cultural knowledge preservation**: Ethnoeconomics focuses on the traditional knowledge and practices of indigenous and local communities. The extent to which these cultural practices are preserved and integrated into SCP can be a vital indicator. This can be measured by assessing the retention and transmission of traditional ecological knowledge, resource management practices, and sustainable technologies.
- **Resource utilization efficiency**: Ethnoeconomics often emphasizes sustainable resource use. Metrics related to resource utilization, such as resource extraction rates, waste generation, and the use of renewable resources, can indicate the extent to which ethnoeconomics principles are integrated into SCP.
- **Community resilience**: The ability of communities to adapt to environmental changes and maintain their well-being is a crucial aspect of SCP. Indicators like

community resilience, vulnerability, and adaptive capacity can be used to assess the impact of ethnoeconomics on sustainable development.

- **Economic viability**: Ethnoeconomics also examines local economic systems and their compatibility with SCP. Metrics related to income generation, employment opportunities, and economic diversification within indigenous and local communities can gauge the economic aspects of ethnoeconomics in SCP.
- **Cultural diversity and identity**: Maintaining cultural diversity and identity is a fundamental aspect of ethnoeconomics. Indicators like language preservation, cultural events, and traditions can measure the impact of ethnoeconomics on cultural sustainability within SCP.

9.2 Data Collection and Analysis

Accurate data collection and rigorous analysis are essential for measuring the impact of ethnoeconomics on SCP. The following considerations are crucial:

- **Fieldwork and ethnographic studies**: Ethnoeconomics often involves close engagement with indigenous and local communities. Ethnographic studies, participant observation, and interviews are common data collection methods. Researchers should establish trust and build relationships with the communities to obtain reliable data.
- **Surveys and questionnaires**: Surveys and questionnaires can help gather quantitative data on various indicators. These tools should be culturally sensitive and adapted to the specific context to ensure accurate information.
- **Secondary data sources**: Existing data, such as government records, environmental assessments, and economic statistics, can complement primary data collection efforts. These sources can provide historical context and baseline data for comparison.
- **Qualitative and quantitative analysis**: Data collected should be subjected to both qualitative and quantitative analysis. Qualitative analysis can help understand the cultural and social dynamics, while quantitative analysis provides statistical insights into the relationships between ethnoeconomics and SCP.
- **Comparative studies**: Comparative studies between communities that embrace ethnoeconomics principles and those that do not can provide valuable insights into the impact of ethnoeconomics on SCP. These studies should control for variables like geography, climate, and historical context.

9.3 Assessing Environmental and Economic Outcomes

a. Environmental impact assessment:

- **Quantifying biodiversity conservation**: One of the major aspects of ethnoeconomics is its emphasis on preserving biodiversity. Assessments should measure the impact of ethnoeconomics on the conservation of biodiversity, including the protection of native species and ecosystems.
- **Ecosystem services**: Evaluate how ethnoeconomic practices contribute to ecosystem services, such as water purification, pollination, and carbon sequestration. This involves analysing the qualitative and quantitative benefits derived from traditional practices.
- **Resource sustainability**: Determine if ethnoeconomic approaches enhance the sustainability of natural resources by examining resource extraction, land management, and their ecological impacts.

b. Economic impact assessment:

- **Income generation**: Assess the ability of ethnoeconomic practices to generate income for local communities. This involves quantifying the economic value of traditional knowledge and products.
- **Local economic development**: Analyse how ethnoeconomics contributes to local economic development, including the creation of small businesses, employment opportunities, and value-added products.
- **Cost-benefit analysis**: Conduct cost-benefit analyses to compare the economic gains from ethnoeconomic practices against potential negative impacts, such as market fluctuations or overexploitation of resources.

c. Social and cultural impact assessment:

- **Cultural preservation**: Evaluate the role of ethnoeconomics in preserving and transmitting indigenous cultures, languages, and traditions. This includes assessing the strength of cultural identity within communities.
- **Social well-being**: Measure the impact of ethnoeconomics on social well-being indicators, such as access to education, healthcare, and overall quality of life.
- **Community resilience**: Assess how ethnoeconomics enhances the resilience of local communities in the face of economic and environmental challenges.

9.4 Long-Term Monitoring and Evaluation

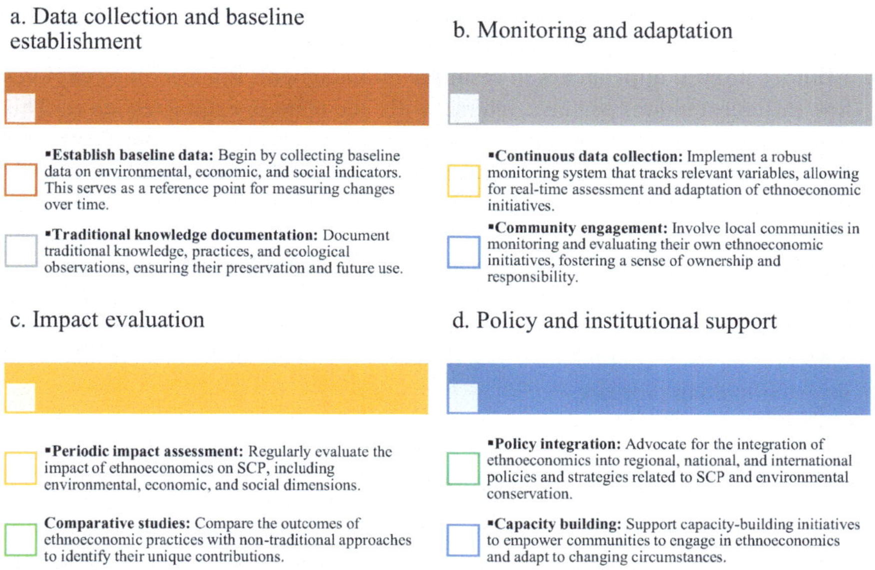

Measuring the impact of ethnoeconomics on SCP involves a multi-dimensional approach that integrates various indicators, data collection, and analysis methods, assesses both environmental and economic outcomes, and sustains long-term monitoring and evaluation to ensure its effectiveness in promoting environmental protection and economic prosperity (Murdock, 2010).

10 Future Directions

10.1 Emerging Trends in Ethnoeconomics

Ethnoeconomics is an interdisciplinary field that combines elements of anthropology, economics, and environmental studies to understand how different cultural practices, beliefs, and traditional knowledge systems influence economic activities and resource management (Lundy, 2009). As we look toward the future, many emerging trends within ethnoeconomics are worth noting.

- **Indigenous economies and local markets**: One main trend is the growing recognition of indigenous economies and their unique contributions to local markets. Indigenous communities often have deep knowledge of their ecosystems, which can be leveraged for sustainable economic development. This trend highlights the importance of understanding and respecting indigenous economic practices.

- **Ethnobotany and sustainable agriculture**: Ethnobotany, the study of the relationship between plants and people, is gaining traction as a means of promoting sustainable agriculture. By documenting and preserving traditional knowledge about plant species and their uses, researchers and policymakers can develop more sustainable agricultural practices and conserve biodiversity.
- **Ethnoecological approaches to resource management**: Ethnoecology explores how different cultures perceive, interact with, and manage natural resources. This approach is becoming increasingly important in the context of climate change and the need for adaptive resource management strategies. Emerging trends include the integration of indigenous knowledge in resource management and land-use planning.
- **Digital ethnoeconomics**: The advent of digital technologies and open-access platforms is transforming the way ethnoeconomic data is collected, analysed, and shared. This trend can lead to more inclusive and participatory research, empowering local communities to actively engage in ethnoeconomic studies and decision-making processes.

10.2 Research Gaps and Opportunities

Ethnoeconomics, while a promising field, still faces many research gaps and opportunities for further exploration in the coming years.

- **Cross-cultural studies**: There is a need for more cross-cultural studies that compare and contrast ethnoeconomic practices across different regions and communities. These studies can shed light on universal principles and specific adaptations to local conditions.
- **Integration of traditional knowledge**: can explore how to better integrate traditional knowledge systems into modern economic and environmental policies. This involves addressing issues related to intellectual property rights, cultural sensitivity, and equitable benefit-sharing.
- **Longitudinal studies**: Ethnoeconomics could benefit from longitudinal studies that track changes in economic and ecological practices over time. This can help identify the impact of globalization, environmental degradation, and economic development on traditional economies.
- **Policy frameworks**: Developing policy frameworks that integrate ethnoeconomic principles into broader sustainability and conservation strategies is a crucial opportunity. Policymakers can benefit from understanding how ethnoeconomics can inform sustainable resource management, ecotourism, and small-scale enterprise development.

10.3 Implications for Sustainable Economics

Ethnoeconomics has profound implications for promoting sustainable economic systems. It can contribute to the development of more holistic and regenerative economic models that prioritize ecological and cultural well-being alongside economic prosperity (Studley, 2007).

- **Community resilience**: By emphasizing local and community-based economic practices, ethnoeconomics can enhance community resilience. It supports the development of small-scale, diversified economies that are less susceptible to external economic shocks.
- **Biodiversity conservation**: Ethnoeconomics can play a vital role in biodiversity conservation by promoting sustainable resource use and preservation of traditional practices that contribute to ecological health.
- **Cultural preservation**: Recognizing and supporting ethnoeconomic practices can contribute to cultural preservation. Economic activities tied to cultural traditions often play a pivotal role in the maintenance of indigenous identities and knowledge systems.

10.4 Ethnoeconomics as a Cornerstone of Ecological Footprint Reduction

Ethnoeconomics can be seen as a cornerstone in the broader effort to reduce ecological footprints and promote SCP patterns.

- **Resource efficiency**: Traditional economic systems often prioritize resource efficiency and waste reduction. Learning from these systems can help modern economies become more efficient and less wasteful.
- **Sustainable agriculture**: Ethnoeconomics can inform sustainable agricultural practices by highlighting the benefits of crop diversity, agroecological knowledge, and localized farming techniques.
- **Sustainable consumption**: By emphasizing locally sourced and culturally relevant products, ethnoeconomics can encourage more sustainable consumption patterns that reduce the carbon footprint associated with global supply chains.
- **Ecotourism and cultural tourism**: Ethnoeconomics can play a pivotal role in the development of ecotourism and cultural tourism, offering travellers the opportunity to engage with and support local economies while fostering a deeper understanding of diverse cultures.

Future of ethnoeconomics holds promise for fostering sustainability, preserving cultural diversity, and advancing economic prosperity. As it evolves, researchers and policymakers must continue to explore emerging trends, address research gaps, and integrate ethnoeconomic principles into broader economic and environmental policy frameworks to truly leverage its potential for a more sustainable and equitable world (Dirin et al., 2023).

11 Conclusion

Sustainable consumption and production (SCP) patterns are crucial for achieving a harmonious balance between environmental preservation and economic development. Through the exploration of the theoretical framework, this has elucidated the significant role of ethnoeconomics in promoting sustainable practices, underscoring its potential as a pathway to both environmental protection and economic prosperity. By examining the interconnection between ethnoeconomics and SCP, this study has shed light on the importance of integrating indigenous knowledge systems and traditional practices into contemporary sustainable development strategies. The discourse on ethnoeconomics and indigenous knowledge has revealed the invaluable contributions of indigenous communities to SCP, emphasizing the preservation and utilization of traditional wisdom as a means to bridge the gap between modern sustainability efforts and ancestral practices. In the realm of sustainable agriculture, the incorporation of indigenous agricultural practices and the emphasis on biodiversity conservation have underscored the pivotal role of ethnoeconomics in ensuring food security and promoting ecologically sound farming techniques.

Furthermore, the exploration of ethnoeconomics in sustainable resource management has demonstrated the effectiveness of indigenous resource management practices in forestry, wildlife, land, and water conservation. This has highlighted the vital lessons that can be gleaned from indigenous resource management, emphasizing the need for a holistic approach to environmental stewardship. Additionally, the discussion on the relevance of the circular economy in SCP has underscored the synergies between ethnoeconomics and waste reduction, emphasizing the significance of indigenous approaches to recycling and sustainability. In the context of sustainable business and entrepreneurship, this has underscored the significance of indigenous entrepreneurship models, ethical sourcing, and green enterprises, highlighting the empowerment of indigenous communities through sustainable economic activities. The elucidation of policy and governance implications has emphasized the need to integrate ethnoeconomics into sustainable policy frameworks and address the challenges and opportunities associated with its implementation. Moreover, this has emphasized the importance of establishing comprehensive metrics and indicators for measuring the impact of ethnoeconomics on SCP, advocating for long-term monitoring and evaluation to assess both environmental and economic outcomes. Looking ahead, this has highlighted future directions for ethnoeconomics, emphasizing emerging trends, research gaps, and the implications for sustainable economics. It has positioned ethnoeconomics as a cornerstone of efforts to reduce ecological footprints, thereby underscoring its potential to shape a more sustainable and equitable future for all.

References

Adhikari, T. (2006). *Lessons from the Equator Initiative: an analysis of partnerships and cross-scale institutional linkages in forestry/agro-forestry related cases.*

Aponte Toro, R. P. (2000). The road ahead: A first week agenda. *Revista Jurídica de la Universidad de Puerto Rico, 69*, 777.

Aurenhammer, P., & Aurenhammer, P. K. (2013). Excursus: Capacity construction and capacity destruction—Whose capacities development cooperation builds upon? In *Development cooperation policy in forestry from an analytical perspective* (pp. 213–275). Springer.

Belshaw, C. S. (Ed.). (2014). *The sorcerer's apprentice: An anthropology of public policy* (Vol. 4). Elsevier.

Bliss, S., & Egler, M. (2020). Ecological economics beyond markets. *Ecological Economics, 178*, 106806.

Butcher, C., & Hallward, M. C. (Eds.). (2019). *Understanding international conflict management.* Routledge.

Callan, H., & Coleman, S. (Eds.). (2018). *The international encyclopedia of anthropology.* Wiley Blackwell.

Cavalcanti, C. (2002). Economic thinking, traditional ecological knowledge and ethnoeconomics. *Current Sociology, 50*(1), 39–55.

Cavalcanti, C. (2006a). 19 Traditional Resource Use. *Human Impacts on Amazonia: The Role of Traditional Ecological Knowledge in Conservation and Development*, 307.

Cavalcanti, C. (2006b). Traditional Resource Use and Ethnoeconomics: sustainable characteristics of the Amerindian lifestyles. In *Human impacts on Amazonia: The role of traditional ecological knowledge in conservation and development* (pp. 307–327). Columbia University Press.

Chandler, P. (2006). *Bound to the Hearth by the Shortest Tether: Village Life in China, Brazil and Points in Between.* University Press of America.

Chapman, V. (Ed.). (2020). *Terrible hard biscuits: a reader in Aboriginal history.* Routledge.

Cheng, L., Rosett, A., & Woo, M. (Eds.). (2003). *East Asian law: Universal norms and local cultures.* Routledge.

Cheng, Y. C. (2022). *School effectiveness and school-based management: A mechanism for development.* Taylor & Francis.

Cole, P. (2006). *Coyote and Raven go canoeing: Coming home to the village* (Vol. 42). McGill-Queen's Press-MQUP.

Comaroff, J., & Comaroff, J. (2022). The wealth of ethno-nations: Notes on the identity economy. *Revue Europeenne Des Migrations Internationales, 373*(3), 31–55.

Cook, S. (2003). Struggling to understand complexity: The sociocultural anthropology of Mexico at the beginning of the twenty-first century. *Mexican Studies, 19*(1), 203–241.

Craig, A. B. (1997). Management of rangelands in the Kimberley high-rainfall zone. *Tropical Grasslands, 31*, 161–187.

Dirin, D., Rasputina, E., Kuklina, M., Krasnoshtanova, N., Trufanov, A., Batosirenov, E., & Lysanova, G. (2023). Potential for Tourism and Recreation in the Todzhinsky Kozhuun (District), Republic of Tyva, RF. *Sustainability, 15*(14), 11087.

Frawley, W., Hill, K. C., & Munro, P. (Eds.). (2002). *Making dictionaries: Preserving indigenous languages of the Americas.* University of California Press.

Gewald, J. B., Luning, S., & Van Walraven, K. (Eds.). (2009). *The speed of change: Motor vehicles and people in Africa, 1890–2000* (Vol. 13). Brill.

GOAL 12: Sustainable consumption and production. (n.d.). UNEP—UN Environment Programme. https://www.unep.org/explore-topics/sustainable-development-goals/why-do-sustainable-development-goals-matter/goal-12

Gould, E. A. (2016). *Ecotourism: Conserving biocultural diversity and contributing to sustainable development* (Doctoral dissertation). University of the Pacific.

Guang, T. (2022). The development of business anthropology in China. *Anthropos, 117*(2), 485–504.

Head, L., Atchison, J., & Fullagar, R. (2002). Country and garden: Ethnobotany, archaeobotany and Aboriginal landscapes near the Keep River, northwestern Australia. *Journal of Social Archaeology, 2*(2), 173–196.

Hisayasu, L. M. (2019). *Mediated Memory and the Internet Indigenous Protagonism in Brazil.*

Horta, G. (2019). From peripatetic anthropology to the ethnography of roads and motorisation in Africa. *Cadernos de Estudos Africanos, 37*, 213–233.

Ignatov, A. (2011a). Three ecologies of consumption. In *APSA 2011 Annual Meeting Paper*.

Ignatov, A. (2011b). Three ecologies of consumption: Practicing the economy differently. In *Western Political Science Association 2011 Annual Meeting Paper*.

Keane, P. (2000). *Tenth Annual Fulbright Symposium on International Legal Problems.*

Kulbok-Lattik, E., & Čopič, V. (2018). Cultural Policies in the Baltic States and Slovenia Between 1991 and 2009. In V. D. Alexander, S. Hägg, S. Häyrynen, & E. Sevänen (Eds.), *Art and the challenge of markets volume 1: National cultural politics and the challenges of marketization and globalization* (pp. 183–215). Springer International Publishing.

Kumar, N., Kushwaha, R. R., Meena, N. R., Mishra, H., & Yadav, A. P. (2023). A study on costs and returns of paddy cultivation in Ambedkar Nagar district of Uttar Pradesh. *International Journal of Statistics and Applied Mathematics, SP-8*(3), 107–111.

Lingham, S., Manning, L., & Maye, D. (2022). Reimagining food: Readdressing and respecting values. *Sustainability, 14*(12), 7328.

Londoño Sulkin, C. D. (2017). Moral sources and the reproduction of the Amazonian package. *Current Anthropology, 58*(4), 477–501.

Lundy, B. D. (2009). *Making a living in Kassumba, Guinea-Bissau.* State University of New York at Buffalo.

Markaryan, V. R., Yakovlevna, L. K., Yurevna, K. E., Alexandrovna, C. V., & Anatolyevna, K. E. (2020). Globalization and problems of modern regional economy. *Systematic Reviews in Pharmacy, 11*(4).

Masarek, A. (2010). Treetop view of the cathedral: Plant variety protection in South and Southeast Asian least-developed countries. *Emory International Law Review, 24*, 433.

McCarthy, D. M. (2011). *An economic history of organized crime: A national and transnational approach* (Vol. 4). Routledge.

McCarthy, D. P. (2006). *International economic integration in historical perspective.* Routledge.

Meagher, K. (2006). Social capital, social liabilities, and political capital: Social networks and informal manufacturing in Nigeria. *African Affairs, 105*(421), 553–582.

Meagher, K. (2011). Informal economies and urban governance in Nigeria: Popular empowerment or political exclusion? *African Studies Review, 54*(2), 47–72.

Meagher, K. A. T. E., Mustapha, A. R., & Ehrhardt, D. (2018). Complementarity, competition and conflict. *Creed & Grievance: Muslim-Christian Relations & Conflict Resolution in Northern Nigeria, 11*, 184.

Mishra, H. (2021). A new era for Indian farming. *Times of Agriculture, 17*, 80–81. www.timesofagriculture.in

Mishra, H., & Mishra, D. (2023a). From comparative advantage to protectionism: Economic effects of trade wars on agricultural markets. *Agriallis, 5*(7), 29–36. www.agriallis.com

Mishra, H., & Mishra, D. (Eds.). (2023b). Artificial intelligence and machine learning in agriculture: Transforming farming systems. In *Research Trends in Agriculture Science* (Vol. I, pp. 1–16). Bhumi Publishing.

Mishra, H., & Singh, M. (2023a). Market liberalization and agricultural sector transformation: Paving the path to a dynamic future. *Times of Agriculture, 3*(7), 67–68.

Mishra, H., & Singh, M. (2023b). Revolutionizing agriculture: Empowering farmers through technological adoption for increased productivity and profitability. *The Agriculture Magazine, 2*(8), 17–22. www.theagricultureonline.com

Murdock, T. L. (2010). *Where new meanings spring: The relationship between Indigenous cultural meanings for freshwater springs and management practices: Analysis of stories from Kalbarri, Western Australia.*

Nama, A. (2008). *Black space: Imagining race in science fiction film*. University of Texas Press.
Nishad, D. C., Mishra, H., Tiwari, A. K., & Pandey, A. (Eds.). (2023). Towards sustainable agriculture: Mitigating the adverse effects of stubble burning in India. In *Research trends in environmental science* (Vol. I, pp. 42–48). Bhumi Publishing.
Pandey, D. N. (2002). Indigenous sustainability science. *Human Ecology*.
Pushpangadan, P., George, V., Ijinu, T. P., & Rajasekharan, S. (2016). Ethnobotany, ethnobiology, ethnopharmacology, bioprospecting of traditional knowledge and evolution of benefit sharing. In *Indian ethnobotany: Emerging trends* (pp. 1–23). The Scientific Publisher.
Reid, A. M., & Murphy, B. P. (2022). Forged by fire: Burning the Australian tropical savannas. *Global Application of Prescribed Fire*, 73.
Robert, C. (2019). Monetizing the mountains: Towards the study of ethno-cultural and demographic aspects of the socio-economic development of the mountain Dagestan. *История, Археология и Этнография Кавказа, 15*(4), 751–768.
Roberts, C. A. (2002). *Palaeopathology and archaeology: The current state of play*. Archaeopress.
Roche, C. (2020). *From hedonistic extraction to human flourishing: Applying disruptive and participatory concepts for a pluralist mining ethic* (Doctoral dissertation). Murdoch University.
Royters, N. M. (2022). *Ghosts amid the gears: Neoliberal subjectivity in 21st century Chinese and American fiction* (Doctoral dissertation).
Senehi, J., Scott, I. M., Byrne, S., & Matyók, T. G. (Eds.). (2022). *Routledge handbook of peacebuilding and ethnic conflict*. Taylor & Francis.
Seppanen, S. (2014). Ideological renewal and nostalgia in China's Avant-garde legal scholarship. *Washington University Global Studies Law Review, 13*, 83.
Singh, M., & Mishra, H. (2023a). Medicinal plant farming to improve farmers' economy. *Agriallis*, 30–36. www.agriallis.com
Singh, M., & Mishra, H. (2023b). Trade development and value chains in agriculture: Unleashing the potential for sustainable growth, *Times of Agriculture*, 56–57. www.timesofagriculture.in
Slikkerveer, L. J. (2019). Towards a Model of integrated community-managed development. *Integrated Community-Managed Development: Strategizing Indigenous Knowledge and Institutions for Poverty Reduction and Sustainable Community Development in Indonesia*, 91–135.
Slikkerveer, L. J., Baourakis, G., & Saefullah, K. (2019). *Integrated community-managed development*. Springer.
Smith, B., & Ouzman, S. (2004). Taking stock: Identifying Khoekhoen herder rock art in southern Africa. *Current Anthropology, 45*(4), 499–526.
Soselisa, H. L. (2002). *Memories and fragments: Resource management in Central Maluku*. Charles Darwin University (Australia).
Studley, J. (2007). *Hearing a different drummer: A new paradigm for the "keepers of the Forest"*. Iied.
Tiwari, A. K., Mishra, H., Nishad, D. C., & Pandey, A. (Eds.). (2023). Sustainable water management in agriculture: Irrigation techniques and water conservation. In *Research trends in agriculture science* (Vol. II, pp. 53–68). Bhumi Publishing.
Turner, K. L. (2010). *Community perspectives on bioeconomic development: Eco-cultural tourism in Hartley Bay, British Columbia*.
Veth, P., Myers, C., Heaney, P., & Ouzman, S. (2018). Plants before farming: The deep history of plant-use and representation in the rock art of Australia's Kimberley region. *Quaternary International, 489*, 26–45.
Vigilante, T., & Bowman, D. M. J. S. (2004). Effects of individual fire events on the flower production of fruit-bearing tree species, with reference to Aboriginal people's management and use, at Kalumburu, North Kimberley, Australia. *Australian Journal of Botany, 52*(3), 405–416.
Yahaya, A. K. (2012). Indigenous knowledge in the management of a community-based forest reserve in the Wa West District of Ghana. *Ghana Journal of Development Studies, 9*(1), 101–114.

Sensemaking and Sustainability: A Sensemaking Perspective on the Ethical Use of Big Data in Marketing Strategizing

Emma (Junhong) Wang, Pierre Berthon, and Yiran Su

Abstract Despite the ethical concerns over the datafication and surveillance of individuals and groups, companies are making ever greater investments in big data. The assumptions underpinning this movement are: (1) organizations are passive implementers of big data—more data is the inevitable consequence of technology and a competitive necessity for business, (2) more data offers a more objective and accurate picture of reality and (3) more data enables better prediction. We argue that this perspective is strategically unsustainable and abdicates ethical responsibility.

In this chapter, we adopt a sensemaking perspective (Weick in (1995) Sensemaking in organizations (Vol. 3). Sage) to challenge each of the assumptions of inevitability, objectivity, and predictability. Building on this critique, we discuss the role that organizations can play in creating alternative sustainable futures with big data and explore the legal and ethical consequences of their actions. In addition, we advocate that, from a sensemaking perspective, organizations can use big data to cultivate sustainable learning and innovating communities of both employees and customers.

Keywords Big Data · Sensemaking · Sustainability · Strategizing · Organization

> We put so much investment in being saved by these objects we create, by these technologies. But our real resource is ourselves, our communities, our relationships, our stories and our narratives.

E. Wang (✉)
School of Business, Southern Connecticut State University, New Haven, CT, USA
e-mail: wangj66@southernct.edu

P. Berthon
Bentley University, Waltham, MA, USA
e-mail: pberthon@bentley.edu

Y. Su
Isenberg School of Management, University of Massachusetts Amherst, Amherst, MA, USA
e-mail: yiransu@isengberg.umass.edu

W. Leal Filho and V. Kuzmanović (eds.), *Sustainable Development Seen Through the Lenses of Ethnoeconomics and the Circular Economy*,
https://doi.org/10.1007/978-3-031-72676-7_7

—Ruha, Benjamin
Founding Director of the IDA B. WELLS Just Data Lab
Associate Professor at Princeton University

1 Introduction

"The technology that connects us also divides us, manipulates us, polarize us, distract us, monetize us and controls us" (Orlowski & Rhodes, 2020). A Netflix documentary *The Social Dilemma* went viral in September, 2020 in the middle of the COVID pandemic. The film highlighted our shared social dilemma (i.e., mental health dilemma, the democracy dilemma, and the discrimination dilemma) caused by social media and the forces controlling these online platforms (i.e. companies, politicians and other interested parties). It features technologists, researchers and activists working to align technology with the interests of humanity, who raised their concerns over the datafication and surveillance of citizens.

Big data is a term for the exponential explosion in the volume, variety and velocity of data we see today. The world now generates an estimated 2.5 quintillion bytes of data every day, (Rayaprolu, 2023). It comes in three forms: (1) Structured data which and exists in predefined formats like credit card numbers and GPS coordinates; (2) Unstructured data such as social media posts and blogs; and (3) Semi-structured data which is a mix of structured and unstructured data such as email addresses. Despite the concerns over the datafication and surveillance of citizens, companies have invested billions of dollars into the harvesting and storage of data (Brown, 2021). This drive is rooted in the belief that data can capture social life in an objective format (Hintz et al., 2018). Big data's ascendance rests on two promises. First, that more data offers a more objective and accurate picture of reality, which can be leveraged for competitive advantage (e.g., Mayer-Schönberger & Cukier, 2013; Rust & Huang, 2014). Second, that "using big data leads to better predictions and better predictions yield better decisions" (McAfee et al., 2012, p. 64). This 'dataism' view of big data, promoted by big tech and consultants, argues for a new era of empiricism, where data, combined with analysis can reveal intrinsic truths, independent of theoretical perspective (Kitchin, 2021).

We argue that mangers have brought into a view of big data that is strategically unsustainable and abdicates ethical responsibility. Moreover, this view marginalizes the negative impacts of Big Data on individuals, organizations, and society. Is there an alternative framing of Big Data that allows for an ethical and sustainable future?

We suggest that Weick's (1995) theory of sensemaking can provide such a framing. Sensemaking involves "placing stimuli into some kind of framework to comprehend, understand, explain, attribute, extrapolate and predict" (Starbuck & Milliken 1988, p. 51). It is seen as a key managerial and leadership ability that enables firms to cope with, and act in, the rapidly changing and complex environments (Ancona, 2012; Becke, 2013).

The rest of the chapter is structured as follows. We start by reviewing the tension in current views of big data. After that, we explore the relationship between sustainability and ethical use of big data. Thirdly, we examine the assumptions underpinning the unsustainable view of big data, and then we introduce a sensemaking perspective. Next, we explore the role that big data can play from a sensemaking perspective. Finally, we draw on this more nuanced framing of big data to discuss the role that organizations can play in creating ethical and sustainable futures.

2 The Tension in Current Views of Big Data

Over past one decade or so, big data has been generating excitement amongst both practitioners and academics. Advocates of big data (e.g., Chen et al., 2012, Constantiou & Kallinikos, 2015, Davenport et al., 2012, LaValle et al., 2011, Mayer-Schönberger & Cukier, 2013, McAfee et al., 2012, Rust & Huang, 2014, Varian, 2010, 2014, Woerner & Wixom, 2015), contend that big data is a revolution that will transform how we live, giving companies a competitive advantage by enabling them to assess, analyze and respond to environmental trends, and offer new types of service. Advocates argue that big data can provide a new era of empiricism where data can 'speak for itself' without theoretical framing of interpretation (Kitchin, 2021). For example, Anderson (2008), former Editor-in-Chief at Wired magazine, contends that "the data deluge makes the scientific method obsolete." Echoing this, Prensky (2009) argues that correlation is enough and we can stop looking for theoretical causal models.

An example was cited in Kitchin (2021)'s work from retail to illustrate this perspective. A retail chain analyzed 12 years of purchase transactions. By discovering correlations between certain items, new product placements and shelf space management were altered, resulting in a 16% increase in revenue per shopping cart in the first month. A hypothesis was not developed or tested to explain why product A was often bought with product B. The data were simply queried to identify correlations that existed. Siegel (2013, p.90) argues, "We ... don't necessarily care (about causation) ... the objective is to predict ...(not) ... understand the world...". As a result, managers know without understanding: the "what" trumps the "why". From this perspective, big data is touted as "a source of new economic value and innovation" (Mayer-Schönberger & Cukier, 2013, p.12, Chen et al., 2012).

However, there are dissenting voices (e.g., Crawford et al., 2014, Crawford, 2014, Naimi & Westreich, 2014, Markus, 2015, Newell & Marabelli, 2015, Richards & King, 2013, 2014, Zuboff, 2015, O'neil, 2017), who critique the hype around big data, and point out the threats big data brings to people's identity, privacy, security, and economic wellbeing. Richards and King (2013) highlights three paradoxes in the rhetoric about big data: the transparency paradox, the identity paradox and the power paradox. Zuboff (2015) argues that we live in an era of 'surveillance capitalism'. While Crawford et al. (2014) argue that the promise of big data as a predictor of social behavior ignores a key insight from sociology: aggregated, individual actions cannot, explain the emergent dynamics of social interaction. O'neil (2017) points out the flaws in big data models:

> many of these models encoded human prejudice, misunderstanding, and bias into the software systems that increasingly managed our lives. Like gods, these mathematical models were opaque, their working invisible to all but the highest priests in their domain: mathematicians and computer scientists. Their verdicts, even when wrong or harmful, were beyond dispute or appeal. And they tended to punish the poor and the oppressed in our society while making the rich richer. (p. 3)

These dissenting voices collectively highlight the manifest flaws in the mainstream perspective on big data. Next, we examine the relationship between sustainability and ethical use of big data.

3 Sustainability and Ethical Use of Big Data

Sustainability involves making decisions that benefit the society, environment, and economy at the same time, rather than trading-off one against the others (Willard & Hitchcock, 2015). The relationship between sustainability and the ethical use of big data presents a complex and multifaceted issue, as it embodies a tension within the current views of big data. This issue can be analyzed from two complementary perspectives: the enablers' side and the barriers' side.

From the enablers' side, big data can facilitate responsible business management, echoing the paradigm shift in the circular economy, altering purchase behavior from ownership to service offerings (Salminen et al., 2017). Big data-enabled digital transformation allows enterprises to capitalize on new business and optimization opportunities using technologies such as cloud, mobile, and social networks with increasing intelligence and automation (Feroz et al., 2021). Digital transformation of supply chain management increases efficiency within the supply network. Furthermore, big data can bridge the gap between supply chain and consumer analytics. Sustainability has emerged as a prevailing marketing and branding strategy, providing companies with a competitive advantage by aligning their values with younger generations' preferences. The increasing accessibility of big data has played a vital role in facilitating this shift towards sustainability practices (Raut et al., 2019). By integrating sustainability practices into their operations and supply chain management, companies can enhance their brand image, appeal to sustainability-conscious consumers, and leverage insights from big data analytics to inform marketing and branding strategies. Companies can use big data to gain insights into consumer preferences and behavior related to sustainability, tailoring their messaging and experiences accordingly to make their sustainability initiatives more effective (Kitchens et al., 2018).

The underexplored aspect of big data lies in the challenges and barriers it presents. As with any technology, the large-scale use of big data will inevitably have some undesirable consequences—both foreseeable and unpredictable. It is crucial to begin exploring the potential unwanted repercussions of the big data revolution, notable, the unique challenges and requirements of warehouse-scale data centers, i.e., large-scale computer systems designed for processing and analyzing massive amounts of data (Schadt et al., 2010). In fact, data centers are the factories of the twenty-first century which consume a tremendous amount of energy (Willard & Hitchcock, 2015). While in technical parlance the "Cloud" might refer to the pooling of computing resources over a network, it has come to signify and encompass the entire gamut of infrastructures that make online activity possible, including services such as Instagram, Hulu, and Google Drive, etc. Monserrate (2022)'s research sketches some of the particular ways that cloud computation contributes to climate change and the Anthropocene. Particularly, this research reveals various material and ecological impacts of computation and digital data storage practices and pinpoints the environmental toll of digital life and the complexity of infrastructures involved in its operation. Thus, the Cloud is not only material, but also ecological in embodiment and effect. As the Cloud expands, its negative impacts on environment increases, despite the best efforts of engineers, technicians, and executives to balance profitability with sustainability. Indeed, the Cloud now has a greater carbon footprint than the airline industry. A single data center can consume the equivalent electricity of 50,000 homes.

Monserrate (2022) further reveals that some of the "hyper-scale" data centers, such as those owned by Google, Facebook, and Amazon, have committed to carbon offsetting, and investing in renewable energy such as wind and solar. However, many smaller data centers lack the resources to pursue sustainability initiatives, and they are often located in old buildings that are not optimized for the ever-changing power, cooling, and data storage needs. Many companies, universities, and others who operate small-scale data centers have begun to transfer their data to hyper-scalers or cloud colocation facilities to cut energy costs.

According to Sattiraju (2020), Google's parent company, Alphabet, is building more data centers across the U.S. to power online searches, web advertising and cloud services. The company has boasted for years that these huge computer-filled warehouses are energy efficient and environmentally friendly. However, there's a cost that the company tries to keep secret. These facilities use billions of gallons of water, often in dry areas with limited water resources. This shift from cooling air to cooling water is an attempt for those data centers to reduce carbon footprint, but it comes at a cost. For example, residents of Bluffdale, Utah, suffer water shortages and power outages due to the nearby Utah Data Center, a facility of the U.S. National Security Agency (NSA) that guzzles seven million gallons of water daily to operate (Monserrate, 2022).

What is worse is that, since customers expect their data and cloud services to be available anywhere, anytime, data centers are designed to be redundant, ensuring that if one system fails, another can take over at a moment's notice, preventing service disruptions. Therefore, data centers require a great deal of energy beyond cooling. It is estimated that only 6–12 percent of computational energy is consumed by active computational processes, and the rest is used for cooling and ensuring redundant fail-safe chains are in place to avoid costly downtime (Monserrate, 2022).

Despite efforts to mitigate the environmental harms of big data, such as carbon emissions, water consumption, noise, and toxic e-waste, there is a vicious cycle where the increasing demand for big data further exacerbates these harmful effects. To complicate matters, managers offload the environmental costs associated with the storage and processing of big data to third parties (such as Amazon's AWS), thus abdicating ethical responsibility. To break this vicious cycle, we need to reexamine the dominant framing of big data. We argue that adopting a sense-making approach can help promote a more sustainable and responsible approach. This approach involves creating, interpreting, and enacting responsible and ethical practices to leverage the full potential of big data for the greater good while minimizing harm to the society, environment, and vulnerable populations.

4 Assumptions Underpinning the Dominant View of Big Data

There is a powerful and attractive set of ideas underpinning the current framing, i.e., the dominant view of big data: inevitability, objectivity, and prediction trumps explanation.

First, organizations are passive implementers of big data—more data is the inevitable consequence of technology and a competitive necessity for business: adopt big data or die (e.g., Mayer-Schönberger & Cukier, 2013; Woerner & Wixom, 2015). In reviewing statement from a White House report on big data (White House, 2014) and a 2009 interview with Google Chairperson Eric Shmidt (Newman, 2009), Zuboff (2015) finds that, "big data is cast as the inevitable consequences of a technological juggernaut with a life of its own entirely outside the social. We are but bystanders" (p. 75).

Second, more data offers a more objective and accurate picture of reality. Here embedded another assumption that, the environment, consists of customers, competitors, markets, advanced technologies, and so on, exists in an objective reality that data reflects (boyd & Crawford, 2012; Crawford et al., 2014). Puschmann and Burgess (2014) reveal the dominant metaphors used in the rhetoric around big data. First, it is "a *resource* to be consumed". Second, it is "a natural *force* to be controlled." They conclude that these metaphors encourage the view that big data as value-neutral resource and an objective force. Indeed, "the rhetoric of objectivity can be very seductive to public policy makers traversing the complex world of social phenomena" (Crawford et al., 2014, p. 1667)".

To compound matters, some data analytics software is sold on the misleading notion that relationships within big data are inherently truthful, and that meaning transcends context or domain-specific knowledge (Kitchin, 2021). For example, the data mining and visualization software Ayasdi claims to be able to "automatically discover insights -- regardless of complexity -- without asking questions." Ayasdi's customers can finally learn the answers to questions that they didn't know to ask in the first place. It further claims to have eliminated the human element of data mining, as well as all the bias that comes with it (Kitchin, 2021).

The third assumption is that prediction trumps explanation. Big data doesn't aim to explain the world, just predict what will happen; correlation patterns are more important than causal relations (Siegel, 2013). More data means greater predictability of customers and markets. "Using big data leads to better predictions and better predictions yield better decisions" (McAfee et al., 2012, p. 64).

Next, we re-examine these assumptions from a sensemaking perspective (Weick, 1995). We discuss how sensemaking works in decision making and then reinterpret big data and the role that organizations play in its use from a sensemaking perspective.

5 Sensemaking and Strategizing

Strategy is not something that an organization *has* but something its members *do* (Johnson et al., 2003) and the strategy-as-practice approach speaks of "strategizing" as the "doing of strategy" (Jarzabkowski, 2004; Whittington, 2006). Indeed, from a sensemaking (Weick, 1995) perspective, strategizing is seen as an ongoing process involving organizational participants' constructing and reconstructing their views of the past, present and future (Kaplan & Orlikowski, 2013). In other words, the process of making strategic decisions is an ongoing, social activity that involves negotiations, discussions, and situated practices that strategists use to accomplish their goals (Jarzabkowski et al., 2007; Kaplan & Orlikowski, 2013).

Organizations begin new strategizing when an existing strategy is disrupted (e.g., a marketing problem or opportunity is detected). Strategists then try to get rid of the 'disordered' situations through creating 'new' orders and making events rationally accountable (Weick, 1995). They get together to exchange ideas about what happened in the past, what is currently at stake now and what is coming up in the future (Kaplan & Orlikowski, 2013). In other words, they used 'sensemaking' to guide them toward identifying substitute actions (Weick et al., 2005) to resolve marketing problems or leverage marketing opportunities.

As previously mentioned, sensemaking means putting stimuli into a framework to comprehend, understand, explain, attribute, extrapolate, and predict things (Starbuck & Milliken, 1988). It consists of three basic components: (1) cues, (2) frames, and (3) the linking of cues and frames (Weick, 1995). "'Cues' are information from current environments and trigger a drive to make sense of the situation. 'Frames' are knowledge or mental structures that include rules and values and serve as a guide to understanding. When people create a relation between frames and cues, they create meaning" (Miles, 2012, p. 242).

Specifically, after strategic decision-makers capture cues from the external or internal environment, they then create ways of comprehending the meaning of the event and fit these cues into their mental frames of understanding (Gioia, 1986; Taylor & Crocker, 1981). While they are translating events and developing a shared understanding among themselves, new constructs are introduced into the collective cognitive map of the organization (Daft & Weick, 1984). They then put these theories or maps into practice, a process that constitutes organizational learning (Argyris &

Schon, 1978; Hedberg, 1981). Taking action is critical because it helps decision-makers and other organization members stay in touch with the changing business environment. Rounds of sensemaking make strategizing an ongoing process. As such, sensemaking essentially serves as a springboard to action (Weick et al., 2005, p. 409) in strategic decision-making.

Next, we consider big data from a sensemaking perspective and contrast this with the dominant view of big data.

6 How Does a Sensemaking Perspective of Big Data Differ?

Recall that the dominant view of big data is underpinned by three assumptions, namely: (1) organizations are passive implementers of big data—more data is the inevitable consequence of technology and a competitive necessity for business, (2) more data offers a more objective and accurate picture of reality and (3) more data enables better prediction. How does a sensemaking perspective differ from this view?

6.1 Big Data Represents an Enactment Rather Than an Objective Picture of Reality

The sensemaking perspective is grounded in two postulates: reality is perspectival and enacted.

First, effective strategizing does not require nor produce an absolute reality; it fundamentally *perspectival.* "Sensemaking is not about truth and getting it right" (Weick et al., 2005, p. 415). In a sensemaking process 'reality' is an ongoing accomplishment that emerges from efforts to create order and make retrospective sense of what occurs (Weick, 1993). Winograd and Flores (1986) describe situations of '*thrownness*', in which "people find themselves *thrown* into ongoing situations and have to make do if they want to make sense of what is happening" (cited in Weick, 1995, pp. 43–44). One of the properties of this thrownness is that strategic decision makers do not have a static representation of a situation. Patterns may be evident in retrospect, but strategists always have to deal with whatever comes up, as it comes up. The process of change is arbitrarily chopped into events. The extracted cures are then organized into a host of different patterns or possibly no pattern at all (Weick, 1995). Objective analysis (or an a-perspectival view) of a situation is impossible because "each representation is an interpretation and there is no way to settle that any interpretation is right or wrong" (Winograd & Flores, 1986, cited in Weick, 1995, p. 44).

Second, reality is enacted rather than discovered (Weick, 1995). This enactment process involves two steps. First, preconceptions are used to set aside portions of the field of experience for further attention, i.e., perception is focused on predetermined stimuli. Second, people act within the context of these portions of experience guided by preconceptions in such a way as to reinforce these preconceptions. Hence, attention to certain stimuli will guide subsequent action so that those stimuli are confirmed as important. This is in stark contrast to the dominant view of big data, which argues that data provides a theory free, objective and unbiased view of reality. This claim is easy to dismiss, as systems are a *priori* designed to capture certain kinds of data and analytics. Such work is guided by an agenda as to what outcomes (e.g., increasing profit or market share) are being sought. Thus, identifying patterns within datasets doesn't happen in a vacuum, but is dictated by what managers deem important and previous research (Kitchin, 2021).

Etymologically, the word data is derived from the Latin *dare*, meaning 'to give' in the sense of a *fact* given as the input into a calculation. This highlight that facts are tantamount to assumptions, and that facts are taken or created from an infinitely complex environment (Kitchin, 2021). We extract elements (data, facts) through observation, computation, experiments and record keeping from an infinite world of possibilities. Thus, data are inherently partial, selective and representative. In fact, from a sensemaking perspective, data are both social and material. They do not merely represent the world but actively produce it. Big data is always used to actively intervene and change the world by its users.

Moreover, the process of interpreting data is always subject to a methodological frame. The meaning of data is inevitably based on context, motives, expectations, and actions of managers (Dourish & Gómez Cruz, 2018). When decision makers interpret big data, what they find depends on the instruments of data collection (sensors), the analytical tools and the questions they ask (methods). Not only the information (cues) that they extract from the present situations, but also their knowledge structures (frames) they acquire from their past experiences, are shaped by the instruments, sensors or tools they use. Their own values and desires influence their choices, therefore, models they build are opinions embedded in mathematics, and, despite the models' reputation for impartiality, reflect goals and ideology. After all, a key component of every model is its definition of success, i.e., what the model builder is trying to accomplish (O'neil, 2017). Patterns found within a data set are not inherently meaningful. There can be random correlations between variables and patterns within a data set, which have little or no causal significance, and they can result in serious ecological fallacies if interpreted that way (Kitchin, 2021).

In short, from a sensemaking perspective, big data represents an enactment of reality rather than an objective picture of reality. Data collection and processing is never removed from human design and bias (Crawford, 2013, O'neil, 2017). Therefore, "having the right data is usually better than having more data." (Borgman, 2015, p.2).

6.2 *Organizations Are Not Passive in Their Adoption or Use of Big Data*

The concept of *enactment* in the sensemaking perspective reminds us that "there is *not* some kind of monolithic, singular, fixed environment that exists detached from and external to the people" (Weick, 1995, p. 31). Rather, as part of the environment, people "act and create the materials that become the constraints and opportunities they face" (p. 31). From this perspective, big data is not an independent 'force of nature,' rather it is actively created by organizations, big and small: managers all too often forget this.

Another characteristic of sensemaking is that it begins with people, thus is grounded in identity construction (Weick, 1995). Specifically speaking, "Once I know who I am then I know what is out there. But the direction of causality flows just as often from the situation to a definition of self as it does the other way." (Weick, 1995, p. 20). What the environment or situation means is defined by who the sense maker becomes while dealing with it or what and who he represents (Weick, 1995). Thus, what big data means to us, is a function of the stories we tell ourselves about ourselves. The fact that sensemaking is self-referential suggests that self might be the text in need of interpretation, rather than the environment (Weick, 1995).

When we talk about our identities, we assume that identity originates from free choice: simply, we chose who we are (Richards & King, 2013). Yet critically, we have to be mindful of how our identity is *shaped* rather than *chosen* in the big data era. In his article, *How Netflix Is Turning Viewers into Puppets*, Andrew Leonard (2013) explains that "the companies that figure out how to generate intelligence from that data will know more about us than we know ourselves, and will be able to craft techniques that push us toward where they want us to go, rather than where we would go by ourselves if left to our own devices." Netflix uses big data shape users choices for greater profit, with little concern for the freedom or wellbeing of its viewers.

In *Social Physics*, Pentland (2014) outlines a vision to gather "the digital bread crumbs we all leave behind as we move through the world—call records, credit card transactions, and GPS location fixes" (p. 16) to predict people's behavior. In his view, big data can be used to avoid market crashes, ethnic violence, political stalemates, widespread corruption, and dangerous concentrations of power. However, to the individuals who are being tracked, such monitoring may be unacceptable, creepy, and ultimately stigmatizing (Markus, 2015): being labeled as a part of 'target' marketing, individuals are liable to discrimination (in housing, education, finance, or insurance) (Markus, 2015; Newell & Marabelli, 2015; Richards & King, 2013). Increasingly, people's choices and identity will be imposed by data processing organizations.

In all these accounts, from a sensemaking perspective, organizations are active creators of big data. Simply, big data is not "the inevitable consequence of a technological juggernaut with a life of its own entirely outside the social (world)" (Zuboff, 2015, p. 75).

6.3 *Strategizing is Driven by Plausibility Rather Than Accuracy*

From a sensemaking perspective, effective strategizing is driven by plausibility rather than accuracy (Weick, 1995). People typically think they are looking for something accurate because pursuing accuracy can sustain motivation (Weick et al., 2005). In fact, in strategic decision-making, "one thing an intelligent executive does not need is totally accurate perception" (Starbuck & Milliken, 1988, p. 40). This highlight another fallacy in the dominant view of big data era, namely that local accuracy and prediction trumps systemic understanding of the world.

In contrast, from sensemaking perspective, plausible reasoning is considered more important than accuracy of perception in managerial thinking. In plausible thinking, cogent ideas or understandings go beyond the directly observable (Isenberg, 1986). Plausible reasoning is not necessarily correct, but it fits the facts, though imperfectly at times. Moreover, it is based on incomplete information (Isenberg, 1986). Indeed, managers may benefit from inaccurate perception under certain conditions if they are able to overcome inertial tendencies and pursue goals that seem insurmountable when viewed 'objectively' (Sutcliffe, 1994). Consider Elon Musk's achievements with electric cars, dismissed at the outset by the entire auto industry.

As Weick (1995) puts it "what is necessary in sensemaking is a good story" rather than an accurate set of facts. In data-driven strategic decision making, although big data may claim to be exhaustive, it's still only a sample, influenced by the technology, platform, data ontology, and regulatory environment (Kitchin, 2021). Moreover, given a set of data, strategists will enact a variety of realities and struggle with competing interpretations of what had happened in the past, what is going on right now and what will be coming up in the future (Kaplan & Orlikowski, 2013). Managers have to developed plausible narratives rather than accurate views of the future to guide an organization in the face of uncertainty (Schryer, 1993). Thus, it is not whether big data can reveal a more accurate picture of consumers or markets, but whether the data is 'right' for strategists to produce 'actionable' intelligence that matters.

Of course, whether data is the 'right' data and whether the intelligence is 'actionable' are not determined by big data, but by the enactment of the reality of their users. As previously discussed, managers' preconceptions shape the nature of the strategic problems that they seek to address and the variables they consider important in their search for answers. As a result, an enacted environment is produced, which comprises 'real' objects -- such as marketing research questions and dataset, etc. These objects, however, are meaningless unless they are acted upon, since their meaning and content will vary. This enacted environment is "a map of if–then assertions in which actions are related outcomes" (Weick, 1988, p. 307) that in turn serve as expectations for future action and focus perception in such a way that these preconceived relationships will be supported.

The stories that managers tell about data, are more important than generating more data in the elusive pursuit of a more accurate picture of a changing reality: stories guide and motive – data does not (Weick, 1995). Indeed, even a mythical 'complete set of data' will not necessarily mean better stories to drive strategy. In fact, too much data can hinder strategists' productivity and decision-making by providing incidental findings that are confusing and misleading (Nease, 2016).

Advocates claim that that big data is truthful, and that meaning transcends context (Kitchin, 2021), this is impossible from a sensemaking perspective. This is because context is an 'ongoing situation' into which strategists are thrown and from which they have to extract the 'cues' (Weick, 1995; Winograd & Flores, 1986). The knowledge or mental structures that include rules and values must serve as the 'frame' in a sensemaking process to guide understanding (Gioia, 1986; Taylor & Crocker, 1981).

In conclusion, from a sensemaking perspective, effective strategizing is driven by plausible reasoning rather than accurate perceptions (Weick, 1995). The data set to be preferred in strategizing is the one that can produce a plausible narrative. It is far from obvious that "more trumps better" (Mayer-Schönberger & Cukier, 2013, p.39); indeed, more may sometimes be less (Bollier & Firestone, 2010; Crawford et al., 2014; Naimi & Westreich, 2014; Nease, 2016).

6.4 Big Data Generates a Retrospection of the Past Rather Than a Prediction of the Future

Predictive analytics comprise a variety of techniques that predict future outcomes based on historical and current data (Gandomi & Haider, 2015). However, from the sensemaking perspective, data aids a retrospective interpretation of what happened in the past, rather than a prediction of the future (Weick, 1995). Managers often overlook the fact that nature of customers and markets are dynamic and enacted. When marketers use big data to predict, for instance, what their customers will do in future, they make the implicit assumption that the future will be like the past, and that it will change in some predictable way. The assumption may be warranted in stable social and market contexts, however in times of change this assumption is highly misleading (Satell, 2015a).

Well documented in the sensemaking literature are the dangers of relying on short term memory at the expense of long term recollection (e.g. Hartshorne, 1962). Big data exacerbates this tendency by offering strategists vast quantities of recent data and a relative paucity of historical data (Chatfield, 2016). This focus on the exponential rise in short term data, coupled with the assumption that future events will closely resemble recent experience can be highly misleading. As a result, managers' reliance on big data is likely to result in poor strategizing.

A case in point is the discovery that Google's big data Flu Trends (GFT) is no longer accurate at predicting flu. Although researchers (e.g., Lazer et al., 2014) blame GFT's method and data, we rather highlight that the dominance of short term retrospection is a major reason why forecasting and strategic planning can be misleading if decoupled from the reflective action and long term memory (Weick, 1995).

In summary: from a sensemaking perspective, the basis upon which big data is being sold to managers, namely that data represents reality, that more data provides greater accuracy, and that data is inherently predictive, are unwarranted. Rather, sensemaking suggests that for strategic decision making, reality is enacted, plausibility of data will always trump accuracy, and that data can help retrospection only. In the next section, we consider how sensemaking perspective may help create alternative sustainable futures with big data.

7 How Can a Sensemaking Perspective Help Create Alternative Sustainable Futures with Big Data?

7.1 A Wake-Up Call

To summarize, a sensemaking perspective suggests that effective strategizing does not require nor produce an objective picture of reality, that strategizing is driven by plausibility rather than accuracy, and that big data generates a retrospection of the past rather than a prediction of the future. In other words, effective strategizing will be no better served by big data than by small data. Big data's potentially transformative power lies not so much in the characteristics of big data, on which its advocates concentrate, as it does in what big data's characteristics afford (Markus, 2015). Indeed, "[t]he myth and the tools mutually constitute each other, and the instruments of data gathering and analysis, too, act as agents that shape the social world" (Crawford, 2014).

More importantly, a sensemaking perspective reminds managers that big data is not the "inevitable consequence of a technological juggernaut with a life of its own entirely outside the social (world)" (Zuboff, 2015, p. 75). Rather, organizations are the creators of big data; to deny this is to succumb to the myth of the Big Other world (Zuboff, 2015); this latter narrative constitutes a new form of power that commodifies, controls, and affects behavior and daily experience in a way that gradually transforms human agency into automaticity. After all, it is organizations that act and create the materials that become the constraints and opportunities they face (Weick, 1995). We should realize that, big data is our tool, not our master. We gave them power, and we can take that power away (O'neil, 2017).

Although all technologies have 'dual effects' which is not inherently problematic (Markus, 2014), "the consequences of technology are rarely distributed evenly or equitably within or across stakeholder groups" (Markus, 2015, p. 58). For instance, whereas some businesses may benefit from using big data and algorithms, others may suffer. Facts show that big data does not benefit every company. The real concern is that the lion's share of big data benefits could go to a few large corporations, while individual citizens could suffer significant harm (Markus, 2015). In general, data is owned and used privately to profit and influence, while the public is kept out of the process and told to behave well and trust the algorithm (O'neil, 2017). According to Zuboff (2019)'s projection, people are deceived and ignorant of the full consequences of surveillance capitalism, which is a form of data capitalism that derives value and profit through datafication and dataveillance of individuals such as consumers and worker. Since the social evolution isn't happening fast enough, we are facing a new kind of sovereign power from the Big Other to be unwittingly changed from human agency into automaticity. When all the behavior of persons and things are monitored and modified for profit and control, there will be no individuals. "Only the world-spanning organism and all the tiniest elements within it" (Zuboff, 2015, p.85) exist. Then, who and what will organizations become? How and by whom the profits and the power will be enjoyed?

7.2 *An Inescapable Responsibility*

A genuine sustainable future with big data, has as its goal *full* sustainability, rather than simply *slowing* the destruction of nature and society (Willard & Hitchcock, 2015). This is an inescapable responsibility for each organization in this society, regardless its size or nature. While making sense of big data from a sensemaking perspective, organizations are urged to recognize the role that they play in the creation and evolution of the big data era, so as not to let surveillance projects become institutionalized into society. Managers need to rethink how they view and use big data, and establish new precedents and laws to promote sustainability (Markus, 2015; Richards & King, 2014; Zuboff, 2015, 2019). As the Netflix documentary *The Social Dilemma* advocates, organizations and individuals can help shape how technology is designed, regulated and used. In a time when technology has become integral to our lives, it is more important than ever that we examine the role that big data plays in our lives and realign it with the interests of people and the environment, not simply profits.

Organizations should carefully consider their investment in big data. On the one hand, big data is, after all, not necessarily superior to small data, and it is not strategically inevitable. More than that, the creation of meaning in sensemaking is an attentional process, in which the attention is directed backward from a specific here and now (Weick, 1995). Yet, in an era of bigger and bigger data, the availability of time and attention from strategists is limited. Therefore, what strategists choose *not* to know, matters just as much as what they chose to know. On the other hand, the retrospective sensemaking of big data tells us that investment in big data contributes to demands for cloud services, which have already outpaced sustainable growth and created harms arising from computing research practices, such as the collection of huge data sets compiled from publicly accessible social media sites (Fiesler, 2021). Monserrate (2022) spells out the dangers that lie ahead if the Cloud is allowed to perpetually expand, unchecked by governments or publics. He also depicts a world in which tech companies continue to grow—seeking profits and remaining largely unregulated—until the cumulative effects of their industry impact global warming to such an extent that governments and publics have no choice but to intervene, albeit too late.

Consequently, when considering big data initiatives, one caveat for organizations is that companies cannot pursue short-term profitability at the expense of environmental impact, economic equity, social democracy and individual freedom. After all, organizations consist of individual employees, who will have no escape from the unsustainable Big Other world. Rather, it is incumbent upon organizations to explore and advocate a legal, transparent, and ethical (big) data practice.

In order to use big data ethically, organizations must re-evaluate their metrics of success, which is often profit, efficiency, or default rates (O'neil, 2017). Whether a transaction is successful depends on what organizations count. For giant web firms, the click on the ad brings in a quarter, fifty cents, or even a dollar or two, which is used to measure success. Therefore, the system is deemed to be functioning efficiently. From society's perspective, a simple search for government services often turns poor people into targets, leading many to take out high-interest loans and receive false promises (debt.org). Lead aggregators lead them into needless transactions, leaving many of them with larger deficits and more dependent on public assistance. Despite the system's efficiency in producing revenue for search engines, lead aggregators and marketers, it operates as a leech on the economy.

Another example of corrupting metrics the maximization of 'time on site' through techniques such as A/B testing which results in addictive behavior by users (Davidowitz, 2018). Through such testing, Facebook, for example, may figure out what particular color of button and font get people to come back to their site more often. Then they change the button to that color and text to that font. They may also find out that emailing people at a certain time gets them coming back to their site more often, and they then follow so. Consequently, Facebook becomes a site optimized to maximize how much time people spend on Facebook. Similarly, despite the system's efficiency in maximizing the frequency of user's visit, Facebook operates as a leech on its users, breaking down users' self-control.

Sustainability thinking calls for organizations to understand all material, social and environmental impacts of the business, establish metrics to measure their success in managing those impacts while succeeding economically and scan the external environment constantly for threats and opportunities (Willard & Hitchcock, 2015). Therefore, a regulatory system should be set up to measure hidden costs by incorporating a host of values. It is necessary to impose human values on data algorithms, even at the cost of efficiency, even though concepts such as fairness and common good reside only in the human mind and can't be quantified.

In addition, O'neil (2017) pointed out that we should start building a regulatory framework to hold organization's data and algorithms accountable for the long term. In the same way that chemical companies must demonstrate they don't damage rivers and watersheds around them, companies that develop and deploy big data need to accept responsibility for their influence and develop evidence that they are not causing harm. They should be required to audit their data and algorithms regularly for legality and fairness. Of course, people with the skills to build data and algorithm auditing initiatives are needed. Academic support for these initiatives is crucial. Their research tools can replicate the immense scale of models and retrieve data sets large enough to reveal the imbalances and injustice embedded in the models. In addition, they can build crowdsourcing campaigns to collect information about the messages people across the society receive from advertisers and politicians. This could illuminate the practices and strategies of micro-targeting campaigns.

Organizations can pro-actively spark and facilitate conversations about the harms of exploitative tech and what to do about it. In addition, they can grow coalition of business and consumers who are, say, boycotting their use of ads on social media until they stop valuing profits over hate, bigotry and disinformation. They can call for a ban on surveillance advertising—the toxic business model depicted in *The Social Dilemma*. While the societal awareness of the dark side of exploitative tech is raised, the public learns more about big data's inner workings and its prejudices. They will then demand more accountability from data and algorithm, while being more motivated to realign their relationship with technology as a tool for connection. For example, they will be mindful of data as well as the exploitative tech used to collect data. They will be able to be determined to take back control with the 7-day Social Media Reboot featuring tips from the experts featured in *The Social Dilemma*. They also will voluntarily help build and advocate for a more humane internet, and so on so forth.

In terms of governmental agencies, they play a powerful regulatory role and can start to adapt and then enforce the laws that are already on the books. Examples are used to illustrate this point in O'neil (2017)'s book. The Fair Credit Reporting Act (FCRA) and the Equal Credit Opportunity Act (ECOA) were meant to ensure fairness in credit scoring. The FCRA guarantees that a consumer can see the data going into their score and correct any errors, and the ECOA prohibits linking race or gender to a person's score. The regulations should be updated to avoid ignoring consumer complaints and explicitly prohibit credit-scoring companies from using zip codes as proxy measures of race. Consumers should have the right to know what information is used to calculate their credit score and to be alerted when it is being used to judge. Whenever there is an error, consumers shall be able to challenge and correct it. Another example is that, big data personality tests, health scores and reputation scores should not be able to sneak around the law to violate the protection of the Americans with Disabilities Act (ADA). On the other hand, government agencies shall make Corporate pledges enforceable to reduce harms to either the environment or society. Given the companies' financial ties to the fossil fuel industry and failure to meet the deadlines of previous pledges to reduce carbon emissions or other kinds of waste, scholars warn against entrusting "Big Tech" with its own regulation (Jardim, 2020).

7.3 Cultivation of 'Experiment for Learning' Communities

As action is a key sensemaking tool it is often wiser to begin with, and learn from, small experiments before broadening the action to drive change across a larger system (Ancona, 2012). Indeed, experiments are a form of 'action', specifically a form of 'acting thinkingly,' whereby managers 'simultaneously' interpret their knowledge with trusted frameworks, yet "mistrust those frameworks by testing new frameworks and new interpretations" (Weick et al., 2005, p. 412). People learn about situations by acting in them and then seeing what happens (Weick, 1985).

Big data makes randomized online experiments, which can find truly causal effects, much easier to conduct. However, the one so-called advantage of "you don't even have to tell users they are part of an experiment" (Davidowitz, 2018, p. 210), is manifestly unethical. What we advocate is enabling 'experimenting for learning' communities. Since companies learn only when individual skills and insights become embodied in organizational routines, practices, and beliefs (Attewell, 1992). Given information systems can change the fabric of social epistemology and the backdrop against which organizations construct, organize, store, distribute, and apply what they learn (Pentland, 1995), companies should focus their information systems on enabling experimenting for learning communities. In this kind of community, not only managers, but employees, customers and other stakeholders can use the company's data and their own knowledge to improve the firm's strategic performance.

The successful business strategy of 'listening to employees' at Best Buy (e.g. Tucker, 2010) presents a rubric for this principle. Years ago, in order to reduce employee turnover and raise their engagement and performances, Best Buy began experimenting with social networking technologies centered upon the company's intranet to create a deeper conversation with their employees across the United States and other countries in the world. When this strategy was activated, their employee turnover rate was 81% (Tucker, 2010). More importantly, this strategy was initiated by a mid-level marketing manager, Jennifer Rock, after she noticed that stores with high employee turnover rates and low employee engagement level suffered from poor sales revenue, while those with low turnover and high engagement showed strong sales performance. Through conducting weekly online polls of employees, setting up wikis for people with common interests to brainstorm together and organizing many other social media activities, Best Buy becomes skilled at communicating with its employees and connect employees with each other (Tucker, 2010). Ultimately, by leveraging networked communities in various forms Best Buy benefits greatly from both the loyalty and creativity of their employees and other stakeholders.

In fact, today there are many different types of social media that are used to support collaborative knowledge work, both within the firm and between the firm and its various stakeholders (Newell, 2015). Companies therefore should deploy these social media to foster flexible experiment for learning communities to further assist strategic sensemaking.

7.4 *Incubation of Innovation*

According to the sensemaking perspective (Weick, 1995), when strategists extract cues from the environment that triggers a drive to make sense of the situation, they use frames, the knowledge or mental structures that include rules and values, as a guide to understanding. When they create a relation between frames and cues, they create meaning (Miles, 2012).

On the one hand, the strategizing process in organizations is dominated by retrospective sensemaking, in which strategists introduce new constructs into the collective cognitive map of organization (Daft & Weick, 1984). They then put cognitive theories into action (Argyris & Schon, 1978; Hedberg, 1981). This new response or action based on the interpretation constitutes organization learning (Argyris & Schon, 1978). In so doing, strategists keep constructing and reconstructing the connections among their views of the past, present and future (Kaplan & Orlikowski, 2013). On the other hand, the dominance of retrospect in sensemaking is a major reason why forecasting, contingency planning, strategic planning and other probes into the future are often found misleading if they are decoupled from the reflective action (Weick, 1995). In a nutshell, their sensemaking is fundamentally about the new interpretation and understanding of the past, present and future, based on the newly emergent situation, though the distinctions between the past, the present and the future situations are too often to be ignored by strategists.

From the sensemaking perspective, data aids a retrospective interpretation of what happened in the past, rather than a prediction of the future. Therefore, the big data era is fundamentally different not for how much information it allows managers to collect for accuracy or prediction, but how it allows them to engineer systems to make new discoveries while making sense of the events and issues (Satell, 2015a). With that being said, the new paradigm of scientific method in an age of big data seeks to incorporate a mode of induction into the research design, although explanation through induction is not the intended goal as it is with empiricism. Instead, it forms a new mode of hypothesis generation before employing a deductive approach. In other words, it uses guided knowledge discovery techniques to identify potential questions (hypotheses) that deserve further examination and testing. Any relationships revealed within the data do not then arise from nowhere and nor do they simply speak for themselves. The insights are not the end-point of an investigation, but the basis for the formulation of new hypotheses. Put it differently, it is a reconfigured version of the traditional scientific method, providing a new way in which to build theory (Kitchin, 2021).

Recalling the legends of innovative marketers, such as Leo Burnett and Steve Jobs, we easily understand why innovation is important at any time. Big data should not be used to replace human creativity, but to inspire creative work or creative thinking (Elliott, 2014). This is why Unilever builds media labs in key markets that provide a platform for innovation, co-creation and incubation of new technologies in marketing programs (Unilever.com). This is also why it is promising for BloomReach to integrate technology and human intuition in its new application to allow marketers to do their best to imagine and test new possibilities. As its marketing manager, Joelle Kaufman, says "A crazy idea isn't so crazy when you can calculate its effect without risking failure in the market." (Satell, 2014).

In addition, data analytics might also help marketers to re-engineer their ways of serving the customer. For example, the website of Neiman Marcus, does not serve their customers by predicting what its customers' preferences are, rather, the system puts its customers in control of their experience and assist them as them shop, by intuitively making suggestions much like a salesperson would do in the store (Satell, 2015b).

8 Conclusion

Over the last decade or so, the media hype around big data has created such a techno-utopia view of big data that it has driven companies to spend huge sums of money on data production and processing, in the hope of uncovering hidden patterns and generating deep insights (O'neil, 2017). Meanwhile, a heated debate over the negative social and environmental impact of big data has emerged.

Indeed, some researchers (e.g., Newell & Marabelli, 2015, Markus, 2015, Zuboff, 2015, O'neil, 2017) have voiced their concerns over the long-term impact of unparalleled tracking and extracting 'everydayness' (Constantiou & Kallinikos, 2015, p. 53) on individuals and wider society. This chapter brings a "sensemaking" (Weick, 1995) perspective to big data and its use in organizations, as strategic decision making is fundamentally a sensemaking process (Kaplan & Orlikowski, 2013; Weick, 1995).

A sensemaking perspective differs from the popular view of big data, and suggests that the basis upon which big data is being sold to managers, namely that big data is an inescapable trend, that data represents reality, that more data provides greater accuracy and that the data is inherently predictive, is unwarranted. Rather, sensemaking suggests that for strategic decision making, big data is created by organizations, it represents an enactment of reality, plausibility of data always trumps accuracy, and big data can only help a reinterpretation of the past. Examples are cited to illustrate these points.

Based on this sensemaking critique, we further discuss how a sensemaking perspective can help organizations to create alternative sustainable futures with big data. The sensemaking perspective suggests that big data's potentially transformative power lies not so much in the characteristics of big data, on which its advocates concentrate, as it does in what big data's characteristics afford (Markus, 2015). Managers should be skeptical of populist rosy mythology of big data and adopt a more sophisticate (and strategically insightful) sensemaking perspective.

We call for a more mindful view of big data. Also, we call for managers to actively curtail institutionalized surveillance projects (Zuboff, 2015). Finally, we call for a legal, transparent, and ethical (big) data practice with focuses on cultivating experimenting for learning communities and incubating innovations among individuals (their customers and employees).

This chapter makes two contributions to our understanding of big data. The first contribution is to offer a theoretical perspective to reinterpret the role of big data in strategic decision making, as well as the role organizations play in creating the big data phenomena. A sensemaking approach brings us return to the nature of strategic decision making activities and reveals what effective strategizing demands and what big data can and cannot deliver.

Second, this chapter follows the call for new critical approaches to big data (Crawford et al., 2014, O'neil, 2017) and the research on the longer term impact of big data on individuals and wider society (Monserrate, 2022; Newell & Marabelli, 2015). Therefore, it contributes to this growing critical conversation. The chapter brings a nuanced and grounded theoretical analysis to engage big data practices, tools, and rhetorics directly and ask how they function, how they build interpretations, and how they could be different, more ethical, and more historically aware.

References

Ancona, D. (2012). Sensemaking: Framing and acting in the unknown. In S. Snook, N. Nohria, & R. Khurana (Eds.), *The handbook for teaching leadership: Knowing, doing, and being* (pp. 3–21). Sage.

Anderson, C. (2008, June 23). *The end of theory: The data deluge makes the scientific method obsolete*. Wired magazine. Retrieved April 28, 2023, from https://www.wired.com/2008/06/pb-theory/

Argyris, C., & Schon, D. A. (1978). *Organizational learning: A theory of acton perspective*. Addison-Wesley.

Attewell, P. (1992). Technology diffusion and organizational learning: The case of business computing. *Organization Science, 3*(1), 1–19.

Becke, G. (2013). *Mindful change in times of permanent reorganization: Organizational, institutional and sustainability perspectives*. Springer Science & Business Media.

Bollier, D., & Firestone, C. M. (2010). *The promise and peril of big data*. Aspen Institute.

Borgman, C. L. (2015). *Big data, little data, no data: Scholarship in the networked world*. MIT Press.

Boyd, D., & Crawford, K. (2012). Critical questions for big data: Provocations for a cultural, technological, and scholarly phenomenon. *Information, Communication & Society, 15*(5), 662–679.

Brown, C. (2021, March 23). *Big data is dead: Long live smart data*. Forbes. Retrieved April 28, 2023, from https://www.forbes.com/sites/forbestechcouncil/2021/03/23/big-data-is-dead-long-live-smart-data/?sh=6acdec22bc39

Chatfield, T. (2016, June 4). *The trouble with big data? It is called "recency bias"*. BBC. Retrieved April 28, 2023, from http://www.bbc.com/future/story/20160605-the-trouble-with-big-data-its-called-the-recency-bias

Chen, H., Chiang, R. H., & Storey, V. C. (2012). Business intelligence and analytics: From big data to big impact. *MIS Quarterly, 36*(4), 1165–1188.

Constantiou, I. D., & Kallinikos, J. (2015). New games, new rules: Big data and the changing context of strategy. *Journal of Information Technology, 30*(1), 44–57.

Crawford, K. (2013, April 1). *The hidden biases in big data*. Harvard Business Review. Retrieved April 28, 2023, from https://hbr.org/2013/04/the-hidden-biases-in-big-data

Crawford, K. (2014, May 30). The anxieties of big data. *The New Inquiry*. Retrieved April 28, 2023, from https://thenewinquiry.com/the-anxieties-of-big-data/

Crawford, K., Gray, M. L., & Miltner, K. (2014). Critiquing big data: Politics, ethics, epistemology. *International Journal of Communication, 8*, 1663–1672.
Daft, R. L., & Weick, K. E. (1984). Toward a model of organizations as interpretation systems. *Academy of Management Review, 9*(2), 284–295.
Davenport, T.H., Barth, P. and Bean, R. (2012, July 30). *How big data is different*. MIT Sloan Management Review. Retrieved April 28, 2023, from https://sloanreview.mit.edu/article/how-big-data-is-different/
Davidowitz, S. S. (2018). *Everybody lies: Big data, new data, and what the internet can tell us about who we really are.* Arper Collins.
Debt.org. *What is predatory lending*? Retrieved April 28, 2023, from https://www.debt.org/credit/predatory-lending/#:~:text=Predatory%20lenders%20typically%20target%20minorities,who%20recently%20lost%20their%20jobs.
Dourish, P., & Gómez Cruz, E. (2018). Datafication and data fiction: Narrating data and narrating with data. *Big Data & Society, 5*(2), 1–10.
Elliott, S. (2014, October 21). At Ogilvy, new unit will mine data. *The New York Times*. Retrieved April 28, 2023, from https://www.nytimes.com/2014/10/21/business/media/at-ogilvy-new-unit-will-mine-data-.html
Feroz, A. K., Zo, H., & Chiravuri, A. (2021). Digital transformation and environmental sustainability: A review and research agenda. *Sustainability, 13*(3), 1530. https://doi.org/10.3390/su13031530
Fiesler, C. (2021). Innovating like an optimist, preparing like a pessimist: Ethical speculation and the legal imagination. *Colorado Technology Law Journal, 19*(1), 1–18.
Gandomi, A., & Haider, M. (2015). Beyond the hype: Big data concepts, methods, and analytics. *International Journal of Information Management, 35*(2), 137–144.
Gioia, D. A. (1986). Symbols, Scripts, and Sensemaking Creating meaning in the organizational experience. In H. P. Sims & D. A. Gioia (Eds.), *The thinking organization* (pp. 49–74). Jossey-Bass.
Hartshorne, C. (1962). Mind as memory and creative love. In J. M. Scher (Ed.), *Theorists of the mind* (pp. 440–463). Free Press.
Hedberg, B. (1981). How organizations learn and unlearn. *Handbook of Organizational Design, 1*, 3–27.
Hintz, A., Dencik, L., & Wahl-Jorgensen, K. (2018). *Digital citizenship in a datafied society*. John Wiley & Sons.
Isenberg, D. J. (1986). The structure and process of understanding: Implications for managerial action. In H. P. Sims & D. A. Gioia (Eds.), *The thinking organization* (pp. 238–262). Jossey-Bass.
Jardim, E. (2020, January 27). *Microsoft, Google, Amazon: Who's the biggest climate hypocrite?* Greenpeace. Retrieved April 28, 2023, from https://www.greenpeace.org/usa/microsoft-google-amazon-energy-oil-ai-climate-hypocrite/
Jarzabkowski, P. (2004). Strategy as practice: Recursiveness, adaptation, and practices-in-use. *Organization Studies, 25*(4), 529–560.
Jarzabkowski, P., Balogun, J., & Seidl, D. (2007). Strategizing: The challenges of a practice perspective. *Human Relations, 60*(1), 5–27.
Johnson, G., Melin, L., & Whittington, R. (2003). Micro strategy and strategizing: Towards an activity-based view. *Journal of Management Studies, 40*(1), 3–22.
Kaplan, S., & Orlikowski, W. J. (2013). Temporal work in strategy making. *Organization Science, 24*(4), 965–995.
Kitchin, R. (2021). *The data revolution: A critical analysis of big data, open data and data infrastructures*. Sage.
Kitchens, B., Dobolyi, D., Li, J., & Abbasi, A. (2018). Advanced customer analytics: Strategic value through integration of relationship-oriented big data. *Journal of Management Information Systems, 35*(2), 540–574.
LaValle, S., Lesser, E., Shockley, R., Hopkins, M. S., & Kruschwitz, N. (2011). Big data, analytics and the path from insights to value. *MIT Sloan Management Review, 52*(2), 21.

Lazer, D., Kennedy, R., King, G., & Vespignani, A. (2014). The parable of Google flu: Traps in big data analysis. *Science, 343*(6176), 1203–1205.

Leonard, A. (2013). *How Netflix is turning viewers into puppets.* Salon.com. Retrieved April 28, 2023, from https://www.salon.com/2013/02/01/how_netflix_is_turning_viewers_into_puppets/

Markus, M. L. (2014). Information technology and organizational structure. In H. Topi & A. Tucker (Eds.), *Computing handbook* (pp. 67–71). Chapman and Hall/CRC.

Markus, M. L. (2015). New games, new rules, new scoreboards: The potential consequences of big data. *Journal of Information Technology, 30*(1), 58–59.

Mayer-Schönberger, V., & Cukier, K., (2013). *Big data: A revolution that will transform how we live, work, and think.* Houghton Mifflin Harcourt.

McAfee, A., Brynjolfsson, E., Davenport, T. H., Patil, D. J., & Barton, D. (2012). Big data: The management revolution. *Harvard Business Review, 90*(10), 60–68.

Miles, J. A. (2012). *Management and organization theory: A Jossey-Bass reader* (Vol. 9). John Wiley & Sons.

Monserrate, S. G. (2022). The cloud is material: On the environmental impacts of computation and data storage. *MIT case studies in social and ethical responsibilities of computing,* Winter 2022 (January). https://doi.org/10.21428/2c646de5.031d4553

Naimi, A. I., & Westreich, D. J.(2014). Big data: A revolution that will transform how we live, work, and think. *American Journal of Epidemiology, 179*(9), 1143–1144.

Nease, B. (2016, June, 16). *How too much data can hurt our productivity and decision-making.* Fastcompany. Retrieved April 28, 2023, from https://www.fastcompany.com/3060945/how-too-much-data-can-hurt-our-productivity-and-decision-making

Newell, S. (2015). Managing knowledge and managing knowledge work: What we know and what the future holds. *Journal of Information Technology, 30*(1), 1–17.

Newell, S., & Marabelli, M. (2015). Strategic opportunities (and challenges) of algorithmic decision-making: A call for action on the long-term societal effects of 'datification.' *The Journal of Strategic Information Systems, 24*(1), 3–14.

Newman, J. (2009, December 11). *Google's Schmidt roasted for privacy comments.* PC World. Retrieved April 28, 2023, from https://www.pcworld.com/article/515472/googles_schmidt_roasted_for_privacy_comments.html#:~:text=%E2%80%9CIf%20you%20have%20something%20that,all%20subject%20in%20the%20United

O'neil, C. (2017). *Weapons of math destruction: How big data increases inequality and threatens democracy.* Crown.

Orlowski, J., & Rhodes, L. (2020). *The social dilemma [Documentary].* Netflix.

Pentland, A. (2014). *Social physics: How good ideas spread-the lessons from a new science.* Penguin.

Pentland, B. T. (1995). Information systems and organizational learning: The social epistemology of organizational knowledge systems. *Accounting, Management and Information Technologies, 5*(1), 1–21.

Prensky, M. (2009). H. sapiens digital: From digital immigrants and digital natives to digital wisdom. *Innovate: Journal of Online Education,* 5(3).

Puschmann, C., & Burgess, J. (2014). Big data, big questions|metaphors of big data. *International Journal of Communication, 8,* 20.

Raut, R. D., Mangla, S. K., Narwane, V. S., Gardas, B. B., Priyadarshinee, P., & Narkhede, B. E. (2019). Linking big data analytics and operational sustainability practices for sustainable business management. *Journal of Cleaner Production, 224,* 10–24.

Rayaprolu, A. (2023, Feburary 27). *How much data is created every day in 2023*? Techjury. Retrieved April 28, 2023, from https://techjury.net/blog/how-much-data-is-created-every-day/#gref

Richards, N. M., & King, J. H. (2013). Three paradoxes of big data. *Stanford Law Review Online, 66,* 41.

Richards, N. M., & King, J. H. (2014). Big data ethics. *Wake Forest Law Review, 49,* 393.

Rust, R. T., & Huang, M. H. (2014). The service revolution and the transformation of marketing science. *Marketing Science, 33*(2), 206–221.

Salminen, V., Ruohomaa, H., & Kantola, J. (2017). Digitalization and big data supporting responsible business co-evolution. In *Advances in human factors, business management, training and education: Proceedings of the AHFE 2016 international conference on human factors, business management and society* (pp. 1055–1067). Springer International Publishing.

Satell, G. (2014, October 12). *The future of marketing combines big data with human intuition.* Forbes. Retrieved April 28, 2023, from https://www.forbes.com/sites/gregsatell/2014/10/12/the-future-of-marketing-combines-big-data-with-human-intuition/?sh=4e4e498d2331

Satell, G. (2015a, November 6). *Marketers need to shift from crafting messages to creating experiences.* Forbes. Retrieved April 28, 2023, from http://www.forbes.com/sites/gregsatell/2015/11/16/marketers-need-to-shift-from-crafting-messages-to-creating-experiences/

Satell, G. (2015b, October 12). *Marketers need to drastically rethink the customer decision journey.* Forbes. Retrieved April 28, 2023, from https://www.forbes.com/sites/gregsatell/2015/10/12/marketers-need-to-drastically-rethink-the-customer-decision-journey/?sh=33129202260a

Sattiraju, N. (2020, April 20). *The secret cost of google's data centers: Billions of gallons of water to cool servers.* Bloomberg. Retrieved April 28, 2023, from https://time.com/5814276/google-data-centers-water/

Schadt, E. E., Linderman, M. D., Sorenson, J., Lee, L., & Nolan, G. P. (2010). Computational solutions to large-scale data management and analysis. *Nature Reviews Genetics, 11*(9), 647–657.

Schryer, C. F. (1993). Records as Genre. *Written Communication, 10*(2), 200–234.

Siegel, E. (2013). *Predictive analytics: The power to predict who will click, buy, lie, or die.* John Wiley & Sons.

Starbuck, W., & Milliken, F. (1988). Executives' perceptual filters: What they notice and how they make sense. *The Executive Effect* (pp. 35–65). JAI Press.

Sutcliffe, K. M. (1994). What executives notice: Accurate perceptions in top management teams. *Academy of Management Journal, 37*(5), 1360–1378.

Taylor, S. E., & Crocker, J. (1981). Schematic bases of social information processing. *Social Cognition: THe Ontario Symposium, 1*, 89–134.

Tucker, R. B. (2010). *Listening to employees is a Best Buy.* Retrieved December 22, 2015, from http://www.business-strategy-innovation.com/2010/03/listening-to-employees-is-best-buy.html

Unilever.com. *Innovating boldly for people and planet.* Retrieved April 28, 2023, from https://www.unilever.com/brands/innovation/

Varian, H. R. (2010). Computer mediated transactions. *The American Economic Review, 100*(2), 1–10.

Varian, H. R. (2014). Beyond big data. *Business Economics, 49*(1), 27–31.

Weick, K. E. (1985). Chaos & Cosmos: sense & nonsense in electronic contexts. *Organizational Dynamics, 14*(2).

Weick, K. E. (1988). Enacted sensemaking in crisis situations. *Journal of Management Studies, 25*(4).

Weick, K. E. (1993). The collapse of sensemaking in organizations: The Mann Gulch disaster. *Administrative Science Quarterly, 38*(4), 628–652.

Weick, K. E. (1995). *Sensemaking in organizations* (Vol. 3). Sage.

Weick, K. E., Sutcliffe, K. M., & Obstfeld, D. (2005). Organizing and the process of sensemaking. *Organization Science, 16*(4), 409–421.

White House. (2014). *Big data: Seizing opportunities, preserving values.* Exceutive Office of the President. Retrieved April 28, 2023, from https://newsroom.unl.edu/announce/bigdata/3919/21901

Whittington, R. (2006). Completing the practice turn in strategy research. *Organization Studies, 27*(5), 613–634.

Willard, M., & Hitchcock, D. (2015). *The business guide to sustainability: Practical strategies and tools for organizations.* Taylorfrancis.

Winograd, T., & Flores, F. (1986). *Understanding computers and cognition: A new foundation for design.* Intellect Books.

Woerner, S., & Wixom, B. H. (2015). Big data: Extending the business strategy toolbox. *Journal of Information Technology, 30*(1), 60–62.

Zuboff, S. (2015). Big other: Surveillance capitalism and the prospects of an information civilization. *Journal of Information Technology, 30*(1), 75–89.

Zuboff, S. (2019). *The age of surveillance capitalism: The fight for a human future at the new frontier of power: Barack Obama's books of 2019*. Profile books.

Preserving the Past, Building the Future: The Role of Adaptive Heritage Reuse in Achieving SDGs Through Tourism

Ahmad Mohammed, Nagwa Zoair, Marwa Abdel-Jalil, and Ayman Abdel-Hakim

Abstract Cultural heritage is recognized as a crucial element in building a sustainable environment that contributes to sustainable economic growth. Adaptive heritage reuse (AHR) is seen not only as a means to safeguard and maintain heritage, but also as a driver for achieving sustainable development goals (SDGs) and promoting sustainable economic growth. However, AHR faces several challenges, including inflexible heritage legislation, lack of clear definitions, financial risks, and the complexity of heritage systems. Despite these challenges, AHR holds great potential for driving sustainable economic growth and SDGs. AHR has been increasingly adopted in the tourism and hospitality sectors in both developed and developing countries, but research in this area is still in its infancy.

This chapter serves to provide a comprehensive understanding of adaptive heritage reuse (AHR) in the context of achieving SDGs. To achieve this, the chapter begins by defining AHR and illustrating its criteria and strategies for heritage buildings. In addition, it presents the drivers and barriers for AHR to SDGs. Furthermore, it explores AHR concept and implementations in the tourism industry through a range

A. Mohammed (✉)
Department of Archaeology, Durham University, Durham, UK
e-mail: ahmad.a.mohammed@durham.ac.uk

A. Mohammed · N. Zoair · M. Abdel-Jalil · A. Abdel-Hakim
Faculty of Tourism and Hotels, Fayoum University, Fayoum, Egypt
e-mail: Nagwa.Zouair@ukf.ac.ae

M. Abdel-Jalil
e-mail: mam32@fayoum.edu.eg

A. Abdel-Hakim
e-mail: a.abdelhakim@ut.edu.sa

N. Zoair
Department of History, College of Art, Science, and IT, University of Khorfkan, Khor Fakkan, UAE

A. Abdel-Hakim
Tourism and Hospitality Management Department, College of Tourism and Hospitality, University of Tabuk, Tabuk, Saudi Arabia

W. Leal Filho and V. Kuzmanović (eds.), *Sustainable Development Seen Through the Lenses of Ethnoeconomics and the Circular Economy*,
https://doi.org/10.1007/978-3-031-72676-7_8

of case studies with different reuse purposes and SDG adaptations. By analysing these case studies, it provides insights into the opportunities and challenges that arise from the adoption of AHR in the tourism industry. Finally, it concludes with extents of AHR implications in tourism industry, highlights future research avenues, and contribute to a better understanding of the potential benefits of AHR in achieving SDGs.

Keywords Adaptive Heritage Reuse (AHR) · SDGs · Sustainable economy · Cultural heritage · Circular economy

1 Adaptive Reuse

Re-Using ancient buildings is a phenomenon that remotes to ancient civilisations. Re-utilisation of ancient temples, tombs, houses…etc., is frequently attested in ancient Egyptian, Phoenician, Babylonian, and Greek civilisations. In Egypt, some of these monuments were remodelled to be suitable to new purposes; as attested in Phila temple, where it was used as a church; walls were plastered and covered by Christian symbols. Other structures were left intact, except for building another structure in its buffer zone; for example, Luxor temple, where a mosque and church were constructed within the temple and its buffer zone. Others were used as dwelling spaces which caused their degradation and destruction.

During the eighteenth century, many ancient monuments in France were sold and transformed into industrial and military zones for economic and financial reasons, consequently leading to their demolition (Plevoets & Van Cleempoel, 2013). The nineteenth century which witnessed some movement to preserve the ancient monuments could be the starting point of what is called 'adaptive reuse'. In France, a restoration movement was led by Eugène Emmanuel (1814–1879), while in England, a conservation movement was held by John Ruskin (1819–1900) and his pupil William Morris (1834–1896) (Plevoets & Van Cleempoel, 2011).

In Egypt, the nineteenth century, is considered the century of reviving, restoring, and conserving ancient monuments The Khedive of Egypt Tawfik (1825–1929) established the 'committee for Arabian antiquities conservation' in 1881, which restored and preserved the Islamic and Coptic monuments (Volait, 2012). This committee undertook many restoration activities, especially during the reign of Khedive Abbas Hilmi II. Their activities varied from strict preservation to some monuments by reinforcing, repairing, or cleaning existing structures. Other monuments were restored by reconstructing the monument to varying extents, which could make them usable again for the community as mosques and churches.

After World War I, the need to restore the demolished building and cities concluded with the adaption of the Athens Charter in 1931, the first document concerning the preservation of the building. With the growing concern of the environment, the concept of adaptive reuse of old buildings has been introduced to the architectural and heritage context during 1960th and 1970th (Cantell, 2005). During that period, there were some attempts to revive some old industrial buildings; the Ghirardelli Square in San Francisco was the most significant example.

Since Venice charter in 1964, Heritage scope continued to be broadened until recently, as it has been internationally agreed to include 'intangible' and 'tangible', and 'environment'. However, heritage definition is still not standardized internationally, which lead to ambiguous definitions for the 'Adaptive heritage reuse (AHR)' concept (Ahmad, 2006). It is worth mentioning that AHR is also known as 'remodelling', 'retrofitting', 'conversion', 'adaptation', 'reworking', 'rehabilitation' or 'refurbishment' (Brooker & Stone, 2004; Giebeler et al., 2009).

Adaptive reuse refers to the process of re-using a structure in a new manner for different purposes (Alikhani, 2009), a strategy to revitalise and sustain a place, building or urban environment (Aytac et al., 2016). The process of remodelled old buildings for new uses (Rodrigues & Freire, 2017). Adaptive reuse is any intervention to change its capacity, function, or performance to adjust, reuse or upgrade a building to suit new conditions or requirements (Yung & Chan, 2012). These definitions stressed the economic, social, and environmental dimensions of adaptive reuse and its role in sustaining the building and its functionality in upgrading the surrounding community.

The definition becomes more complex when it concerns reusing heritage buildings for their nature and importance; reusing a historic building should have minimum impact on the heritage significance of the building and its setting (Alikhani, 2009; Arfa et al., 2022). Keeping its architectural and artistic characteristics and involving in the community and environmental sustainability is the ultimate goal for reusing such buildings. UNESCO's definition of Adaptive reuse of heritage buildings highlighted the value of preservation while using them in the present to transfer them to the future.

The ICOMOS Burra Charter indicates that the Adaptive reuse of heritage buildings is a strategy to enhance its present and future profitability by sustaining its heritage value (Truscott, 2014). The significant importance of preserving the value of adaptive reuse of heritage buildings and involving its use in sustainable development provides the concept of green adaptive reuse (Langston, 2011). In accordance with the appearance of green cities to build the environment (Cohen, 2011). The strategy of green adaptive reuse is concerned with extending the facility life while decreasing the drawback of reusing heritage buildings as decreasing carbon footprint (Langston, 2011).

1.1 Scope

In ancient times, old buildings were remodified and altered pragmatically for new purposes, mainly for financial reasons; with no heritage intentions, the reusing was driven mainly by financial and functional concerns. However, the reflection on adaptive reuse is recent (Plevoets & Van Cleempoel, 2011).

Adaptive Heritage Reuse (AHR) refers to the process of adapting and reusing existing historic buildings for modern-day purposes while preserving their cultural and historical significance (Caves, 2005). AHR has been developed as a tool/method to safeguard heritage buildings through reusing and repurposing these building to sustain their heritage asset (Cantell, 2005; Machado, 1976). In AHR, function is the most obvious change. However, the building itself can be altered as well, including the circulation route, orientation, relationship between spaces; additions can be constructed, and other parts can be demolished (Brooker & Stone, 2004).

Riegl has recognized the intrinsic value of reusing historic buildings in contemporary conservation practices, after he included the use-value in his assessment of monuments (Riegl, 1903). Thus, adaptive reuse must always be prioritized over demolition and redevelopment (Cantell, 2005). It is considered as an interdisciplinary endeavour; conservation, architecture, interior architecture, and engineering (Plevoets & Van Cleempoel, 2011).

The scope of adaptive heritage reuse is broad, encompassing various aspects of design, construction, preservation, and community engagement. It requires a delicate balance between preserving historic significance and meeting contemporary needs, while also generating community support and ensuring the long-term sustainability of the building.

1.2 Purpose

The main purpose of adaptive heritage reuse is to find new uses for old buildings that are no longer being utilized or are underutilized, and to breathe new life into these buildings by repurposing them for contemporary needs. This process not only helps to preserve the cultural and historical value of these buildings but also contributes to sustainable development by reducing the need for new construction and promoting the reuse of existing resources (Veldpaus et al., 2022).

According to Schittich (2003), the goal of adaptive reuse is to find a balance between the preservation of cultural heritage and the creation of contemporary, functional spaces (Schittich, 2003). Similarly, Powell (1999) emphasizes the importance of creating new uses for old buildings that are relevant to the needs of modern society (Powell, 1999). In the same view, Machado (1976) argues that adaptive heritage reuse should aim to create a "palimpsest," where the original layers of history are still visible but new layers of functionality are added over time (Machado, 1976). Furthermore, Plevoets and Van Cleempoel (2011) suggest that authenticity is a key concept in adaptive heritage reuse, as the process should aim to respect the original character and significance of the building while also adapting it to meet contemporary needs (Plevoets & Van Cleempoel, 2011).

Overall, the purpose of adaptive heritage reuse is to create sustainable, functional spaces that respect and preserve the cultural and historical significance of existing buildings. This process requires a delicate balance between preservation and adaptation, as well as a commitment to sustainability and respect for cultural heritage.

1.3 Uses and Reuses

Adaptive reuse improves environmental sustainability by reducing material and resource consumption, economic sustainability by reducing costs, and social sustainability by retaining workers (Cantell, 2005; Plevoets & Van Cleempoel, 2011) have reviewed the literature on adaptive heritage reuse and have identified the main types of buildings that has been adaptively reused; industrial, religious, public and semi-public, residential, military, and commercial buildings) (Plevoets & Van Cleempoel, 2011). While Fisher and Powell have given emphasis on the contemporary reuse purpose of the historical buildings; dwellings, museum, exhibition, library, theatre, education, retail, office, leisure, care, industry, religious, military, and mixed-use development) instead of the old use of the buildings (Fisher, 1992; Powell, 1999).

Scholars have neglected, or limitedly, presents the 'meaning' of the historical buildings being reused, the genius loci, in describing the adaptive reuse process (Plevoets & Van Cleempoel, 2013). Modern conservation is based on values so each rehabilitation project should be based on assessment of these values (Lemaire & Stovel, 1994). The socio-economic value of a building is often the most important factor for owners and developers; in particular, this may threaten the preservation of 'soft values,' such as history, sociology, psychology, art, culture, morality, and religion, especially for buildings which are not protected as monuments (Van Hooydonck, 2006).

2 Approaches and Strategies

Researchers have searched and proposed many strategies of AHR. These strategies are essentially the same. Nevertheless, researchers have used many terms to discuss them (Arfa et al., 2022). Furthermore, they have given great interest in labelling these strategies which is based on their culture-value not based on critical analysis of their potential effect on other heritage value of these buildings (Arfa et al., 2022).

Plevoets and Van Cleempoel (2011) reviewed literature on AHR and find different design and architectural strategies proposed by scholars (Brooker & Stone, 2004; Cramer & Breitling, 2007; Jäger, 2010; Robert, 1989). These strategies are abstracted and illustrated in Fig. 1. However, the most reviewed three contributions are; Roos (2007) who has identified seven phases of AHR; (1) inventarisation, (2) analysis, (3) principle, (4) models, (5) design choice, (6) development, and (7) execution (Roos, 2007). Then Hendriks et al. (2009) have also proposed six phases for AHR; (1) initiative, (2) definition, (3) design, (4) elaboration, (5) execution, and (6) following up (Hendriks & der Hoeve, 2009). Later, Kuipers and de Jonge (2017) has also defined four main steps; chrono-mapping, value-mapping, mapping level of significance, and defining diemmas (Kuipers & De Jonge, 2017).

Arfa et al. (2022) noticed that many of the above-mentioned proposed models are overlapped. Therefore, they have reviewed literature on adaptive reuse, and suggested

Design Strategies				Architectonic Expressions
Robert 1989	**Brooker & Stone 2004**	**Jäger 2010**	**Cramer & Breitling 2007**	
Building within	Insertion	Transformation	Modernisation	Correspondence
Building over		Addition	Adaptation	Unification
Building around	Intervention			
Building alongside				
Adapting to a new function		Conversion		
	Installation			Junction and delineation
Building in the style of			Replacement	
Recycling materials of vestiges			Corrective maintenance	

Fig. 1 Design and Architectural strategies in Literature (Plevoets et al., 2011)

an 'ideal' model that should considered as a compresence model for AHR- however, it needs to be tested in practice- which consist of four main phases (pre-project phase, preparation phase, implementation phase, and post-implementation phase), with ten steps; (1) initiative, (2) analysis of heritage buildings, (3) value assessment, (4) mapping level of significance, (5) definition of adaptive reuse potential, (6) definition of design strategy, (7) final decision-making, (8) execution, (9) maintenance, and finally (10) evaluation after years (Fig. 2) (Arfa et al., 2022).

In order to repurposing these building many changes have to be made, which have been summarized by Plevoets and Van Cleempoel (2011) as follows; loadbearing structure (frames, floors, walls, roofs, underpinning, and heavy-lifting), building envelope (internal surface, new floors, façade, accessibility and circulation), and comfort, safety, and energy efficiency (fire-resistance, thermal performance, acoustic performance, preventing moisture and dampness, and indoor air quality (Plevoets & Cleempoel, 2011).

Cucco et al. (2023), have developed a model that can be used to evaluate the adaptive reuse strategies of the heritage buildings. This model is based on the SDGs and the European Quality Principles. It has three level of assessment; level 1 has 3 criteria that includes social, cultural, and financial criteria; level 2 has 5 criteria that includes community involvement, level of employment, impact on the community, impact on the asset, and financial performance of investment; level 3 has 4 criteria namely, public benefit, sustainability, computability, and proportionality (Cucco et al., 2023). They have demonstrated that this model 'multi-criteria analysis' is a valid scientific tool for policy and decision makers regarding the best adaptive reuse strategy to

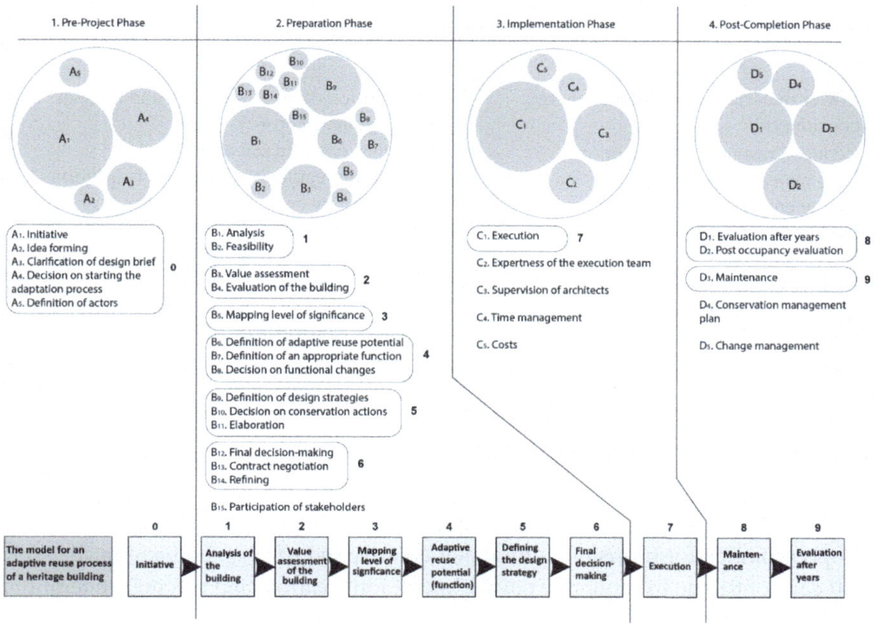

Fig. 2 Comprehensive model of AHR, referred to as '10-steps' (Arfa et al., 2022)

be adopted for historical buildings by taking into consideration all historical, architectural, social, economic, and environmental parameters and values (Cucco et al., 2023).

3 Drivers and Barriers to Heritage Reuse

The adoption of heritage reuse strategies can be influenced by various drivers and barriers. For instance, developing a model to assist practitioners in making decisions regarding reusing or demolishing existing built assets, Bullen and Love (2011) conducted 81 in-depth interviews over a six-month period with a variety of stakeholders, including architects, developers, planners, building managers/owners, and property consultants. According to their findings, reuse is driven by a variety of factors and is challenged by a variety of barriers (Table 1). In addition to capital investment, asset condition, and regulation, researchers underlined three underlying factors influencing adaptive reuse decisions (Bullen & Love, 2011).

Based on previous studies (Bullen & Love, 2011; De Silva et al., 2019), we summarized the common drivers and barriers to heritage reuse as follows:

Table 1 Drivers and barriers of AHR, after Bullen and Love (2011: 37)

Drivers	Barriers
• Lower material, transport and energy consumption • Reduced resource consumption • Less material wastes • Rising energy costs • Building functionality • Less disruption • Reduce negative impact of poor buildings • Changing work patterns • Requirement for multiple use Financial incentives	• Condition of external fabric and finishes • Maintenance costs • Higher rental in reuse buildings • Building regulations/planning restrictions • Complexity • Lack of skilled tradesmen • Building layout (e.g., space efficiencies) • Health and safety requirements • Commercial risk and uncertainty Low quality construction

3.1 Drivers for Adaptive Heritage Reuse

1. Economic benefits: Heritage reuse can generate economic benefits by creating opportunities for tourism, cultural and creative industries, and local businesses. It can contribute to economic development, job creation, and revenue generation, which can be a significant driver for adopting heritage reuse.
2. Sustainability and conservation: Heritage reuse can be seen as a sustainable practice as it promotes the conservation and preservation of historic buildings or sites, reducing the need for new construction and minimizing environmental impacts. It can also help revitalize declining or underutilized areas, contributing to urban regeneration and revitalization.
3. Cultural value and identity: Heritage reuse can help maintain cultural value and identity by preserving and showcasing historic buildings or sites that hold cultural significance to local communities. It can promote a sense of pride, ownership, and attachment among the community members, driving the adoption of heritage reuse.
4. Adaptive reuse potential: Historic buildings or sites may have unique architectural features, design elements, or strategic locations that make them suitable for adaptive reuse. These inherent characteristics can serve as drivers for adopting heritage reuse, as they offer opportunities for creative and innovative repurposing.

3.2 Barriers to Heritage Reuse

1. Regulatory and legal challenges: Regulatory and legal challenges such as complex heritage preservation laws, zoning restrictions, and building codes can pose barriers to heritage reuse. These challenges may require extensive approvals, permits, and compliance processes, adding complexity and cost to heritage reuse projects.

2. Financial constraints: Heritage reuse projects may require significant investments for restoration, renovation, and adaptive reuse, which can pose financial constraints. Limited funding sources, high costs of heritage preservation, and potential uncertainties about returns on investment can be barriers to heritage reuse.
3. Lack of expertise and skills: Heritage reuse projects may require specialized knowledge, skills, and expertise in historic preservation, architectural conservation, and adaptive reuse. The lack of such expertise and skills among stakeholders, including developers, designers, and local communities, can be a barrier to heritage reuse.
4. Stakeholder conflicts and concerns: Stakeholder conflicts, concerns, and resistance can pose barriers to heritage reuse. Local community opposition, conflicts among different stakeholders with varying interests, and concerns about changing the character or integrity of historic buildings or sites can hinder the adoption of heritage reuse.
5. Market demand and viability: The market demand and viability of heritage reuse projects can be a barrier. Limited market demand for certain types of adaptive reuse, lack of market research or feasibility studies, and uncertainties about the economic viability of heritage reuse projects can hinder their adoption.
6. Physical condition and challenges: Historic buildings or sites may have physical challenges such as structural deficiencies, environmental contamination, or deterioration, which can pose barriers to their adaptive reuse. Overcoming these physical challenges may require additional investments, technical expertise, and resources.

It's important to note that the drivers and barriers to heritage reuse can vary depending on local contexts, regulations, and stakeholders involved. Overcoming these challenges and leveraging the drivers can help facilitate the adoption of heritage reuse and contribute to sustainable development and cultural preservation (De Silva et al., 2019).

4 AHR and SDGs

Adaptive reuse is seen as a critical strategy towards the preservation of cultural heritage (Ghaderi et al., 2020). In addition, it is an important constituent of sustainable development (Yung & Chan, 2012). The adaptive reuse approach is designed to preserve both the building and its inherent values as well as make the necessary preparations to host a new activity, also it may add some contemporary layers to the building values as part of keeping it safe (Masoud & Gharipour, 2022). AHR have not been explored comprehensively in relation to the three tenets of sustainability, which leads to a conflict between the preservation of heritage values and advancement of sustainable urban design (Bullen & Love, 2011). However, Cucco et al. (2023) has stated that achieving the 2030 SDGs, architectural conservation, economic and environmental values should be merged in a mixed approach 'unicum' which will enhance its attractiveness and promoting circular economy practices (Cucco et al., 2023).

Ghaderi et al. (2020) state that adaptive reuse is any work done on a building in addition to basic maintenance to change its capacity, function or performance (i.e., it is an intervention to modify, reuse or upgrade a building to suit new conditions or requirements) (Ghaderi et al., 2020). Therefore, ARH transforms heritage buildings into reachable and usable places besides providing benefits for redeveloping an area in a sustainable way and adjusting with public safety principles, well-being and significant legislative requirements (Bucher & Kolbitsch, 2019; Mısırlısoy, 2020; Ragheb & Naguib, 2021; Yung & Chan, 2012). This is due to the important historical, aesthetic, cultural and economic values of buildings, in addition to the size, space character and some structural reasons for instance handling ever-growing lists of heritage buildings, supporting creative industries, which need immediate protection (Ghaderi et al., 2020; Mérai et al., 2022; Mısırlısoy, 2020).

According to Yung and Chan (2012) and Mérai et al. (2022), ARH is used as part of a broader climate emergency program to decrease carbon dioxide emissions and waste materials, contain the embodied energy of materials and labour and be more sustainable than new construction (Mérai et al., 2022; Ragheb & Naguib, 2021). This makes ARH considered from an approach that pulls defined boundaries and goals within itself, to a context that has been explored for purposes as diverse as a sense of place, tourist development, environmental sustainability, sustainable development and usability, social unity, urban renewal, and cultural variety (Mérai et al., 2022; Mısırlısoy, 2020). Thus, as the number of these factors increases, the decision-making process becomes more complex, which makes different countries put high efforts into assimilating and restructuring policies and regulations (Masoud & Gharipour, 2022; Mérai et al., 2022; Ragheb & Naguib, 2021). This in line with the context of the United Nations SDGs, makes framing sustainability for adaptive reuse a more attractive practice for policymakers.

5 Sustainable Development Goals (SDGs)

In September 2015, the General Assembly of the United Nations take on the 2030 Agenda for Sustainable Development which made up of 17 SDGs, and 169 targets (Cucco et al., 2023). These goals develop the precept of "leaving no one behind" and highlights a holistic method to reaching sustainable development for all (United Nations, 2023), all goals are clearly illustrated in Fig. 3 (United Nations Development Programme, 2023).

As indicated by Ragheb and Naguib (2021) the preservation and reuse of heritage buildings have extensive social benefits, as well as significantly benefiting upcoming generations (Ragheb & Naguib, 2021). Besides refining the lifestyle and providing job chances, manifold investments to improve the liveability and sustainability in the community and providing an enduring source of financing.

Fig. 3 Sustainable development goals. After, https://favpng.com/png_view/sustainable-development-goals-sustainability-millennium-development-goals-united-nations-development-programme-png/iyiy19tY, accessed on April 29, 2023

6 Case Studies

This section aims to explore the concept of Alternative Host Resource (AHR) and its implementation in the tourism industry through a series of case studies. The three case studies presented here have been chosen based on their diverse reuse purposes and their adaptation to the Sustainable Development Goals (SDGs). By analyzing these case studies, we hope to provide insights into the opportunities and challenges that arise from the adoption of AHR in the tourism industry.

The case studies presented in this section aim to highlight the different ways in which AHR can be implemented in the tourism industry. The first case study explores the reuse of abandoned royal res house/lodge as AHR accommodation (Hotel). The second case study examines the adaptation of traditional a royal palace to AHR museum, while the third case study focuses on the use of private palace as AHR museum, art gallery, and events place.

6.1 First Case Study: Mena House Hotel

6.1.1 Location and History

Mena House Hotel is a luxury hotel with a direct view of the pyramids located in Giza, Egypt (coordinates: 29°59′08″N 31°07′58″E). The five-star hotel is currently owned by the Egyptian General Company for Tourism and Hotels and is operating under the "JW Marriott" brand (Enterprise, 2022; Ibrahim, 2018).

The palace has a rich history and many adaptive reuses since it has been constructed by Khedive Ismail in 1869. His majesty built the rest lodge/house, which is later known as "Mina House" hotel, in front of the pyramids of Giza on an area of 40 acres, to serve as a private hunting lodge and rest house that was named the "Mud Hut". Khedive Ismail expanded the rest house and reused it as a palace for the guests of the Suez Canal opening ceremony (Salem, 2022).

In 1883, Khedive Ismail's debts increased, so his son Khedive Tawfiq sold the palace to a wealthy British man and his wife, "Frederick and Jesse Head," and the palace became their private resting residence. Then, the 'Honeymoon' expanded its construction and named it 'Mina house', after King Mina, the founder of Egypt's first dynasty (Ibrahim, 2018).

Frederick added English touches from the great fireplaces in the corners, which were unusual in Egypt at the time, but gave a wonderful inspiration to the place when mixed with 'mashrabiyas', handmade blue tiles, mosaics, and hand-carved wooden doors inlaid with copper and mother-of-pearl (Ibrahim, 2018; Rabie & Ahmed, 2018), and in 1885 they sold the palace to an Englishman and his wife, "Ethel and Hughes Locke King," a family famous for its love of ancient Egyptian antiquities, and decided to convert the palace into 'the Mena House Hotel', which opened to the public in 1886 (Rabie & Ahmed, 2018).

The hotel started with 80 distinguished rooms and suites, and in 1920 another 30 rooms were added to the hotel, and in 1964 the hotel was sold to the Oberoi Group, and it began renovation in 1972 and was completed in 1975. Then in 1978 work began on the garden suite, where 200 renovated rooms were added, and in 2007 and 2008 the hotel was renewed again. The number of hotel rooms now reaches 486 rooms and suites (7 junior suites and 4 master suites, each with a private balcony overlooking the pyramids (Rabie & Ahmed, 2018).

6.1.2 Heritage Assets

According to Hua (2010), the heritage assets of the Mena House Hotel can be categorised into intangible and intangible cultural heritage (Hua, 2010). Based on many related literatures reviewed (Arab News, 2023; Humphreys, 2015; Nelson, 1997, 2003; Rabie & Ahmed, 2018; Salem, 2022). The several heritage assets of Mena House Hotel can be classified into: Architectural atheistic: The Mena House Hotel is housed in a historic palace dating back to the nineteenth century. Originally built as a hunting lodge for Khedive Ismail, the palace was converted into a hotel in 1869. It has since been a preferred destination for royalty, dignitaries, and celebrities from around the world. Furthermore, the hotel features two Royal Suites, named after King Farouk and Queen Nazli, originally used by the Egyptian royal family. These suites are beautifully preserved and showcase the opulence and grandeur of the bygone era. They feature exquisite furnishings, elegant decor, and panoramic views of the Pyramids of Giza.

Historical Artifacts: The Mena House Hotel is home to a vast collection of historical artifacts, including ancient Egyptian art and antiques. The hotel's public areas are

Fig. 4 The Mena House hotel; (left) panoramic view for the hotel with Giza pyramids, After, https://pin.it/3xpC1FF; (right) the layout of the hotel and its gardens, After, https://pin.it/2yIzhko, accessed on April 28, 2023

adorned with striking pieces of art, such as intricate carvings, murals, and paintings. These pieces provide a glimpse into Egypt's rich cultural heritage.

Gardens: The hotel is surrounded by lush gardens meticulously landscaped and maintained, showcasing a variety of exotic plants, flowers, and trees. These gardens are not only aesthetically pleasing but also hold historical significance, as they were originally designed by a prominent landscape architect in the late nineteenth century. They have been a part of the hotel's heritage for over a century.

Historical Events: The Mena House Hotel has witnessed several historical events. During World War II, it served as a hospital for British and Allied forces, and later as headquarters for the French Army. Many famous personalities, including Winston Churchill, have stayed at the hotel during their visits to Egypt, adding to its unique significance.

Cultural Activities: The Mena House Hotel offers various cultural activities to guests, such as Egyptian dance performances, music concerts, and traditional culinary experiences. This provides an opportunity to immerse in Egypt's rich heritage and culture (Fig. 4).

Moreover, the Mina House administration was keen to name the names of the important personalities who resided in it, including monarchs, heads of state, and world celebrities, in its rooms and suites, such as the Churchill suite, the suite of the commander of the victorious forces in the Battle of Al-Alamin and one of the most famous leaders in World War II, Montgomery, and the Umm Kamthum suite. Along with other pavilions, for example, but not limited to Aga Khan, Princess Diana, Queen Elizabeth, President of France Sarkozy, Charlie Chapman, Agatha Christie, Bill Gates (Rabie & Ahmed, 2018).

Surprisingly, according to the most famous hotels in the world (2023), Mena House was managed by 27 managers staring with Ernst Baron Rodakowski: 1887–1896 until today by Omar Tantawy. The managers used to write their dairies which used later to understand the different aspects of the history of Mena House (Nelson, 1997).

Finally, the Hotels were the location where many films, including the international film “Valley of the Kings” and a number of Egyptian films, including “A Love Story” by Abdel Halim Hafez, Abdel Salam Al Nabulsi, Maryam Fakhr El Din, “A Day of My Life” by singer Abdel Halim Hafez, and “Her Majesty” by Farid Shawky. In addition, a number of international films by James Bond were filmed at the hotel (Humphreys, 2015; Ibrahim, 2018; Arab News, 2023).

6.1.3 The Hotel and SDGs

According to the Marriott International (2019), the company is committed to sustainable practices in its all hotels in the chain, including JW Marriott Cairo Mena House. The sustainable practices of the Marriott are in line with SDGs. The achieved SDGs are reflected in the following practices. To reduce the chain’s environmental footprint, the first step is to minimize the chain’s energy and water consumption. The company planned to reduce the environmental footprint by 15%|30%*|45%|50% across the portfolio by 2025 (from a 2016 baseline; for water/carbon/waste/food waste). In this concern and worth mention that JW Marriott Cairo Mena House has achieved the required carbon footprint: 64.49 kg per room night and water footprint: 7168.36 L per room night (Marriott Mena House, 2023). (SDG-6- Clean water and sanitation, and SDG-7- affordable and clean energy). In addition, the company and the communities in which it operates benefit from adopting innovative technologies to plan, implement, track, and communicate how to mitigate climate-related risk (SDG-8- Decent work and economic growth, and SDG-13- Climate action). Furthermore, in regard to education and awareness, Mena House Hotel raises awareness about sustainability among its guests and staff through educational programs, training, and information dissemination about sustainable practices and their importance (SDG-4 ‘Quality education’) (Marriott Mena House, 2023; Marriott International, 2019). El-behary (2018) underlined that meeting the SDGs requirements and other factors like quality, originality, innovation, sustainability and influence were crucial in selection of the Marriott Mena House hotel among the most famous world’s greatest hotels by the Times Magazine in 2018 (El-Behary, 2018).

In summary, the Mena House Hotel in Egypt is not only a luxury hotel but also a repository of rich heritage assets, including its historic building, royal suites, historical artifacts, gardens, historical events, and cultural activities, which make it a unique case for adapted heritage reuse and destination for tourists interested in Egypt’s history and culture.

6.1.4 Second Case Study: Manyal Palace

This palace is located on Roudah Island, in Manyal district of southern Cairo (coordinate: 30°01′39″N 31°13′49″E). Prince Mohamed Ali Pasha (1875–1955), the younger brother of Khedive Abbas Hilmi II, built this palace between 1901 and 1929.

Fig. 5 (Left) Manyal Section View;(Right) Manyal Palace Layout. After; https://www.sitesint.com/projects/manyal-palace-museum/ accessed April 28, 2023

The palace was designed in a mixed European and Islamic Style. It includes architectural and artistic rococo features with many traditional Islamic styles: Mamluk, Ottoman, Andalusian and Persian (Fig. 5).

6.2 Heritage Assets

The palace is considered a significant example of natural and cultural heritage significance. It reflects the lifestyle of royal family during the nineteenth and twentieth centuries The palace consists of six buildings with a vast garden. The buildings including the throne hall, the residence hall, the reception hall, the clock tower, the mosque, the Sabil, the hunting museum, the private museum and the golden hall. Every building has its distinctive features. The Persian garden, about 34,000 m^2, is designed with some features of English style with rare plants and trees that has been brought by the prince himself from different countries; such as Syria, Iran, Iraq and Zanzibar (Abdel-Rahman, 2016; Hamdy, 2010).

The most prominent building is the throne hall; it consists of two floors. The ground floor is a long hall ended by the throne. A splendid sunburst, the symbol of the Mohamed Ali dynasty, occupies the ceiling. The two longitudinal walls are decorated with a portrait of members of the Mohamed Ali dynasty and landscape paintings; on the sides are gilded furniture with red upholstery. The reception hall, consisting of two floors, is designed to revive the Islamic of Maro and Syria and Syrian features. it was the reception place of distinguished visitors and official guest. The residence building is impressive with its architectural elements and prestigious furniture. It consists of two floors with mant rooms such as bedroom. Mirror room and prince office. The golden hall which was move from Ibrahim Pasha residence was for official celebration. The mosque has a rococo ceiling and its pulpit decorated with ceramic tiles. The clock tower is inspired by Andalusian and Moroccan features (Mohammed, 2018).

6.3 Adaptive Reuse of the Palace

The palace was initially constructed to be the residence of Prince Mohamed Ali. The owner left an instruction to turn the palace into museum after his death. In 1955 it was subjected to Council of Egyptian Antiquities which opened to pubic. This stage of reusing exposed the palace to some degradation especially the gardens. In 1964, the garden was subjected to the Egyptian Company of Tourism and Hotels; they constructed a hotel but in 1992 that the Prime minister issued a decree to demolish the hotels and to transfer the management to museum authority. Due to its degradation, the palace was closed in 2005 and restoration works started for ten years when it was reinaugurated. Some building was added as the restoration laboratory, lecture hall and textile hall: The garden is used today to organize photo sessions of wedding and parties; training workshops and educational lectures are organised beside it is open for the public to visit buildings (Connolly-Cove, 2022).

6.3.1 The Palace and SDGs

After being restored, transformed, and adaptively reused to be a museum and cultural hub. The palace has meet many SDGs; SDG-4 'Quality education', SDG-7 'Clean energy', SDG-13 "Climate action' and SDG-17, the overall goal. SDG-4, the palace become an educational hub for school and university students, in addition to local residents through their educational programs offered, and visitors tours. Using energy saving lighting systems, natural ventilations system, and using bright colour materials for pavements have led to reduce the energy consumption of the palace, and achieve SDG-7, which is also considered as a climate action, so that it has achieved SDG-13 as well.

7 The Third Case Study: Baron Empain Palace

7.1 Location and History

Baron Empain Palace ('*Qasr el Baron Emban*' in Arabic), located in the Heliopolis district of Cairo, Egypt (*coordinates*: 30°05′12″N 31°19′49″E). Located opposite the Presidential Guest House, the Hindu Palace was built by Marcel and Georges-Louis Claude and served as the residence of Sultan Hussein Kamel between 1914 and 1917 (Raafat, 1995). The palace is a historical iconic palace that was built by Belgian industrialist Baron Édouard Empain in 1907. The palace was built in 1911 as a private residence for Belgian industrialist Baron Edouard Empain (Elyamani, 2018).

7.1.1 Heritage Assets

The Baron Empain Palace is a significant heritage asset due to its historical and architectural asset. Marcel's unique interpretation of the temple, Angkor Wat temple complex in Cambodia, architecture and his innovative use of modern materials make the palace a one-of-a-kind structure and its unique architectural style, which combines elements of Indian, Islamic, and European design; Neo-Moorish style was introduced into Egypt by European colonialists and orientalists, influenced by Islamic decorative arts and grandiose scenography (Abdel-Rahman, 2016; Aboulnaga et al., 2021). Despite the buildings' mixture of styles and forms, the "baroque" aspect is evident on their facades (Tresilian, 2010). Thus, the palace becomes the Cairo's most distinctive buildings, and made it an important heritage asset in the region, resulting in cultural impact and nostalgia among local residents (Aboulnaga et al., 2021).

7.2 Architectural Description: The Palace Interior Design

The palace has three floors (basement, ground and first) and a roof, and is surrounded by a garden on all sides. The palace's interior consists of a basement, two floors, and a roof. A large garden surrounds the palace on all sides. In the basement, palace servants lived in rooms connected by corridors and doors. All palace floors are connected to the basement by a spiral staircase and elevator. A reception room, a dining room, and a billiard room are located on the ground floor. Four rooms, each with its own balcony and bathroom, are located on the first floor. Finally, the palace roof appears as an open space with a tower, giving the palace its characteristic appearance (Elyamani, 2018) (Fig. 6).

7.2.1 Adaptive Reuse

The palace has a long history for adaptive reuse; it was initially used as the residence of Baron Empain but was later sold and used for various purposes (2022). During World War II, the palace was used as a hospital by the British army (2019). Afterwards, the palace served as a government guest house and later as the headquarters of the Egyptian Electric Authority (2022); The palace fell into disrepair and was abandoned for several years until it was acquired by the Egyptian government in 2005.

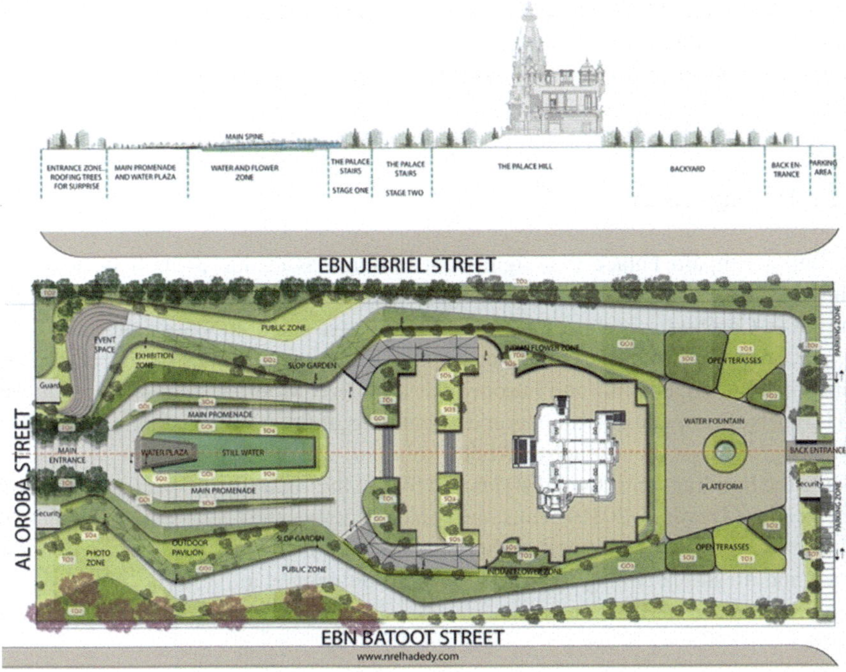

Fig. 6 Baron Empain Palace Architectural Design and landscape (After nrelhadedy; https://www.behance.net/gallery/85499707/Baron-Palace-Land-space-design/modules/494994349)

Elyamani (2018) has visually investigated and document the status of the palace after being abandoned. He proposed re-use model; 'the ground floor is re-used as a small museum after being furnished on the historical style. The first floor is re-used as a museum and/or a motel. The roof is re-used in holding cultural seminars, and as a place for distinctive imaging types. The palace garden is to be re-used similar to its historical usage as an open space for celebrations and parties' (Elyamani, 2018).

The palace's historical and cultural significance has led to its restoration and transformation into a cultural centre and museum, which represents the cultural sustainability of the palace (Aboulnaga et al., 2021). In 2017, the Egyptian government has worked to preserve the palace's unique architecture and showcase its history and importance to visitors. The restoration cost is EGP 175 million (US$ 11.2 million at time of restoration) (Aboulnaga et al., 2021). Today, the palace serves as a cultural landmark in Egypt, visitors can tour the palace and explore its unique architecture and historical significance, the total estimated revenue of the palace is about EGP 242,880 (US$ 15,560) (Aboulnaga et al., 2021). The successful restoration and reopening of the place, proves that the palace retained its cultural memory over the break in time (obsolescence) and break in space accessibility (caesura) (Aboulnaga et al., 2021).

7.3 The Palace and SDGs

Aboulnaga et al (2021) have assessed the palace sustainability in terms of environmental, social, economic, and cultural sustainable pillars. The assessment has been carried out after the restorations, transformations and adaptive reuse of the place. They found that the palace meets 4 SDGs, namely SDG-4 'Quality education', SDG-7 'Clean energy', SDG-11 'Sustainable cities', and SDG-13 'Climate action' (Aboulnaga et al., 2021).

Training restoration parties on how to utilize efficient tools like BIM can improve the quality of education by better managing their resources as well as educational trips, SDG-4 has been attained. Through using smart equipment, and bright coloured materials for pavements, energy consumption reduced, and SDG-7 is achieved; in terms of SDG-11, it is achieved by providing an example of sustainable community development; lastly, SDG-13 is achieved by minimising the amount of energy used for operational purposes (Aboulnaga et al., 2021).

The adaptive reuse of the palace impacted the social sustainability of the district by promoting the nostalgia among different age-groups, especially the working groups. It has also direct impact on the economic sustainability through creating new jobs. Furthermore, it promotes the cultural sustainability through sustaining a cultural asset to the country' capital, restoring a main landmark of Heliopolis city, the visibility of the palace to international visitors as it is located on the road leads to Cairo airport, and for the locals as well (Aboulnaga et al., 2021).

8 Conclusion

In the last three decades, Egypt took measures to preserve its cultural heritage and, therefore, many projects were implemented to restore and conserve historic buildings and monuments. To create a sustainable community, Egypt was moved from conservation to a new approach: adaptive reuse. This approach aims at sustaining social, cultural, and economical attributes of heritage buildings and preserve its characteristics simultaneously. Moreover, it helps achieve Egypt's 2030 strategic plan that is based on the UNESCO SDGs.

We presented three case studies from Cairo, Egypt's capital, to illustrate how AHR can be a catalyst for SDGs in tourism. The first is Mena House Hotel, a historic palace dating back to the nineteenth century. In its long history, it has been transformed from being a hunting lodge to becoming one of Cairo's most famous hotels. Secondly, The Manyal Palace served as the residence of Prince Mohamed Ali, who was appointed crown prince. The palace was built as a royal palace, it is now a museum displaying artefacts from different eras and countries. The third is Baron Empain Palace, which was abandoned for many years until it has been restored to be a museum.

After in-depth investigation of these three case studies, we found that they have meet at least 7 gools of the UNESCO SDGs, including SDG-4 'Quality education', SDG-7 'Clean energy', SDG 8 (Decent Work and Economic Growth), SDG 9 (Industry, Innovation, and Infrastructure), SDG 11 (Sustainable Cities and Communities), SDG-13 'Climate action' and SDG-17. All three cases help improve education quality by offering training programs and field trips. However, the benefits of student visits go beyond just education quality. They also promote sustainability by fostering community loyalty and building their identity; there it enhances the achievement of SDG-11. Furthermore, The SDG-7 'affordable and clean energy' is also a common achievement of three cases. Therefore, heritage buildings can be repurposed and revitalized through adaptive reuse, promoting sustainable urban development, economic opportunities, and achieving SDGs.

The tourism industry can benefit from adaptive reuse by offering unique and authentic experiences to tourists, while also preserving cultural heritage and supporting local communities. However, successful adaptive reuse requires careful planning, community engagement, and sustainable management practices. By integrating adaptive reuse into their sustainability strategies, tourism stakeholders can contribute to the achievement of the SDGs, while also promoting responsible tourism and preserving cultural heritage for future generations. Finally, we suggest that this chapter is a call for future comprehensive research on the Adaptive reuse of heritage buildings in both developed and developing countries.

References

Abdel-Rahman, N. (2016). Egyptian historical parks, authenticity vs. change in Cairo's Cultural landscapes. *Procedia—Social and Behavioral Sciences, 225*, 391–409. https://doi.org/10.1016/j.sbspro.2016.06.086

Aboulnaga, M., Puma, P., & Elsharkawy, M. (2021). Sustainability assessment of restored historic buildings: Case study of Baron Empain Palace in Heliopolis, Cairo, Egypt—Representation analysis of the building and site. In *IOP conference series: Earth and environmental science* (pp 1–9). IOP Publishing.

Alikhani, A. (2009). Assessing sustainable adaptive re-use of historical buildings. In: *Proceedings of the 7th IASME/WSEAS International conference on heat transfer, thermal engineering and environment, HTE* (pp. 239–246).

Arab News. (2023). Mena House: Cairo's most legendary 'family hotel'|Arab News. *Arab News*. https://www.arabnews.com/node/1504871/lifestyle. Accessed 30 April .2023

Arfa, F. H., Zijlstra, H., Lubelli, B., & Quist, W. (2022). Adaptive reuse of heritage buildings: From a literature review to a model of practice. *Historic Environment: Policy and Practice, 13*, 148–170. https://doi.org/10.1080/17567505.2022.2058551

Aytac, D. O., Arslan, T. V., & Durak, S. (2016). Adaptive reuse as a strategy toward urban resilience. *European Journal of Sustainable Development, 5*, 523–532. https://doi.org/10.14207/ejsd.2016.v5n4p523

Baron Empain Palace. (2019). In *Ministry of tourism and antiquities*. https://egymonuments.gov.eg/monuments/baron-empain-palace/. Accessed 9 April 2023.

Baron Empain Palace. (2022). In *Wikipedia encyclopedia*. https://en.wikipedia.org/wiki/Baron_Empain_Palace. Accessed 9 April 2023.

Brooker, G., & Stone, S. (2004). *Re-readings. Interior architecture and the design principles of remodelling existing buildings.* RIBA Enterprises.

Bucher, B., & Kolbitsch, A. (2019). Coming to terms with value: Heritage policy in Vienna. *Heritage and Society, 12*, 41–56. https://doi.org/10.1080/2159032X.2021.1878990

Bullen, P. A., & Love, P. E. D. (2011). Adaptive reuse of heritage buildings. *Structural Survey, 29*, 411–421. https://doi.org/10.1108/02630801111182439

Cantell, S. F. (2005). *The adaptive reuse of historic industrial buildings: Regulation barriers.* Virginia Polytechnic Institute and State University.

Caves, R. W. (2005). *Encyclopedia of the city.* Routledge.

Cohen, N. (2011). *Green cities: An A-To_Z Guide.* Sage Publications.

Connolly-Cove. (2022). Mohamed Ali Palace in Manial: Home of the king who never was—ConnollyCove. In *Connolly-Cove.* https://www.connollycove.com/mohamed-ali-palace-egypt/. Accessed 30 April 2023.

Cramer, J., & Breitling, S. (2007). *Architecture in existing fabric.* Birkhäuser.

Cucco, P., Maselli, G., Nesticò, A., & Ribera, F. (2023). An evaluation model for adaptive reuse of cultural heritage in accordance with 2030 SDGs and European Quality Principles. *Journal of Cultural Heritage, 59*, 202–216. https://doi.org/10.1016/j.culher.2022.12.002

De Silva, G. D. R., Perera, B. A. K. S., & Rodrigo, M. N. N. (2019). Adaptive reuse of buildings: The case of Sri Lanka. *Journal of Financial Management of Property and Construction, 24*, 79–96. https://doi.org/10.1108/JFMPC-11-2017-0044

El-Behary, H. (2018). Cairo's Marriott Mena House among world's greatest places: Times Magazine - Egypt Independent. In *Egypt independent.* https://egyptindependent.com/cairos-marriott-mena-house-among-worlds-greatest-places-times-magazine/. Accessed 30 April 2023.

Elyamani, A. (2018). Re-use proposals and structural analysis of historic palaces in Egypt: The case of baron Empain palace in Cairo. *Scientific Culture, 4*, 53–73. https://doi.org/10.5281/zenodo.1048245

Enterprise. (2022). JW Marriott officially becomes manager of Mena House|Enterprise. In *Enterprise: The state of the nation.* https://enterprise.press/stories/2017/02/01/jw-marriott-officially-becomes-manager-of-mena-house/. Accessed 30 April 2023.

Fisher, A. (1992). *New life in old buildings.* Verlag.

Ghaderi, Z., Dehghan Pour Farashah, M. H., Aslani, E., & Hemati, B. (2020). Managers' perceptions of the adaptive reuse of heritage buildings as boutique hotels: Insights from Iran. *Journal of Heritage Tourism, 15*, 696–708. https://doi.org/10.1080/1743873X.2020.1756834

Giebeler, G., Krause, H., Fisch R, et al. (2009). *Refurbishment manual; maintenance, conversions, extensions.* Refurbishment Manual. https://doi.org/10.11129/DETAIL.9783034614337/HTML

Hamdy, R. S. (2010). A study of plant distribution in nine historic gardens in Egypt. *Garden History, 38*, 267–314.

Hendriks, L., der Hoeve, J. van (2009). *Guideline for building archaeological research.* Cultural Heritage Agency (Rijksdienst voor het cultureel Erfgoed).

Hua, S. (2010). World heritage classification and related issues—A case study of the "Convention concerning the protection of the world cultural and natural heritage." In *Procedia social and behavioral sciences* (pp. 6954–6961).

Humphreys, A. (2015). *Grand hotels of Egypt: In the golden age of travel.* American University in Cairo Press.

Ibrahim, K. (2018). *Information in a photo—The story of Mina House, which was transformed from the Khedive's resting place into a famous hotel.* https://tinyurl.com/yc3ju3cm. Accessed 30 April 2023.

Jäger, F. (2010). *Old & new design manual for revitalizing existing buildings.* Birkhäuser

Kuipers, M., & De Jonge, W. (2017). *Designing from heritage-strategies for conservation and conversion.* BK Books.

Langston, C. A. (2011). Green adaptive reuse: Issues and strategies for the built environment. In *Modeling risk management in sustainable construction* (pp. 199–209). Springer.

Lemaire, R., & Stovel, H. (1994). *Nara document on authenticity.* World Heritage Convention.

Machado, R. (1976). Old buildings as palimpsest. Towards a theory of remodeling. *Progressive Architecture, 11*, 46–49.
Marriott Mena House. (2023). 5 Star Luxury Hotel|Marriott Mena House, Cairo. https://www.marriott.com/en-us/hotels/caimn-marriott-mena-house-cairo/overview/. Accessed 30 April 2023.
Masoud, E., & Gharipour, M. (2022). Developing a model to weigh cultural values in the adaptive reuse of heritage buildings: The case of the Risbaf Factory in Isfahan, Iran. *Journal of the Institute of Conservation, 45*, 105–121. https://doi.org/10.1080/19455224.2022.2065689
Mérai, D., Veldpaus, L., Pendlebury, J., & Kip, M. (2022). The governance context for adaptive heritage reuse: A review and typology of fifteen European countries. *The Historic Environment: Policy & Practice, 13*, 526–546. https://doi.org/10.1080/17567505.2022.2153201
Mısırlısoy, D. (2020). Towards sustainable adaptive reuse of traditional marketplaces. *Historic Environment: Policy and Practice,* 1–17. https://doi.org/10.1080/17567505.2020.1784671
Mohammed, B. (2018). El-Manial Palace: Where passion for taking the throne. *PressReader*. https://www.pressreader.com/egypt/the-daily-news-egypt/20180208/281629600724968. Accessed 30 April 2023.
Nelson, N. (2003). *The history of Mena house hotel*. The Palm Press.
Nelson, N. (1997) .*The Mena house: A short history of a remarkable hotel*. Mena House Oberoi Hotel.
Plevoets, B., & Van Cleempoel, K. (2011). Adaptive reuse as a strategy towards conservation of cultural heritage: A literature review. *WIT Transactions on the Built Environment, 118*, 155–164. https://doi.org/10.2495/STR110131
Plevoets, B., & Van Cleempoel, K. (2013). Adaptive reuse as an emerging discipline: An HISTORIC SURVEY. *Reinventing architecture and interiors: A socio-political view on building adaptation* (pp. 13–32). Libri Publishers.
Powell, K. (1999). *Architecture reborn*. Rizzoli International Publications, Inc.
Raafat, S. (1995). Who built the palace. In *Egyptian mail*. https://web.archive.org/web/20100804000901/http://www.egy.com/landmarks/97-05-01.shtml. Accessed 25 March 2023.
Rabie, S. H., & Ahmed, H. H. (2018). Mena house hotel (1863–1952) historical study. *Journal of Association of Arab Universities for Tourism and Hospitality, 15*, 10–12.
Ragheb, G. A., Naguib, I. M. (2021). Empowering criteria for effective adaptive reuse of heritage buildings in Egypt. *International Journal of Sustainable Development and Planning, 16*, 1061–1070. https://doi.org/10.18280/ijsdp.160607
Riegl, A. (1903). *Der moderne Denkmalkultus sein Wesen und seine Entstehung*. Verlag.
Robert, P. (1989). *Adaptations. New uses for old buildings*. Editions du Moniteur.
Rodrigues, C., & Freire, F. (2017). Adaptive reuse of buildings: Eco-efficiency assessment of retrofit strategies for alternative uses of an historic building. *Journal of Cleaner Production, 157*, 94–105. https://doi.org/10.1016/J.JCLEPRO.2017.04.104
Roos, J. (2007). *Discovering the assignment*. VSSD.
Salem, A. (2022). All you need to know about the development of the "Mina House" palace, after it was renovated at 550 million pounds. . In El-Youm El-Sabaa. https://tinyurl.com/yc8ebxez. Accessed 30 April 2023.
Schittich, C. (2003). *Building in existing fabric: Refurbishment, extensions, new design (In Detail)*. Birkhäuser.
Tresilian, D. (2010). Memories of Baron Empain. *Al-Ahram Weekly*.
Truscott, M. C. (2014). Burra charter: The Australia ICOMOS charter for places of cultural significance (1999). *Encyclopedia of Global Archaeology,* 1078–1082. https://doi.org/10.1007/978-1-4419-0465-2_1046
Van Hooydonck, E. (2006). Soft values of seaports. A plea for soft values management by port authorities. In: *Proceedings of the European sea ports organisation's annual conference* (pp. 93–145). Stockholm.
Veldpaus, L., Lossifidis, M., Mason, A., Hofman, M. W. (2022). *A roadmap for the EU and Europe; Integrating adaptive heritage reuse in wider EU policies, programmes and practices.*

Volait, M. (2012). *Maisons de France au Caire : le remploi de grands décors mamelouks et ottomans dans une architecture moderne*. Institut français d'archéologie orientale

Yung, E. H. K., & Chan, E. H. W. (2012). Implementation challenges to the adaptive reuse of heritage buildings: Towards the goals of sustainable, low carbon cities. *Habitat International, 36*, 352–361.

Organizational Ethnography and Anthropology

José G. Vargas-Hernández, María F. Higuera-Cota, and M. C. Omar C. Vargas-González

Abstract This study aims to analyze some of the theoretical, conceptual and methodological implications between organizational anthropology and ethnography. Starting from the assumption that ethnographic analysis and interpretive research in organizational anthropology has an emergent and symbolic role rooted in social processes and without a priori assumptions, with explanations and categories defined by organizational actors. The method used is based on analytical and descriptive questions from the theoretical and empirical review of the literature that leads to reflective analysis. It is concluded that the ethnographic methodology is pertinent to be used in the analysis of its interactions with organizational anthropology as a new specialty in organizational studies.

Keywords Ethnography · Organizational anthropology · Organizational studies

1 Introduction

The origin and establishment of organizational anthropology responds to situations, conditions, different but articulated anthropological visions that lead to diverse perspectives and approaches. Where organizations are conceived as a legitimate research laboratory in fields such as organizational anthropology, psychology and

J. G. Vargas-Hernández (✉)
Tecnológico Nacional de México, ITS Fresnillo, Avenida tecnológico, Fresnillo, Zacatecas, México
e-mail: jose.vargas@zapopan.tecmm.edu.mx; joseguadalupe.vh@fresnillo.tecnm.mx

M. F. Higuera-Cota
Faculty of Social Work and Postgraduate, Universidad Autónoma de Sinaloa, Av. los Sauces, Los Fresnos S/N. 80019, Culiacán, Sinaloa, México
e-mail: Higuera.maria@uabc.edu.mx

M. C. O. C. Vargas-González
Instituto Tecnológico de México, Campus Cd. Guzmán Cd., Guzmán, Jalisco, México
e-mail: omar.vg@cdguzman.tecnm.mx

W. Leal Filho and V. Kuzmanović (eds.), *Sustainable Development Seen Through the Lenses of Ethnoeconomics and the Circular Economy*,
https://doi.org/10.1007/978-3-031-72676-7_9

sociology. That is why organizational anthropology studies have become relevant to make contributions to the organizational and administrative school of thought and provide complementarity to sociology, psychology, biology and history.

Organizational anthropology is an inclusive administrative discipline of knowledge processes in the management of organizations to increase efficiency. Anthropology together with ethology, ethnology, sociology and psychology in organizational and managerial studies are relevant for the analysis of administrative relations such as production-consumer-consumption management.

Diverse contexts in a differentiated socioeconomic world are demanding new anthropologically oriented organizational forms as specific responses for survival and adaptability. In the words of Gonnet (2012) the organizational space from an emic perspective of its own members is in charge of nurturing anthropology and organizational theory.

2 Problem Statement

The relationship between the academic and professional fields of anthropology contribute to the theoretical framework supported to contribute to organizational psychology. In this regard, Fotaki et al. (2020) point out that the reference to the discipline of anthropology is still conspicuously absent in organizational studies.

Even though the interdisciplinarity of organizational anthropology is marked by the interrelated work carried out by industrial psychology, social anthropology, ethnology, sociology, etc., it is still necessary to continue working on studies focused not only on the knowledge of man, but also on through these it is possible to contribute to organizational development, build a dialogue and dissertation of organizational studies. That is, cultivating learning that addresses behavioral problems at work in organizations.

The term Anthropology comes from the Greek ἄνθρωπος, ánthrópos, which means man or human being, and λόγος, logos, which means word, treaty, knowledge, study. Anthropology is a science with a holistic approach to study humanity as a human being, people, human groups in terms of values, norms, lifestyles, patterns, etc. of homosocialis and culture. The study of the human being has a long tradition carried out by Herodotus (484–425 BC), Hippocrates (460–377 BC) and Aristotle (384–322 BC). The word Anthropology was used by Aristotle and was used to designate knowledge for the study of spiritual human nature, that is, doctrine.

Anthropology is the scientific study of man and his culture, contemplating social behavior, beliefs, languages, modes of behavior. In addition, it considers the origin and historical evolution of the human being. In fact, anthropology has been consolidated as a social science with the colonization processes. For example, Menéndez (1996) asserts that the industrial revolution caused deep anthropological transformations in the context of organizations based on modes of industrial production and capitalist development processes as a consequence of colonial expansion that led to the international division of intellectual labor.

3 Importance of the Study

The conceptualizations of organizational anthropology to define the object of study are framed in the capitalist international division of intellectual labor. Anthropological metaphors such as character, tribe, clan, etc., among others, are attributed to Ohnismo, considered a folkloric trap by Berg and Faucheux (1982) and Alvesson and Berg (1992), leaving aside the capitalist concepts of performance and efficiency based on the Toyota organizational paradigm.

Smirnova (2016) states that anthropology has developed in physical and organizational settings to include administrative, cultural, and social anthropology. On the other hand, there are other types of anthropology such as industrial, organizational and business anthropology which, according to Roca i Girona (2001), make up a discipline whose unit of study is the industrial organizational business environment. For his part, Roca (1998) specifies that industrial anthropology is different from economic anthropology. Industrial anthropology refers to the economy of societies, that is, to their activity as a social individual who produces, buys, sells and interacts with others in their economic environment. It is also known as business anthropology.

For Roca (1998) industrial anthropology limits specialization beyond the anthropology of work with an interest in social aspects based on productive labor practices, which lead to industrial anthropology being an anthropology of industrial society with an interest in the problems historical that are related to industrialism and its social anthropology. So, the work of anthropology deals with industrial and non-industrial work, being the object of study the industrial organization, store, farm, artisan workshops, inserted either in the formal or informal economy.

The applied concepts of anthropology in industrial societies can be defined in relation to their practical use in a historical setting. Anthropology's interest in studying complex industrial societies includes interventions in different areas of organizational studies influenced by ideological and material power in industrial organizations (Maestre Alfonso, 1983). Thus, the process of formation and development of organizational anthropology under the approach of applied anthropology is linked to the phenomena of industrialization of societies.

Organizational anthropology studies human organizations, and through empirical work it is possible to explain the opportunities and limitations associated with the use of anthropological methods in organizations and management. However, the texture of organizational anthropological research also includes actor-centered context, history, and process. That is, organizational anthropology separates between research and intervention.

On the other hand, García Canclini (1982) explains that sociology, psychology, anthropology, communication studies and other social sciences converge in multidisciplinary research on organizations. That is, the study of organizations must be framed in a multidisciplinary approach from a micro perspective to human groups subject to anthropology, paleontology, historiography, sociology pointing to the anthropology of organizations.

4 Method

This analysis begins in the first place by describing, analyzing and reflecting on issues and concerns related to the emerging topic of organizational anthropology in organizational studies, to continue with the topic of organizational ethnography, as the relevant methodology to use. Finally, some final comments are made from the reflective analysis.

5 Organizational Anthropology

Organizational anthropology is considered an emerging field, which has emerged as a discipline in convergence with sociology and psychology and the intersections between the local and the global to analyze the organizational components of complex societies, as well as their transformative effects on cultural dynamics in traditional models of capitalist organization. The connection between anthropology and organizational studies in a discipline of organizational anthropology accounts for the social diversity of the meanings of the human being. And these types of studies are applicable to all types of organizations regardless of their nature and identity.

Authors such as Corsín Jiménez (2007), Caulkins et al. (2013) and Garsten et al. (2013), mention that administrative and organizational anthropology, also known as organizational anthropology, is a science that studies the interactions between objects and people. of management. For Kottak (2011) organizational anthropology studies the diversity of human conditions that entails the adaptability in space and time of organizations, biology, society, culture and language, etc.

About the fundamental concepts of the theoretical framework of organizational anthropology, these are oriented to analyze the reality of organizations as an object of study of anthropology leading to processes of change in professional programs of various disciplines tending to apply anthropology in the organizational studies of industrial societies. Specifically, organizational anthropology provides support to human realities, such as social constructions, symbolic, cultural and ideological aspects of organizations. The theories and methodologies of organizational anthropology must be compatible with the reality of organizations developed through processes of transformation and formation of companies and companies.

Likewise, organizational anthropology contributes to analyze the perspectives of the actors, contributing to the human side of organizations made up of human beings. Organizational anthropology is a means of providing a background for the study of human beings in organizations that focuses on management and on profitability, efficiency, and effectiveness. For Richardson (1955) anthropology in organizations supports the focus on human relations in organizations, along with psychology and non-systematized knowledge.

About the field of organizational anthropology Roca (1998) considers that this focuses on the investigation of human relations, behaviors and cultures between the different processes of organizations, businesses, industries, companies, ventures, corporations, etc., as systems to provide knowledge, reveal its nature and contribute to criticize, change, improve, denounce, etc. It should be emphasized that the production of organizational anthropology knowledge focused on the diversity of applied organizations requires changes towards more collaborative efforts in professional tasks. The production of one's own knowledge in the anthropological organization as a discipline with its various approaches requires collaboration with change and professional work in parallel.

Regarding the above, Chanlat (1994) emphasizes that the anthropology of organizations is a symbolic ideological, cultural, meaning and identity aspect that creates and develops multiple realities. In other words, the anthropology of organizations is perceived through symbols that reveal internal relationships such as unified elements for work, social culture, organizational and corporate culture, and subcultures within the members of the organization. In such a way that the theoretical knowledge of organizational anthropology is provided in objective tools to industrial psychology aimed at understanding the problems and human aspects in organizations.

The study of organizations from anthropology considers behavior, structure, group values, etc., which leads to analyzing the functioning of organizations (Jordan, 2013). Rather, organizational anthropology describes the sociopolitical relations in the structures of organizations aimed at modifying and transforming forms of commitment, times and new spaces, information and communication technologies. It should be emphasized that the dimensions of organizational anthropology have been modified by information technologies from the perspective of actors within related disciplines who are interested in working in organizations.

Organizational anthropology studies human organizations. That is to say, the anthropological dimension of the human being accounts for a more humanistic organization and the social sense and identity, giving rise to the diversity of human groups. Which leads to the creation and development of mostly human organizations.

Anthropology emphasizes the specificities of human groups in organizations, differentiating itself from sociology by participating with the people studied. The classical theory of anthropology in organizations described as political entities in which various groups pursue their interests and objectives, analyzes the existence of competition between multiple cultural groups, forming a social structure designed to translate demands into culture.

Classical anthropology claims an anthropology of the current world with critical positions and methodological crossovers in both materialist and idealist versions of interpretativism in common core on the familiarization of the exotic to build otherness as a form of practical construction of knowledge for participatory practices as proposed by the approach ethnomethodological (Menéndez, 2006). The foregoing allows building processes of reflection and questioning of classical anthropological theories and their role in society framed in the scientific approach of Marxism.

For Baer (2014) the anthropological vision of organizations provides a perspective that big data fails to fully analyze and interpret the data related to the different organizational stakeholders as customers think, since the human sciences allow us to understand human subjectivity as for Decipher the functions of the technology used to create goods and services.

The concept of business anthropology supported by Jordan (2013) leaves anthropological practice not only for the benefit of organizations on issues related to group behavior, work processes, organizational change, diversity, globalization, etc. In this regard, Caulkins and Jordan (2013) and Morales Inga and Morales Tristán (2018) point out that organizational anthropology is a dynamic field in organizational studies that, more than a unified theory, is made up of multiple theoretical approaches with various methodologies developed and used. in various contexts.

In line with the above, the organizational anthropology methodology aims to collect and use primary information to design an experiential and feedback workshop supported by classic tools such as the SWOT, the group interview, the problem tree, etc., that lead to diagnose problems and find solutions. In turn, the analytical tools of organizational anthropology are used to analyze hierarchies and relationships between and within groups and organisms (Lomnitz, 1975). In addition, the quantitative methodology of organizational anthropology is the conjunction of techniques such as participant observation and psychometrics to achieve the necessary qualifications to obtain objective numerical data on the participants and obtain comprehensive individual results.

From organizational anthropology, the imaginary is the individual perception and beliefs that build the process of social construction of reality generated by interactions between humans, enabling the organizational anthropological perspective created by humans in society of the symbolic world beyond the reality (Cely-López, & Gómez-Niño, 2016). In this regard, Jaumier (2020) warns that anthropology plays a role in understanding alternative organizations and the acts of imagining new ones that lean towards the local experiences and meanings of the members of the organization as a field of problematization rather than theory driven.

The role of organizational anthropology by focusing more on human relations than on production processes. It indicates that the organization is a community aimed at building and strengthening an identity, which, sustained through an organizational culture, values, norms, rites, myths, etc., develops a vision to generate value. Individuals and communities in organizational anthropology promote intervention practices to identify the necessary community perceptions about program design processes to foster the development of community organizations.

Regarding the anthropology of organizations and history, according to Llobera (1975) these contribute to appreciate epistemic cycles. Giving rise to flexible epistemic shelters focused on the construction of alterity supported by other disciplines tending to question relativistic ethnocentric rationalities that lead to the context of creative imagination.

For Czarniawska (2012), organizational anthropology is positioned in business and management research programs, by focusing on analyzing practices in co-evolution with market institutions. In turn, organizational anthropology has reached a stage of maturity focusing on the analysis of organizational theories, based on the emergence of the discipline that provides historical characteristics in the development of theories, traditional and innovative methodologies, and philosophical approaches to organizations and management research. Kunda (1986) and Weeks (2004) state that anthropological journeys establish explicit connections between anthropology and the study of organizations.

In this regard, Fotaki et al. (2020) claim that the analysis of spirituality, symbolism, and storytelling in organization studies are explicitly committed to anthropology. That is, organizational anthropology prioritizes symbolic meanings over more rational thought, makes the human side of the organization relevant and contributes to a holistic perspective of human behavior in organizations (Páramo, 2018; Roca i Girona, 2001).

Interpretive research in organizational anthropology has an emerging and symbolic role rooted in social processes and without a priori assumptions, with explanations and categories defined by organizational actors (Cely-López, & Gómez-Niño, 2016). The symbolic magical meanings on human rationality lead to show the human side of organizations. On the other hand, the lack of interest of symbolic anthropology in the organizational process is due to the fact that technocracy is obsessed with efficiency and effectiveness has imposed organizational thinking (Chanlat, 1994).

Anthropology and sociology have the social aspect in common, but differentiating between them is that the anthropological approach makes the concerns of each human group more specific, leading to a better analysis of organizational phenomena such as organizational culture, which goes against the positive approach. Both anthropology and sociology study and analyze human and social issues and concerns in organizations leading to establishing general and universal social laws. However, anthropology is not concerned with the general laws that account for the diversity of human groups manifested in specific characteristics, analyzing social and cultural details, giving them identity and meaning.

The sociology and anthropology of organizations have the social aspect in common, although the latter gives meaning to the cultural and ideological identity specificities of the various groups that build multiple realities (Chanlat, 1994). Anthropological and sociological sensitivity analyzes human beings in contemporary organizations responsible for the future. Anthropology accounts for the social aspect of the diversity of individuals and human groups and studies, searching for the hidden differences that lead to their meaning and characteristics, with emphasis on specificities.

The specialties of organizational anthropology aim to study various aspects of the constitution of the human being. In other words, an organizational anthropology applied in organizational settings is concerned with organized individuals. Well, it focuses on the study horizon of organizations through intervention and research processes to generate new knowledge with the aim of solving social problems. For Thomas Barfield (2000) applied anthropology focuses on solving practical problems, creating guidelines, providing information and taking action, in categories of applied research and intervention.

Consequently, apply the knowledge of organizational anthropology to the different fields of organizational action, focusing on the analysis of the development of organizational life within the sociocultural context, if the researchers are participants, they contribute to the creation of theoretical knowledge. On the other hand, both anthropology and sociology deal with the social aspect of the organization, the universal and general laws of the social considering the positivist aspect. For example, anthropology studies the social organization of societies, language, beliefs, etc., in organizations. Thus, the analysis of organizational anthropology contributes to the study of issues related to the company and entrepreneurs, tools, methods, categories, etc.

The pioneering analysis in organizational and business anthropology was in the analysis of simple societies to complex societies. Business anthropology studies as a social science aim to explain the behavior of elites by addressing theoretical and methodological challenges using anthropological methods and tools to analyze practices and referents of positions of power whose study subjects are marginal subordinates (Cerutti, 2003; Hernández, 2013). In other words, the studies of entrepreneurship under an organizational anthropology had the objective of explaining the behaviors of the elites.

Socio-anthropological sensitivity removes the administration theory from linear causality of action-benefit (Muñoz, 2011) and provides the elements reproducing the logic of the organizational management leading to the agency of financialization of the economy as the protagonist of social creation instead of considering it as a fatality. Administration is supported by anthropology, sociology, psychology, etc. The administrative thought includes the socio-anthropological sensitivity leading to sharpen the vision for sustainable action contextualized and modulated of the dialectic public—private interests.

The organizational factors are analyzed in the analytical theoretical approaches of organizational and administrative anthropology and symbolic interactionism that deal with the categories of environments and organizational contexts that come from the information and confirmation emanating from semi-structured interviews, dimensions and subdimensions (Cely-López, & Gómez-Niño, 2016).

In this regard, Cely-López and Gómez-Niño (2016) emphasize that organizational anthropology contributes to the administrative process of planning, organization, integration, direction and control; to social accounting that deals with issues related to employees, social community, social responsibility, environmental and ethical issues, etc. For Baba (2012) organizational management structures are supported by social and organizational anthropology to seek effectiveness in private companies and public organizations. In other words, public administration influenced by anthropology has the purpose of humanizing training in organizations.

Anthropological and sociological sensitivity identifies the phenomena and objects of the complexity of human beings who carry organizational collective life. Studies like that of Jamie Uys lead to the theoretical and methodological accumulation of anthropology and organizational sociology. And although the interaction time to study groups in organizational sociology is shorter and sporadic than in organizational anthropology that is dedicated to an intimate study of the group for a longer period. Institutional time management was able to fulfill the positional functions with advantage to plan from an anthropological perspective of organizations.

Traditional and organizational anthropology link technology to broaden the organizational focus and apply knowledge that contributes to the generation of initiatives for the construction of local and autochthonous meanings. It should be noted that technologies contribute to organizational systems in the creation and promotion of new companies, evaluation of technological intervention projects through the formulation of policies and strategies framed in organizational anthropology, contribute to the creation and capture of value in public–private partnerships, etc.

In this regard, Roberts and Grabowski (1996) state that organizational anthropology analyzes different technologies with emphasis on traditional technologies developed contextually with their own resources, and Western technologies classified as mechanical, human, and knowledge. And it is through the theoretical study through documentary and bibliographical analysis that it is intended to explore the relationships between organizational anthropology and traditional technology as part of the organizational space.

The term anthropology was coined by François Auguste Péron, a French naturalist and explorer (1775–1810). And it refers to the science born of the nineteenth century, which studies man. At present, research on the relationships between anthropology and organizational studies, introducing the theory and management of organizational anthropology, begins in the middle of the last century, anthropology displaced from its traditional core of the object of study based on knowledge, from pre-industrial times and non-industrial communities towards a disciplinary interest in more organizational concerns and problems (Marzal, 1996). It might be worth noting that the development of organizational, labor, and industrial anthropology are interrelated. And that, as a scientific discipline, anthropology becomes an applied science that is proposed as an applied industrial anthropology to study problems of the anthropology of work and its functional relationship with society, such as the phenomenon of rural migration to urban areas. (Esteva, 1984, 1955).

The history of organizational anthropology and business organizations in the academic field are complementary developments to the theoretical knowledge in the development of organizational psychology applied to specific practices such as the diversification of products and services. In relation to the above, Harvey (2004) declares that historical reality prompted science and technology to establish the Fordist production system that strengthened the bureaucratic organizational system to control production from the perspective of rationality characterized as instrumental by the perspective criticism.

For authors such as Corsín Jiménez (2007), Caulkins et al. (2013) and North and Gita (2014), organizational studies require new concepts, approaches and technologies such as organizational and management anthropology, creative and knowledge management, etc.., conducive to personal and social development. A review of organization theory and organizational studies and their different approaches and relationships with anthropology highlights the anthropological perspective that leads to the humanistic aspect of organizations.

Organizational anthropology was established in 1927 with the Western Electric Company project at industrial plants in Hawthorne, Chicago as a scientific discipline led by sociologist and industrial psychologist Elton Mayo of the Harvard Business School. And it is related to the school of administration called neo-human relations or human resources created and developed by the same psychologist with his research in the Hawthorne plants between 1927 and 1932 (Chanlat, 2019; Roca i Girona, 2001).

Mayo's interest was to study workers' job satisfaction from the socio-psychological perspective. Authors such as Malinowski (1944), Radcliffe-Brown (1952) and Lloyd Warner (1952) participated in this project, laying the foundations of the theory of organizational anthropology. Considering the latter as the father of organizational anthropology for the work carried out as an ethnologist and sociologist (Bélanger & LeBlanc, 2011). The studies and analyzes built from organizational anthropology contribute to clarify the differences between the referents to support arguments and solve problems that arise between management and workers. In addition, organizational anthropology includes questions and issues related to the welfare of workers assumed as political development organizations.

Based on experiments with the workforce and its productivity, Mayo develops industrial psychology to support the human dimension of organizations, a milestone that marks the beginning of organizational anthropology. Organizational anthropology demonstrated that job satisfaction and worker productivity are determined by their human relationships developed by the contribution of anthropological, ethnographic and participant observation techniques (Richardson, 1955). Given the concept of organizational anthropology, organizations train internally for the productivity, motivation and training of members to create and develop an identity based on organizational capacity.

Organizational anthropology topics began to gain relevance from the famous Hawthorne research project and later with the Society Applied Anthropology research giving rise to the Applied Anthropology Journal renamed Human Organization (Santibáñez, 1994). This emerged in the early 1950s as an expected priority in organizational research interrupted by the crisis in the human relations school that led to the adoption of the managerial perspective. The first anthropological studies were carried out by Caudill (1958) in a psychiatric hospital.

The first organizational anthropology was carried out by Munizaga (1988). During the 1970s, organizational anthropology presented unfavorable academic and scientific production, struggled to become institutionalized and implement programs to train organizational anthropologists to study processes of organizational work dynamics, transculturation in organizational fields, social development, etc.

Organizational anthropology was established as a social science discipline based on ethnographic research methodologies during the 1980s (Bate, 1997) with the aim of studying and analyzing the nature and functioning of public and private organizations. Some classics in the business anthropology literature are Holzberg and Maureen (1981), Pérez-Lizaur (2010), Basaldúa (2005) and Urban and Koh (2013).

Years later, organizational anthropology became a subdiscipline in management research, focusing on working conditions, the burden of work and schedules, the management of organizational processes, etc. Among the new knowledge interests attract the development of the disciplines of organizational and management anthropology, knowledge management and creativity aimed at promoting the formation of people development, creating skills and relationships between personality and the socio-ecological system including society and nature. Organizational anthropology carries out the organizational analysis of the development of organizational management.

The perspectives of organizational psychology in the analysis of organizational behavior are thought more as dysfunctional behaviors, fears and dilemmas, etc., to be addressed as problems and options to strategically position consistently to deal with anthropology for management. While anthropology contributes to satisfy the management needs and demands of organizations, giving rise to organizational anthropology from the management perspective, methods, tools and instruments for management. In other words, organizational anthropology should contribute to designing and developing managerial tools and instruments for the analysis of the organization.

The orientation of organizational anthropology towards the managerialist approach distances itself from the humanist approach that leads to practical application outside of the tensions between labor and capital, prioritizing the maximization of benefits and profitability. The relationships between both disciplines, anthropology and organizations, are a consequence of the interactions found in the management of behavioral limits to make potential contributions to learn and apply on issues of people's well-being aligned with capital and work.

Organizational anthropology broadens the interactions between individuals and the complicated social environment exerting the impact of human formation, care and respect for people. Therefore, the organizational anthropology approach is complementary to the organizational approach to assess job competencies by producing different types of information and data than if only one were used.

Concerning the instrumental conception of the human being, Chanlat (1994) describes it as manipulative, although other anthropologists maintain that organizational behavior has been strengthened with homo economicus as the dominant conception. It is precisely because of these differences that the categories of the economic model are endorsed to understand the characterization of symbolic, mythical, magical, normative and religious phenomena of organizational life and family affairs that can coexist simultaneously. Where the focus of the anthropological organization in the selection of personnel alleviates some of the problems.

In other words, an anthropological approach to organizations contributes to expanding and complementing knowledge in talent management. For this reason, practical organizational anthropology serves management in the management of knowledge of the specific problems of organizations from the theoretical and methodological frameworks of anthropology and anthropological techniques. What makes them necessary for organizational development.

Anthropological organizational facilitation is the professional external intervention aimed at improving the institutional management practices of the actors who pursue their own objectives based on the concepts and objects of study of organizational anthropology, such as the construction of alterity and reflexivity. And it is assigned as a function of organizational management urging higher education institutions to prepare knowledge.

From an organizational anthropology perspective with a specific contribution to organizational facilitation through a reconversion of ways of positioning in the face of problems. There is participatory action in social processes, collective actions with specific formal and informal purposes. Participatory and facilitation processes as transfer instruments are methodological challenges that present themselves as opportunities and difficulties to situate non-traditional actions as objects of organizational anthropology from different asymmetric rationalities. These challenges must be addressed in accordance with the anthropological contribution of methodological principles to facilitation and organizational participation aimed at creating and changing the organizational and management culture.

Reflections on management practices lead the framework of organizational anthropology to the point of becoming a discipline in organizational studies. This alternative must be included in the academic questions and concerns to strategically position itself in the theoretical and practical deepening of an anthropology for management. The theoretical framework of organizational anthropology and the referents involved have a place in the anthropology of practice. Well, the practice of anthropology in organizational dynamics confronts processes between management and workers in order to change the methodological approach, affecting the entire human being inscribed in organizational behavior, demanding commitment and responsibility with oneself.

Social anthropology studies social relationships and structures. The analysis from the social anthropology of the family, the businessman and the company are linked actors. Studies on simple societies in anthropology analyze the kinship systems of society, such as the case of Lebanese businessmen in southeastern Mexico (Ramírez Carrillo, 1992), the determinants of the family pattern of businessmen (Nader, 1972) in a comparative analysis. Practice for social agents applying anthropological imagination (Gravano, 1995) and the case method in organizational management in institutions, organizations and movements.

Organizational anthropology studies of organizations, entrepreneurship and the family refer to the family-organization. The family and the company from the perspective of anthropology is resolved around analyzing the articulation of the company and the labor participation of the family members and the relationships established between them and pointing to issues related to the members of the family, family who are workers and owners at the same time in organizations. An analysis from the social anthropology of the family business is a business domestic unit that emphasizes the functions of the family as a primary network. Organizational anthropology firms equate the family as the domestic unit of members who contribute relationships, resources, practices, etc.

The field of social management through the anthropology of organizations contributes to build the options, including the relevant methodological and ideological ones. Organizational anthropology seeks to describe and analyze the structuring of social relationships at work, presentation and body appearance, duration, forms of commitment, experiences, new spaces and times, and other elements in the management of organizations.

Mexican anthropology, like the Manchester School of Anthropology, tries to overcome the prejudice of the managerial approach of organizational anthropology. Regarding the above, the organizational crisis coincided with the emergence of the Manchester School in organizational anthropology influenced by Gluckman (1940) on the research carried out on industrial organizations, including participant observation that led to the contradiction of harmony in the work proposed by the School of Human Resources, the social fit situations from a broader structure. Where the link between two organizations, the economic unit and the domestic unit, expands that family in the analysis of social networks characterized as a structure and represented by individuals or other networks since 1960 according to García and Oliveira.

Mexican anthropology has more recent origins, but it has obtained a high impact and scope in economic, social, political and cultural achievements. Anthropological studies in Mexico originated with the colonization process in the sixteenth century followed by social and cultural contradictions in the need to describe and interpret indigenous cultures. In the independent Mexico of the nineteenth century, anthropology focused on issues and concerns related to the interpretation of the existing social reality in search of a common identity, creating a stable and strong state and the origin of the professionalization of anthropology.

At the beginning of the nineteenth century, physical anthropology and ethnology began in Mexico. And with this at the end of the same century, the development of empirically applied organizational anthropology begins, articulating work niches, although professional practice is more related to management actions of academic institutions. In 1910, the National School of American Archeology and Ethnology was founded, introducing the paradigm of indigenous anthropology with Manuel Gamio, becoming one of the lasting currents of anthropological thought (Gonzàlez Gamio, 2003; Matos Moctezuma, 1987; Villanueva et al., 1999). In this, themes such as the issues, problems and concerns of applied anthropology in Mexico aimed at recovering national identity and local history revolving around the analysis to understand one's own were developed.

In the 1920s and 1930s, the integrationist conception of anthropology was formed, called New Anthropology committed to nationalist interests with the teaching of anthropology in the academic programs of the National Polytechnic Institute and the National School of Anthropology and History (Olive Negrete, 1981). In which the traditional limits of anthropology as a discipline focused on the study of social groups such as peasants, migrants, workers, etc., during the 1970s, complementing the Mexican anthropology carried out by Esteban Krotz (1993) and García and Krotz (1988) with an emphasis on the cultural heritage of the national state.

Marxist theory and critical perspective have a strong influence on the theoretical framework that supports the development of Mexican anthropology. While critical organizational studies are inspired by anthropology, it has not been credited that the contributions remain implicit and elusive, revealing an incomplete story (Mir & Fayard, 2021). However, anthropological criticality contributes the focus on the dynamics of power and front, and its empirical focus on managerial practices in the contexts of indigenous organizations and informal settings. In turn, the contributions of the organizational anthropological approach complement feminist economies by making unpaid domestic work visible (Domínguez Folgueras, 2019).

In correspondence with the above, Roca i Girona (2001) indicates that the study of anthropology in organizations is considered more complex for anthropologists because they are implicitly under criticism for being involved in a contractual relationship for a salary in exchange for work. Nonetheless, despite organizational anthropology's imperfections in organizational studies that are characterized by the potential for opportunities for further cross-fertilization and scholarly scrutiny. This approach should focus on the organizational sciences that can benefit from organizational anthropology and ethnography as a method (Bate, 1997).

Latin American organizations and work situations are a laboratory of organizational anthropology aimed at researching, analyzing, formulating and applying policies in public and private formal structured organizations (Bermúdez, 2017). Well, the organizational anthropological production in Latin America is at the beginning of a dialogue and discussion based on the differences between history, regions, ethnic groups and other specificities of methodologies, research practices, convergences and detected differences.

In addition, organizational anthropology is an interdisciplinary professional whose specificity begins to develop by focusing on the design of an integral model considering the neighborhood as a symbol, and the semiotic mechanisms established in the construction of meaning. Hence, the anthropology consultancy of organizations needs a global and more objective tool capable of shortening the time to develop field research for comprehensive results with an emphasis on organizational analysis.

Gravano (1992) describes organizational anthropology as the intervention and facilitation of organizational processes using methodological tools that are not necessarily applied and practical anthropology for the implementation of listening, interpolation, objectification and transfer caused by the practices of the participants to make decisions about actions to achieve effectiveness. Likewise, Cely-López and Gómez-Niño (2016) affirm that organizational anthropology ventures into the analysis of behaviors, values, beliefs, customs in all organizational practices and activities related to work life, lifestyles, human development, education and training etc. That is to say, trends in educational disciplines are aimed at sharing knowledge on organizational anthropology assigned as a separate subject on administrative, cultural and social anthropology.

To summarize, the agency of people and social movements in social structures is the new current in anthropological studies to reveal dynamic changes with the commitment to explain integration processes through research.

6 Organizational Ethnography

Organizational anthropology and organizational sociology are privileged in the referential framework of management by the methods of ethnography and ethnology to carry out research on their respective objects of study tending to acquire more useful anthropological and sociological sensitivity to organizational administration and management. The ethnography of sociocultural anthropology in organizational contexts supports problem solving and provides theoretical-conceptual elements of organizational anthropology oriented to the analysis of behaviors and institutional relationships.

Organizational anthropology and ethnography offer a theoretical and conceptual framework and practical tools for studying and analyzing organizational functions, practices, activities, processes, and relationships. In the words of Bate (1997), organizational anthropology is a discipline that uses ethnographic research methodologies aimed at analyzing the nature and functioning of organizations as an object of study established since the 1980s. For its part, ethnography is the technique most representative anthropological and ethnographic research aimed at understanding and holistic observation of the system of phenomena and organizational behavior through the description of the elements that interact (Hammersley & Atkinson, 2007).

So, organizational ethnography is the application of methodological techniques developed by anthropologists Malinowski and Radcliffe Brown. Thus, organizational anthropology and ethnography have become relevant in the use of methodological insights into organizational and management theory and research. So, organizational ethnography and anthropological studies have created the field of organizational behavior by taking it into a separate field and losing touch with the essential qualities of anthropology. Anthropology remains the forgotten science in organizational studies (Bate, 1997).

There is a growing interest in the ethnographic methodology used in organizational anthropology to be applied in a formal and structural way in organizations, policies and public and private structures such as associations, companies and cooperatives. The anthropological reflexivity of organizations conceives ethnography to investigate and implement intervention processes capable of facilitating the understanding of behaviors and practices to record the voice of the voiceless.

The writing of anthropological ethnographies of organizations is distinguished from organizational science. Regarding the above, Van Maanen (1987) indicates that the influence of research is reflected in organizational anthropology and organizational ethnography. Also, Turco (2016) and Anteby (2013) consider organizational ethnography as fertile in anthropological research in organizational and management studies in the use of ethnographic methods as indicated by Barley (1986) and Orlikowski (2002), in sharing meanings. in organizational communities (Bechky (2003).

Hawthorne's study evidences the anthropological approach to the study of culture using the ethnological method applied by Warner under the direction of Mayo to the analysis of the human side of the organization in a group of workers as a small society. It should be noted that Mayo's ethnographic work is a practical approach to the study of human problems and behaviors in organizations, which supports important contributions to organizations such as objective observation, the participatory method, the social group, etc.

Organizational ethnographies contribute to theoretical development. It also improves organizations and businesses by resorting to the study of anthropology to collect the information that big data is not capable of obtaining to understand people's life patterns (Lebeau, 2017). In relation to the ethnographic approach to organizational improvement, it was nourished by a dialectical-institutional project towards a conflict theory model centered on contradiction and negativity (Lourau, 1979).

Organizational anthropology studies began with tools and methodologies developed by traditional ethnography, which have been criticized by Roca i Girona (2001), as poorly defined and as the result of heresy or contradiction.

On the other hand, the new tools of organizational ethnography and anthropology today represent the foundations for theoretical empirical research in the economic atmosphere to analyze patterns, perspectives, and rhythms of organizational life incorporated into mainstream organizational research.

Lastly, the ethnographic study of gender politics in the global movement like the published work on para-ethnography in business organizations making gender equality policies by Fisher (2012a, 2012b), remains a research challenge organizational.

7 Conclusions

The objective of the study was to analyze some of the theoretical, conceptual and methodological implications and contributions between organizational anthropology and ethnography, based on the assumption that the ethnographic analysis of organizations and interpretative research on organizational anthropology have an emerging and symbolic role rooted in social processes and without a priori assumptions, with explanations and categories defined by organizational actors. The analysis concludes that the ethnographic methodology is pertinent to be used in the analysis of its interactions with organizational anthropology as a new specialty in organizational studies.

The anthropological contribution to organizational studies leads to the dimensions of the human side of the human being to account for individual understanding and meaning in its context. In addition, organizational anthropology has contributed to the advancement of organizational studies, the company, business, management and business anthropology. The main contributions of organizational anthropology are academics and professionals who complement each other in organizational analysis to clarify the vision of organizations and apply them to specific products and services under new paradigms.

Organizational anthropology addresses the reality to be studied considering time. At the same time, they contribute to creating more humane organizations and more social skills in management. Likewise, it analyzes the reality of social behavior to capture the integral and general character of organizational social life. In short, it rescues the dimensions of the human being, relying on anthropological tools to study and analyze the specific details of human groups as the dimensions of being in the organizational phenomenon.

8 Recommendations

The construction of a conceptual framework of organizational anthropology to study and analyze the phenomenon in theoretical depth supported by more widespread methodological contributions to give meaning to organizational studies. This organizational anthropological conceptual framework must be put into practice and applied to organizational management issues.

In the anthropological organization, knowledge transmission processes and events using ethnographic methods require a lot of time to be considered as a laboratory for organizational anthropology. What makes it necessary to incorporate anthropological components such as artifacts and processes full of meanings to structure organizational transformations that facilitate the creation, transmission and reproduction of knowledge. Hence its usefulness, since organizational, business, corporate or industrial anthropology is characterized by an ethnographic approach focused on shared meanings that include spiritual and material manifestations.

For their part, higher education institutions should promote the humanization of management by supporting new concepts, technologies and approaches to influence self-development and social development. In other words, the new fields of knowledge are organizational anthropology, knowledge, and creative management that contribute to human formation, the development of social relationships, and creative abilities.

Finally, the anthropology of organizations contributes to the study that allows deepening, detailing and revealing the basic individual dimensions of the human being. That is, the dimensions of the human being that account for the human side of organizations are anthropological contributions to the analysis of human behavior in the context of organizational studies. For example, a research object is the analysis of organizational anthropology related to traditional technology as a space for reflection to generate future research.

References

Alvesson, M., & Berg, P. O. (1992). *Corporate culture and organizational symbolism: An overview*. Walter de Gruyter.

Anteby, M. (2013). *Manufacturing morals: The values of silence in business school education*. University of Chicago Press.

Baba, M. (2012). Anthropology and business: Influence and interests. *Journal of Business Anthropology, 1*(1), 20–71.

Baer, D. (27 de marzo de 2014). *Business Insider*. Recuperado de https://www.businessinsider.com/heres-why-companies-aredesperatetohireanthropologists-2014-3

Barfield, T. (Ed.). (2000). *Diccionario de Antropología*. Siglo XXI Editores.

Barley, S. R. (1986). Technology as an occasion for structuring: Evidence from observations of CT scanners and the social order of radiology departments. *Administrative Science Quarterly, 31*(1), 78–108.

Bate, S. P. (1997). Whatever happened to organizational anthropology? A review of the field of organizational ethnography and anthropological studies. *Human Relations, 50*(9), 1147–1175. https://doi.org/10.1177/001872679705000905
Basaldúa, M. (2005). *Los empresarios de la compañía industrial cerillera de san Juan del Rio: Antropología de la industria cerillera.* Tesis de doctorado en antropología s/p Universidad Iberoamericana.
Bechky, B. A. (2003). Sharing meaning across occupational communities: The transformation of understanding on a production floor. *Organization Science, 14*(3), 312–330.
Bélanger, A. et LeBlanc, M.-N. (2011). *Socio-anthropologie de la culture populaire. Séminaire de Doctorat en sociologie. SOC 9004-40.* Université du Québec à Montréal (UQÀM). [inédito].
Berg, P. O., & Faucheux, C. (1982). *The symbolic management of company cultures.* INSEAD.
Bermúdez, H. L. (2017). Sociology and anthropology in administrator training. In: *Forum doctoral* (No. 7, pp. 27–27).
Caudill, W. (1958). *Some uses of anthropology: Theoretical and applied. American Anthropologist* New Series, *60*(4), 762–764 (3 pages).
Caulkins, D. D., & Ann, J. (2013). *Companion to organizational anthropology.* Blackwell Publishing.
Caulkins, D., & Jordan, A. T. (Eds.). (2013). *A companion to organizational anthropology.* Wiley-Blackwell.
Chanlat, J. F. (2019). Antropología de las organizaciones. *Revista del Centro de Estudios de Sociología del Trabajo, 11*, 17–39.
Chanlat, J. (1994). Hacia una antropología de la organización. In *Gestión y política pública* (Vol. III, núm. 2, segundo semestre, pp. 317–364).
Cely-López, C. L., & Gómez-Niño, O. (2016). An anthropological perspective of organizations from sociocultural characterization, management, and social accounting. The case of a tertiary education institution. *Cuadernos de Contabilidad, 17*(43), 184.
Cerutti, M. (2003). Los estudios empresariales en América Latina ¿el debate interminable?. *Boletín de Historia Económica*, año 1, 2, junio. México (pp. 3–9). Disponible en: http://www.audhe.org.uy/Boletin_Audhe/Boletin_2/Boletin_02_Cerutti.pdf
Corsín Jiménez, A. (2007). *The anthropology of organizations.* Ashgate Publishing Limited.
Czarniawska, B. (2012). Organization theory meets anthropology: A story of an encounter. *Journal of Business Anthropology, 1*(1), 118–140.
Domínguez Folgueras, M. (2019). ¿Cuánto vale el trabajo doméstico en España? *Observatorio Social de La Caixa.* Accedido 11 de enero de 2020. https://bit.ly/2Rmnhyg
Esteva Frabegat, C. (1984) [1973]. *Antropología industrial.* Anthropos
Esteva Fabregat, C. (1955). *Carácter social y familia obrera en México.* Tesis de Maestría en etnología, presentada en la Escuela de Antropología e Historia de México.
Fisher, M. (2012a). *Wall street women.* Duke University Press.
Fisher, M. (2012b). Toward a feminist para-ethnography on gender equality policy making in business. *Collaborative Anthropologies, 5.*
Fotaki, M., Altman, Y., & Koning, J. (2020). Spirituality, symbolism, and storytelling in twentyfirst-century organizations: Understanding and addressing the crisis of imagination. *Organization Studies, 41*(1), 7–30.
García Canclini, N. (1982). *Las Culturas Populares en el capitalismo.* Nueva Imagen.
García Mora, C., & Krotz, E. (1988). *La antropología en México: panorama histórico* (Vol. 9). Instituto Nacional de Antropología e Historia.
Garsten, Ch., & Anette, N. (2013). *Organizational anthropology: Doing ethnography in and among complex organizations.* Pluto Press.
Gluckman, M. (1940). *Analysis of a social situation in Zululand, Manchester*. Manchester University.
Gonnet, J. (junio de 2012). Cultura, organizaciones y antropología. Una revisión crítica. Avá. *Revista de Antropología* (21), 151–170. Recuperado de http://www.redalyc.org/articulo.oa?id=16903026800

Gonzàlez Gamio, A. (2003). *Manuel Gamio: una lucha sin final*. Universidad Nacional Autónoma de México.
Gravano, A. (1995). La imaginación antropológica; interpelaciones a la otredad construida y al método antropológico. Publicar en *Antropología y Ciencias Sociales, 5*, 71–91.
Gravano, A. (1992). Antropología Práctica, muestra y posibilidades de la Antropología Organizacional. Publicar en *Antropología y Ciencias Sociales*, Buenos Aires, n. 1, pp. 95–126.
Hammersley, M., & Atkinson, P. (2007). *Ethnography*. Routledge.
Harvey, D. (2004). *La condición de la posmodernidad*. Amorrortu editores.
Hernández, V. (2013). Genealogía de una elite rural: elucidación antropológica de una práctica de poder. *Mundo Agrario, 13*(26), junio. Argentina. Disponible en: https://www.redalyc.org/pdf/845/84527468004.pdf
Holzberg, C., & Maureen, G. (1981). Anthropology and Industry reappraisal and new directions. *Annual Review of Anthropology, 10*. Estados Unidos (pp. 317–360). https://doi.org/10.1146/annurev.an.10.100181.001533
Jaumier, S. (2020). Why does the study of alternative organizations (so badly) need anthropology? In: R. Mir, A.-L. Fayard (Eds.), *The Routledge companion to anthropology and business* (pp. 414–432). Routledge. https://doi.org/10.4324/9781003052456-22
Jordan, A. (2013). *Bussines anthropology*. Waveland Press, Inc.
Kottak, C. P. (2011). *Antropología cultural*. McGrawHill.
Krotz, E. (1993). Antropología y antropólogos en México: elementos de balance para construir perspectivas: (pp. 361–380). In: *Balance de la Antropología en América Latina y el Caribe Universidad Nacional Autónoma de México*.
Kunda, G. (1986). *Engineering culture: Control and commitment in a high-tech corporation*. Temple University Press.
Lomnitz, L. (1975). Anthropology of scientific research at UNAM. In: *Science and development* 6. CONACYT.
Lourau, R. (1979). *El análisis institucional*. Amorrortu.
Lebeau, S. (2017 24 de julio de). *Minnesota Business*. Recuperado de https://www.minnesotabusiness.com/anthropology-business
Llobera, J. (1975). *La antropología como ciencia*. Anagrama.
Maestre Alfonso, J. (1983). *Introducción a la Antropología social*. Akla.
Malinowski, B. (1944). *A scientific theory of culture and other essays*. University of North Carolina Press.
Marzal, M. M. (1996). *Historia de la anthropologìa. Volume I. Anthropologìa indìgena*. Ediciones Abya-Yala.
Matos Moctezuma, E. (1987). Román Piña Chan y la Escuela Nacional de Antropología e Historia (pp. 81–90). In: *Homenaje a Román Piña Chan*. Universidad Nacional Autónoma de México—Instituto de Investigaciones Antropológicas.
Menéndez, E. (2006). Participación social en salud: las representaciones y las prácticas. In: E. Menéndez, H. Spinelli (Eds.), *Participación social ¿para qué?*, pp. 81–115. Lugar Editorial.
Menéndez, E. (1996). *Fundamentals of economics*. Buenos Aires.
Mir, R., & Fayard, A.-L. (2021). Anthropology and organizational studies: A symbiotic connection. In R. Mir & A.-L. Fayard (Eds.), *The Routledge companion to anthropology and business* (pp. 1–13). Routledge.
Morales Inga, S., & Tristán, O. M. (2018). Capturando la cultura: tres aportes de la antropología a la selección de personal. *Palermo Business Review, 18*, 261–280.
Munizaga, B. J. (1988). La violencia doméstica y la sociedad. *Revista De Sociología, 3*, 35–43. https://doi.org/10.5354/0719-529X.1988.27565
Muñoz, R. (2011). *Formar en administración. Por una nueva fundamentación filosófica*. Siglo del Hombre. Fondo Editorial Universidad EAFIT.
Nader, L. (1972). *Up me anthropologist: perspectives gained from studying up*, mimeo, 28p. Disponible en: https://files.eric.ed.gov/fulltext/ED065375.pdf

North, K., & Gita, K. (2014). *Knowledge management. Value creation through organizational learning*. Springer International Publishing.
Olive Negrete, J. C. (1981). *Antropología Mexicana*. Plaza y Valdés—Instituto Nacional de Antropología e Historia—Colegio Mexicano de Antropólogos.
Orlikowski, W. J. (2002). Knowing in practice: Enacting a collective capability in distributed organizing. *Organization Science, 13*(3), 249–273.
Páramo, D. (2018). Antropología organizacional. *Revista científica Pensamiento y Gestión, 1*(45).
Pérez-Lizaur, M. (2010). *Empresa y Familia en México, una visión desde la antropología*. Universidad Iberoamericana.
Radcliffe-Brown, A. (1952). *Structure and function in primitive society*. Oxford University Press.
Ramírez Carrillo, L. (1992). Estratificación, clase y parentesco: empresarios libaneses en el sureste de México. *Nueva Antropología*, vol XIII no. 43. México (pp. 123). Disponible en: https://www.redalyc.org/pdf/159/15904311.pdf
Richardson, F. (1955). Anthropology and human relations in business and industry. *Yearbook of Anthropology* (pp. 397–419). Recuperado de http://www.jstor.org/stable/3031158
Roberts, K., & Grabowski, M. (1996). Organizations, technology and structuring. In S. R. Clegg, C. Hardy, & W. Nord (Eds.), Handbook of organization studies (pp. 409–423). Sage.
Roca i Girona, J. (2001). Antropólogos en la empresa? A propósito de la mal llamada cultura de la empresa. *Etnográfica, 1*. Colombia. (pp. 69–99). Disponible en: http://ceas.iscte.pt/etnografica/docs/vol_05/N1/Vol_v_N1_69-100.pdf
Roca, J. (1998). *Antropologia Industrial y de la Empresa*. Ariel.
Santibáñez, D. (1994). *Una aproximación sistémico- cultural a la organización com unitaria*. Memoria para optar al título profesional de Antropólogo social, Universidad de Chile, Santiago.
Smirnova, V. (2016). *Organizational culture* (pp. 42–43). Yurayt Publishing.
Turco, C. J. (2016). *The conversational firm: Rethinking bureaucracy in the age of social media*. Columbia University Press.
Urban, G., & Koh, K. (2013) Ethnographic research on modern business corporation. *Annual Review Anthropology, 42*. Estados Unidos (pp. 139–158). https://doi.org/10.1146/annurev-anthro-092412-155506
Van Maanen, J. (1987). *Tales of the field: On writing ethnography*. University of Chicago.
Villanueva, M., Serrano, C., & Vera, J. L. (1999). *Cien años de antropología física en México: inventario Bibliográfico*. Universidad Nacional Autónoma de México—Instituto de Investigaciones Antropológicas.
Warner, W. L. (1952). *Structure of American Life*. Edinburgh University Press.
Weeks, J. (2004). *Unpopular culture: The ritual of complaint in a British bank*. University of Chicago Press.

Prosumer Economy in Practice: Building a Community of Smes with Deepened Circular Supply Networks

Ayşe Defne Korğalı, Duru Uslu, and Uygar Özesmi

Abstract The dominant economic paradigm is dysfunctional, both in its ecological and social dimensions. A planetary boundaries framework update reports that currently, 6 out of 9 boundaries are already transgressed, indicating the earth isn't a safe space for humanity anymore (Richardson et al. in Science Advances 9, 2023). The normalization of unjust economic practices is the root cause of the polycrisis humanity experiences. Solving the polycrisis may only be possible by shifting the dominant economic paradigm. We set out to create a prosumer economy as an alternative sustainable economic paradigm. The prosumer economy is defined as "a macroscale circular economy with minimum negative or positive ecological and social impact, an ecosystem of producers and prosumers, who have synergistic and circular relationships with deepened circular supply networks, where leakage of wealth out of the system is minimized" (Özesmi in The prosumer economy—Being like a forest, 2019). This prosumer economy system was implemented in Good4Trust.org where more than 25.000 prosumers and 770 producers (SMEs) came together and are working together. Good4Trust is an online bazaar that brings ecologically and socially fair producers and prosumers together to create a full ecosystem. It doesn't reinforce competition like a marketplace but solidarity and symbiosis like a local bazaar where producers all help each other and work together. Exchanges include retail, wholesale, services, and contractual sales. Good4Trust also has an inbuilt community currency called "Trust". Every time a prosumer supports a producer, by buying a product from them, they create "Trust". These trusts then, can be gifted, transferred, or used in other exchanges. We discuss Good4Trust as a viable sustainable ecosystem and demonstrate how the prosumer economy may help in the creation of a needed paradigm shift to solve the polycrisis.

A. D. Korğalı (✉) · D. Uslu
Prosumer Economy Society, İzmir, Turkey
e-mail: ayse.defne@turetimekonomisi.org

D. Uslu
e-mail: duru@turetimekonomisi.org

U. Özesmi
Centre for Energy and Sustainable Development, Kadir Has University, İstanbul, Turkey
e-mail: uygar@good4trust.org

W. Leal Filho and V. Kuzmanović (eds.), *Sustainable Development Seen Through the Lenses of Ethnoeconomics and the Circular Economy*,
https://doi.org/10.1007/978-3-031-72676-7_10

Keywords Prosumer · Prosumer economy · Post-humanism · Alternative economies · Trust · Prefigurative organisations

1 Introduction

The dominant economic paradigm seeks for infinite growth on a finite planet. Yet, it is simply against physics. (Özesmi, 2019) The consequences of human activities driven by the anthropocentric mindset destroy planetary life support systems. The global surface temperature has increased by 1.1 °C since the pre-industrial period. In 2019, the CO2 concentrations in the atmosphere reached the highest level within two million years. Changes in the atmosphere, ocean, cryosphere and biosphere are unprecedentedly rapid and destructive. Weather and climate extremes occur everywhere around the globe. These result in the degradation of biological diversity and deepening social inequalities by impacting disproportionately the most vulnerable communities (IPCC, 2023). The root cause of these polycrises is the dominant economic paradigm based on profit maximization and consumption.

The growing industrialization and economic scale have been one of the fundamental drivers of global and local climate change, since it requires the transformation of Earth's resources into wealth through industrial activity, leading to a rapidly increasing level of consumption of materials and energy (Linnenluecke & Griffiths, 2013). Currently, nature is under the combined pressure of human population growth and the growth in the wealth per capita (Lutz et al., 2004). Being aware of the situation, "[s]cientists and policymakers have argued in varying terms that this challenge can only be met if *system innovations* are realized" (Tukker & Butter, 2007). Therefore, a change towards a sustainable economic system is necessary for the survival of humanity on Earth.

A sustainable economy can be defined as an economy that acknowledges the limitations of the planet and planet's ability to meet present and future needs as well as ensuring everyone, especially the world's poor has access to their fundamental needs (Lorek & Spangenberg, 2014). It is essential that we abandon the traditional twentieth century growth model, and focus on creating a new sustainable economy through a low carbon economic model and lifestyle and realize sustainable social development (Xiaowei et al., 2011).

Thankfully, there is a rising consciousness on the harmful practices and demand for change, reflected both in consumer behavior and institutional regulations. However, individual efforts or solutions similar to corporate social responsibility, financial initiatives and sanctions still remain within the current system. Fortunately, numerous people questioned the dominant mindset which then transformed into grassroot movements proposing solutions for systemic change. For instance, the degrowth movement emerged by questioning the compatibility of the earth's balance with the capitalist system (D'Alisa et al., 2015). Similarly, Solidarity Economies, Commons Movement, Peer to Peer Movement, Transition Network, social enterprises or cooperatives as an older model are all grassroot movements that differ in form but that are all against the dominant socio-economic paradigm based on growth, competition, consumption, and profit maximization. They imagine and build economies of ecology and social justice; new prefigurative organisations emerge (Schiller-Merkens, 2022).

One of those grassroot movements that challenge capitalism is the prosumer economy. The prosumer economy is defined as "a macroscale circular economy with minimum negative or positive ecological and social impact, an ecosystem of producers and prosumers, who have synergistic and circular relationships with deepened circular supply chains/networks, where leakage of wealth out of the system is minimised" (Özesmi, 2019). "While most human activities may present negative consequences, a BM may be designed to limit its externalities" (Lecocq et al., 2023, p. 126). The significance of the prosumer economy is that it creates an ecosystem that doesn't consume, in other words creates positive ecological and social externalities, or minimizes the negative externalities by encouraging sustainable production. The prosumer economy is an ecosystem in which every member of the ecosystem is in symbiosis with other community members. Symbiosis defined as "association, for significant portions of the life cycle, of individuals that are members of different species" (Margulis, 1981, p. 161). Since prosumer economy is based on collaboration, it is a symbiotic ecosystem.

Even though the prosumer economy is relatively new, the origin and history of the concept of prosumer dates back to the 1980s. The word "Prosumer" was first used by futurologist Alvin Toffler (1980), who predicted the roles of consumers and producers would blur and merge. Toffler defined "Prosumers" as people who are "neither producers nor consumers in the usual sense" (Toffler, 1980, p. 266). They consumed what they produced themselves. According to Toffler, there are three different stages of production and consumption activity. The first stage was before the industrial age, when people were mostly prosumers; they produced their needs themselves to survive. The second wave started with the industrial age. In the second stage, most people were consumers and produced for other people's consumption. The production processes were more focused on efficiency and tried to provide that by industrialization and marketization. The third and last stage is the post-industrial age. In the third wave, prosumers are back on the rise, and their focus is individuation, therefore leading to de-massification, deindustrialization, and de-marketization (Toffler, 1980).

As the world became digitized, the term "prosumer" slightly evolved. In the new digital world, as Toffler has foreseen, the prosumer is also described as an active consumer. Thanks to the implementation of new information technologies, consumers can actively engage in production processes, such as designing new products, improving materials, product reliability and durability, commercialization of products and services, designing promotional campaigns, and managing customer service. This idea of having a say in the production is very attractive for (especially young) consumers and is closely related to the concept of crowdsourcing. "It is based on constant cooperation with consumer environments and uses the knowledge and skills of their participants to obtain creative content, generate new ideas, and collect user opinions about a product, service, or brand" (Bednarz, 2022, p. 32).

Prosumer is also an important term in the field of renewable energy, where individuals produce the energy they use with photovoltaic panels (PV) on the roofs of their houses. Building on the concept of prosumer, who both produce and consume energy, the term "prosumage" has further emerged. Combining the words prosumer and storage, prosumage simply defines the process of producing electricity and storing the excess amount (Green & Staffell, 2017). Prosumagers, people who prosumage, are defined as "grid-connected electricity consumers who own small-scale PV generators as well as batteries, and use these installations to produce their own electricity at times, draw electricity from the grid at other times, and feed electricity to the grid at yet other times" (Schill et al., 2017, p. 2).

Other than sustainable energy production, the term prosumer is also a significant part of sharing economies. In the last decade, many peer-to-peer platforms have arisen, challenging the common social paradigm of corporate production. Those peer-to-peer exchanges not only provide an alternative to consumerism but also encourage both providers and consumers to become prosumers, which are defined as people who both consume and provide. By converting one-sided users (only providers or consumers) to prosumers, the members of the sharing economy create a collective benefit, because the range and choice of service or product increases for the consumers, and the demand for those sustainable products or service alternatives increases. By increasing prosumers in a sharing economy and encouraging one-sided users to become providers, the economy provides benefits for both the people and the ecology (Lang et al., 2020).

On the other hand, from an ecological perspective, every organism is a prosumer. The only providers are the Sun and the Earth; everything else prosumes. When we look at a food web, we notice that photosynthetic organisms create biomass from the Sun and the Earth (Lithosphere, Hydrosphere, and Atmosphere). This biomass is then food for others, and those others are food for others, and so on, until they become the Earth again through the action of decomposers. Ironically the decomposers themselves are eventually decomposed. So everything turns in a circle and circles in circles forming a web of prosumers, all powered by the Sun and the Earth (Lindeman, 1942).

Inspired by all the previous definitions, we take a different route, where we define prosumer not only as a portmanteau of the words producer and consumer, but give it an ethical and social quality. Prosumers in our definition are people or entities "who treat others as they would like to be treated themselves (Golden Rule) hence create value with their actions for society and the planet. They support social and ecologically just productions directly" and most importantly collectively (Özesmi, 2019). In a similar approach Good4Trust Council Member and Founder of Slow Food in Turkey, Defne Koryürek says "prosumers are the ones who refuse the bipolar definition of the growth economy knowing that every producer is also a consumer and every consumer is a producer. They adopt the conservation of fauna, flora, and thereby the future with a longing for a good, clean, and just civilisation. They take these values as a compass for inquiring modes of production and consumption."

Prosumers aren't only passive prosumers, who source their needs from sustainable producers, but they are also involved in the governance, supply chains, and the cooperation in the ecosystem. Prosumers are the ones to decide who will govern the ecosystem, who is qualified and sustainable to get into the ecosystem as a producer, and the ones to attract other consumers into the prosumer economy system, to be prosumers. They'll also encourage other producers to get into the ecosystem and source their raw materials from other producers in the ecosystem, therefore becoming prosumers (Satıcı & Özesmi, 2023). They are the driving force behind a sustainable new socio-economic paradigm, deepening supply chains, creating circularity, and minimizing leakage out of the system.

Since the prosumer definition in prosumer economy is not limited to a role in economy but also gives the term an ethical perspective, the prosumer economy is able to address both social and ecological problems, thus sustainable. In its ideal state, the prosumer economy does not harbor exploitation of people or the environment/nature. The main goal in the prosumer economy is maximizing ecological and social impact, not profit. The prosumer economy ensures that by being an ecological economic system like a lake or a forest, every member of the ecosystem is helped and is helping other members of the community or ecosystem at a larger scale.

For an economy to be classified as a prosumer economy there are four basic rules the economy must follow. Those are:

The economic system, the ecosystem, and the community should be established upon ethics. The system must embrace the Golden Rule which is "Do unto others as you would have them do unto you." Others include all the other organisms and planetary life support systems, considering the biodiversity crisis we experience nowadays.

All members of the ecosystem aim for solidarity, collaboration, cooperation, and ecological and social justice, and work towards that shared goal.

The sustainable supply chains in the ecosystem are deepened and reinforced by the support systems built in the prosumer economy ecosystem.

The community is governed by a democratic local governance.

As economies and ecosystems around the world become more and more like prosumer economies, more prosumer economies may be generated around the world. We hope that the dominant paradigm will be the prosumer economies of the future that are both socially and ecologically just. We believe the current dominant economies will be the minority and eventually disappear, or civilization or even humanity may be at risk.

For the prosumer economy to be the common paradigm and to be adopted by different communities, the Prosumer Economy Society has been working in Turkey since 2015 (*Türetim Ekonomisi Derneği*, n.d.). Prosumer Economy Society's goal is to research ecologically and socially just business models, reinforce and strengthen good practices, and inform the public about the prosumer economy's positive impacts on ecology and building a sustainable society.

In this article, we are going to examine the implementation of prosumer economy through the prosumer economy lab Good4Trust in Turkey. We are going to explain the business model, how it contributes and deepens the sustainable supply chains between local SMEs, prosumers and producers and the methods we used in detail and discuss the social and ecological impact the prosumer economy created through building a community of ecologically and socially mindful prosumers. In discussion, we are going to evaluate the challenges and limitations of prosumer economy as well as its future prospects and potential. We are going to discuss the possibility of the prosumer economy as the new sustainable economic ecosystem the world needs throughout the paper.

2 Good4Trust as a Laboratory of Prosumer Economy

The prosumer economy, as stated above, has an empirical implementation through which the theoretical framework is applied, therefore can be tested and developed. Thus, we chose to analyze the laboratory of prosumer economy "Good4Trust.org", a "virtual field" (Hammersly & Atkinson, 2007). Our method can be defined as "observer participation" (Duverger, 2015) as we are implicated and have direct access to our field. Our findings are the results of our observations of the system and community building of Good4trust.org. We also used documentary sources which "construct 'facts', 'records', 'diagnoses', 'decisions', and 'rules' that are crucially involved in social activities". (Hammersly & Atkinson, 2007) These sources include formal organisational reports and articles but also any informal published material produced by the community members. These empirical findings combined with the literature allowed us to examine both theoretical and practical aspects of the prosumer economy. We should also note here that being aware of the "reflexivity of research" (Hammersly & Atkinson, 2007) amplified by our personal implications, we deliberately chose to employ "we" in this article which allowed us to not hide our implication yet minimize any distortion of our findings by practical interests (Hammersly & Atkinson, 2007).

Good4Trust.org was established in 2014 as a prefigurative organisation in Turkey, as a laboratory of the prosumer economy, to bring an organiszed prosumer economy ecosystem to life and explore its implementation. Good4Trust.org operates as a digital public utility. It is an online bazaar and a community hub for ecologically and socially just producers and prosumers who base their principles on values derived from the Golden Rule (as defined in the introduction) including trust, transparency, justice, and peace. The prevailing discourse in the existing economy is on the effectiveness, even the necessity, of competition. However, Good4Trust follows Kropotkin who demonstrates the evolution of living beings through collaboration and mutual support (Kropotkin, 2009). Similarly we follow Margulis (1981), who has shown that major breakthroughs in ecology have come thru symbiosis and any functioning ecosystem is full of symbiotic relationships. Good4Trust has found its philosophical partner in Posthumanism (Çevirme et al., 2023). This partnership necessitates not only seeking planetary symbiotic existence for humans, but also an individual awareness that ought to bring humility and care for others (living and non-living beings). We assume that every individual joining the community aligns with shared values of goodness. To make this visible and sustain it within the community, Good4Trust incorporates a social solidarity component on the platform, allowing prosumers to share their actions that adhere to the Golden Rule. This can include a good deed such as volunteering, donations to NGOs, providing scholarships or simply tutoring someone for their exams. Purchases through which prosumers support ecologically and socially just producers are also considered good deeds to be shared.

In the Good4trust community, prosumers support each other to transform current socio-economic paradigms. The dominant narrative makes consumers feel small and helpless (Miller, 2004). Prosumers on the other hand are powerful and hopeful. "They establish a governance system among themselves while also collaborating to build this new circular economy at the macro-level" (Satıcı & Özesmi, 2023). Good4trust is governed by prosumers. When a prosumer joins the platform, they are given a seed. With every good deed they share, they receive drops of water for the seed. The seed is watered by every purchase or good deed shared and grows to be a seedling, then a sapling, becoming a young tree, then a mature tree, a flowering tree, and finally a fruit bearing tree. This growing tree gives a status to prosumers which in return gives them the right to participate in the governance of the platform. The more a prosumer is engaged in the system, the more rights they obtain. The Council of Seven gives advice and suggestions, cautions if necessary and shows the way for the Good4Trust administration. This council, while also ensuring gender equity within itself, is elected among prosumers who reach the status of fruit bearing tree (Özesmi, 2019).

Producers derive their production principles from the Golden Rule, intending to ensure that their products or services align with principles of ecological symbiosis, non-toxicity, zero waste, clean energy, and fair working conditions. Producer is an inclusive conceptual designation encompassing entities such as small producers, Small to Medium Enterprises (SME), Cooperatives, Social Enterprises, Association Economic Enterprises etc. They set up their shops on the platform to sell their products and services, both retail and wholesale. Good4Trust producers' purpose isn't to maximize their profit but to maximize their positive impact on nature and society.

2.1 Inclusion and Development System in Good4Trust

Initially, producers were integrated into the system after an assessment of whether they were just or not. In this way, the bazaar was considered to be ecologically and socially just. However, this situation disregarded social inequalities and the bazaar wasn't fully inclusive. It failed to reach producers who lacked the knowledge, experience, or financial means for just production and were unable to access them. In this way, the system wasn't transformative of harmful practices. As the "system changers are more likely to change their strategy" (Wilf, 2018) we renounced the gatekeeping strategy and established the inclusion system. It is only when the economic system is inclusive that "the production of goods and services is optimized to meet the expectations of, and to create opportunities for, all segments of society" (Satıcı & Özesmi, 2023).

The inclusion system allows every producer who intends to engage in ecologically and socially just production and declare their intention to join the community and open their shops in the bazaar. In this way, the community can support and transform producers who are not yet fully capable of minimizing their own harm. Every producer is evaluated by the Council of Seven to determine whether their product or service is ecologically and socially fair. The resulting assessment, which includes the producer's shortcomings and recommendations for the roadmap, is added to the producer's declaration page. Additionally, based on this evaluation, the producer receives one of three distinct symbols:

Just Producer: These are the producers who produce ecologically and socially just products or services, fully in line with Good4Trust.org principles. They minimize their negative impact and maximize impact through their production. They were assessed a minimum 6 points out of 7 by the Council of Seven. The contribution fee taken from their orders is %3.

Dedicated Producer: These are the producers who have begun to enhance their productions, reduced their negative impact, and are recognizing their need for improvement and have started to act upon it. They were assessed 4–5 points out of 7 by the Council of Seven. The contribution fee taken from their orders is %5.

Intentional Producer: These are producers who are committed to improve their production processes, declaring their intention to themselves and prosumers, and aiming to reduce their negative impact. They were assessed less than 3 points out of 7 by the Council of Seven. The contribution fee taken from their orders is %7.

Producers can transition between levels when they improve their practices. This system has been designed to motivate and support producers in their just transformation processes. With periodical evaluations, their improvements are followed and suggestions are made when necessary. This inclusive and transformative system allows the elimination of ecological and social externalities within the ecosystem. However, a macro-level transformation of the system can only be achieved if the leakage from the system is prevented.

As a prefigurative organisation at Good4Trust, we planted the seeds of the prosumer economy in the existing economic system. If the wealth entering the prosumer economy exceeds the wealth leaving it, the consumer economy will eventually stop expanding and start shrinking. Thus, when the prosumer economy will encompass the whole system, the economy will be regenerative, increasing circularity, synergies and welfare of all beings (Özesmi, 2019).

2.2 *Trust Transformation Tool for Non-leakage*

A transformation tool unique to Good4trust, called "Trust", was developed to tackle the issue of leakage out of the system. Trust is an incentive mechanism to reduce the leakage of wealth and materials to the outside of prosumer economy. It contributes to creating circular and synergic supply networks among producers.

Trust in essence is the first digital community currency in Turkey. It is produced whenever something is purchased with another currency. It can be used again and again as it passes from prosumer to producer and from producer to prosumer. Let us explain how Trust operates through a practical exposition (Yakut & Özesmi, 2023):

- Trust is generated and transferred as purchases are made through Good4Trust by prosumers and producers.
- Trust is generated for the prosumer through purchases (5% of the purchase amount) and social interactions within the community.
- Generated Trusts can be used for up to 50% of all purchases.
- Trusts can be gifted to other prosumers within the community by both producers and prosumers.
- Trust cannot be accumulated. If Trusts are not used or gifted, they expire (after 90 days)
- The most closely expiring Trusts will be used first by the system at the time of purchase
- All past transactions and current information about Trusts are available on the Trust Details page.

Through the circulation of Trust by its acquisition (%5) and redemption (%50), the purchases within the system are incentivized. Besides revitalizing the economy internally, Trust addresses four pillars of sustainability. Ecological, because trust helps minimizing the ecological impact by connecting ecologically and socially just producers, becoming local through shorter supply chains and reducing the transportation quantity with wholesale. Cultural, as it creates mutual support and interconnected networks. Social, through the act of sharing information, expertise, and experience in prosumers' interactions with Trust. Economic, as Trust is "an instrument of financial inclusion that can strengthen local businesses by preventing money from flowing out of the Good4Trust ecosystem" (Yakut & Özesmi, 2023). Trust doesn't only prevent leakages and create loyalties but it also proves that, contrary to the existing monetary system, a transformation tool can provide trust and strengthen social networks. It also supports localization of needs which is another important pillar of the prosumer economy that needs more exploration (Yakut & Özesmi, 2023).

In the "idolatry of gigantism" (Schumacher, 1973) of the consumer economy, it's not a coincidence that all alternative economies "emphasize local solutions before anything else: they bond economic construction with its environment" (Miller, 2004). The needs should be identified through local knowledge. What we take should never exceed the self-renewing capacity of nature, and this capacity can only be determined by local knowledge (Özesmi, 2010). Localizing needs also reduces ecological footprint as they lead to shorter supply chains (Yakut & Özesmi, 2023). It also establishes social networks.

2.3 Becoming Glocal

Another portmanteau word is *glocal*, formed from *global* and *local*. The global vision of another economy can only be realized thru local action and local organisations coming together through shared principles. Reaching to local producers, understanding their capacity and needs, guiding them in their improvements, building a community and empowering disadvantaged groups require a deep understanding of the local context. In that matter, local governments play a significant role, as through their services and regulations, they have a direct impact on people's daily lives (*Spínola*, n.d.). Therefore, as Good4Trust, we collaborated with the İzmit Municipality. Together, we established the "İzmit Bazaar" as a special-bazaar within Good4Trust.org in 2019. Its success led to establishing a second collaboration with Merkezefendi Municipality to open "Merkez Bazaar" in 2020. This municipality bazaar model is created exclusively for the producers living within the municipal boundaries. Producers work in solidarity by getting their supplies from each other, producing joint products, sharing knowledge and experience through circular supply networks. The municipality also can prioritize to focus on a particular objective, which is in occurrence, empowering women producers. Through this model, we can also build up solutions to problems such as shipping. In collaboration with Prosumer Economy Society, Good4Trust.org and İzmit Municipality, we designed the "Izmit Bazaar Bicycle Courier Network". This network shows an alternative way to courier transportation by ensuring time and cost saving for the individuals by minimizing their carbon emissions. On the other hand, the increased bicycle mobility will be beneficial for the urban transportation systems and both individual and societal health. Through this access to municipal space, the municipality bazaar also gives the opportunity to physical gatherings. Producers come together for physical bazaars, festivals or educational programs that we organise (*Türetim Ekonomisi Derneği*, n.d.).

We need prosumer economy communities to emerge in different locales, cities, regions and countries to tackle the polycrisis. Therefore, our objective is to become *glocal* that we define as locally organised prosumer economy communities interdependent through a global economic ecosystem and movement. To enable this expansion, Good4Trust.org is an open source software replicable with a non-profit social license agreement (Özesmi, 2019).

Regarding our business model, Good4Trust.org operates as a prefigurative social enterprise. In Turkey, social enterprises don't have a separate legal status taking different legal forms such as cooperatives, limited companies, sole proprietorship, association, foundation or corporations (British Council, 2019). As such, Good4Trust.org is registered under "İyilik İletişim ve Yazılım Ticaret Ltd." which is a limited company consisting of exclusively investment shares. Therefore, the company doesn't distribute profit. Good4trust has operational revenues including contribution fees where the rate depends on the producer's status (%3 just, %5 determined, %7 intentional), supporters through newsletter subscriptions, own product sales and municipality bazaar fees. In addition, we generate income through consultancy services, lectures and other non-operational activities. The income is injected into the ecosystem to ensure its continuity and scalability.

3 Discussion

It's obvious that we need to shift our common socioeconomic paradigm from consumerism to prosumerism since the root cause of the polycrises we face is the result of consumerism and a growth-based economy with competition as a norm. We suggest an alternative social and ecological economic system, the prosumer economy, to change the common goal of economic entities from profit maximization to impact maximization, from greed to ethics, from growth to degrowth, and from competition to symbiosis. As it is seen in the Good4Trust example, the prosumer economy is a sustainable economic model as it is both ecologically and socially sustainable, and creates a common ground where every member of the ecosystem has access to their needs. Therefore, the shift from the linear consumer economy to the circular prosumer economy and its implementation may be the solution to the pressure of growth on ecology. For such a paradigm shift to occur, the change has to start from within the system. That's why, Good4Trust.org was established to implement the prosumer economy in Turkey. As more prosumer economies are established and create circular ecosystems, the inflow to the system will exceed the outflow eventually, and the dominant paradigm will become the prosumer economy.

Even though the seed of Good4Trust was planted in the conventional system as a prefigurative organisation, and it transforms the existing by expanding day by day, creating a new ecosystem has some limitations and struggles. One of the struggles of creating a just ecosystem is that the producers have to be considerate of their ecological and social impact. However, in the dominant socioeconomic paradigm, some types of products are still not produced in both ecologically and socially sustainable ways, an obstacle in the way of a sustainable economy. Therefore, prosumers may find some fair products and not others. For example, the prosumers can find sustainable cosmetic products, organic food, and some clothes. But they can't find sustainable electronics or oddly enough shoes in the Turkish context currently. As more people are considerate of their ecological impact and demand fair products more ways to produce sustainable products will be found. And maybe then they can find fair or fairer products like readily available fairphones (Akemu et al., 2016; Haucke, 2018) or shoes such as Allbirds (Pavlovich et al., 2020), Able, Veja (Cohen & Muñoz, 2017), etc. produced locally and maybe even with higher standards.

In Good4Trust, most prosumers' daily needs have an alternative, but since they are sustainable and need sustainable inputs for just production, the prices of sustainable alternatives are usually higher than the common unsustainable products that can be found everywhere. That price difference doesn't form a problem for high-income people. But Turkey "stands at the bottom of the roster of industrialized states or toward the top of the ranks of the lesser-developed economies of the world" (Harris,

2023). That's why the current economic situation in Turkey, high inflation rates, and economic crises don't allow low income people to prefer sustainable alternatives. A study conducted in Turkey found that demand for organic products is higher among wealthy, middle-aged, females. 85.8% of participants in the same study agreed that the reason for them not preferring organic products is the products' price, and 86.2% of participants said that they would prefer organic products if they were less expensive (Aygen, 2012). Since currently, low income people can't afford the price difference between sustainable and healthier alternatives and the common products, Good4Trust.org seems to appeal mostly to high-income people. While the policy environment does not penalize ecological and social externalities, it will be hard to overcome the price differences (Becchetti & Huybrechts, 2007), although we are trying to develop coping mechanisms.

As mentioned before, Good4Trust.org created the transformation tool "Trust" that creates additional internal value to cope with high prices, encourages local prosumption, decreases the negative effects of transportation such as carbon emissions, since "logistics is one of the main contributors to environmental degradation" (Karia, 2020). However, one constraint of Good4Trust.org as an online bazaar is that most producers are situated in the western part of Turkey. Specifically Marmara, Aegean, and Mediterranean regions. Thus, the supply chains for prosumers in Anatolia are still not sustainable enough, because the locality includes the whole country, not the town or city. There aren't many just producers from Anatolia in Good4Trust.org, thus a prosumer in Anatolia has to acquire a just product after a long journey of transportation which isn't ecologically just. That's why for the prosumer economy to reach its goal of creating a sustainable ecosystem that is both ecologically and socially just, shorter supply chains and sustainable logistics alternatives are crucial. To implement the prosumer economy in every aspect, and create a complete symbiotic ecosystem, a transformation in the logistics industry (aviation, ocean shipping, trucking, railways, warehouses, etc.,) is needed, such as reducing energy consumption, using renewable energy instead of fossil fuels, creating centralized and decentralized distribution structures, and replacing single-use plastics with recyclable or biodegradable materials (Karia, 2020). Unless all those changes are completed and greener logistics firms are in the market, current logistics firms have no place in a prosumer economy ecosystem, since they are both ecologically and socially destructive.

All of these changes need finance but the finance system itself is broken. The general goal in finance is to invest in a way that will maximize the return. The portfolio optimization method is based on risk and the return of the investment, and aims "for maximizing mean return while also minimizing the variance of portfolio returns" (Kim et al., 2022). But that approach to investing isn't sustainable and just because of how those returns are obtained. Since the profit-maximization-focused financial approach cannot address modern global problems, for the last two decades the demand for socially responsible investments and responsibility has been growing rapidly and has become a mainstream investment strategy from the niche it used to be (Białkowski & Starks, 2016). A study conducted on impact investors' expectations of returns found that impact investors are willing to forego profit to create impact through their investments (Barber et al., 2021). Thus, as impact investors and socially responsible investment strategies increase, the funds needed for sustainable changes will start to be funded.

In addition to logistics and may be more so the biggest challenges to this prefigurative future is the war industry. War itself goes against the prosumer economy because it goes completely against the "Golden Rule". The war industry is neither ecologically nor socially just. A study conducted on G7 countries concluded that "the increase in military expenditure that stems from the tendency of countries to adopt high-technology weapons and equipment which uses large amounts of fossil fuels and emits large quantities of carbon dioxide in order to protect their geopolitical and local interests brings environmental degradation" (Konuk et al., 2023) Also, throughout the history, conflicts caused consequential social and economic costs besides human suffering (Rodrik, 1999). The consequences of war such as "the loss of human life, destruction of infrastructure, disruption of the labor force and human capital, weakening of government institutions, political instability, and increased uncertainty" (Le et al., 2022) makes the concept of war opposite to the "Golden Rule". Therefore, military industry doesn't align with the philosophy of the prosumer economy, and disrupts its goal of creating an ecologically and socially just ecosystem.

The fossil fuel industry is also non-compatible with the prosumer economy. "If today's energy infrastructure was to be operated until the end of the typical lifetime[...], [it is] estimate[d] that [the amount of] cumulative energy-related and industrial process CO_2 emissions between 2020 and 2050, [will be] around 30% more than the remaining total CO_2 budget consistent with limiting global warming to 1.5 °C with a 50% probability" (Bouckaert et al., 2021, p. 39) The phase-out of fossil fuels is central to the process of achieving a decarbonized economy and net-zero emissions by 2050 (Vieira et al., 2022). International Energy Agency asserts that neither new oil and gas fields nor new coal mines or mine extensions should be approved after 2021 (Bouckaert et al., 2021, p. 26). Thus for an ecological and just economy fossil fuel companies should transform their energy production processes into solar energy and its contemporary derivatives such as wind and currents for a place in the new, just economic paradigm.

Another non-compatible sector in need of transformation is the agrochemicals industry, a contributor to global warming and the biodiversity crisis. The use of agrochemicals such as reactive nitrogen to increase food productivity causes damage to people, climate, biodiversity, and the environment since it disrupts the neutral mineral cycles of nature (Galloway et al., 2021). Hence the agrochemical companies go against Golden Rule as they aren't considerate of other organisms, and cannot exist in a prosumer economy. Prosumer economy supports local and organic farming, without any chemical intervention, producing by trusting nature's own processes, farmers doing more manual work and bonding with nature and trusting their knowledge of nature without interference. That's why the agrochemical companies don't have a place in the prosumer economy as they function currently.

Those issues are some of the struggles we face in implementing the prosumer economy as a new, alternative sustainable ecosystem. Some of the reasons for those struggles arise from the common paradigm and the policy environment. That's why, a sustainable and permanent change, can only come from a change in perception. That's where the prosumer economy and Good4Trust need philosophical support because only implementing the prosumer economy doesn't necessarily create a significant change in perception.

The philosophical partner of the prosumer economy in changing the paradigm and perception is posthumanism. Posthumanism aligns and adds on the Golden Rule by being against anthropocentrism and defending rights of not only people but the whole of nature. The intellectual partnership doesn't only help the prosumer economies to shift the common perspective, but helpful for post-humanism too. "[T]he combination of these ideas would be mutually beneficial—the philosophical depth of the posthumanist movement would enrich the prosumer economy, while putting the posthumanist perspective into practice and establishing an economy based on those values would strengthen the philosophical movement" (Çevirme et al., 2023).

The findings acquired through observation of implementation of prosumer economy through a virtual field, Good4Trust, in Turkey by participants show that the prosumer economy is obtainable in reality and creating a local, socially and ecologically just and sustainability ecosystem similar to a forest's is possible. But still it has limitations such as transforming logistics, agrochemical and military industry to be sustainable to get involved in an ecologically and socially just ecosystem.

How will the challenges be overcome? How will this prefigurative movement become mainstream? How will incompatible sectors transform? These, and many more, are still questions to be explored, researched, and experimented. They will unfold and be challenged as the roots of the prosumer economy start taking hold.

4 Conclusion

In this paper we have discussed the prosumer economy, the origins of the concept of prosumer, the virtual field Good4Trust as a lab of prosumer economy, some of the challenges prosumer economy faces and the possible questions to be answered as well as the importance of a new sustainable paradigm.

The paradigms that humanity will choose to form an economy around, will determine the extent to which the planet and all beings will experience a different world. For people the future will be either ecologically just or bust. Prosumer economy proposes a new economic system to create an ecologically and socially just future. Through a prefigurative organisation called Good4Trust.org, it is seen that the prosumer economy is achievable in real life. Currently more than 25.000 prosumers and 770 producers (SMEs) are working together towards transforming the common paradigm to prosumer economy. This number is increasing every day. Thanks to them the prosumer economy is seeded into the existing economy and will eventually grow into it. However, we need the transition to occur before the consumer economy balloon explodes and destroys biodiversity including humans on the planet.

As demonstrated above, in order to achieve this new symbiotic state, the structure of companies must transform into ecological and social impact-oriented companies instead of being profit-oriented in the future so that humanity can keep on living on Earth (Gücüm & Özesmi, 2023).

As prosumer economy has conditions such as being socially and ecologically just, or at least having the intention of becoming socially and ecologically just as a producer, the industries such as military, fosil fuel based logistics, agrochemicals or current finance industry cannot be involved in such ecosystem unless they transform themselves into planetary symbiosis. The Good4Trust example proves that the prosumer economy is viable and can be implemented around different regions with SMEs and prosumers, as in Turkey. The working system in Turkey and 770 SMEs is a sign that people are looking for alternative sustainable economies.

To be able to shift the common paradigm we need different prosumer economies encouraging local prosumption and collaboration, to then become the common paradigm. That's why more labs similar to Good4Trust should emerge around the globe and encourage local and sustainable production, as well as more scientific and experimental research should be conducted on the field of prosumer economy and its implementation to adress the limitations and let more people know about the potentials of prosumer economy.

References

Akemu, O., Whiteman, G., & Kennedy, S. (2016). Social enterprise emergence from social movement activism: The fairphone case. *Journal of Management Studies, 53*(5), 846–877. https://doi.org/10.1111/joms.12208

Alisa, G. D., Demaria, F., & Kallis, G. (2015). *Degrowth: A vocabulary for a new era*. Routledge, Taylor & Francis Group.

AR6 Synthesis Report: Climate Change. 2023. (2023, March). IPCC. https://www.ipcc.ch/report/ar6/syr/

Aygen, F. G. (2012). Attitudes and behavior of Turkish consumers with respect to organic foods. *International Journal of Business and Social Science, 3*(18), 262–273.

Barber, B. M., Morse, A., & Yasuda, A. (2021). Impact investing. *Journal of Financial Economics, 139*(1), 162–185. https://doi.org/10.1016/j.jfineco.2020.07.008

Becchetti, L., & Huybrechts, B. (2007). The dynamics of fair trade as a mixed-form market. *Journal of Business Ethics, 81*(4), 733–750. https://doi.org/10.1007/s10551-007-9544-8

Bednarz, J. (2022). Who is a consumer in the digital era? Still a consumer or a prosumer? In M. Bartosik-Purgat & N. Filimon (Eds.), *European consumers in the digital era: Implications of technology, media and culture on consumer behavior* (pp. 27–42). Routledge Taylor & Francis Group.

Białkowski, J., & Starks, L. T. (2016). SRI funds: Investor demand, exogenous shocks and ESG profiles. *American Finance Association Annual Meeting*, 1–47.

Bouckaert, S., Pales, A. F., McGlade, C., Remme, U., Wanner, B., Varro, L., D'Ambrosio, D., Spencer, T., Abergel, T., Arsalane, Y., Bains, P., Menendez, J. M., Connelly, E., Crow, D., Dasgupta, A., Delmastro, C., Goodson, T., Gouy, A., Hugues, P., …, Wetzel, D. (2021, October). *Net Zero by 2050 a roadmap for the global energy sector* (E. Hosker, Ed.). IEA. https://www.iea.org/reports/net-zero-by-2050

Çevirme, E. T., Satıcı, E. E., & Özesmi, U. (2023). Can the prosumer economy be a posthumanist economy? *Journal of Posthumanism, 3*(3). https://doi.org/10.33182/joph.v3i3.3005

Cohen, B., & Muñoz, P. (2017). Entering conscious consumer markets: Toward a new generation of sustainability strategies. *California Management Review, 59*(4), 23–48. https://doi.org/10.1177/0008125617722792

Duverger, M. (2015). *Introduction to the social sciences with special reference to their methods* (M. Anderson, Trans., Vol. 34). Routledge (Original work published 1964).

Galloway, J. N., Bleeker, A., & Erisman, J. W. (2021). The human creation and use of reactive nitrogen: A global and regional perspective. *Annual Review of Environment and Resources, 46*(1), 255–288. https://doi.org/10.1146/annurev-environ-012420-045120

Green, R., & Staffell, I. (2017). "Prosumage" and the british electricity market. *Economics of Energy & Environmental Policy, 6*(1). https://doi.org/10.5547/2160-5890.6.1.rgre

Gücüm, S., & Özesmi, U. (2023). İyi Şirket. Bağcılar, İstanbul: Yeni İnsan.

Hammersley, M., & Atkinson, P. (2007). *Ethnography: Principles in practice* (3rd ed.). Routledge (Original work published 1983)

Harris, G. S. (2023). *Turkey coping with crisis*. Routledge. https://doi.org/10.4324/9781003354611

Haucke, F. V. (2018). Smartphone-enabled social change: Evidence from the fairphone case? *Journal of Cleaner Production, 197*, 1719–1730. https://doi.org/10.1016/j.jclepro.2017.07.014

İzmit Çarşısı Bisiklet Kurye Ağı Projesi [İzmit Bazaar Bicycle Courier Network Project]. (n.d.). *Türetim Ekonomisi Derneği*. Retrieved January 2, 2024, from https://turetimekonomisi.org/izmit-carsisi-bisiklet-kurye-agi-projesi/

Karia, N. (2020). Green logistics practices and sustainable business model. *Handbook of research on the applications of international transportation and logistics for world trade*, 354–366. https://doi.org/10.4018/978-1-7998-1397-2.ch019

Kim, J. H., Lee, Y., Kim, W. C., & Fabozzi, F. J. (2022). Goal-based investing based on multi-stage robust portfolio optimization. *Annals of Operations Research, 313*(2), 1141–1158. https://doi.org/10.1007/s10479-021-04473-7

Konuk, F., Kaya, E., Akpınar, S., & Yıldız, Ş. (2023). The relationship between military expenditures, financial development and environmental pollution in g7 countries. *Journal of the Knowledge Economy*. https://doi.org/10.1007/s13132-023-01122-1

Kropotkin, P. A. (2009). *Mutual aid: A factor of evolution*. Cosimo Classics.

Lang, B., Botha, E., Robertson, J., Kemper, J. A., Dolan, R., & Kietzmann, J. (2020). How to grow the sharing economy? Create prosumers! *Australasian Marketing Journal, 28*(3), 58–66. https://doi.org/10.1016/j.ausmj.2020.06.012

Le, T.-H., Bui, M.-T., & Uddin, G. S. (2022). Economic and social impacts of conflict: A cross-country analysis. *Economic Modelling, 115*, 1–13. https://doi.org/10.1016/j.econmod.2022.105980

Lecocq, X., Demil, B., & Warnier, V. (2023). Moving business models forward for positive social, environmental and economic outcomes: Managing externalities (and internalities) for sustainability innovation. *Journal of Business Models, 11*(3), 117–132. https://doi.org/10.54337/jbm.v11i3.8128

Lindeman, R. L. (1942). The trophic-dynamic aspect of ecology. *Ecological Society of America, 23*(4), 399–417. https://doi.org/10.2307/1930126

Linnenluecke, M. K., & Griffiths, A. (2013). Firms and sustainability: Mapping the intellectual origins and structure of the corporate sustainability field. *Global Environmental Change, 23*(1), 382–391. https://doi.org/10.1016/j.gloenvcha.2012.07.007

Lorek, S., & Spangenberg, J. H. (2014). Sustainable consumption within a sustainable economy—Beyond green growth and green economies. *Journal of Cleaner Production, 63*, 33–44. https://doi.org/10.1016/j.jclepro.2013.08.045

Lutz, W., Sanderson, W. C., & Scherbov, S. (Eds.). (2004). *The end of world population growth in the 21st century. New challenges for human capital formation and sustainable development*. Earthscan.

Margulis, L. (1981). *Symbiosis in cell evolution*. W. H. Freeman.

Miller, E. (2004). *Solidarity economics strategies for building new economies* [Pamphlet]. Grassroots Economic Organizing (GEO) Collective.

Özesmi, U. (2010). *Yasak Meyve Cehennemden Çıkış*. TB.
Özesmi, U. (2019). *The prosumer economy—Being like a forest* (Doctoral dissertation). Arxiv. https://arxiv.org/abs/1903.07615
Pavlovich, K., Bowden, S., Simnadis, T., Connolly, H., Collins, E., & Gibb, J. (2020). *Allbirds: Sustainable innovation disrupting the casual shoe industry*. SAGE Publications: SAGE Business Cases Originals. https://doi.org/10.4135/9781529713206
Richardson, K., Steffen, W., Lucht, W., Bendtsen, J., Cornell, S. E., Donges, J. F., Drüke, M., Fetzer, I., Bala, G., von Bloh, W., Feulner, G., Fiedler, S., Gerten, D., Gleeson, T., Hofmann, M., Huiskamp, W., Kummu, M., Mohan, C., Nogués-Bravo, D., ..., Rockström, J. (2023). Earth beyond six of nine planetary boundaries. *Science Advances, 9*(37). https://doi.org/10.1126/sciadv.adh2458
Rodrik, D. (1999). Where did all the growth go? External shocks, social conflict, and growth collapses. *Journal of Economic Growth, 4*(4), 385–412.
Satıcı, E., & Özesmi, U. (2023). *The Prosumer Economy*. DIXI Books (Uk) Limited.
Schill, W. P., Zerrahn, A., & Kunz, F. (2017). *Prosumage of solar electricity: Pros, cons, and the system perspective*. DIW Berlin.
Schiller-Merkens, S. (2022). Prefiguring an alternative economy: Understanding prefigurative organizing and its struggles. *Organization*. https://doi.org/10.1177/13505084221124189
Schumacher, E. F. (1973). *Small is beautiful: Economics as if people mattered*. Harper and Row Publishers.
Spínola, T. (n.d.). *Cities and social entrepreneurs report*. Ashoka. https://www.ashoka.org/en-us/files/cities-social-entrepreneurs-report-catalyst2030-ashoka-2pdf
The State of Social Enterprise in Turkey. (2019). British Council. https://www.britishcouncil.org.tr/programmes/education/social-enterprise-research
Toffler, A. (1980). *The third wave*. Bantam Books.
Türetim Ekonomisi Derneği [Prosumer Economy Society]. (n.d.). *Türetim Ekonomisi Derneği*. Retrieved December 25, 2023, from https://turetimekonomisi.org/
Tudi, M., Daniel Ruan, H., Wang, L., Lyu, J., Sadler, R., Connell, D., Chu, C., & Phung, D. T. (2021). Agriculture development, pesticide application and its impact on the environment. *International Journal of Environmental Research and Public Health, 18*(3), 1112. https://doi.org/10.3390/ijerph18031112
Tukker, A., & Butter, M. (2007). Governance of sustainable transitions: About the 4(0) ways to change the world. *Journal of Cleaner Production, 15*(1), 94–103. https://doi.org/10.1016/j.jclepro.2005.08.016
Vieira, L. C., Longo, M., & Mura, M. (2022). From carbon dependence to renewables: The european oil majors' strategies to face climate change. *Business Strategy and the Environment, 32*(4), 1248–1259. https://doi.org/10.1002/bse.3185
Wilf, S. (2018). How Ashoka fellows create systems change: New learnings and insights from the 2018 global fellows study. *Social Innovations Journal*, (52). https://socialinnovationsjournal.org/editions/issue-52/75-disruptive-innovations/2905-how-ashoka-fellows-create-systems-change-new-learnings-and-insights-from-the-2018-global-fellows-study
Xiaowei, J., Qi, S., & Yanfeng, G. (2011). New approaches to the green economy of china in the multiple crises. *Energy Procedia, 5*, 1365–1370. https://doi.org/10.1016/j.egypro.2011.03.236
Yakut, Z., & Özesmi, U. (2023, November 3). In Good we Trust: Transforming the way we understand 'money' [White paper]. *Good4Trust.org*. Retrieved December 31, 2023, from https://blog.good4trust.org/2023/11/18/in-good-we-trust/#more-3500

A Review of Consumer Understanding of Green Marketing and Deceptive Green Marketing

Deepti Jog and Vivek Pani

Abstract Ecological sustainability has risen to the topmost of global political conversations in recent decades and is now identified as a crucial factor driving innovation. As a result, there is a rise in the number of companies working to develop green products, and more and more consumers are increasingly interested in these products (Dangelico and Vocalelli in Journal of Cleaner Production 165:1263–1279, 2017). Although the number of eco-sensitive consumers is increasing, the growth in green consumer numbers must be more substantial in the overall consumer segment. The primary reason could be the inability to differentiate between green and deceptive green marketing efforts. This chapter investigates the consumer acceptance and understanding of green marketing and the deceptive green marketing efforts of the organizations. Compared to the green attitude, the purchase rate of green products is comparatively lower (Dangelico and Vocalelli in Journal of Cleaner Production 165:1263–1279, 2017). A potential explanation for this scepticism amongst consumers to opt for green products may be their need for exposure to green marketing. This lack of understanding could also lead to consumers needing help to differentiate between green marketing and deceptive green marketing (i.e. greenwashing), resulting in a green attitude not being culminated in green purchase behaviour in the case of many consumers.

Further, literature has identified that, over time, consumers' understanding of greenwashing has increased. This understanding of the greenwashing practices of the brands among consumers could be a significant factor contributing to the lower rate of green product purchases (Jog and Singhal in Strategic Direction 35:4–7, 2019; Jog and Singhal in Greenwashing understanding among Indian consumers and its impact on their green consumption, 2020). Past empirical research in the area of green and deceptive green marketing has examined how consumer understanding impacts several antecedent and consequent variables (e.g., purchase of green or eco-friendly products, new green product development, and recycling programs). By analyzing the relevant literature surrounding consumer perspectives on green marketing and deceptive green marketing, this chapter will study the consumer understanding of

D. Jog (✉) · V. Pani
Department of Management Studies, NALSAR University of Law, Hyderabad 500101, India
e-mail: deepti.jog@nalsar.ac.in

W. Leal Filho and V. Kuzmanović (eds.), *Sustainable Development Seen Through the Lenses of Ethnoeconomics and the Circular Economy*,
https://doi.org/10.1007/978-3-031-72676-7_11

green and deceptive green marketing. This is assessed by reviewing the existing literature based on the green marketing orientation theory proposed by Papadas et al. (2019). This theory attempts to classify firms' green marketing strategies at three levels—strategic, tactical, and internal. According to this theory, the green marketing efforts of organizations can be classified into three measured areas stated above. Further, drawing from the existing consumer-centric literature, this chapter attempts to understand how such efforts of organizations are perceived at a consumer level through the lens of green marketing theory. Managers, academics, and students can all benefit greatly from understanding the organization's orientations and tactics for overcoming obstacles.

1 Introduction

Environmental concern is rising and is presently a significant interest area for consumers in developing nations. Particularly in highly populated economies like India, such rising concern has shaped ecologically conscious consumers who desire to do their part to contribute towards the environmental improvement through their purchases. These customers examine the environmental impact of products before making a purchase and consider themselves to be green or environmentally conscious. Responding to consumers' demands for environmental product information, environmental claims have exponentially increased in the marketplace. However, customers are frequently misled or confused by environmental claims owing to the complexity of environmental concerns, the ambiguity of words, and the need for environmental understanding affecting consumers' green purchase decisions. Thus, due to the difficulty in decoding the environmental ads, consumers are deceived by such communication mainly due to their pervasiveness and appeal to consumers to contribute towards the environment through their purchases (Scarpaci et al., 2016). Such complexities in the understanding necessitate the need to re-look at the literature by linking it backwards through the inception of the notion of green marketing to date to bring coherence in the understanding of green marketing and deceptive green marketing (greenwashing) communication.

After the rise of the 1960 environmental movement, consumer concerns about environmental pollution and degradation have risen. Since the 1960s and the early 1970s, a visible increase in consumer concern was seen due to the production and consumption patterns directly affecting the environment. This was further evident through the work of Kinnear et al. (1974), whose findings suggested that businesses and marketers should explore the ecologically concerned consumer segment since it is a larger cohort expected to grow over time. The impacts of such concerns were evident through another study by TerraChoice,[1] which found that between 2008 and 2009,

[1] Based in Canada, TerraChoice is a private marketing and environmental consulting firm. It assists customers from many industries and business divisions in incorporating sustainability objectives and principles into their business plans. Greenwashing - Wikipedia.

there was a 79% increase in green product offerings, and between 2009 and 2010, there was a 73% increase (Mulch, 2009). United Nations marked this in the sustainable development goals (SGG-12) proposed in the year 2015, focusing on "ensuring sustainable consumption and production patterns". Many organizations are abiding by these criteria set by the United Nations to improve their environmental image and positioning in the eyes of the public. To achieve this objective, organizations are implementing green marketing as their core corporate agenda through efforts such as corporate social responsibility, helping organizations gain a competitive advantage and reach ecologically conscious consumers.

However, it is observed that not all green practices are accurate and are depicted falsely to portray a firm's positive environmental conduct. Such actions are identified in academic and mainstream media as deceptive green actions of the firms that companies engage in by way of communicating the ecological conservational issues without significantly addressing them in actions (For academic research, see Ramus and Montiel (2005); among the mainstream media, Terrachoice, an environmental marketing company, is becoming more and more visible).

Environmental management has thus risen to the top of many company agendas due to growing environmental concerns and pressure to act responsibly (King & Lenox, 2002). Previous research on organizations indicates that stakeholder pressures have acted as important drivers of corporate environmental response (Hoffman & Ventresca, 2002, p. 398). On the other hand, consumers are essential stakeholders; past empirical research has examined their pivotal role in several facets, including (e.g. green product purchase, creating green product development-related needs and participation in reverse logistics). To cater to such demands, many large businesses try making their environmental initiatives public and try to strengthen their environmental stances. Additionally, businesses embrace green marketing initiatives in an effort to inform consumers about their green strategy and competitive advantage and as an appeal to environmentally sensitive consumers.

Green marketing has now been used as an essential tool for sustainable business strategy. Green marketing is defined by Peattie (1995) as "the holistic management process responsible for identifying, anticipating and satisfying the requirements of customers and society profitably and sustainably". An organization to be classified as green is required to perform on three parameters—strategic green marketing orientation, tactical green marketing orientation and internal green marketing orientation. Consumers today know the importance of implementing holistic environmental strategies that can gauge business risks and the importance of today's environmental challenges. Consumers are also cognisant of the necessity of companies working towards societal well-being, a strategy that helps to build a positive image in the minds of consumers over time. Such efforts of companies pay off in the long run by way of lowered costs of production, profit maximization, competitive advantage and business development (Gordon et al., 2011). However, such pressures on businesses to implement green practices might encourage greenwashing. This is because, although industry pressures strengthen the internalization of proactive environmental practices for some who can and those who cannot end up engaging in superficial adoption, commonly referred to as greenwashing. Notably, customer pressures tend to encourage organizations to adopt superficial and misleading environmental practices (greenwashing). Greenwashing is thus a side effect of greening market offers (Parguel et al., 2015). Greenwashing is defined as "disinformation disseminated by an organization to present an environmentally responsible public image" (Concise Oxford English Dictionary, 2010) and "the act of misleading consumers regarding the environmental practices of a company or the environmental benefits of a product or service" (Parguel et al., 2015, p. 2). Greenwashing poses a greater risk in the long run as it decreases green trust and consumer confusion and negatively affects green purchase intention.

Multiple factors are observed to impact consumers' understanding of green marketing and the deceptive green marketing practices of the firms, including various external, organizational, and individual issues. Although studies assessing green consumption are many, the literature on greenwashing is limited. Therefore, more study is needed to understand the perception of consumers towards both green and deceptive green marketing practices, as such efforts have the capacity to undermine consumer perception of green marketing and eventually company profitability and may cause ethical harm to organizations engaging in such practices (Nyilasy et al., 2014). Thus, the present study is an extension of past research that examines how green and deceptive green marketing communication is perceived by consumers in the existing literature and how this communication consequently impacts their behaviour (including strategic perception, environmental and product perceptions, as well as objective behavioural outcomes). In particular, we investigate the impact of green communication (using interactive green and deceptive green elements). Understanding interactive communications' persuasive power is crucial to understanding how to communicate green marketing effectively and morally.

Thus, considering consumers' perspective, although consumers prefer to purchase products from brands that have constantly put in efforts to take action against environmental issues, green consumers have become more conscious of understanding marketing communication, making it further challenging for corporations. Corporations thus feel challenged as consumers' perception of companies primarily depends upon the companies' green messages in advertisements. Over time, it is observed that more consumers are sceptical about their green purchase-related decisions. As a result, it is recommended that businesses limit back on their greenwashing practices and demonstrate their "greenness" by providing evidence of their eco-friendly products in addition to making such claims. These practices would lessen danger and uncertainty for customers.

2 Conceptual Understanding of Green Marketing Orientation of Corporations

Over time, as the attitude and behaviour of consumers have moved into the more environmentally and socially conscious domain, green marketing efforts have gained momentum. Although environmental and social issues are associated with multiple human- centric activities, a few studies have attempted to assess the problems with green marketing and consumption (Chen & Chang, 2012). This visible change in society regarding the increased consumer concern regarding the natural environment and societal welfare has led businesses to alter their strategies to address such rising societal concerns. However, companies that initially produced green products incurred losses in their ventures. This was particularly associated with limitations associated with availability, features and, functionality and higher prices. This led to reduced purchase of green products, thus leading to reduced prominence of green marketing concepts in the common debates. This necessitated organizations to establish their image in the market as green and required that the consumers be educated. Such efforts were expected to help the organizations build brands, products and services that are environmentally friendly. Over time, the concept was expanded to include healthy, advantageous, encouraging or conducive.

Multiple businesses globally have started imbibing change in their strategies, considering practices such as environmental management, minimisation of waste, reduced usage of non- biodegradable components, incorporation, and recycling activities. Businesses look for a range of occasions by which they can pursue green strategies to address the wants of various stakeholder groups (Cronin et al., 2011). At the forefront, green strategies are classified in the marketing literature as green innovation, greening the technique and green alliances. Over time, the three areas are considered central tenets of control. They are strategic, tactical and internal green marketing orientations in standard terms (refer to Fig. 1). Among the three components, the efforts taken by the firms in the green marketing or environmental marketing domain that contribute towards the formulation of strategy are identified as strategic green marketing orientation initiatives.

Further, those efforts that consider small, consistent efforts of organizations that help them switch from the conventional marketing mix into an eco-friendly green marketing mix are classified as tactical green marketing organizations. These actions are practically based on the marketing mix and work towards converting the traditional marketing mix into a green one (Papadas et al., 2017). Such efforts are most challenging as marketers keep designing short- term innovative techniques to contribute well towards sustainability principles. Finally, marketing orientation that considers spreading messages across internal audiences to ensure a broad corporate green culture is termed internal green marketing orientation. Papadas et al. (2019) proposed a green marketing orientation theory that conceptualizes green marketing from a corporate-wide perspective, capturing an organization's modern strategic and internal initiatives towards a holistic green marketing strategy.

Fig. 1 Dimensions of green marketing

- **Thought Point (1):** *By keeping in view of the green marketing orientation, based on any of your recent purchases, enlist the characteristics elements of your purchase that helped you identify the product as a green product and the characteristic elements showcased by organizations (in the form of marketing communications) that were green or deceptive green marketing claims that guided your choice.*

2.1 *Strategic Green Marketing Orientation*

Strategic green marketing is long-term, top management strategies and practices that focus on the environmental strategies of businesses in consensus with external environmental stakeholders. These strategies include companies engaging in the design and execution of environmental activities at the entrepreneurial level that, in turn, have the capacity to generate revenue (satisfying firms' social and economic objectives). Such green strategic orientations refer to "the strategic instructions implemented via a company to create the appropriate behaviours for the continuous gold standard performance of the business" (Gatignon & Xuereb, 1997). These strategies include following ecological guidelines, strengthening their green claims, building brands, and restructuring the enterprise to design products and services that are ecologically pleasing. Further green strategies also include organizations' green or eco-friendly branding, packaging, labelling and marketing efforts that contribute to creating demand for green or eco-friendly products.

Such a strategy is an apt response that challenges the age-old marketing orientation of increased sales and profit maximization. It is evident that such efforts conflict with agendas surrounding sustainability and responsibility. This broadens the scope for firms to include being considerate towards environment and social stakeholders in their marketing scope and strategic marketing objectives. Although customers are at the forefront of green marketing, other stakeholders are employees, investors, suppliers, legislators, governmental agencies, shareholders, competitors and the general public.

Strategic green marketing is long-term, top management strategies and practices that focus on the environmental strategies of businesses in consensus with external environmental stakeholders. These strategies include companies engaging in the design and execution of environmental activities at the entrepreneurial level that, in turn, can generate revenue (satisfying firms' social and economic objectives). Such a strategy is an apt response that challenges the age-old marketing orientation of increased sales and profit maximization. It is evident that such efforts conflict with agendas surrounding sustainability and responsibility. This broadens the scope for firms to include being considerate towards environment and social stakeholders in their marketing scope and strategic marketing objectives. Although customers are at the forefront of green marketing, other stakeholders are employees, investors, suppliers, legislators, governmental agencies, shareholders, competitors and the general public.

- **Thought Point (2):** *Assume that green marketing has yet to live up to the hopes and dreams of many consumers and consumer activists. By being in the position of a consumer during your last purchase, can you enlist how you were forced to make trade- offs between product attributes or helping the environment?*

2.2 *Tactical Green Marketing Orientation*

A tactical green marketing plan outlines the precise instruments, short-term actions, and methods businesses will employ to achieve their objectives. This dimension discusses quick fixes to make the conventional marketing mix more environmentally friendly. On a broad scale, tactical orientation focuses on the actions to improve environmental performances, inclusive of supply chains. These decisions would also focus on products and services that aid in reducing environmental performance, which include the usage of environmentally responsible raw material or packaging, use of recyclable or re-usable raw materials, use of renewal energy sources in the production process, engaging in the reverse logistics or re- examination of the product life cycle.

Green tactics of the organizations include identifying the production network partners, including customers to follow proactive ecological methodology, few actions that transform the traditional marketing mix into a more environmentally friendly one, marketing actions such as naturally capable bundling and fixing among the product offerings, using or recyclable and reusable substance, shifting towards the more sustainable production and raw material alternatives (Cronin et al., 2011), Focusing on ancillary practices such as easy biodegradable packaging—paper or any other biodegradable waste, removing excessive packaging, decreased quantity of non-biodegradable material in the production and packaging efforts. Additional tactical green marketing decisions include discovering the right market segments with more profound environmental concerns and a green distribution mechanism that incorporates steps to reduce/eliminate environmental damage and waste. Green distribution further considers a list of operational activities, including product type, frequency of transportation operations, distance to the customers and packaging traits such as weight, structure and material (Sarkis, 2003).

- **Thought Point (3)**: *Considering that a growing number of people are willing to pay a premium for green, sustainable and organic products, whether it is true or not, they believe organic food to be healthier, tastier and safer. Enlist the marketing tactics organisations use that particularly appeal to consumer's self-interests.*

2.3 Internal Green Marketing Orientation

Internal green marketing orientation aims to disseminate environmental values across the organization to establish a more comprehensive corporate green culture. Internal green marketing is considered an effort to promote environmental awareness inside the organization by sharing environmental knowledge and implanting an environmental culture in the organization. Some of the major activities under this strategic orientation include rewarding employees for their efforts to improve the environment, communicating and handling critical environmental issues, starting environmental programs and policies, and allocating organizational resources to environmental projects.

To put it another way, it is an internal green marketing plan that ties into the environmental culture of the internal stakeholders that needs to permeate the entirety of the business and business image. Internal green operations include actions such as employee training, environmental conservation actions inside the organizational practices, environmental leadership activities.

Developing a corporate culture embedded with shared green values and integrity and communicating the environmental values across the departments. Internal green marketing practices include more giant corporations establishing independent departments dedicated to environmental conservation and corporate social responsibility. Considering all the actions under the internal green marketing domain, it is essential to comprehend that such actions must be adequately visible to the consumers.

- **Thought Point (4)**: *In the realm of corporate social responsibility (CSR) and green marketing, the question arises whether companies should openly communicate their internal practices to larger consumer groups. Discuss.*

3 Three-Dimensional Understanding of the Green Marketing Orientation

This study discusses the theory of green marketing orientation, which comprises three dimensions: strategic green marketing orientation, tactical green marketing orientation and internal green marketing orientation. Green marketing orientation is "the extent to which an organization engages in strategic, tactical and internal processes and activities which aim to create, communicate and deliver products and services with minimal environmental impact".

The three dimensions reiterate the need to reinvent the interdisciplinarity of the three dimensions that help to responsibly balance growth goals with environmental sustainability and harmonize actions with principles and ethical business culture. Consequently, environmental values must be shared and communicated across divisions. According to Wells et al. (2015), promoting a company's green values to its employees is just as vital as marketing its purpose to customers. Progressive companies will create a separate department committed to CSR and sustainable development.

- **Thought Point (5)**: *Look at* Fig. 1 *shows the three functional blocks: strategic green orientation, tactical green orientation and internal green orientation. Considering both short-term tactical initiatives and internal organisational practices, how can a company effectively implement green orientation in its marketing strategy to promote eco-friendly products? Provide examples of successful green marketing campaigns that embody these dimensions.*

Greenwashing, although it is looked at as a short-term solution or as a shortcut effort to portray a better image in front of their stakeholders. However, in the bargain, it undermines corporate accountability towards consumers and the credibility of environmental initiatives (Testa et al., 2018). Over time, accurate appearances regarding corporate sustainability can lead to clarity among consumers and lead them to lose confidence in the brand, particularly among consumers and the general public, which has increased difficulties in identifying truly socially responsible firms. In the long run, greenwashing can lead to an increased gap between talk and action regarding corporate sustainability by organizations, leading to public criticism in the media and NGO circles.

Consequently, greenwashing may create a short-term gain for the deceptive companies, but in the long run, the whole green market will experience a fall (Polonsky et al., 2010). That is a loss–loss situation for the market and consumers.

4 Conclusion and the Way Forward

Moving forward with green marketing focus will require a comprehensive and flexible strategy to match corporate operations with sustainable environmental principles. The cornerstone is strategic green orientation, which encourages businesses to incorporate environmentally conscious ideas into their primary business plan. The organizations have to plan their green strategies for their consistent long-term growth and well-being. To highlight environmental responsibility entails reinventing supply chain management, product creation, and market positioning. Companies could allocate resources to develop sustainable materials, implement renewable energy sources, and emphasize their dedication to environmentally friendly practices in their corporate communications.

To enhance a company's environmental commitment, tactical green orientation refers to the daily choices and actions that support it. This could involve introducing targeted eco-friendly advertising efforts, implementing recycling plans, or embracing innovative package designs that reduce their adverse environmental effects. In order to ensure that green programs connect with target audiences and encourage positive behavioural change, practical, tactical green orientation necessitates striking a balance between consumer education and engagement.

The triad is completed by internal green orientation, highlighting the necessity of a corporate culture firmly anchored in sustainability. Employers must help employees develop a green attitude by promoting eco-friendly behaviours at work. This could entail establishing internal sustainability targets, implementing training programs, and praising and awarding staff members for their eco-friendly actions. Long-term adherence to green marketing concepts is ensured by fostering a corporate culture where sustainability is deeply embedded in the organization's DNA.

Therefore, a smooth integration of all three dimensions is necessary. Innovation and constant adaptability are necessary for a successful green marketing strategy. It is critical to embrace new technologies, remain aware of changing customer preferences, and take proactive measures to solve environmental issues. Working with suppliers, consumers, and government agencies is essential for navigating the complicated sustainability landscape.

In summary, advancing green marketing orientation will require a continuous process that calls for tactical accuracy, strategic foresight, and a solid internal commitment. Businesses that effectively follow this route help create a sustainable future and establish themselves as industry leaders in a market where consumers are increasingly concerned about the environment.

5 Further Questions

- Think of a well-known green brand you are familiar with. Can you recollect the green marketing strategies (Fig. 1) that were at the focus of the brands marketing efforts?
- How do you think velocity of conversations and other information flows both internal and external (Fig. 1) that could affect current or future position of the brand in the market?

Key Further Reading

Gordon, J. A., Balta-Ozkan, N., Haq, A., & Nabavi, S. A. (2024). Coupling green hydrogen production to community benefits: A pathway to social acceptance? *Energy Research & Social Science, 110*, 103437.

Jog, D., & Singhal, D. (2019). Pseudo green players and their greenwashing practices: A differentiating strategy for real green firms of personal care category. *Strategic Direction, 35*(12), 4–7.

Mukhtar, B., Shad, M. K., Woon, L. F., Haider, M., & Waqas, A. (2024). Integrating ESG disclosure into the relationship between CSR and green organizational culture toward green Innovation. *Social Responsibility Journal, 20*(2), 288–304.

References

Chen, Y. S., & Chang, C. H. (2012). Enhance green purchase intentions: The roles of green perceived value, green perceived risk, and green trust. *Management Decision, 50*(3), 502–520.

Cronin, J. J., Smith, J. S., Gleim, M. R., Ramirez, E., & Martinez, J. D. (2011). Green marketing strategies: An examination of stakeholders and the opportunities they present. *Journal of the Academy of Marketing Science, 39*, 158–174.

Dangelico, R., & Vocalelli, D. (2017). "Green arketing" An analysis of definitions, strategy steps, and tools through a systematic review of the literature. *Journal of Cleaner Production, 165*, 1263–1279.

Gatignon, H., & Xuereb, J. M. (1997). Strategic orientation of the firm and new product performance. *Journal of Marketing Research, 34*, 77–90. https://doi.org/10.1177/002224379703400107

Gordon, R., Carrigan, M., & Hastings, G. (2011). A framework for sustainable marketing. *Marketing Theory, 11*(2), 143–163.

Hoffman, A. J., & Ventresca, M. J. (2002). *Organizations, policy, and the natural environment: Institutional and strategic perspectives*. Stanford University Press.

Jog, D., & Singhal, D. (2020). Greenwashing understanding among Indian consumers and its impact on their green consumption. *Global Business Review*, 0972150920962933.

King, A., & Lenox, M. (2002). Exploring the locus of profitable pollution reduction. *Management Science, 48*(2), 289–299.

Kinnear, T. C., Taylor, J. R., & Ahmed, S. A. (1974). Ecologically concerned consumers: Who are they? Ecologically concerned consumers can be identified. *Journal of Marketing, 38*(2), 20–24.

Mulch, B. (2009). The seventh sin. *Alternatives Journal, 35*(5), 40–41.

Nyilasy, G., Gangadharbatla, H., & Paladino, A. (2014). Perceived greenwashing: The interactive effects of green advertising and corporate environmental performance on consumer reactions. *Journal of Business Ethics, 125*, 693–707.

Papadas, K. K., Avlonitis, G. J., & Carrigan, M. (2017). Green marketing orientation: Conceptualization, scale development and validation. *Journal of Business Research, 80*, 236–246.

Papadas, K. K., Avlonitis, G. J., Carrigan, M., & Piha, L. (2019). The interplay of strategic and internal green marketing orientation on competitive advantage. *Journal of Business Research, 104*, 632–643.

Parguel, B., Benoit-Moreau, F., & Russell, C. A. (2015). Can evoking nature in advertising mislead consumers? he power of 'executional greenwashing.' *International Journal of Advertising, 34*(1), 107–134.

Peattie, K. (1995). *Environmental marketing management: Meeting the green challenge* (pp. 705–726).

Polonsky, M. J., Grau, S. L., & Garma, R. (2010). The new greenwash?: Potential marketing problems with carbon offsets. *International Journal of Business Studies: A Publication of the Faculty of Business Administration, Edith Cowan University, 18*(1), 49–54.

Ramus, C. A., & Montiel, I. (2005). When are corporate environmental policies a form of greenwashing?. *Business & society*, *44*(4), 377–414.

Sarkis, J. (2003). A strategic decision framework for green supply chain management. *Journal of Cleaner Production, 11*, 397–409. https://doi.org/10.1016/S0959-6526(02)00062-8

Scarpaci, J. L., Sovacool, B. K., & Ballantyne, R. (2016). A critical review of the costs of advertising: A transformative consumer research perspective. *Journal of Consumer Policy, 39*, 119–140.

Testa, F., Boiral, O., & Iraldo, F. (2018). Internalization of environmental practices and institutional complexity: Can stakeholders pressures encourage greenwashing? *Journal of Business Ethics, 147*, 287–307.

Dangling Between Frontier Market and Emerging Market, the Demarketing of a Potential African Market: Demographic Implications and the Effects on Sustainable Development

Remi Chukwudi Okeke, Jude Odigbo, and Kingsley Nnorom

Abstract The world is invariably ruled by the developed markets but some nationalistic public policy pundits may challenge such assertions. However, these challengers still inwardly know that in real economic terms, this group of countries still leads while others follow. There are still countries that are structurally and operationally impaired and debarred from being classified as developed markets. Policy makers and implementers in these other countries are not essentially cynical about the status of the leading economies. Still, the tasks of jettisoning their subsisting national categorizations are enormous. Here we find the frontier and emerging markets. Then a very peculiar state-scenario arises in Africa of all places. In this specific country, the economy is neither strictly a frontier case nor an emerging market type, and indisputably not among the developed markets. In comparative terms, this country possesses a humongous population. Then the internal dynamics of generic policy articulation and implementation in the location lead towards a summative evaluation of demarketing. This chapter examines the national, regional and worldwide demographic implications of this unusual case in Africa. Moreover, it discusses the effects of the country's atypical subtleties on sustainable development.

Keywords Frontier markets · Emerging markets · Developed markets · National demarketing · Sustainable development · Sustainable development goals · Strong institutions

---

R. C. Okeke (✉)
Department of Public Administration, Madonna University, Okija, Nigeria
e-mail: okekerc@madonnauniversity.edu.ng

J. Odigbo
Department of Political Science, Madonna University, Okija, Nigeria

K. Nnorom
Department of Sociology, Federal University, Wukari, Nigeria

W. Leal Filho and V. Kuzmanović (eds.), *Sustainable Development Seen Through the Lenses of Ethnoeconomics and the Circular Economy*,
https://doi.org/10.1007/978-3-031-72676-7_12

1 Introduction

In the intricate web of global economic interactions, developed markets wield significant influence in shaping the trajectory of the world economy (Coe & Yeung, 2015). The term "developed markets" typically refers to advanced industrialized nations with well-established infrastructures, robust financial systems, and high levels of per capita income. Such developed markets, including the United States, European Union countries, and Japan, collectively hold a disproportionate share of global economic output (IG Uk, 2024) Their dominance is evident in key economic indicators such as gross domestic product (GDP), trade volume, and financial market capitalization. As hubs of technological innovation, production, and consumption, these economies set trends that reverberate worldwide. The policies and decisions made within these markets often have far-reaching consequences for other nations, creating a system where economic power is concentrated in the hands of a few. The financial systems of these developed markets serve as the nerve center of global finance. Their dominance in international finance is reinforced by the prevalence of their currencies, such as the US dollar and the euro, as preferred reserve currencies. This affords them significant leverage in shaping international monetary policies, influencing exchange rates, and determining the terms of international trade and finance.

Furthermore, developed markets often dictate the rules of the game in global trade and investment through mechanisms such as free trade agreements, bilateral investment treaties, and multinational trade organizations like the World Trade Organization (WTO). These arrangements are often crafted to safeguard the interests of developed market economies, enabling them to gain preferential access to foreign markets while imposing barriers on imports from less developed countries. Moreover, multinational corporations headquartered in developed markets wield considerable influence in shaping global supply chains, exploiting disparities in labor and environmental regulations to maximize profits (Desai, 2023).

Invariably, technological advancements originating from developed markets have profound implications for the global economy. Innovations in information technology, biotechnology, and renewable energy not only drive economic growth within developed economies but also reshape industries and redefine competitive dynamics worldwide. Access to these technologies is often uneven, exacerbating disparities between the developed and developing nations (Helsper, 2021). Current concerns about data privacy, intellectual property rights, and digital sovereignty underscore the need for a more equitable distribution of technological benefits. In essence, while the dominance of developed markets has undoubtedly contributed to global prosperity and progress, it also poses significant challenges and risks. Persistent income inequality, environmental degradation, and financial instability are among the pressing issues exacerbated by the concentration of economic power in the hands of a few (Li et al., 2022; van Niekerk, 2020). But beyond every other critical consideration, the tendencies and characteristics of the developed markets are marked by the prevalence of strong institutions.

On the reverse side of the embedded issues, an assertion that the world economy is ruled by developed markets may oversimplify the intricate dynamics of global economic governance. This is because, while developed markets undoubtedly wield significant influence, it is essential to recognize the plurality of actors and forces that currently shape the global economic landscape. Consequently, the narrative of developed market dominance is challengeable. The past few decades have witnessed the remarkable rise of emerging economies, such as China, India, Brazil, and several Southeast Asian nations (Goel et al., 2022). These countries have become key drivers of global economic growth, leveraging their abundant labor force, natural resources, and strategic investments in infrastructure and technology. The economic ascent of emerging markets has led to a rebalancing of economic power, challenging the traditional dominance of developed markets and fostering greater multipolarity in the global economy (Gürcan, 2023; Kukreja, 2020).

Furthermore, regional economic blocs and initiatives have gained prominence as mechanisms for fostering economic cooperation and integration among countries with shared geographical proximity or common interests. Examples include the Association of Southeast Asian Nations (ASEAN), the African Union (AU), and the Eurasian Economic Union (EAEU). By deepening trade ties, harmonizing regulatory frameworks, and facilitating cross-border investment, regional integration initiatives are intended to diversify economic linkages and reduce dependence on developed markets. Additionally, the concept of South-South cooperation emphasizes collaboration among countries in the Global South to address common development challenges, promote trade, and share knowledge and expertise. Through initiatives such as bilateral trade agreements, development aid, and technical assistance programs, emerging economies are forging mutually beneficial partnerships that bypass traditional power structures dominated by developed markets (Oyedele & Firat, 2020).

Besides, the democratization of technology has leveled the playing field in many industries, enabling startups and entrepreneurs from emerging economies to compete on a global scale. The proliferation of digital platforms, open-source software, and decentralized finance has reduced barriers to entry and empowered individuals and small businesses to participate in the global economy without reliance on traditional intermediaries or established market players (Lekhi, 2024; Turi, 2020). Moreover, innovations such as blockchain, artificial intelligence, and renewable energy hold the potential to reshape industries and create new avenues for economic growth beyond the control of developed markets (Daraojimba et al., 2023; Mosteanu & Faccia, 2021). Current calls for reforming global economic governance structures accordingly reflect growing recognition of the need for greater representation and inclusivity in decision-making processes. All proposals aimed at reforming institutions such as the International Monetary Fund (IMF), the World Bank, and the United Nations Conference on Trade and Development (UNCTAD) seek to amplify the voices of emerging economies and ensure that their interests are adequately represented in the formulation of international economic policies and norms.

Ultimately, while developed markets continue to exert significant influence over the world economy, their dominance is being increasingly challenged by the rise of emerging economies, regional integration efforts, South-South cooperation, technological innovation, and calls for global governance reform (Molinari et al., 2022; Yang, 2021). Acknowledging the plurality of actors and forces shaping the global economic landscape is essential for fostering a more balanced, inclusive, and sustainable model of economic development. Embracing economic pluralism offers a pathway towards a more resilient and equitable global economy that reflects the diversity of human aspirations and aspirations. However, in current net economic terms, the developed markets still lead while others speedily follow (Focus Economics, 2024). Even at that, there are still countries that are structurally and operationally impaired and debarred from being classified as developed markets. Policy makers and implementers in these other countries are not essentially cynical about the status of the leading economies. Still, the tasks of jettisoning their subsisting national categorizations are enormous. Here we find the frontier and emerging markets.

2 Between Frontier Market and Emerging Market

Frontier markets and emerging markets represent two categories of economies that occupy different positions along the spectrum of development and investment attractiveness. While both offer opportunities for growth and investment, they exhibit distinct characteristics, risks, and potential rewards. Emerging markets refer to economies that display characteristics of rapid industrialization, urbanization, and economic growth (Zhang, 2021). These countries typically exhibit higher levels of income per capita, industrialization, and financial market development compared to frontier markets. Examples of emerging markets include Brazil, Russia, India, China (BRIC), South Africa (BRICS), Mexico, and Turkey. Frontier markets, on the other hand, represent economies that are at an earlier stage of development, characterized by lower income levels, less developed financial markets, and greater political and economic volatility (Stereńczak et al., 2020). These markets often possess untapped potential for growth but also face significant challenges related to governance, infrastructure, and institutional capacity. Examples of frontier markets include Nigeria, Vietnam, Pakistan, Bangladesh, and several countries in sub-Saharan Africa and the Middle East.

Frontier markets typically offer higher potential returns but also entail greater risks compared to emerging markets (Larrabee, 2012). The lack of institutional capacity, political instability, and susceptibility to external shocks make frontier markets more volatile and unpredictable (Stereńczak et al., 2020). Emerging markets, while still exhibiting volatility, tend to have more established institutions and regulatory frameworks, reducing some of the investment risks associated with frontier markets. Emerging markets generally have more liquid and accessible financial markets, making it easier for investors to buy and sell securities. Frontier markets may have limited liquidity and market infrastructure, which can pose challenges for investors seeking to enter or exit positions. However, frontier markets offer the opportunity for early-mover advantage and potential higher returns for investors willing to tolerate illiquidity and higher risk (Larrabee, 2012).

Emerging markets often have more diversified economies with developed manufacturing, service, and export sectors. In contrast, frontier markets may be heavily reliant on natural resources or agriculture, exposing them to commodity price fluctuations and external shocks. This reliance on primary sectors also presents opportunities for investment in sectors with untapped potential for growth and value creation. Then emerging markets tend to have more mature regulatory frameworks and investor protections compared to frontier markets. Investors in frontier markets may face greater regulatory uncertainty, weaker property rights enforcement, and less transparency, requiring careful due diligence and risk management strategies. All the same, frontier markets offer unique opportunities for investors to participate in the early stages of economic development and capitalize on rapid growth potential. These markets may benefit from demographic trends, urbanization, and technological leapfrogging, creating new consumer markets and business opportunities. Moreover, investment in frontier markets can contribute to poverty alleviation, infrastructure development, and sustainable economic growth (Ofosu-Mensah Ababio et al., 2021).

Emerging markets continue to attract significant investment inflows due to their size, growth prospects, and increasing integration into the global economy (Horvat et al., 2021). These markets offer opportunities for diversification, access to new consumer markets, and exposure to industries driving global growth such as technology, healthcare, and consumer goods. Moreover, investment in emerging markets can foster economic development, job creation, and poverty reduction. (Horvat et al., 2021). Understanding the differences between frontier markets and emerging markets is essential for investors seeking to navigate global markets effectively and capitalize on diverse investment opportunities. Invariably, the generic scenarios of the emerging markets are characterized by the manifold presence of national economic institutions of promise. At the frontier markets, such institutions are noted for the weirdness of their tendencies and net negative contributions. Incontrovertibly, fostering economic development and stability in both frontier and emerging markets is crucial for promoting inclusive and sustainable global growth. Demarketing can make a potential emerging market to dangle perpetually between a frontier market and emerging market categorizations.

3 Theoretical Framework: Institutional Theory

Institutional theory is a prominent perspective in management and organizational studies that focuses on understanding how institutions—defined as systems of rules, norms, and shared beliefs—shape the behavior and actions of individuals and organizations within a society or industry. Institutional theory emerged as a response to the recognition that organizations are not just rational entities operating in isolation but are deeply embedded within broader social and institutional contexts (Jepperson & Meyer, 2021).

There are several key concepts and components of institutional theory, which include the following:

- Institutional Environment: It is held here that institutions provide the broader context within which organizations operate. This environment consists of formal institutions (such as laws, regulations, and government agencies) and informal institutions (such as cultural norms, values, and traditions) that influence organizational behavior (Furusten, 2023).
- Institutional Isomorphism: Institutional theory suggests in these regards that organizations tend to become more similar to each other over time due to institutional pressures (Cardona Mejía et al., 2020).
- Organizational Legitimacy: Legitimacy refers here to the perception that an organization's actions, structures, or behaviors are appropriate, proper, or desirable within its institutional context. Legitimacy is crucial for organizational survival and success because it influences stakeholders' trust, support, and cooperation (Acquah et al., 2021).
- Institutional Entrepreneurship under which institutional theory recognizes the role of actors known as institutional entrepreneurs who seek to influence or change existing institutional arrangements. Institutional entrepreneurs may challenge established norms, advocate for new practices, or create alternative institutional arrangements to address societal problems or advance their interests (McMullen et al., 2021).
- Institutional Change, whereby institutional theory acknowledges that institutions are not static but can change over time in response to external pressures, internal dynamics, or deliberate efforts by actors. Institutional change may involve the emergence of new institutions, the transformation of existing institutions, or the decline of outdated institutions (Furusten, 2023).

Institutional theory actually has its roots in sociology, with subsequent contributions from scholars across various disciplines. Its development can then be traced back to several key influences and historical contexts. It invariably draws heavily from the sociological tradition, particularly the work of Max Weber, Emile Durkheim, and Talcott Parsons (Weiss & Gomes Neto, 2021). Weber's concept of "rationalization" highlighted the increasing importance of formal rules and bureaucratic structures in modern society, while Durkheim's notion of "social facts" emphasized the existence of shared norms and values that regulate social behavior. Parsons' structural-functionalism provided a framework for understanding how institutions maintain social order and stability (Weiss & Gomes Neto, 2021). But overall, the origin of institutional theory can be traced to interdisciplinary efforts to understand the role of institutions in shaping social, economic, and organizational phenomena.

Consequently, by drawing on insights from sociology, economics, political science, and organizational studies, institutional theory provides a valuable framework for analyzing the complex interplay between formal rules, informal norms, and organizational behavior within diverse institutional contexts. It provides a valuable framework for understanding how organizations are shaped by and respond to their institutional environments, including the norms, rules, and beliefs that govern behavior within specific social or industry contexts. By examining the influence of institutions on organizational behavior, strategies, and outcomes, researchers and practitioners can gain insights into the complex dynamics of organizational life and the broader social systems in which they are embedded. Using institutional theory, this chapter analyzes how institutional factors shape the demarketing tendencies in this African market and their implications for sustainable development.

4 The De-Marketing of a Potential African Market in Nigeria

Nigeria, with its vast population, abundant resources, and strategic geographical location, holds immense potential as a market for domestic and foreign investors (Adeniyi et al., 2021; Idowu, 2021). However, despite its promising prospects, Nigeria faces significant challenges that impede its attractiveness for investment and economic growth (Abubakar & Ayuba, 2022). This section of the chapter essentially delves into the concept of de-marketing, exploring the factors contributing to the negative perception of Nigeria as a stunted market. De-marketing refers to the deliberate efforts to reduce demand for a product, service, or market due to various reasons, such as overcapacity, negative externalities, or unfavorable market conditions (Alsamydai., 2015). In the context of Nigeria, de-marketing manifests through institutional malfunctions and the consequent negative movements and developments in the country's business environment, governance, security, and infrastructure. The challenges contributing to de-marketing in Nigeria include the following:

5 Governance and Corruption

Governance and corruption in Nigeria have long been intricately intertwined, posing significant challenges to the country's development and stability (Azoro et al., 2021; Nwogbo & Ighodalo, 2021). Despite every effort to combat corruption in the country, it remains pervasive at various levels of government and society, undermining the effectiveness of governance structures and impeding socio-economic progress. Corruption in Nigeria often involves bribery, outright embezzlement of public funds and nepotism. Several initiatives have been instituted to address corruption in Nigeria, including the establishment of anti-corruption agencies like the Economic and Financial Crimes Commission (EFCC) and the Independent Corrupt Practices and Other Related Offences Commission (ICPC). However, these efforts have faced numerous obstacles, including political interference, inadequate funding, and slow judicial processes. Corruption has accordingly become deeply entrenched in the country's political culture, with many public officials exploiting their positions for personal gain, further eroding public trust in government institutions. Nigeria's reputation for corruption and weak governance accordingly undermines investor confidence and erodes trust in the country's institutions (Nwozo & Afolabi, 2023). Persistent corruption in the nation consequently hampers business operations, increases transaction costs, and deters foreign investment.

6 Security Concerns

Security concerns in Nigeria present significant challenges to the stability and well-being of the nation. The country grapples with a myriad of security threats, including insurgency, terrorism, communal violence, kidnapping, and armed robbery (Akinyetun et al., 2023). The Boko Haram insurgency which started in the northeast region of the country and aims to establish an Islamic caliphate has resulted in widespread displacement, loss of lives, and humanitarian crises. Despite efforts by the Nigerian military and multinational coalitions, such as the Multinational Joint Task Force (MNJTF), to combat the insurgency, Boko Haram continued to carry out attacks in Nigeria, demonstrating the persistent security challenges facing the country. Although the attacks that are directly ascribable to the dreaded terrorist group has subsided, mass killings which are reminiscent of the Boko Haram atrocities have since continued (Obiezu, 2023).

In addition to the insurgency in the northeast, Nigeria faces escalating violence in other regions, fueled by ethnic, religious, and socio-economic tensions. Communal clashes between herders and farmers over land resources have claimed numerous lives and displaced communities, particularly in the Middle Belt region. Inter-ethnic conflicts, such as those between the Fulani and various ethnic groups, further exacerbate the security situation, underscoring the need for holistic approaches to address underlying grievances and promote peaceful coexistence. Furthermore, the proliferation of small arms and light weapons exacerbates insecurity, enabling criminal elements to perpetrate violence and undermine state authority (Aja, 2023; Yahaya, 2020).

Moreover, the issue of kidnapping has become increasingly prevalent across Nigeria, with both criminal gangs and terrorist groups resorting to abductions for financial gain or political leverage (Ogunode et al., 2024). The Nigerian government faces immense pressure to enhance security measures, strengthen law enforcement capabilities, and improve intelligence gathering to effectively counter the various security threats plaguing the country and restore confidence in its ability to protect its citizens. The prevalence of insecurity including insurgency, terrorism, and communal conflicts, poses significant risks to businesses and investments in Nigeria. Such security challenges not only disrupt business operations but also deter foreign investment and tourism and demonstrate the prevalence of weakened institutions in the country.

7 Infrastructure Deficits

Infrastructure deficits in Nigeria pose significant obstacles to the country's economic growth and development (Anam et al., 2024). Despite being one of Africa's largest economies, Nigeria's infrastructure remains inadequate and often in a state of disrepair, hindering productivity, stifling investment, and impeding socio-economic progress. Key sectors such as transportation, energy and water supply, suffer from chronic underinvestment, outdated technologies, and poor maintenance culture, exacerbating inequalities and constraining the country's potential for sustainable development.

One of the most pressing infrastructure challenges in Nigeria is the transportation sector, where terribly bad roads, decrepit seaports, and abandoned railways hamper the efficient movement of goods and people. Congested roads, poorly maintained highways, and insufficient public transport systems not only result in increased transportation costs but also contribute to traffic accidents and delays, further undermining productivity and competitiveness. Additionally, the country's seaports and airports suffer from congestion and substandard facilities, hindering trade and investment opportunities and limiting Nigeria's connectivity with global markets.

In the energy sector, Nigeria faces persistent power shortages and unreliable electricity supply, despite being one of the leading oil producers in the world. The inadequate power infrastructure, coupled with systemic issues such as gas supply constraints, transmission losses, and outdated distribution networks, hampers industrial productivity, stifles entrepreneurship, and exacerbates poverty. Many businesses in the country rely on costly diesel generators to meet their energy needs, increasing operational expenses and reducing profitability (Adedeji et al., 2024). Addressing the infrastructure deficits in the energy sector is therefore crucial for unlocking Nigeria's economic potential and ensuring inclusive growth by providing reliable and affordable electricity to households and businesses across the country. The country's inadequate infrastructure, particularly in the area of power supply, constrains economic growth and productivity. Poor infrastructure increases costs for businesses, reduces efficiency, and hampers competitiveness.

8 Regulatory Environment

Regulatory challenges in Nigeria, characterized by complex and inconsistent regulatory frameworks, present formidable barriers to investment, innovation, and economic diversification. (Oguejiofor et al., 2023). The regulatory environment in the country is often marked by bureaucratic red tape, opaque processes, and regulatory overlaps, creating uncertainty and dis-incentivizing both domestic and foreign investors. Entrepreneurs and businesses in the country face significant hurdles in navigating the intricate web of regulations across various sectors, leading to delays, increased costs, and a lack of confidence in the business environment. The complexity and inconsistency of regulatory frameworks in Nigeria not only deter investment but also stifle innovation and entrepreneurship. Complex and inconsistent regulatory frameworks, bureaucratic red tape, and legal uncertainties create obstacles for businesses operating in the country. They are also the manifestations of institutional disorientation.

9 Demographic Implications of Nigeria's De-Marketing: Effects on Sustainable Development

This section explores the concept of de-marketing of the Nigerian market in the context of its demographic implications and the effects on sustainable development. It commences with a reminder that in continental comparative terms and equally in global perspectives, the Nigerian state possesses a humongous population. Nigeria is the most populous country in Africa, with an estimated population exceeding 222 million people and its population is expected to surpass 400 million by 2050, making it the third most populous country globally (Akinyemi, 2023; UNFPA, 2023). Nigeria has accordingly long been viewed as a potential powerhouse in Africa and a lucrative market for domestic and foreign investors. Despite its promising demographic profile, the country continues to face numerous challenges that hinder its attractiveness for investment and sustainable development. The country boasts a youthful demographic profile, with a significant proportion of its population under the age of 30 (Akinyemi, 2023). This demographic portrait presents opportunities for economic growth, innovation, and human capital development if properly harnessed.

Rapid urbanization and internal migration trends have reshaped Nigeria's demographic landscape, with millions of people moving from rural to urban areas in search of economic opportunities and better living standards that are hardly available, consequent upon the country's demarketing. The demographic implications of this demarketing extend to the issue of brain drain and talent flight. The attendant negative perceptions and challenging business conditions arising from demarketing in Nigeria contribute to brain drain and talent flight, as skilled professionals and entrepreneurs seek opportunities abroad. This brain drain deprives Nigeria of valuable human capital and impedes its capacity for innovation and sustainable development (Enibe et al., 2021). Furthermore, despite its youthful population, Nigeria grapples with high rates of youth unemployment and underemployment (Olubusoye et al., 2023). De-marketing exacerbates this issue by deterring investment, limiting job creation, and stifling economic opportunities for young people, potentially fueling social unrest and instability.

Additionally, de-marketing of Nigeria widens socio-economic disparities, as investment concentrates in select sectors and regions, exacerbating inequalities and marginalizing vulnerable populations. This exacerbates social tensions, undermines social cohesion, and hinders inclusive and sustainable development efforts. Nigeria's burgeoning population invariably strains public services, infrastructure, and resources, exacerbating challenges related to healthcare, education, housing, and sanitation. The country's de-marketing further compounds these pressures by deterring investment in critical sectors of the economy and inhibiting the delivery of essential services to the population. In the meantime, inflation rate in the country remains on upward swing, as the average citizen becomes increasingly restless. The inflation rate accelerated to 29.90% in January 2024, from 28.92% recorded in the preceding month. The increase of 0.98% showed that the country's inflation rate was yet to record decreases (Aina, 2024).

10 Effects on Sustainable Development

Indeed, the effects of the foregoing scenario on sustainable development, center on economic stagnation and domestic dependency. De-marketing undermines Nigeria's prospects for sustainable economic growth, perpetuating a cycle of underdevelopment and dependency on extractive industries and the country's volatile crude oil resources. This dependency limits diversification efforts, stifles entrepreneurship, and perpetuates reliance on unsustainable economic models. Furthermore, the pursuit of short-term gains amid de-marketing pressures often disregards environmental considerations, leading to deforestation, pollution, and resource depletion. This compromises Nigeria's ecological resilience, exacerbates climate change impacts, and undermines long-term sustainability dreams. In additional critical terms, the country's demarketing exacerbates social tensions, economic disparities, and governance failures, increasing the incidences of social unrest, communal conflicts, and political bickering. The occasioning instability undermines peacebuilding efforts, hampers social cohesion, and threatens the achievement of sustainable development goals in Nigeria.

11 Worldwide Demographic Implications

A finally de-marketed Nigerian market would certainly have significant worldwide demographic implications, due to Nigeria's position as the most populous country on the African continent and one of the largest economies in Africa. On global migration patterns, Nigeria has a very large population, and if economic opportunities continue to diminish in the country due to demarketing, there could be continuous emigration from Nigeria to other countries, both within Africa and beyond. The emigration trend is already enormous (Okunade & Awosusi, 2023). This could lead to demographic shifts in destination countries as well as potential social and political tensions related to immigration. Then related to regional economic impact, Nigeria plays a crucial role in the economic dynamics of the West African region in particular. Demarketing of Nigeria could disrupt regional trade and economic integration efforts, affecting neighboring countries and potentially leading to economic downturns and demographic changes in the broader West African region. Against the background of global supply chains, Nigeria is not an insignificant player in this area, particularly in industries such as oil and gas. Demarketing the country could disrupt these supply chains, impacting global trade patterns and potentially leading to demographic shifts in regions that rely on Nigerian imports.

Again, because of its large population, Nigeria's demographic trends, including population growth, health outcomes, and education levels, have implications for global health and development efforts. Demarketing Nigeria could hinder progress on key development indicators, such as maternal and child health, education, and poverty reduction, affecting global demographic trends and development outcomes. With a further focus on security and stability, Nigeria's stability and security have implications beyond its borders, particularly in the context of regional security dynamics in West Africa. Demarketing Nigeria could exacerbate existing security challenges, leading to increased instability in the region and potentially influencing migration patterns and demographic trends in neighboring countries. In summary, the demarketing of the Nigerian market in Africa could have far-reaching worldwide demographic implications, impacting migration patterns, regional economic dynamics, global supply chains, health and development outcomes, and security and stability in the broader West African region and beyond.

12 Strategies for Redressing the De-Marketing of Nigeria

The principal strategy for redressing the demarketing tendencies in Nigeria is governance reform and the strengthening of all national institutions to operate at the level of desired capacities. Implementing comprehensive governance reforms to enhance transparency, accountability, and the rule of law is critical for restoring investor confidence and promoting sustainable development in the country. It fundamentally needs institutional rejuvenations. Investment in human capital is also imperative. Prioritizing investment in education, relevant skills development, and in healthcare is essential for harnessing Nigeria's demographic potentials and fostering inclusive and sustainable development. Promoting economic diversification through targeted industrial policies, innovation incentives, and spirited support for small and medium enterprises (SMEs) can reduce dependence on volatile sectors and stimulate inclusive growth. Investing in critical infrastructure, including transportation, energy, and digital inclusion is unquestionably vital for unlocking Nigeria's economic potential, enhancing competitiveness, and facilitating sustainable development.

13 Conclusion

Overcoming the de-marketing of Nigeria as a potential emerging market requires concerted efforts to address governance challenges and institutional failures enhance security and stability, invest in infrastructure, and reform regulatory frameworks (regulatory institutions). By implementing strategic reforms and promoting Nigeria's potential, the country can attract relevant domestic and foreign investment, foster economic growth, and unlock opportunities for sustainable development. Building a conducive business environment grounded in transparency, stability, and good governance is essential for Nigeria to realize its aspirations for prosperity and global competitiveness. The de-marketing of Nigeria as a potential African market poses significant demographic implications and undermines efforts towards sustainable development. Addressing the root causes of de-marketing, including governance failures, insecurity, and infrastructure deficits, is essential for harnessing Nigeria's demographic potentials, promoting inclusive growth, and achieving sustainable development goals. By prioritizing governance reforms institutional rejuvanation, investment in human capital, economic diversification, and infrastructure development, Nigeria can unlock its full potential and emerge as a catalyst for progress and prosperity in Africa.

References

Abubakar, H. A., & Ayuba, B. (2022). Effect of unfavourable environmental factors on Foreign Direct Investments Inflow (FDII) and Nigeria's economic growth. *Journal of Global Economics and Business, 3*(8), 125–155.

Acquah, I. S. K., Essel, D., Baah, C., Agyabeng-Mensah, Y., & Afum, E. (2021). Investigating the efficacy of isomorphic pressures on the adoption of green manufacturing practices and its influence on organizational legitimacy and financial performance. *Journal of Manufacturing Technology Management, 32*(7), 1399–1420.

Adedeji, A. A., Ogunbayo, I., Ajayi, P. I., & Adeniyi, O. (2024). Energy security, governance quality, and economic performance in sub-Saharan Africa. *Next Energy, 2*(-), 1–10.

Adeniyi, A. G., Ighalo, J. O., & Adeyanju, C. A. (2021). Materials-to-product potentials for sustainable development in Nigeria. *International Journal of Sustainable Engineering, 14*(4), 664–671.

Aina, D. (2024). *Inflation rate jumps to 29.90% as food prices rise.* https://punchng.com/just-in-nigerias-inflation-rate-jumps-to-29-90-nbs/

Aja, U. A. (2023). Merchants of terror: Proliferation of small arms and light weapons and human security challenges in Nigeria. *African Security Review, 33*(1), 49–63.

Akinyemi, A. I. (2023). *Nigeria's growing population can be an advantage, with better data and a policy focus on young people.* https://theconversation.com/nigerias-growing-population-can-be-an-advantage-with-better-data-and-a-policy-focus-on-young-people-209530

Akinyetun, T. S., Ebonine, V. C., & Ambrose, I. O. (2023). Unknown gunmen and insecurity in Nigeria: Dancing on the brink of state fragility. *Security and Defence Quarterly, 42*(2), 16–34.

Alsamydai, M. J. (2015). *The Impact of Ostensible Demarketing Strategy on Improving Product Reputation in Customer's Minds International Review of Management and Business Research, 4*(4), 973–988.

Anam, B. E., Ijim, U. A., Ironbar, V. E., Otu, A. P., Duke, O. O., & Achuk Eba, M. B. (2024). Economic recovery and growth plan, economic sustainability plan and national development plan (2021–2025): The Nigerian experience under President Muhammadu Buhari. *Cogent Social Sciences, 10*(1), 1–15.

Azoro, C. J., Onah, C. A., & Agulefo, Q. O. (2021). Weak Institutions and Poor Governance in Nigeria: A Socio-Legal Perspective. *African Journal of Law, Political Research and Administration, 4*(2), 61–70.

Cardona Mejía, L. M., Pardo del Val, M., & Dasí Coscollar, M. D. S. (2020). The Institutional Isomorphism in the Context of Organizational Changes in Higher Education Institutions. *International Journal of Research in Education and Science, 6*(1), 61–73.

Coe, N. M., & Yeung, H. W. C. (2015). *Global production networks: Theorizing economic development in an interconnected world*. Oxford University Press.

Daraojimba, C., Abioye, K. M., Bakare, A. D., Mhlongo, N. Z., Onunka, O., & Daraojimba, D. O. (2023). Technology and innovation to growth of entrepreneurship and financial boost: A decade in review (2013–2023). *International Journal of Management & Entrepreneurship Research, 5*(10), 769–792.

Desai, A. (2023). Global supply chain resilience and risk management: Navigating a fragile system. *Journal of Philosophical Criticism, 6*(02), 235–244.

Enibe, O. G., Umeh, C. R., & Eze, I. J. (2021). Brain drain and sustainable development in Nigeria, 2000–2015. *University of Nigeria Journal of Political Economy, 11*(1), 278–292.

Focus Economics, (2024). *The Top 5 Economies in the World by 2028*.https://www.focus-economics.com/blog/the-largest-economies-in-the-world/

Furusten, S. (2023). *Institutional theory and organizational change*. Edward Elgar Publishing.

Goel, R., Gautam, D., Natalucci, F., & Natalucci, M. F. M. (2022). *Sustainable finance in emerging markets: evolution, challenges, and policy priorities*. International Monetary Fund.

Gürcan, E. C. (2023). The Multipolar Challenge: Implications for Dollar Dominance and the Shifting Tides of US Hegemony. *Belt & Road Initiative Quarterly, 5*(1), 40–59.

Helsper, E. J. (2021). *The digital disconnect: The social causes and consequences of digital inequalities*. Sage Publications

Horvat, T., Bendix, H., Bobek, V., & Skoko, H. (2021). Impacts of investments in infrastructure projects on emerging markets' growth: The case of East African countries. *Economic Research, 34*(1), 2135–2161.

Idowu, S. S. (2021). Eclectic theory and foreign direct investment in Nigeria: A contextual overview. *The African Review, 48*(2), 395–412.

IG UK. (2024). *Developed markets definition.* https://www.ig.com/uk/glossary-trading-terms/developed-markets-definition

Imam, N. (2022). *Imperatives of maintaining Nigeria's dilapidated roads.* https://punchng.com/imperatives-of-maintaining-nigerias-dilapidated-roads/

Jepperson, R. L., & Meyer, J. W. (2021). *Institutional theory: The cultural construction of organizations, states, and identities*. Cambridge University Press.

Kukreja, V. (2020). India in the emergent multipolar world order: Dynamics and strategic challenges. *India Quarterly, 76*(1), 8–23.

Larrabee, D. (2012). *Frontier market investing: Inefficiency equals opportunity*. https://blogs.cfainstitute.org/investor/2012/05/03/frontier-market-investing-inefficiency-equals-opportunity/

Lekhi, P. (2024). Megatrends and innovations shaping the future of finance. In *Innovation, sustainability, and technological megatrends in the face of uncertainties: Core developments and solutions* (pp. 41–53). Springer Nature Switzerland.

Li, N., Ulucak, R., & Danish. (2022). Turning points for environmental sustainability: The potential role of income inequality, human capital, and globalization. *Environmental Science and Pollution Research, 29*(27), 40878–40892.

McMullen, J. S., Brownell, K. M., & Adams, J. (2021). What makes an entrepreneurship study entrepreneurial? Toward a unified theory of entrepreneurial agency. *Entrepreneurship theory and practice, 45*(5), 1197–1238.

Molinari, A., Mena, F., & Ghiglione, J. (2022). South-South cooperation: Building productive bridges between Latin America and Africa. *Third World Quarterly, 43*(9), 2091–2111.

Mosteanu, N. R., & Faccia, A. (2021). Fintech frontiers in quantum computing, fractals, and blockchain distributed ledger: Paradigm shifts and open innovation. *Journal of Open Innovation: Technology, Market, and Complexity, 7*(1), 1–19.

Nwogbo, D. C., & Ighodalo, A. (2021). Governance and corruption in Nigeria. *Journal of Good Governance and Sustainable Development in Africa, 6*(2), 81–97.

Nwozor, A., & Afolabi, O. (2023). Keeping up appearance? Nigeria's anti-corruption crusade and image dilemma in the global arena. *Journal of Financial Crime, 30*(3), 813–827.

Obiezu, T. (2023). *Death toll rises to 150 following Christmas Eve attack in Nigeria.* https://www.voanews.com/a/death-toll-rises-to-150-following-christmas-eve-attack-in-nigeria/7414856.html

Ofosu-Mensah Ababio, J., Attah-Botchwey, E., Osei-Assibey, E., & Barnor, C. (2021). Financial inclusion and human development in frontier countries. *International Journal of Finance & Economics, 26*(1), 42–59.

Oguejiofor, B. B., Omotosho, A., Abioye, K. M., Alabi, A. M., Oguntoyinbo, F. N., Daraojimba, A. I., & Daraojimba, C. (2023). A review on data-driven regulatory compliance in Nigeria. *International Journal of Applied Research in Social Sciences, 5*(8), 231–243.

Ogunode, N. J., Ayeni, E. O., & Olorundare, A. S. (2024). Roles of tertiary institutions in curbing banditry kidnapping and terrorism in Nigeria. *International Journal of Sharia Economics and Financial Literacy, 1*(1), 19–34.

Okunade, S. K., & Awosusi, O. E. (2023). The Japa syndrome and the migration of Nigerians to the United Kingdom: An empirical analysis. *Comparative Migration Studies, 11*(1), 1–18.

Olubusoye, O. E., Salisu, A. A., & Olofin, S. O. (2023). Youth unemployment in Nigeria: Nature, causes and solutions. *Quality & Quantity, 57*(2), 1125–1157.

Oyedele, A., & Firat, F. (2020). Institutions, small local firms' strategies, and global alliances in sub- Saharan Africa emerging markets. *International Marketing Review, 37*(1), 156–182.

Stereńczak, S., Zaremba, A., & Umar, Z. (2020). Is there an illiquidity premium in frontier markets? *Emerging Markets Review, 42*(-), 1–19.

Turi, A. N. (2020). *Technologies for modern digital entrepreneurship: Understanding emerging tech at the cutting-edge of the web 3.0 Economy*. Apress.

UNFPA. (2023). *United Nations Population Fund Country programme document for Nigeria.* https://nigeria.unfpa.org/en/publications/united-nations-population-fund-country-programme-document-nigeria

van Niekerk, A. J. (2020). Inclusive economic sustainability: SDGs and global inequality. *Sustainability, 12*(13), 5427.

Weiss, R., & Gomes Neto, J. (2021). Talcott parsons and the sociology of morality. *The American Sociologist, 52*(1), 107–130.

Yahaya, J. U. (2020). An overview of the security implication of inflow of small arms and light weapons: A Nigeria perspectives. *Journal of Social and Political Science, 1*(11), 1–48.

Yang, Y. E. (2021). China's strategic narratives in global governance reform under Xi Jinping. *Journal of Contemporary China, 30*(128), 299–313.

Zhang, K. (2021). Economic structural transformation in emerging market countries. *Global Journal of Emerging Market Economies, 13*(2), 216–238.

Considerations on the Socio-Ecological Management of Agrobiodiversity Within Community Tourism

Ángel Eduardo Vázquez-Martin and Noé Aguilar-Rivera

Abstract Nowadays, various studies around the world agree on the importance of agrobiodiversity derived to its high ecological vulnerability. In addition to, the community tourism represents a valuable source for its preservation, dissemination, and conservation. Therefore, our paper documented the state of the scientific art of the main tourism studies that studied the socio-ecological management of agrobiodiversity as biocultural heritage. Consequently, our study objective was to identify agrobiodiversity management through an interdisciplinary approach. Our findings allowed us to recognize the main tourism case studies about the modern management of this biocultural resource. Furthermore, we found that community tourism affects the management of this resource mainly within rural tourism, ecotourism, agritourism and gastronomic tourism. As result, we observed that the ethnobiological knowledge of communities is an exceptional element that must be studied in its complexity by areas such as food anthropology, bioeconomic, ecology, ethnobiology, agricultural sciences, and sociology. Finally, this document presents the bases for its study within the science of sustainability. These considerations could serve as a source for public policy decision-making for the sustainable management of agricultural biodiversity.

Keywords Ethnobiological knowledge · Biocultural resource · Tourism

1 Introduction

Recently, various scientific studies are agreed on the importance of the high ecological vulnerability of global agrobiodiversity (Baumann, 2021; Cissé et al., 2022; Duflot et al., 2022; Porcuna-Ferrer et al., 2023; Rocchi et al. 2016). Specifically,

Á. E. Vázquez-Martin (✉) · N. Aguilar-Rivera
Universidad Veracruzana, Xalapa, México
e-mail: zs19019419@estudiantes.uv.mx

N. Aguilar-Rivera
e-mail: naguilar@uv.mx

W. Leal Filho and V. Kuzmanović (eds.), *Sustainable Development Seen Through the Lenses of Ethnoeconomics and the Circular Economy*,
https://doi.org/10.1007/978-3-031-72676-7_13

Matthies et al. estimated that a relatively small change in agrobiodiversity on European extensive agricultural lands could lead to disproportionate declines in agricultural biodiversity, causing an average local loss of 26% and 17% of threatened species richness (Matthies et al., 2023). Also, Khumalo et al. determined that in southern Africa the main cause of genetic erosion of crops and other forms of agrobiodiversity is the replacement of local varieties with exotic or improved varieties (Khumalo et al., 2012). Currently, we can observe that in the Anthropocene the main changes in land use have been caused by population, urbanization, and globalization. This is possibly caused by easier access to information and markets, more frequent natural hazards such as climate change, technological and economic advances (Antrop, 2005; Eiter & Potthoff, 2016).

Historically, the biodiversity of food systems and agriculture has supported their development and expansion for at least 4000 to 7000 years (Fuller et al., 2011; Smith & Zeder, 2013). Subsequently, changes in the industrial period since 1800 have rapidly transformed the biodiversity of agriculture and food systems (Foley et al., 2013). In recent decades, the study of the interaction between humans and agricultural resources is increasingly recognized as central to changes on a planetary scale since they involve the social and environmental dimensions of sustainability (Zimmerer & De Haan, 2017). However, the study of agrobiodiversity has been scarce and there are gaps regarding its scientific and academic implications (Ruddiman, 2013; Steffen et al., 2011; Zalasiewicz et al., 2017).

Today, the community tourism stands out within research on human management of biological resources due to its different scope. Therefore, the tourism could represent a valuable source for the preservation, dissemination, and conservation of biocultural heritage (Liu et al., 2022). This activity is caused by the establishment of a community, which includes common living spaces, community consciousness, cultural and historical emotions, quality of interaction of relationships, active participation, and other factors (Etzioni, 1993). Chang mentions that community-based tourism has been becoming a type of tourism with social care, although tourism development in communities has brought some problems for communities (Chang, 2021). Moreover, community tourism must consider the overall development of the community, sustainability, and self-sufficiency (Giampiccoli & Jugmohan, 2016). Therefore, our chapter presents a compilation of scientific literature, in which we show the relationship between agrobiodiversity into the community tourism. Which allowed us to define the social and ecological implications of agrobiodiversity as biocultural heritage. In addition to integrating a classification and discussion on the management carried out within tourism. Finally, these considerations could serve as a source of information for decision-making in multidisciplinary research and public policy within the sustainable management of agrobiodiversity. Furthermore, multidisciplinary research within the science of sustainability is of vital importance for the study of the processes involved in the management of agrobiodiversity within community tourism.

Fig. 1 Agrobiodiversity provides flora, fauna, fungi as ecosystem services (photographs taken in Veracruz, Mexico)

1.1 Definition of Agrobiodiversity

Currently there is no consensus on the definition of agrobiodiversity. Possibly this is a result of its close relationship with other concepts such as agroecosystem services -tangible or intangible benefits of agroecosystems that are determined by human agricultural practices and by the functions of agroecosystems— (Liu et al., 2022). Furthermore, as Kremen and Miles studied, agrobiodiversity provides agriculture with key ecosystem services, which reduces the need for non-agricultural inputs (Kremen & Miles, 2012). In a study by Bilz et al. defined it as "the genetic diversity of food crops". Therefore, among the most recognized definitions are the one provided by the Food and Agriculture Organization of the United Nations—variety and variability of animals, plants, and microorganisms—(FAO, 1999) and that of the United Nations—all the components of biological diversity relevant to food and agriculture— (Fig. 1) (UN, 2000).

1.2 Ecological Implications of Agricultural Biological Diversity

Agricultural biological diversity promotes the diversity of crop habitats, and the set of crop varieties and livestock breeds which are fundamental to maintaining the stability of food systems. (Negi et al., 2012). In addition, different research has shown that agrobiodiversity can promote sustainable land management, improve food security, improve soil quality, support biodiversity, and support ecosystem services (Agnoletti & Santoro, 2022; Chaudhary et al., 2020; Liu et al., 2022). Agricultural biological diversity is considered crucial and relevant for farmers who cultivate relatively small areas for cultural, food security, environmental, and climate adaptation reasons (Bukchin & Fishman, 2021; Zimmerer et al., 2019). Currently there are various factors that affect agrobiodiversity, the main ones being the decline of native livestock and traditional food crops and livestock. Another determining factor is the change in land use—mainly through the intensification and expansion of agriculture (Batáry et al., 2020). In addition to, the migration of the population of agricultural communities around the world has had negative impacts on the biodiversity related to agricultural lands (Herzog et al., 2013). Moreover, to the climate change-induced factors, as the adoption of high-yield crops to compensate for climate-induced productivity loss, and land and pasture degradation (Adhikari et al., 2017).

In a study by Bahadur, determined that agrobiodiversity has served as a survival mechanism in times of scarcity. In addition, it has traditionally served as insurance against diseases, pests, and climatic fluctuations (Bahadur et al., 2016). As suggested by Hussan and Qamer, agrobiodiversity is key to maintaining the sustainability -economic, ecological, and environmental- food systems. This could be possible through the reintegration of traditional food crops—agronomic crops, fruits, nuts, and medicinal plants—and native livestock. Hussan & Qamer suggest that traditional crops should be reintegrated into food systems without replacing any other livestock or crops because existing ones are equally important for maintaining diversity in the food system. (Hussain & Qamer, 2020). Agrobiodiversity as a resource provides various ecosystem services, which for certain population groups represent a resource for their survival (Liu, 2021). Despite this, these biological resources represent a collective good that is distinguished in each culture (Cao et al., 2020). However, the current food consumption of the world population and its trends (food packaging, vegan nutrition, consumption of superfoods, healthy eating with low fat and sugar content, healthy, natural, and organic snacks) call into question the subsistence of agrobiodiversity. Therefore, this chapter integrates the elements of agrobiodiversity management in community tourism.

1.3 Tourist Implications of Agrobiodiversity

The central component that motivates tourists and hikers to visit a place is identified as a tourist resource. Therefore, we could recognize within tourism any element of nature, culture, history, research, gastronomy, etc. (Muñoz-Benito, 2023) A tourist resource includes the set of natural, cultural, and social elements, which can be used as a sufficient cause to provoke, prolong, or repeat the tourist displacement (Rodríguez, 1982). The varied range of tastes, inclinations and preferences of the traveler could the unexpected into a tourist resource or attraction. The flora and fauna in each community represent elements of an agrarian or pastoral life. In this segment we can place agrobiodiversity as part of the biocultural heritage. Based on a study by Ekblom et al. It is possible to identify agrobiodiversity within tourism. This author suggested classifying them as natural attractions—flora, fauna, hydrography, orography—historical heritage—traditions, habits, history, others—folklore and manifestations of traditional culture—agricultural traditions (Ekblom et al., 2019).

The traditional knowledge about biological diversity has been integrated into the knowledge of society throughout its history. This knowledge is a fundamental part of cultural manifestations around the world (Lindholm & Ekblom, 2019). Therefore, the main objective of community tourism is to preserve in a sustainable way—economically, ecologically, and socially—the use and protection of world ethnobiological knowledge and heritage. Thus, biocultural heritage has been described by different authors within the cultural landscape as part of the survival of human beings (Petina et al., 2015). In a study by Long et al. suggests the complexity of the systematization and codification of the ethnobiological heritage of the communities (Long et al., 2021). The above supports the fact that the population's ethnobiological knowledge is susceptible to multiple threats, such as biopiracy (Dutfeld, 2020). Furthermore, the biocultural heritage of agrobiodiversity is part of popular wisdom, which legally belongs to the public domain (Chambers, 2000). This condition fosters the weakness of legal frameworks on intellectual property rights over biological resources (Volenzo, 2018). As a result of this situation, in several countries, their legislation has sought to include traditional knowledge in different legal instruments (Chakrabarty & Kau, 2021). There are various ecological and social risks when making agrobiodiversity available to a free market. Therefore, community-based tourism must be implemented by specialists in strict adherence to professional ethics and including diverse professional approaches. In its use, familiarization, knowledge, and cultural relevance are shown as a predominant element of culture. This biocultural heritage, as Comaroff and Comaroff mention, is a means to find true beings individually and collectively, "through the appropriation of the past" (Comaroff & Comaroff, 2009).

2 Community Based Tourism Characteristics

Around the world, communities of all sizes have showed a growing fascination with tourism, which has been motivated by its potential economic benefits. Qian et al. estimated that each year tourism contributes approximately 10% of world GDP and 6% of total world exports (Qian et al., 2017). However, tourism creates vulnerabilities within local communities despite substantial economic benefits at the expense of natural resources, social unrest, environmental damage, and traditional cultural activities (Butler, 2018). Rozo and Velez suggest that tourism could become a strategy for territorial articulation of areas with high natural and cultural wealth, where ethnic minorities or peasant communities live, who historically have depended on the use of natural resources (Rozo & Vélez, 2012).

As an alternative to the impact of mass tourism, community-based tourism emerged in recent decades. Which is a type of alternative tourism considered as a management model that includes community participation as the main element of this activity to achieve the objective of sustainable tourism development. (Telfer & Sharpley, 2008). Consequently, this type of tourism promotes social commitment, equitable distribution of benefits and respect for the environment. This activity promotes tourism development and community resilience through the mobilization of six types of community capital: human, social, natural, physical, financial, and psychological: which strengthen the capacity of the community during crises or unrest (Wakil et al., 2021). One of the main characteristics of community-based tourism highlights the role of social capital in the collaborative management of natural resources, where community resilience development activities contribute to the well-being and quality of life of the community (Musavengane & Kloppers, 2020). Therefore, community capital within community tourism fosters the community's ability to address different conditions through collective efforts and diversified resources (Magis, 2010).

3 Community-Based Tourism as a Sustainable Management Model

In this section, we describe the functioning of community tourism based on the theory of sustainability with the purpose of identifying its possible impacts on communities. The scientific concern within sustainability provides various methodological approaches to determine the effects of humanity's intervention on the planet through different disciplines such as ecology and social sciences (Kates, 2001). Based on the theory, a modern, holistic, and transdisciplinary scientific approach on the dynamic character of the anthropogenic nature-society inference within tourism is what is offered by the study of socio-ecological systems within sustainability. This approach is also called coupled natural and human systems (An, 2012; Liu et al., 2007a, 2007b). Therefore, community-based tourism responds to the characteristics of a socio-ecological system. This type of system is composed of at least two subsystems—an ecological subsystem and a social subsystem—both constantly interacting in a reciprocal manner. As proposed by Carpenter and Brock, the study of the theory of sustainability to explain the complexity of the man-society. This relationship could facilitate the study of problems regarding the management of natural resources in an ambivalent way through different temporal and special scales (Carpenter & Brock, 2004).

In a study by Walker suggested that any socio-ecological system provides different services to the actors of the system, but these, in turn, are limited and can generate competition for them (Walker, 2006), as is observed to happen with the conventional tourism. As Sotolongo suggests, a socio-ecological system such as community tourism can be recognized as a non-linear dynamic system. Then, a system is delimited based on its interactions between its ecological and social subsystems, it is susceptible to being defined as a socio-ecological system (Salas-Zapata et al., 2011). This results in an exchange of energy and mass, as well as information. Consequently, ontologically it has a reflective identity that allows it to recognize itself. Therefore, this character manifests itself in both biotic and abiotic systems (Sotolongo, 2012). In addition to these interactions at the global system level, attributes emerge that characterize socio-ecological systems. In a study by Chapin et. they identified the attributes of social-ecological systems, which they identify as: (1) emergent properties, (2) non-linearity of dynamics, (3) the existence of several scales and (4) loops of retroactivity. These authors also indicated that the emergent properties of systems are

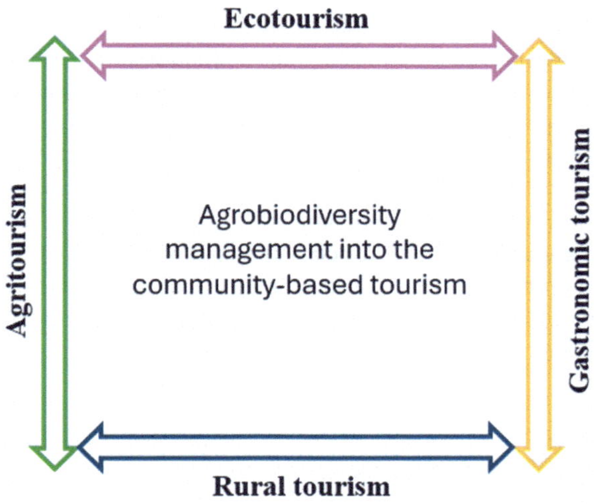

Fig. 2 Agrobiodiversity management into the community-based tourism classification

characteristics that result unpredictably from the interactions between the elements of the system. Furthermore, they mentioned that the non-linearity of dynamics is conceptualized by sudden changes based on temporal thresholds. Consequently, this makes experimentation for the study of socio-ecological phenomena such as community-based tourism complex for economic, ethical, and logistical reasons. In addition, beliefs, stories, myths, and personal references are recognized as a source of information for communities (Amorozo & Viertler, 2010; Poderoso et al., 2017). Below, based on the community tourism management model, we include the main activities where tourism has affected the agrobiodiversity (Fig. 2).

3.1 Ecotourism

Ecotourism is also recognized as green tourism, sustainable tourism, ecological tourism. The most widely accepted definition is given by in areas virtually undisturbed and which should contribute to the conservation of nature. In a concept by the Global Ecotourism Network (GEN), "ecotourism is responsible travel to natural areas that conserves the environment, sustains the wellbeing of the local ecology, and understanding through interpretation and education of all involved (GEN, 2016). Around the years 1984 1985, the Ecotourism was born, both as practice, in United States, together with the development of tourism for the naturalists in the most remote fragile and remote ecological areas (Ioan, 2013). The interdependence and interconnection between ecosystems and human society continue to deepen in the fast-growing context of tourism around the world development (Arif et al., 2022).

The following activities are mentioned among the most popular: studying the flora and fauna, photography and landscape painting, cultural sightseeing (Shi et al., 2019). Therefore, the ecotourists are mainly interested in relatively undisturbed ecosystems and want to learn more about natural phenomena (Hornoiu et al., 2014). Miller et al. indicated that ecological tourism focuses on not only humans' impact on the environment but also ecosystem-human–ecosystem interaction (Miller et al., 2022). In addition, the ecotourism helps maintain the function and structure of the tourist destination's ecosystem, improving resilience, strength, and organizational vitality (Yang et al., 2019). Also, the management of ecological tourism allows ensuring sustainability development of tourist destinations (Li et al., 2013). In this respect, the ecotourist have a special interest in environmental responsibility in tourism and support the green tourism suppliers (Juvan & Dolnicar, 2016). Therefore, the result of global interest in ecotourism, based on natural and cultural resources, has increased the marketing challenges in these areas.

3.2 Gastronomic Tourism

In terms of tourism, food can be conceived as a resource due to its historical and cultural character (Sormaz et al., 2016). The food is an essential element for the tourist experience (Cagli, 2012). Gastronomic tourism is one of the most dynamic, which it the tourist the main motivation when travelling is the gastronomy of the city visited, its tradition culinary-(Berbel-Pineda et al., 2019). Nowadays, the gastronomy has a privileged place in tourism development since it is a reason for strengthening the tourist offer. Therefore, gastronomy has become a source of interest for tourists (McKercher & Okumus, 2008). This offer satisfies the basic biological need for food in which the cultural identity of a place is expressed (Avielim, 2013; Richards, 2002). In recent decades, gastronomy has become an emblem of tourist destinations as an attraction and special interest has been devoted to it within the economy, academy and research. (De Jesús-Contreras et al., 2017; Hall et al., 2003). An example of this is the enhancement of local gastronomy and its traditional foods in countries such as Italy, France, Portugal, Spain, and Argentina. In which studies demonstrated the interest of tourists in the consumption of local cuisine (Arzeno & Troncoso, 2012).

The tourist promotion of gastronomic and culinary heritage not only includes local consumption, but also the acquisition of regional food products, which makes it possible to increase the profitability of native products (Hall & Mitchell, 2005). In community tourism it has been observed that those involved offer their own agricultural production to tourists. In this way, the close link between the food sector and tourism is observed (Calıskan, 2013). Therefore, an important aspect for the development of gastronomic tourism is a region's population protecting local products belonging to that region (Alonso & Yiliu 2011).

3.3 *Rural Tourism*

Rural tourism has been conceived to utilize community management opportunities and the sustainable use of biocultural resources (Yachin & Ioannides, 2020). The World Tourism Organization defines rural tourism as a tourism valuation strategy of natural resources, agricultural spaces, popular traditions, cultural heritage, rural housing, local products (UNWTO, 2023). Particularly in China and Europe, the rural tourism constitutes an important market segment worldwide (An & Alarcon, 2021; World Tourism Organization, 2017). This activity aims to meet society's demand for leisure with a focus on sustainable local development, within a new social solidarity between urban centers and rural areas (Leite et al., 2023). Consequently, rural tourism contemplates traditional economic activities and allows positive exchange between visitors and recipients (Pigram & Jenkins, 2005).

As a characteristic of this type of tourism, it has been observed that it promotes good quality services, diversifying rural economies, and is promoted by the formation of productive chains in places of origin, promoting balanced development between productive activities (Diaz & Zielinski, 2022). These benefits allow the training of the community, reinforces the capacity of the association of local actors and privileges contemplative activities by tourists (Ross & Saxena, 2019). In a study by Putu et al. They observed that another characteristic of rural tourism is the importance of harmony between people and nature, the reinterpretation of resources and the customary participation of actors in tourism (Putu et al., 2023). In rural tourism, the fundamental elements within resource management include the interaction of interested parties, mutual benefits, communication, public sector support, active community participation, shared objectives, planning, trust, structuring, financing, product development, learning and self-assessment.

3.4 *Agritourism*

Agritourism is one of the forms of tourism in which activities such as ecotourism, adventure tourism and rural tourism are usually integrated. Its many facets and offerings reflect in its diverse connotations including agrotourism or agritourism, agricultural tourism, farm tourism, agri-entertainment, tourism, farm vacation, wine tourism, etc. (Kolawole et al., 2023) In a study Flanigan et al., 2010 defined the term agrotourism as tourist activity in agricultural production, farms, or plantations (Fig. 3) (Flanigan et al., 2010). In which the actors complement their income with some form of tourism, who provide accommodation, food, and the opportunity to familiarize themselves with agricultural work to visitors (Busby et al., 2000).

As an experience in this tourist activity, the visitor can interact and obtain knowledge of agriculture, uses, customs, local products, traditional food, and the daily life of the rural population (Fischer, 2019). The activities that highlight this type of tourism are the preparation of preserves, harvesting, milking, rodeo, assistance

Fig. 3 Agritourism as tourist activity in the agricultural production, farms, or plantations (photographs taken in Madrid, Spain)

in feeding and caring for the animals. Furthermore, in the tourist experience it is possible to combine them with other recreational activities such as bird watching, horseback riding, walks around the farm, among other activities (Ungureanu, 2008). Agri-food tourism privileges the valorization of agrobiodiversity and its sustainability within community management (Guan et al., 2019; Kaswanto, 2015). The agritourism experience is characterized by the production of food, its gastronomic preparation and tasting. In addition, the rural community shares the intrinsic value of food—history, its originality, and its belonging. In a study by Rodríguez et al. suggested that agri-food tourism could influence the development of socially and economically marginalized communities. He also indicated that in the communities there could be reactivation of productive activities, job creation and the recovery of customs and traditions (Rodríguez et al., 2017). Therefore, agritourism represents a sustainable alternative for the modern management of agrobiodiversity around the world. Damnet et al. suggested that it is possible agricultural learning centers with integrated tourism innovations that combine knowledge from traditional sources, flower such as animal farming tourism, garden innovation and architecture, agricultural technology, tourism in rice fields, flower garden tourism,, highland tourism, innovations in agritourism and accommodation, picturesque salt fields marine fishing farms, tourism that combines spirituality, and city simulators as tourist attractions (Damnet et al., 2023).

4 Conclusions

This chapter corroborates about the implications of the socio-ecological management of agrobiodiversity within community tourism. The state of the art reflected the epistemological bases on its sustainable management. Our findings suggested a close relationship between community tourism and its relationship with agrobiodiversity. Furthermore, this study showed us that in recent decades there has been a growing interest in the study of ecotourism, gastronomic tourism, rural tourism, and agritourism as an alternative for the sustainable management of agrobiodiversity. In this context, the multidisciplinary study could be promoted in this area, which could promote the diversification of activities within tourism. As well as the promotion of biocultural heritage and ethnobiological knowledge of the communities. Furthermore, we can theoretically establish a complex system of relationships between natural resources and human management. Therefore, research could integrate the approach proposed by science on sustainability, integrating anthropology, bioeconomy, ecology, ethnobiology, agricultural sciences, and sociology. Given the vulnerability of the biocultural heritage of agrobiodiversity, tourism could offer multiple benefits. Such as the promotion, preservation, and rescue of agrobiodiversity through promoting alliances between academic, scientific, cultural, and private organizations. Finally, new approaches to the management of agrobiodiversity within tourism could represent an alternative for the preservation and conservation of agroecological biocultural heritage.

References

Adhikari, L., Hussain, A., & Rasul, G. (2017). Tapping the potential of neglected and underutilized food crops for sustainable nutrition security in the Mountains of Pakistan and Nepal. *Sustainability.*, *9*(2), 291. https://doi.org/10.3390/su9020291

Agnoletti, M., & Santoro, A. (2022). Agricultural heritage systems and agrobiodiversity. *Biodiversity and Conservation, 31*. https://doi.org/10.1007/s10531-022-02460-3

Alonso, A. D., & Liu, Y. (2011). The potential for marrying local gastronomy and wine; the case of the fortunate islands. *International Journal of Hospitality Management, 30*, 974–981.

Amorozo, M. C. M., & Viertler, R. B. (2010). The qualitative approach in data collection and analysis in ethnobiology and ethnoecology [A abordagem qualitativa na coleta e análise de dados em etnobiologia e etnoecologia.] In U. P. Albuquerque, R. F. P. Lucena, and L. V. F. C. Cunha (Eds.), *Metodos e Tecnicas na Pesquisa Etnobiologica e ´Etnoecologica*, 65–82. NUPPEA, Recife, PE.

An, L. (2012). Modeling human decisions in coupled human and natural systems: Review of agent-based models. *Ecological Modelling, 229*, 25–36.

An, W., & Alarcon, S. (2021). Rural tourism preferences in Spain: Best-worst choices. *Annals of Tourism Research, 89*, Article 103210. https://doi.org/10.1016/j.annals.2021.103210

Antrop, M. (2005). Why landscapes of the past are important for the future. *Landscape and Urban Planning, 70*. 21–34. https://doi.org/10.1016/j.landurbplan.2003.10.002

Arif, M., Behzad, H. M., Tahir, M., & Li, C. (2022). The impact of ecotourism on ecosystem functioning along main rivers and tributaries: Implications for management and policy changes. *J. Environ. Manage., 320*.

Arzeno, M., & Troncoso, C. A. (2012). Traditional andean foods, tourism and place: Defining the new geography of La Quebrada de Humahuaca (Argentina). [Alimentos Tradicionales Andinos, Turismo y Lugar: Definiendo La Nueva Geografía de La Quebrada de Humahuaca (Argentina).] *Revista de Geografia Norte Grande 90*(52), 71–90

Avieli, N. (2013). What is 'local food?' dynamic culinary heritage in the world heritage site of Hoi an, Vietnam. *Journal of Heritage Tourism, 8*(2–3), 120–132.

Bahadur, K. C. K., Pant, L. P., Fraser, E. D. G., Shrestha, P. K., Shrestha, D., & Lama, A. (2016). Assessing links between crop diversity and food self-sufficiency in three agroecological regions of Nepal. *Regional Environmental Change, 16*, 1239–1251.

Batáry, P., Báldi, A., Ekroos, J., et al. (2020). Biologia Futura: Landscape perspectives on farmland biodiversity conservation. *Biologia Futura, 71*, 9–18. https://doi.org/10.1007/s42977-020-00015-7

Baumann, M. (2021). Agrobiodiversity's caring material practices as a symbolic frame for environmental governance in Colombia's southern Tolima. *Geoforum, 128*. https://doi.org/10.1016/j.geoforum.2021.01.002

Berbel-Pineda, J. M., Palacios-Florencio, B., Ramírez-Hurtado, J. M., & Santos-Roldán, L. (2019). Gastronomic experience as a factor of motivation in the tourist movements. *International Journal of Gastronomy and Food Science*, 100171. https://doi.org/10.1016/j.ijgfs.2019.100171

Bukchin, S., & Fishman, R. (2021). Should long-term climate change adaptation be focused on smallholders? *Environmental Research Letters, 16*. https://doi.org/10.1088/1748-9326/ac2699

Busby, G., & Rendle, S. (2000). The transition from tourism on farms to farm tourism. *Tourism Management—Tourism manage, 21*. 635–642. https://doi.org/10.1016/S0261-5177(00)00011-X

Butler, R. (2018). Resilience in the face of changing circumstances: Fair Isle, Shetland. In J. M. Cheer, & A. A. Lew (Eds.), *Tourism, resilience and sustainability: Adapting to social, political and economic change*, 116–131. Routledge

Caglı, IB. (2012). *Turkiye'de Yerel Kulturun Turizm Odaklı Kalkınmadaki Rolu: Gastronomi Turizmi Ornegi*, İstanbul Technical University, Institute of Science and Technology, Department of Urban and Region Planning, Region Planning, MA Thesis, İstanbul.

Calıskan, O. (2013). Destinasyon rekabetciligi ve seyahat motivasyonu bakımından gastronomik kimlik. *Journal of Tourism and Gastronomy Studies, 1*(2), 39–51.

Cao, Y., Li, R., Zhou, S., Song, L., Quan, R., & Hu, H. (2020). Ethnobotanical study on wild edible plants used by three trans-boundary ethnic groups in Jiangcheng county, Pu'er, southwest China. *Journal of Ethnobiology and Ethnomedicine, 16*(1). https://doi.org/10.1186/s13002-020-00420-1

Carpenter, S. R., & and. Brock WA,. (2004). Spatial complexity, resilience, and policy diversity: Fishing on lake-rich landscapes. *Ecology and Society, 9*(1), 8.

Chakrabarty, S. P., & Kaur, R. (2021). A primer to traditional knowledge protection in India: The Road Ahead. *Liverpool Law Review, 42*, 401–427, https://doi.org/10.1007/s10991-021-09281-4

Chambers, D. W., & Richard, G. (2000). Locality in the history of science: Colonial science, technoscience, and indigenous knowledge. *Osiris, 15*(1), 221–240.

Chang, K. (2021). The affecting tourism development attitudes based on the social exchange theory and the social network theory. *Asia Pacific Journal of Tourism Research, 26*(2): 167–182, https://doi.org/10.1080/10941665.2018.1540438

Chaudhary, P., Bhatta, S., Aryal, K., Joshi, B., & Gauchan, D. (2020). Threats, drivers and conservation imperative of agrobiodiversity. *The Journal of Agriculture and Environment, 21*, 44–61.

Cissé, A., Clermont-Dauphin, C., Sall, S., Gie, S., Groupement, M., Ndiaye, A., Diouf, M., Traore, B, Ndir, K., Kane, N., & Berthouly, C. et al. (2022). Sahelian smallholders' varietal mixtures reconcile yield and agrobiodiversity conservation. *Basic and Applied Ecology, 67*. https://doi.org/10.1016/j.baae.2022.12.006

Comaroff, J., & Comaroff, J. (2009). *Ethnicity*. The University of Chicago Press, Chicago.

Damnet, A., Sangnak, D., & Poo-Udom, A. (2023). Thailand's innovative agritourism in the post COVID-19 new normal: A new paradigm to achieve sustainable development goals. *Research in Globalization*, 100171

De., Jesús-Contreras, Thomé-Ortiz, H., Espinoza-Ortega, A., & Vizcarra-Bordi, I. (2017). Turismo Agroalimentario, Una Perspectiva Recreativa de Los Alimentos Emblemáticos Desde La Geografía Del Gusto. *Estudios y Perspectivas En Turismo, 26*, 549–567.

Diaz, L. H., & Zielinski, S. (2022). Community-based tourism, social capital, and governance of post-conflict rural tourism destinations: the case of Minca, Sierra Nevada de Santa Marta, Colombia. *Tourism Management Perspectives, 43*. 100985. https://doi.org/10.1016/j.tmp.2022.100985

Dutfeld, G., Wynberg, R., Laird, S., & Ives, S. (2020). *Beneft sharing and traditional knowledge: Unsolved dilemmas for implementation.* The Challenge of Attribution and Origin: Traditional Knowledge and Access and Beneft Sharing. Voices for BioJustice, Policy Brief. https://doi.org/10.13140/RG.2.2.30347.52002

Duflot, R., San-Cristobal, M., Andrieu, E., Choisis, J. P., Esquerré, D., Ladet, S., Ouin, A., Rivers-Moore, J., Sheeren, D., Sirami, C., Fauvel, M., & Vialatte, A. (2022). Farming intensity indirectly reduces crop yield through negative effects on agrobiodiversity and key ecological functions. *Agriculture, Ecosystems & Environment, 326*. 107810. https://doi.org/10.1016/j.agee.2021.107810

Eiter, S., & Potthoff, K. (2016). Landscape changes in Norwegian mountains: Increased and decreased accessibility, and their driving forces. *Land Use Policy, 54*, 235–245. https://doi.org/10.1016/j.landusepol.2016.02.017

Ekblom, A., Shoemaker, A., Gillson, L., Lane, P., & Lindholm, K. J. (2019). Conservation through biocultural heritage—Examples from Sub-Saharan Africa. *Land, 8*(5). https://doi.org/10.3390/land8010005

Etzioni, A. (1993). *The spirit of community: Rights, responsibilities and the communitarian agenda, political science quarterly, 108*(3), 577. https://doi.org/10.2307/2151727

FAO. (1999). *Agricultural biodiversity multifunctional character of agriculture and land conference.* Background paper 1.

Fischer, C. (2019). Agriculture and tourism sector linkages: Global relevance and local evidence for the case of South Tyrol. *Open Agriculture, 4*(1), 544–553.

Flanigan, S., Hunter, C., & Blackstock, K. (2010). A typology for defining agritourism. *Tourism Management, 31*. 754–758. https://doi.org/10.1016/j.tourman.2009.08.001

Foley, S. F., Gronenborn, D., Andreae, M. O., Kadereit, J. W., Esper, J., Scholz, D., Pöschl, U., Jacob, D. E., Schöne, B. R., Schreg, R., & Vött, A. (2013). The Palaeoanthropocene-The beginnings of anthropogenic environmental change. *Anthropocene, 3*, 83–88.

Fuller, D. Q., Van Etten, J., Manning, K., Castillo, C., Kingwell-Banham, E., Weisskopf, A., Qin, L., Sato, Y. I., & Hijmans, R. J. (2011). The contribution of rice agriculture and livestock pastoralism to prehistoric methane levels: An archaeological assessment. *Holocene, 21*, 743–759.

Giampiccoli, A., Saayman, M., & Jugmohan, S. (2016). Are 'Albergo Diffuso' and community-based tourism the answers to community development in South Africa? *Development Southern Africa, 33*. 1–14. https://doi.org/10.1080/0376835X.2016.1180968

Global Ecotourism Network. (2016). *What is (not) ecotourism?* https://www.globalecotourismnetwork.org/what-itis-not-ecotourism

Guan, J., Gao, J., & Zhang, C. (2019). Food heritagization and sustainable rural tourism destination: The case of China's Yuanjia village. *Sustainability (Switzerland), 11*(10), 2858. https://doi.org/10.3390/su11102858

Hall, M., & Mitchell, R. (2005). Gastronomic tourism: comparing food and wine tourism experiences. In İcinde M. Novelli (Ed.), *Niche tourism, contemporary issues, trendsand cases*, ss. 89–100

Hall, C., Sharples, L., Mitchell, R., Macionis, N., & Cambourne, B. (2003). Food tourism around the world. *Food tourism around the world*, 1–373

Herzog, F., Jeanneret, P., Ammari, Y., Angelova, S., Arndorfer, M., Bailey, D., Bal´ azs, K, Zanetti T, et al. (2013). Measuring farmland biodiversity. *Solutions, 4*(4), 52–58.

Hornoiu, R. I., Pădurean, M. A., Nica, A. M., & Maha, L. G. (2014). Tourism consumption behavior in natural protected areas. *Amfiteatru Econ., 16*, 1178–1190.

Hussain, A., & Qamer, F. M. (2020). Dual challenge of climate change and agrobiodiversity loss in mountain food systems in the Hindu-Kush Himalaya. *One Earth, 3*. 539–542. https://doi.org/10.1016/j.oneear.2020.10.016

Ioan, S. (2013). Ecological tourism and public administration in Romania. *Procedia—Social and Behavioral Sciences*, (81), 235–240. https://doi.org/10.1016/j.sbspro.2013.06.419

Juvan, E., & Dolnicar, S. (2016). Measuring environmentally sustainable tourist behaviour. *Annals of Tourism Research, 59*, 30–44.

Kaswanto, R. (2015). Land suitability for agrotourism through Agriculture, Tourism, Beautification and Amenity (ATBA) Method. *Procedia Environmental Sciences, 24*. https://doi.org/10.1016/j.proenv.2015.03.006

Kates, R. W. (2001). Environment and development: Sustainability science. *Science, 292*(5517), 641–642. https://doi.org/10.1126/science.1059386

Khumalo, S., Chirwa, P., Moyo, B. H., & Syampungani, S. (2012). The status of agrobiodiversity management and conservation in major agroecosystems of Southern Africa. *Agriculture, Ecosystems & Environment, 157*. 17–23. https://doi.org/10.1016/j.agee.2012.01.028

Kolawole, O., Hambira, W., & Gondo, R. (2023). Agrotourism as peripheral and ultraperipheral community livelihoods diversification strategy: Insights from the Okavango Delta, Botswana. *Journal of Arid Environments, 212*. https://doi.org/10.1016/j.jaridenv.2023.104960

Kotler, P., Bowen, J., & Makens, J. (2010). *Marketing for hospitality and tourism*, (5th ed.), Pearson Prentice Hall.

Kremen, C., & Miles, A. (2012). Ecosystem services in biologically diversified versus conventional farming systems: benefits, externalities, and trade-offs. *Ecology and society, 17*(4), 40–66

Leite, H., Binotto, E., Padilha, M., & Hoeckel, P. (2023). Cooperation in rural tourism routes: Evidence and insights. *Journal of Hospitality and Tourism Management, 57*, 84–96. https://doi.org/10.1016/j.jhtm.2023.09.005

Li, Y. J., Chen, T., Hu, J., & Wang, J. (2013). Tourism ecological security in Wuhan. *J. Resour. Ecol., 4*(2), 149–156. https://doi.org/10.5814/j.issn.1674-764x.2013.02.007

Lindholm, K. J., & Ekblom, A. (2019). A framework for exploring and managing biocultural heritage. *Anthropocene, 25*, 100195–. https://doi.org/10.1016/j.ancene.2019.100195

Liu, J. T., Dietz, C. R., Carpenter, M., Alberti, C., Folke, E., Moran, A. N., Pell, P., Deadman, T., Kratz, J., Lubchenco, E., Ostrom, Z., Ouyang, W., Provencher, C. L., Redman, S. H., & Schneider and Taylor WW,. (2007a). Complexity of coupled human and natural systems. *Science, 317*(5844), 1513–1516.

Liu, J. T., Dietz, S. R., Carpenter, C., Folke, M., Alberti, C., Redman, S. H., Schneider, E., Ostrom, A. N., Pell, J., Lubchenco, Taylor W. W., Ouyang, P., Deadman, T., Kratz & Provencher, W. (2007b). Coupled human and natural systems. *AMBIO: A Journal of the Human Environment 36*(8), 639–649

Liu, J., Li, W., Kang, X., Zhao, F., He, M., She, Y., & Zhou, Y. (2021). Profiling by HPLC-DAD-MSD reveals a 2500-year history of the use of natural dyes in Northwest China. *Dyes and Pigments, 187*. https://doi.org/10.1016/j.dyepig.2021.109143

Liu, Q., Sun, X., Wu, W., Liu, Z., Fang, G., & Yang, P. (2022). Agroecosystem services: A review of concepts, indicators, assessment methods and future research perspectives. *Ecological Indicators, 142*, 109218.

Long, J. W., Lake, F. K., & Goode, R. W. (2021). The importance of indigenous cultural burning in forested regions of the Pacific West, USA. *Forest Ecology and Management, 500*(3), 119597. https://doi.org/10.1016/j.foreco.2021.119597

Magis, K. (2010). Community resilience: An indicator of social sustainability. *Society and Natural Resources, 23*(5), 401–416. https://doi.org/10.1080/08941920903305674

Matthies, A., Fayet, C., O'Connor, L., & Verburg, P. (2023). Mapping agrobiodiversity in Europe: Different indicators, different priority areas. *Ecological Indicators, 154*. 110744. https://doi.org/10.1016/j.ecolind.2023.110744

McKercher, B., Okumus, F., & Okumus, B. (2008). Food tourism as a viable market segment: It's all how you cook the numbers! *Journal of Travel and Tourism Marketing, 25*(2), 137–148.

Mill, R. C., & Morrison, A. M. (2002). *The tourism system*. Kendall Hunt.

Miller, A. B., Blahna, D. J., Morse, W. C., Leung, Y. F, Rowland, M. M. (2022). From recreation ecology to a recreation ecosystem: A framework accounting for socialecological systems. *Journal of Outdoor Recreation and Tourism-Research Planning and Management, 38*.

Muñoz-Benito, R., Navajas-Romero, V., & Hernande, R. D. (2023). Traditional gastronomy in Alto Guadalquivir: Origin of contemporary recipes in cordovan cuisine. *International Journal of Gastronomy and Food Science, 32*, 100720. https://doi.org/10.1016/j.ijgfs.2023.100720

Musavengane, R., Kloppers, R. (2020). Social capital: An investment towards community resilience in the collaborative natural resources management of community-based tourism schemes. *Tourism Management Perspectives, 34*, 100654. https://doi.org/10.1016/j.tmp.2020.100654
Negi, G. C. S., Samal, P. K., Kuniyal, J. C., Kothyari, B. P., Sharma, R. K., & Dhyani, P. P. (2012). Impact of climate change on the western Himalayan Mountain ecosystems: An overview. *Tropical Ecology, 53*, 345–356.
Pert, P. L., Hill, R., Maclean, K., Dale, A., Rist, P., Schmider, J., Talbot, L., & Tawake, L. (2015). Mapping cultural ecosystem services with rainforest aboriginal peoples: Integrating biocultural diversity, governance and social variation. *Ecosystem Services, 13*, 41–56. https://doi.org/10.1016/j.ecoser.2014.10.012
Pigram, J. J., & Jenkins, J. M. (2005). *Outdoor recreation management* (2nd ed.). Routledge.
Poderoso, R. A., Peroni, N., & Hanazaki, N. (2017). Gender influences in the perception and use of the landscape in a rural community of German immigrant descendants in Brazil. *Journal of Ethnobiology, 37*(4): 779–797. https://doi.org/10.2993/0278-0771-37.4.779
Porcuna-Ferrer, A., Labeyrie, V., Alvarez-Fernandez, S., Calvet-Mir, L., Faye, N. F., Ouadah, S., & Reyes-García, V. (2023). Crop biocultural traits shape seed networks: Implications for social-ecological resilience in south eastern Senegal. *Agricultural Systems*, Vol. 211, Elsevier.
Putu, D. R., Wang, Y., Dupre, K., Darma, N., & Jin, X. (2023). Rural tourism in Bali: towards a conflict-based tourism resource typology and management. *Tourism Recreation Research.* https://doi.org/10.1080/02508281.2023.2223076
Qian, C., Sasaki, N., Jourdain, D., Kim, S., & Shivakoti, G. (2017). Local livelihood under different governances of tourism development in China—A Case study of Huangshan Mountain Area. *Tourism Management, 61.* https://doi.org/10.1016/j.tourman.2017.01.006
Richards, G. (2002). Gastronomy: An essential ingredient in tourism production and consumption. *Tourism and Gastronomic*, 1–39.
Rocchi, L., Paolotti, L., Cortina, C., & Boggia, A. (2016). Conservation of landrace: The key role of the value for agrobiodiversity conservation. An application on ancient tomatoes varieties. *Agriculture and Agricultural Science Procedia, 8*. 307–316. https://doi.org/10.1016/j.aaspro.2016.02.025
Rodríguez, M. (1982). *General theory of tourism.* [Teoría General del Turismo], p. 83. Southwestern Publishing Co. Ohio, E.U.A.
Rodríguez, R. M., & Pulido-Fernández, and Herrera IMR,. (2017). The tourism product in magic towns of Mexico. A critical analysis of its components. [El Producto Turístico En Los Pueblos Mágicos de México.Un Análisis Crítico de Sus Componentes]. *Revista De Estudios Regionales, 108*, 125–163.
Ross, D., & Saxena, G. (2019). Participative co-creation of archaeological heritage: Case insights on creative tourism in Alentejo, Portugal. *Annals of Tourism Research, 79*, Article 102790. https://doi.org/10.1016/j.annals.2019.102790
Rozo, E., & Vélez, M. (2012). Rural tourism: Experiences and challenges in Latin America. Rural tourism: Strategy for poverty reduction of peasant families in the province of Alto Ricaurte, Boyacá, Colombia [Turismo Rural: Experiencias y desafíos en Iberoamérica. El turismo rural: Estrategia para la reducción de la pobreza de las familias campesinas de la provincia del Alto Ricaurte, Boyacá, Colombia]. Colegio de Postgraduados, pp. 39–64.
Ruddiman, W. F. (2013). The anthropocene. *Annu Rev Earth Plan Sci, 41*, 45–68.
Salas-Zapata, W. A., Rios-Osorio, L. A., & Alvarez-Del Castillo, J. (2011). Conceptual bases for a classification of socioecological systems of sustainability research. [Bases conceptuales para una clasificación de los sistemas socioecológicos de la investigación en sostenibilidad]. *Rev. Lasallista Investig, 8*(2), 136–142.
Smith, B. D., & Zeder, M. A. (2013). *The Onset of the Anthropocene. Anthropocene, 4*, 8–13.
Sormaz, U., Akmese, H., Gunes, E., Aras, S. (2016). Gastronomy in tourism. *Procedia Economics and Finance, 39*, 725–730. https://doi.org/10.1016/s2212-5671(16)30286-6
Sotolongo, P. (2012). Looking Through Ulanowicz's "Third Window". *Journal Article Axiomathes, 22*(2), 207–221 Springer Netherland. https://doi.org/10.1007/s10516-011-9175-7

Steffen, W., Grinevald, J., Crutzen, P., & McNeill, J. (2011). The anthropocene: Conceptual and historical perspectives. *Philos T R Soc A, 369*, 842–867.

Shi, F., Weaver, D., Zhao, Y., Huang, M. F., Tang, C., & Liu, Y. (2019). Toward an ecological civilization: Mass comprehensive ecotourism indications among domestic visitors to a Chinese wetland protected area. *Tourism Management, 70*, 59–68.

Telfer, R., & Sharpley, D. J. (2008). *Tourism and development in the developing world*. Routledge.

Ungureanu, D. (2008). Sustainable development alternatives by rural tourism and agritourism in the romanian mountain rural area. *Amfiteatru Economic., 10*, 207–212.

United Nations. (2000). *COP decision: Agricultural biological diversity: review of phase I of the programme of work and adoption of a multi-year work programme*, V5, appendix.

Volenzo, T., Odiyo, J., & Kimambo, O. (2018). *Integrating endemic medicinal plants into the global value chains: The ecological degradation challenges and opportunities*. Preprints, 2018110053. https://doi.org/10.20944/preprints201811.005.v1

Walker, B. et al. (2006). A handful of heuristics and some propositions for understanding resilience in social-ecological systems. *En: Ecol Soc.* (11), 1–13.

Wakil, Md., Sun, Y., & Chan, E. (2021). Co-flourishing: Intertwining community resilience and tourism development in destination communities. *Tourism Management Perspectives, 38*. 100803. https://doi.org/10.1016/j.tmp.2021.100803

World Tourism Organization. (2017). *International rural tourism development—An Asia Pacific perspective*. UNWTO.

World Tourism Organization United Nations (2023). *Tourism and rural development: A policy perspective, UNWTO, Madrid*, https://doi.org/10.18111/9789284424306

Yachin, J. M., & Ioannides, D. (2020). 'Making do' in rural tourism: The resourcing behaviour of tourism micro-firms. *Journal of Sustainable Tourism, 28*(7), 1003–1021. https://doi.org/10.1080/09669582.2020.1715993

Yang, X. Y., Dong, L., Li, C. S. (2019). Microclimate tourism and microclimate tourism security and safety in China. *Tourism Manage, 74*. 110–133. https://doi.org/10.1016/j.tourman.2018.12.012

Zalasiewicz, J., Waters, C. N., Summerhayes, C. P., Wolfe, A. P., Barnosky, A. D., Cearreta, A., Crutzen, P., Ellis, E., Fairchild, I. J., Gałuszka, A., & Haff, P. (2017). The working group on the anthropocene: Summary of evidence and interim recommendations. *Anthropocene, 19*, 55–60.

Zimmerer, K. S., & De Haan. S. (2017). Agrobiodiversity and a sustainable food future. *Nat Plants 3*, 1–3. https://doi.org/10.1038/nplants.2017.47

Zimmerer, K., Haan, S., Jones, A., Creed-Kanashiro, H., Tello, M., Carrasco, M., Meza, Kr., Plasencia, A., Jimenez, Y. et al. (2019) The biodiversity of food and agriculture (Agrobiodiversity) in the anthropocene: Research advances and a conceptual framework. *Anthropocene, 25*. 100192. https://doi.org/10.1016/j.ancene.2019.100192

The manufacturer's authorised representative in the EU is Springer Nature Customer Service Centre GmbH, Europaplatz 3, 69115 Heidelberg, Germany. If you have any concerns regarding our products, please contact ProductSafety@springernature.com

Printed and bound by CPI Group (UK) Ltd, Croydon, CR0 4YY
01/10/2026
02225910-0005